PROJECT APPRAISAL AND PLANNING
FOR DEVELOPING COUNTRIES

PROJECT APPRAISAL AND PLANNING FOR DEVELOPING COUNTRIES

by

I. M. D. Little

and

J. A. Mirrlees

H·E·B

HEINEMANN EDUCATIONAL BOOKS
LONDON

Heinemann Educational Books Ltd

LONDON EDINBURGH MELBOURNE AUCKLAND TORONTO
SINGAPORE HONG KONG KUALA LUMPUR
IBADAN NAIROBI JOHANNESBURG
NEW DELHI LUSAKA

ISBN 0 435 84500 4
Paperback edition ISBN 0 435 84501 2

First published 1974

Published by
Heinemann Educational Books Ltd
48 Charles Street, London W1X 8AH

Printed in Great Britain by
Morrison and Gibb Ltd, London and Edinburgh

Contents

PART TWO

PROJECT ANALYSIS AND PLANNING

Contents

PART FOUR

SOME RELATED ISSUES

Introduction and Acknowledgements

This is a successor volume to the *Manual of Industrial Project Analysis for Developing Countries, Volume II, Social Cost–Benefit Analysis*, published by the OECD Development Centre, Paris, 1968.

It is something more than a second edition, and partly for this reason has a quite different title. Nevertheless, although very largely rewitten, it cannot be said to be an altogether different work. Thus, while the present volume differs too much from the OECD *Manual* to be regarded as a second edition, the repetition of material is too great for it not to have been an infringement of copyright, had not the OECD given permission to publish. We are very grateful to the OECD for this release of copyright.

The basic concepts and principles used in this work were evolved for the writing of the *Manual*, which was an OECD Development Centre project, although the views and recommendation of the *Manual* were essentially those of the present authors, and could not be regarded as adopted by the OECD.

Much of the *Manual*, indeed the more important part, was devoted to fairly detailed guidelines concerning the estimation of accounting prices. Broadly speaking, the guidelines in this work remain close to those of the *Manual*, but there are some fairly important changes. The most notable concern the treatment of the shadow wage, which is now made to depend more explicitly on income distribution. There are other changes of emphasis.

There are considerable additions of material. The organization of project planning and evaluation, and how it relates to sectoral and macro-economic planning, is discussed at much greater length. The scope of the work has been enlarged by discussions of agricultural and infrastructural projects, so that the word 'industrial' has been eliminated from the title. There is more discussion of how to measure the benefits of the production of non-traded goods and services. Income distribution, and the why and wherefore of allowing for it in project analysis, is dealt with more explicitly and at much greater length. This is partly a consequence of the work now being aimed at agricultural and rural infrastructural projects as well as industrial projects. Much the same is true of employment.

The application of the principles to private investment, particularly private overseas investment, has been spelled out in considerably more detail than before. The use of project evaluation by donor agencies is also discussed. Two new chapters, one comparing our methods with those of others, and one on the Theory of the Second Best have been added. Only a few chapters remain substantially the same, those on the need for accounting prices, on scarce resources, on objectives, and on externalities (Chapters II, III, IV, and XVI in this work).

Certain subtractions have been made. In line with the reduced emphasis on industrial projects, the discussion of protection has been largely eliminated: it is, in any case, echoed in *Industry and Trade in Some Developing Countries*[1]. We have also, with some regret, eliminated the two case studies of the *Manual*. But there was a need to keep the length reasonable, and we believe there is now a sufficient number of published and available case studies using the principles of the *Manual* and of this volume (see Bibliography). The 'Appendix for Professional Economists' has also been eliminated, much of it now being incorporated in the text, or in other short mathematical notes.

Since writing the *Manual*, the authors have learned much from the Nuffield College Project, supported by the Leverhulme Foundation, and organized by I. M. D. Little and M. FG. Scott, which had the essential purpose of promoting case studies of investments in developing countries, and discussion of the principles. This project has led to the publications of the case studies mentioned above, including those four which the OECD Development Centre has published as follow-ups of the *Manual* (see Bibliography).

Our greatest debt is to Mr M. FG. Scott, the co-director with Mr Little of the Nuffield College Project. He has been a continuous and sympathetic critic, and has contributed greatly to our understanding of some of the problems involved, both in conversation and as a result of his forthcoming work. The authors have also benefited from all those who have been associated with the Nuffield College Project; apart from the authors of the case-studies referred to in the Bibliography, these include particularly J. S. Flemming, V. Joshi, S. Mulji, and P. Sadler. We have also learnt from the critical articles on the OECD *Manual* which are listed in Section 2.2 of the Bibliography. We have held and attended a great many conferences and seminars on the subject in many parts of the world, but those who have contributed in this way are too numerous to mention. We have received valuable comments on the draft from P. Diamond, V. Joshi, D. Newbery, G. Ohlin, and M. FG Scott. We should also like to thank Mrs Baidoun for her typing, Mrs Dowley for help with the Bibliography, and Miss Schott for preparing the Index.

---

[1] Little, Scitovsky, and Scott, 1970.

Part One

THE ECONOMICS OF SOCIAL COST–BENEFIT ANALYSIS

CHAPTER ONE

Project Analysis—Private and Social Profitability

Projects are the building blocks of an investment plan. All investment is planned by someone; factories and canals do not just happen. The plan cannot be good if its constituent parts are faulty. This applies whether we are considering the investment plan of a corporation, or a country. Some investment plans may consist of a single project: but often there are many projects, more or less inter-related. This book is basically concerned with the evaluation of projects: but since projects are often parts of plans it is inevitably also a book about economic planning.

1.1 THE DEFINITION OF A PROJECT

We mean by a project any scheme, or part of a scheme, for investing resources which can reasonably be analysed and evaluated as an independent unit. The definition is thus arbitrary. Almost any project could be broken down into parts for separate consideration: each of those parts would then be by definition a project. But it would not be sensible to consider separately two projects if they were so closely linked that one could not be operated, or fulfil its purpose, without the other. In such a case the two parts must be considered as a whole—that is, as one project.

Some examples will suggest when it is sensible to break down what would otherwise be a project into smaller projects for separate consideration, or build up what would otherwise be smaller projects into a larger one. A transmission system is essential to the functioning of a motor-car; but it is possible to buy transmissions, whose production can be considered as a separate project; furthermore, if it was decided to make transmissions it might be right to make them for other car manufacturers as well as for oneself. On the other hand, it would not make sense for an irrigation authority to present as two projects, for separate consideration, a dam and the main canal to distribute the water. These are both cases where one part cannot work without the other. The difference is that transmissions may be more economically made by another manufacturer, perhaps even in another country, possibly because he has spare capacity, or because they can be made on a scale which is not linked to the particular motor-car whose production is under consideration; while the canal is precisely linked to the size of the dam, and its construction cannot be economically integrated with other construction work.

One can give other examples where the separability or otherwise of parts of a project is more in doubt. Let us suppose an airport authority is considering turning a landing ground, with no runway and a few old huts, into a small civil airport. Should it expect its planning staff to present the proposed runway and terminal building as two projects or as one? A civil airport can hardly operate with no passenger facilities at all, but the huts could be used as a make-shift. Without the terminal there would be some traffic and many complaints: with it, traffic would build up a little more, and there would be fewer complaints. This makes it possible to assess the terminal independently: it is a separable part of the airport, and its inclusion or exclusion makes a difference to costs and revenue. In theory, then, it should be a separate project. In practice, in such a case it is very possible that it would not be submitted to the board of management as a separate project.

The above example brings out the important point that projects are considered at many levels. The fact that the planner might submit only a design for a runway–terminal complex, together with a profitability analysis, to his board, does not necessarily imply that he has not himself considered the terminal as a separate project (and if he has not done so, he should have). It is possible that a very cursory consideration convinced him that it was not worth the detailed work required to present it separately to the board. Or again, he might be correct in assuming that the 'intangible' factor of complaints would weigh so heavily with the board that the decision would be a foregone conclusion.

Thus designers and planners themselves accept and reject many sub-projects before making any formal submission of a project to higher authority. This is really part of the process of design, or formulation of a project. It is also inevitable. Higher authority cannot be consulted about everything. But we should further note that, in accepting and rejecting sub-projects, planners, down to quite junior levels, inevitably make judgments which are commonly thought of as judgments of policy. For instance, in failing to submit the terminal as a separate project, the planner may have been partly guided by the thought that air-passengers ought to be provided with certain standards of service. Moreover, in the design of the terminal itself, he must himself have taken many decisions of the same kind.

Planners, of course, must keep broadly in line with policies laid down from above. It is an essential part of good economic management, both at the national and lower levels, that policies should be laid down in such a way that planners and administrators feel able to go ahead without constant reference upwards, and yet feel that they are not usurping political authority to an undue extent. Nevertheless, they must usurp political authority to *some* extent. Economic advisers and administrators are, for instance, constantly influencing and taking decisions which benefit one person at the expense of another, and which are not predetermined by any rigid rule—decisions which are in the nature of value judgments. The planner who is too chary about making such judgments is not worth his salt.

What have we now established? First, a project is not just some grand design for a steelworks, a river valley, or a supersonic passenger plane which will be described (and normally recommended) in several tomes, and be considered (and normally approved) by a Cabinet Committee. It is any item of investment which can be separately evaluated. Thus projects are considered and evaluated at all levels from a junior engineer to the Planning Commission or the World Bank. They are also analysed at all depths, from the back of the envelope to many volumes of erudite programming and scientific guesswork or prediction. Secondly, project *decisions* are taken at all levels: the process of design consists of rejecting and accepting alternatives, many of which are projects in our sense of the term.

It is clearly desirable that all projects should be evaluated, so far as possible, by applying the same principles. Otherwise inconsistent decisions are certain to be made. Thus our junior engineer, or settlement planner, should be guided by the same rules and methods as are used in the final appraisal of the steelworks or the river valley scheme.

The above kind of planning harmony should not be too difficult to achieve in the case of a corporation whose sole aim is to maximize its profits (or, more accurately, its present value—see below). The planning engineer then knows that he should design with this aim in view. He will have to predict market prices in so doing, these being the prices which the corporation faces. As against this, it quite often happens that executives get a hunch about some scheme, and become personally committed to promoting or opposing it as the case may be. It is not then difficult for them to steer their predictions to support their case. The board is often in no position to check the predictions, and may well not understand how they were arrived at. The same applies in the case of a nationalized industry and its responsible ministry; and in the case of spending ministries and the planning department or finance ministry.

In general, we shall see that harmony is much more difficult to achieve when one is trying to plan to maximum social advantage for a whole country. This book can be considered as an exploration of the means of achieving this very difficult aim.

1.2 A General Defence of Project Appraisal

Before turning to the analysis of projects, it is worth mentioning that a few economists, mostly those who put great faith in broad macroeconomic strategies, have tended to belittle the subject. One line of argument is that what matters for development is simply more investment, the kind of investment being of little importance. It is difficult to see how anyone can still believe this when there is so much evidence of investment in LDCs which has yielded little or nothing. A more sophisticated reason given is that the whole is greater than the sum of the parts. This enigmatic proposition can be explained with reference to our airport. If one evaluated the terminal without the runway, and the runway without the terminal, and added the two together, one would understate the value of the airport. It is undoubtedly true that very many projects help each other—in economists' jargon they have external benefits. Others may damage each other. Where this is obvious, one will consider such interlinked projects together (one thus internalizes the externalities of the sub-projects by considering them together as a single project). It is also true that a new project may help or damage existing investments. What is being claimed therefore is that project evaluators will habitually neglect the less obvious externalities —and that these are important enough to make project analyses dangerous or even valueless.

We believe this attitude has done enormous damage in developing countries. It strains the imagination to believe that these unclear external effects (if they are clear they can be allowed for) vary so much from project to project as to make the analysis of individual acts of investment valueless. The logical end to this line of argument is to say either that it does not matter what a country invests in or how it does it; or to put one's faith in God or in the insight of some other central planner. Since few, if any, really believe either of these conclusions, the effect has been not to eliminate project evaluation, but to cause it to be undervalued and hence to be badly done. There are many monuments to this neglect in the developing world (and some in all countries).

It is often argued that management is very important: and with this we certainly agree. But the importance of good management in no way reduces the need to have well-designed projects which, if they are operated properly, will substantially increase the national welfare. Many investments are made, which work as they were designed to do, being well managed, and are yet very poor investments because they produce the wrong things or satisfy only a low priority need. Indeed, we would think that good management usually tends to be discouraged if the managers know that they are working at something which was ill-conceived: no doubt cases can be cited where an ill-conceived investment turns out to be quite good, because an imaginative and flexible management solves the problems which are thrown up, and in so doing learns something which may be of further use; but that 'company doctors' may learn a thing or two is hardly a good reason for producing handicapped infants.

1.3 THE BASIC DATA REQUIRED

It is easiest to approach the subject of the social cost–benefit analysis of a project by first considering how a private profitability analysis is conducted.

The starting point of the analysis is to specify all the expected inputs and outputs of the project, and to put a price to each such input and output. In this way, one arrives at anticipated expenditures and receipts. These will be spaced over time from the inception of planning to the economic demise of the project (that is, when it ceases to be profitable to operate it), or to eternity. These guesses are then combined into some measure of profitability. It is now generally accepted that, from the point of view of an enterprise, the best method of thus combining the data is that known as 'discounted cash flow' (DCF), which will be explained in 1.4.

Reverting to profitability analysis, the basic figures required annually in order to conduct a DCF analysis are as follows:

(i) all payments received from the sale of outputs of the project for each year of the life of the project, these including the sale of any buildings and equipment remaining at the end of the life of the project; and

(ii) all payments made for goods and services used by the project according to the year in which they are made, from the date of the first expenditures until the end of the life of the project.[1] These include payments of capital costs, whether for initial equipment or for replacement, as well as all current costs.

For purposes of prediction and for assessing the reliability of such prediction, all the values of the above receipts and expenditures should wherever possible be split into quantities and prices. To ensure that all related receipts and expenditures are taken into account, the total effect of the project upon the enterprise must be considered. The key question is: what would the annual receipts and expenditures of the enterprise be if the project were undertaken, compared with what they would be if it were not?

These figures of annual receipts and incomes, split into quantities and prices, are required for a social cost–benefit analysis just as much as for a profitability analysis. While, as we have seen, a social cost–benefit analysis may revalue the quantities of goods and services used and produced (that is, use different prices from those appropriate to an estimate of profitability), nevertheless such shadow prices will often be based on the prices which enter into the profitability analysis.

The above figures are thus the raw material with which the economic evaluator works, whether he works for an enterprise or in a planning bureau. If these basic predictions are to be as accurately established as possible, a great deal of preliminary work is required. It cannot be too strongly emphasized that such work is as essential for social cost–benefit analysis as it is for profitability analysis.

The reliability of the basic figures—the quantities and prices of inputs and outputs—depend upon three kinds of considerations: (*a*) technical, (*b*) human and managerial, and (*c*) economic.

It is a technical matter whether the physical inputs and outputs, which are presupposed by the figures for receipts and expenditures,

---

[1] Strictly speaking, the life of a project is not a technological datum. The project should 'die' when it no longer pays to operate it, making such repairs and replacements as are necessary. Sometimes it is easiest to estimate on the basis of an infinite life, allowing sufficient replacement expenditure to make it so. Accuracy is not, however, important in assigning a life to a project, unless the discount rate used is exceptionally low.

are consistent with each other. For instance, is it true that the stated quantities of raw materials, components, and fuels, when properly fed into the designed plant will produce the stated quantities of outputs for the number of years for which the project is supposed to endure? This all concerns quantities, not prices, and is a matter for engineers. Its importance is obvious. Dams do break and plants have technical troubles. The quality of inputs may be wrongly assessed, with disappointing results—and so on. With advanced technical processes, for example, in the chemical and metallurgical industries, economic failure has quite often been due to technical failure. But, considering investment as a whole, it is probably true that technical miscalculation is a cause of major economic failure in a minority of cases.

Turn now to the question of management and skills. This is a more frequent cause for disappointment. One should distinguish four different ways in which over-optimistic assumptions about the quality of management and the skill of the labour force affect the predicted figures for inputs and outputs. First, the period of construction is underestimated. Despite exceptions, it has been the rule in developing countries (and common in all countries) that major projects take longer to complete than is allowed for in the project report. This has probably been because neither the consultant engineers nor the host government departments had much experience of industrial projects in developing countries and therefore underestimated the difficulties. Secondly, the period between when a plant is finished and when the new management team and labour force are sufficiently skilled to be able to operate it at its rated capacity, has usually been underestimated. Again, the reason has probably been that there was little experience to go on. Thirdly, of course, it is always possible that the rated capacity is never attained, despite there being no reason for this, from a technical point of view, because of insufficient demand or insufficient supply of materials. Fourthly, although the rated capacity is attained, it may be attained only with the use of more inputs, especially labour, than was allowed for. This excess use of labour is extremely common, and is not always the fault of the management itself. It is often forced upon the management for political reasons, or because labour laws make it virtually impossible to sack anyone.

We turn now to the economic assumptions which lie behind the basic figures used for the economic evaluation of profitability or cost–benefit, and first consider the receipts. First, the figures naturally imply that a certain amount of output can be sold, and at a certain price, for every year of the project's economic life. This presupposes that a sound demand analysis has been made. Demand will always depend to a lesser or greater extent on government policies and/or planning. This subject will be reconsidered in 6.21, since the government's proper influence on demand is very closely linked with social cost–benefit analysis. From a cost–benefit point of view, outputs may be valued at different prices from those actually obtained, but this in no way interferes with the need to establish that the outputs can be sold at the actual prices assumed in the project analysis.

Secondly, of course, the basic figures also presume that realistic prices have been attached to current inputs of materials, components, and labour, throughout the life of a project: and that these inputs will be obtainable when wanted. The chief reasons for their sometimes not being obtainable are (*a*) exchange control forced on the government because of a failure to be realistic in foreign exchange planning, and (*b*) delays in the establishment of other projects which should have supplied these inputs, and/or a failure to supply inputs of the right specifications.

As far as this initial capital investment goes, the reality of the cost estimates depends largely on the advice of the engineers, and also upon the nature of the contracts with the supplying firms. Particular attention must be paid to construction costs and estimated construction periods, since underestimation and long delays are commonplace. It should also be noted that changes in design may release supplying firms from the original contract prices.

In saying that all the above matters are presupposed in the basic figures which confront the economic evaluator or evaluation team, it should not be assumed that their function does not include that of asking nasty questions about all of these assumptions. Certainly, in the case of major projects, it must be someone's function to do just this. Indeed, it is of great importance that some central staff should undertake this essential probing. This is because projects will come up from many different sources, from different departments of government employing their own different staffs, or from different consulting engineers. In these circumstances it is almost inevitable that different degrees of care will have been exercised. Moreover, different, even conflicting, assumptions will often have been made. We shall return again to this subject in 6.5.

From now on, since our subject is the *evaluation* of projects, not their design and formulation, it is assumed that the basic engineering and demand and cost analyses have been properly conducted for every project and every variant of every project which is to be evaluated.

1.4 DCF ANALYSIS, AND MEASURES OF PROFITABILITY

We first outline the procedure from the point of view of a firm or enterprise, and then turn to social cost–benefit analysis.

The principle upon which DCF evaluations are based is that money has a time value. $100 received now is worth more than $100 received in a year's time, because it can be used meanwhile to earn a return. For example, if it could be invested at 10% p.a., it would be worth $110 after a year and $121 after two years. In these circumstances $121 received in two years' time can be said to have a 'present value' of $100, the future sum being 'discounted' at the rate of 10% p.a. The discounting process is thus simply compound interest worked backwards.

The first step in carrying out a DCF evaluation is to record, year by year throughout the expected life of the project, all expected expenditure payments for goods and services for the project (including capital expenditures) and all expected receipts from the project. For each year, the subtraction of the former from the latter shows how much cash the firm gains or loses as a result of the project. Borrowing and lending, and interest or dividend payments, are normally excluded from the concept of 'cash flow' when this is used for the purpose of assessing the profitability of a new investment. The fairly common exception to the above rule is when the financial flows, or some part of them, are tied to the project and thus cannot be separately considered. It should also be noticed that direct tax payments are, from a firm's point of view, a use of resources: from the social point of view, as we shall see later, this is not so.

The difference between cash flow accounting and most forms of normal commercial accounting are as follows:

(i) In normal accounting income and expenditure represent the values of goods or services delivered (sometimes into stock) and received; not the cash received and paid out for them.

(ii) Normal accounting shows financial liabilities, with respect to interest and tax, not payments. There are sometimes large differences of timing here.

(iii) A financial allowance for depreciation and obsolescence of capital is made in normal accounting. In cash flow accounting there is no such provision, but anticipated renewals and replacements will be included as well as the scrap value of the equipment.

The second step is to discount future cash flows back to the present. For this purpose the enterprise must select a rate of discount. This is the rate of return which, given the financial conditions for obtaining cash and the investment opportunities likely to be open to the firm in future years, it deems prudent to aim to earn on its new investments.

As already explained, the process of discounting is simply compound interest worked backwards. In general, the present value of any future receipt or expenditure is calculated by multiplying it by $1/(1+d)^t$, where $100\ d$ is the percentage rate of discount and t is the number of years ahead.[1] Thus, by this process of discounting, expenditures and receipts which occur at different times throughout the construction and operation of the project (and are to this extent incomparable) are all revalued to make them comparable to present expenditures and receipts. They can then all be added up to give a single figure which is therefore named the *present value of the project* (PV). It comes to the same thing, and is more convenient, to subtract expenditures from receipts to give a net cash flow for each year, and then discount these cash flows back to the present. This also gives the PV of the project—hence the term 'discounted cash flow'. PV is one important measure of profitability. It assumes that capital funds, and receipts on current account, need not be distinguished from each other. They are, both of them, just money. This lack of distinction between the two is fully justified if the firm can borrow (or lend) as much as it chooses at a fixed rate of interest equal to the discount rate used to arrive at the PV. If this is the case, there can be no special shortage of investible funds.

But if investment funds are constrained in any way (other than by their price) then it becomes impossible to give any simple investment rule. This is because there is no rate of discount, given from outside

---

[1] We have assumed, for simplicity, a constant rate of discount over time. But it is possible that changes in the rate of discount will be anticipated. More generally, a future item may be multiplied by

$$\frac{1}{(1+d_1)(1+d_2)\ \ldots\ (1+d_t)}$$

where d_1 is the fractional discount rate between now and next year, d_2 the rate between next year and the one after, and so on. If the ds are all equal this collapses to $1/(1+d)^t$ as in the text.

the enterprise, which expresses the value of capital and is independent of its own investment opportunities (which will themselves partly govern its future investible funds). In these circumstances the enterprise will need to guess a discount rate which will, it hopes, be a sufficient measure of the financial constraints it suffers and yet will not be so high as to stop investments which would have been beneficial. Such a rule, using some arbitrary discount rate rather higher than the market rate, is certainly useful, perhaps essential, but cannot be regarded as better than a 'rule of thumb'.

It is also useful to calculate a second measure of profitability, the *internal rate of return* (IRR)—that is, the 'yield'—of the project. By definition this is the rate of discount which makes the PV of the project zero.[1] It can be called the 'yield', because it is closely analogous to the yield of a security. Thus if a $100 bond pays a dividend of $5 per annum for ever, one says that it yields 5%. But the IRR of a purchase of this bond is also 5%, because $5 for ever discounted at 5% gives a PV of $100, equal to the purchase price of the bond—so that the PV is zero.

One reason for calculating the yield is that entrepreneurs and other investors are more used to judging investments by their yield than by either of the other measures put forward. Another reason is that the PV gives no indication of whether a project is close to the margin of acceptability. Two projects may have the same PV, one being a large project with an IRR only just above the discount rate, while the other is a very small project with quite a high IRR. If the management is unsure of its target rate of discount, then it is useful to have this information. Finally, the enterprise may not have decided on a rate of discount to use, and in this case the PV cannot be calculated: on the other hand, the IRR is of limited use if decision-makers do not have a target yield to compare it with; and, in effect, a target yield is the same thing as a rate of discount.

Moreover, the IRR is not always a reliable guide. This can be seen by turning to the ways in which measures of profitability may be used to select and reject projects. In discussing this we shall assume that the enterprise has unlimited access to funds at a given interest rate.

Suppose the enterprise has to choose between, say, a small factory and a large one. Now it is possible that the small factory would give

---

[1] In the case of some projects there may be several discount rates which make the PV zero. In that case, it is probable that none of these discount rates is very useful for comparing it with other projects. This is one of the reasons why general reliance cannot be placed on the internal rate of return.

the higher yield, but the smaller PV. In this case, the firm should of course borrow more and build the larger factory, for it is its PV that it wants to maximize. The point is that the IRR, being a pure number, gives no indication of size. Sometimes it is best to make a large investment at a lower yield rather than a small one with a higher yield.

Why not make both investments, the reader may well ask? But that would not be possible if the large and small factories were mutually incompatible—and each was evaluated on the assumption that the other would not be built. Other examples of mutual incompatibility arise when comparing the same factory this year and next year; or a large and small dam on the same river; or any number of alternative schemes for settling the same agricultural region. In all these cases, the IRR may give the wrong answer. It is necessary to stress this. Only very recently a famous firm of consultants told us that they had been instructed by the IBRD to maximize the internal rate of return when designing an irrigation scheme: no doubt there was some misunderstanding.

Thus the IRR can be safely used only if there is no incompatibility:[1] it then makes no difference whether one follows the rule 'do everything which yields 11% or more', or the rule 'do everything which has zero or more PV at a discount rate of 11%'; the same projects would qualify under either rule—and the same ones fail.

1.5 THE CONSIDERATION OF ALTERNATIVES

In the case of incompatible alternatives, confusion sometimes arises because of the dictum that a profitability (or social cost–benefit) analysis is essentially comparing the future stream of profits of the enterprise (or society) with and without the project under examination. This seems to imply that the alternative to doing the project is to do nothing. Yet, of course, the alternative of doing nothing is frequently unrealistic. For instance, the realistic alternative to building a new factory may be to enlarge and refurbish an existing one. This particular confusion is easily resolved. Each option, refurbishing or building anew, is compared with doing nothing: the PVs of the difference which each option makes as compared with doing nothing can then be compared with each other.

Even so, some ambiguity as to the meaning of 'doing nothing' can

---

[1] Except when the possibility mentioned in the previous footnote arises.

arise. For instance, does 'doing nothing' imply that the old factory would not even be maintained? In the case of an on-going business contemplating expansion, it could be taken that 'doing nothing' meant going on as before—that is, using and maintaining the old factory. However, it is quite possible to compare the PV of continuing as before with closing down the business. The moral is that one should be quite clear what is being compared with what. Usually the comparison will be as between some new investment, or several alternative new investments, and carrying on as before.

Neglect of possible alternatives can be regarded as a case of making the wrong comparison. Suppose a country is contemplating a new port, because an existing one is rapidly falling into disrepair. The PV of the new port might look very great if, without it, the country would lose much of its foreign trade. It may still be a bad project, because rebuilding the old port might show a still higher PV—both being compared with letting the old port go to ruin. Equally, some repair work may show a high PV: but this does not prove that the asset should not have been allowed to fall to pieces, and a new one built.

1.6 Short-cuts

In 1.4 we explained what may be termed the full treatment. This should always be carried out for any very large investment expenditure (in public sector industries in the U.K., for example, it is mandatory for all investments submitted for government approval—which in most cases are those of over £1 million). But we have also emphasized that designers make many decisions on a scale which would not warrant the full treatment: they may also want to make a rough check where intuition suggests the answer anyway.

One of the most obvious short-cuts is to compare the gross return on capital invested, for a single year's presumably normal operation, with the annual rate of capital cost (interest, plus an allowance for depreciation). Such a measure is imperfect on two counts. First, it makes no allowance for the length of time which elapses before the project reaches a normal year's operation, which can vary greatly between projects. Second, depreciation is an essentially arbitrary financial measure, loosely related to the life of the project.

Another short-cut is known as the pay-off (or pay-back) period.

Since this attempts to allow for risk, which has been deliberately neglected in this chapter, it is discussed in 15.7.

We do not recommend either of the above methods, even as a short-cut. It seems better to aim at the right sort of calculation in as abbreviated a manner as circumstances dictate. As an example, one might guess the capital cost at the date of commencement of operations, allowing for interest if the gestation period is much more than a year. Then one can put in a constant figure for annual operating costs, and give the project a certain life, say 15 years. With compound interest tables it is then only a few minutes' work to deduce a figure for average annual earnings which, when discounted to the date of commencement of operations, gives a total equal to the capital cost. This estimate of required earnings can then be compared with the likely reality, and if it seems implausibly high, the project need not be considered further.

1.7 DISCOUNTED RESOURCE FLOWS, AND SOCIAL PROFITABILITY

Turning finally to social cost–benefit analysis, we can be brief because it takes exactly the same form as a profitability analysis. Indeed, a profitability analysis is a private cost–benefit analysis—although, to save words, we shall use the phrase 'cost–benefit analysis' always to refer to the social variety. The easiest way to understand social cost–benefit analysis is therefore to examine the differences.

Two differences have already been referred to. The first was that inputs and outputs may be differently valued. For instance, the output may or may not be valued net of indirect taxes; similarly, payment for current inputs will probably include some indirect taxes, which may be subtracted. We emphasize the word 'may'— the treatment of indirect taxes is dealt with in 12.5. Nor, as we shall see, are taxes the only reason for putting different values on inputs and outputs from those which are relevant for the enterprise's own accounts.

The second difference already mentioned was that there may be some benefits or costs resulting from the project's operation which would not appear as inputs or outputs in the ordinary accounts. Any such benefits or costs have to be separately added or subtracted for every year of operation during which they occur.

The third difference is one of timing. For instance, in a project's DCF accounts, payment for items of equipment will occur well after the dates when resources were used in its construction, which is when the social costs are incurred. It would be a counsel of undue perfection always to try to allow for this, but sometimes it could be important (see 9.6).

Only one further point requires to be made at this stage, which is that the discount rate used to arrive at the *present social value* (PSV) will usually differ from the market rate of interest which might be used by a private firm.

CHAPTER TWO

The Need for Cost–Benefit Analysis

It is a tenet of laissez-faire capitalism that profits measure the gain which society derives from a project. The acceptance of this view seems to permit capitalists to claim the moral plaudits of society as they line their pockets. Yet it cannot be dismissed as intolerable hypocrisy, for the theory that profits measure social (and not merely private) gains has no necessary connection with capitalism at all. Indeed, many would think the theory more valid for a socialist society; and it is generally recognized that profits have an important, even essential, role to play in a socialist society. But just what role?

2.1 The Function of Profits

Profit (or loss) can be thought of as a necessary feature of any decentralization of economic decisions. If institutions and people (these inevitably include local and central government departments and agencies, private people who sell their services and buy consumption goods, and foreigners; and also, in a mixed economy, private firms) are free to buy or sell then they must have an effect on the profit of any project—for there must always be a profit or loss if *any* output or input is bought or sold, rather than allocated without charge. But these offers and demands can be made effective only if some positive response is made to them, such as making investments which promise to be profitable and rejecting those which do not. It is clear that such a response may be the wrong one if profits in fact fail to reflect social gains. Thus profits are an almost essential signalling mechanism for guiding decentralized investment decisions—but they may or may not be a *good* signalling mechanism. They are good only if expenditures closely measure social costs and receipts closely measure social benefits.

The reader may well ask at this stage if it does not make a difference that public sector profits accrue to the state, and private sector profits to individuals (to the extent that they are not taxed away). It may well seem more plausible that profits can be a good measure of social gain if they are, in the first instance, received by the government rather than going, in part, directly to individuals. We shall discuss this argument later. Here we need only remark that if profits which go to individuals are worth less to society than those which go to the government then a cost–benefit analysis can make allowance for this.

The essence of a cost–benefit analysis is that it does *not* accept that actual receipts adequately measure social benefits, and actual expenditures social costs. But it does accept that actual receipts and expenditures can be suitably adjusted so that the difference between them, which is therefore very closely analogous to ordinary profit, will properly reflect the social gain. The prices used, after such adjustments have been made, will be called 'social accounting prices', or for short 'accounting prices'. The difference between receipts and costs measured at accounting prices is, therefore, most appropriately called 'social profit'. A rider to this is that a further adjustment may be thought necessary in the light of the previous paragraph depending on who receives the actual profits.

We sum up the above discussion by saying that cost–benefit analysis is the more necessary the greater the extent to which project expenditures differ from the social costs which, according to the theory of laissez-faire, they ought to measure—and similarly for project receipts.

2.2 The Requirements for Private and Social Profit to Coincide

First, then, we ask under what conditions costs to a firm exactly measure costs to society. To put it another way, we ask 'What assumptions do we need to make about the real world, if the theory that actual costs measure social cost is to be exactly true?' For simplicity of exposition we shall first deal with a society which has no foreign trade. The complications of foreign trade and payments are considered later. Even without this complication readers with no economic training may find the rest of 2.2 a little esoteric.

2.21 *Full Employment*
The basic requirement is that if Firm A buys a good or service, to the value of $1, then that will result in the loss of $1 worth of benefit elsewhere in the economy; for the loss to society of a benefit of $1 is, of course, a cost to society of $1.

Suppose that the service bought is 1 man-day of unskilled labour. The man, if not employed by Firm A, might have sat idle. Now if he would have been only just willing to give up a day of leisure for a $1, it is true that there is a real social cost of $1 in employing him, and the theory holds. But this example points to one important assumption of the theory, which is that *there should not be involuntary unemployment or underemployment* for then the man will not have valued his leisure at $1, since he would have preferred to work.

2.22 *No Influence on Prices and Profit Maximization*
If the man would have had other employment (say, in Firm B), then the requirement is that he would have increased the production of Firm B so as to benefit society by $1. That this should be so requires:

   (i) that Firm B would also pay him $1, and would employ him for $1 only if the resultant extra product sold for $1, no more and no less;
   (ii) that the sale of this extra product for $1 implies a benefit to society of $1.

We shall return to the second requirement (ii) under the discussion of benefits, but (i) needs elaboration as follows. First assume that Firm B has to pay the man $1. Presumably, it would *not* employ him unless the extra receipts from the resulting rise in production were equal to $1 or more. Now the extra receipts equal the price obtained for the extra product, *provided that* it is possible to sell this extra product without reducing the price previously obtained. Given this proviso, it appears that the sales value of the extra product must equal or exceed the wage that had to be paid in order to get that extra product.

But if the sales value exceeds the wage paid ($1), then it is worth employing yet another man, and so on until the sales value is equal to the wage paid, *provided that* there is no need to raise the wages of those already employed, when taking on an extra man for $1. Thus the firm might know that wage rates will rise if employment is increased, in which case it would need to subtract this extra cost from the extra sales proceeds before deciding whether to employ another man.

But, given the above two provisos, it follows that the extra product from an extra man-day costing $1 will sell for exactly $1. The two provisos can be generalized as follows: if a firm has no influence on the price of anything it buys or sells, then (assuming that it tries to make as much money as it can), the extra product resulting from the employment of a dollar's worth of extra labour (or anything else) will sell for $1. Where these conditions hold true a firm employing many men makes no profit on the last man it employs, and its profits do not change as a result of losing a man to another firm. So Firm B's profits would not change as the result of Firm A taking a man from it, and the social cost of employing the man in Firm A is therefore the value of his alternative product in Firm B. The condition of 'no influence on prices or wages', together with the assumption of 'no voluntary unemployment', also imply that Firm B would have had to pay the man the same as Firm A, i.e. $1.

The conditions given above (*maximizing profits*, and *no influence on prices, including wages*) are, in economic jargon, those of 'perfect competition'.

Mutatis mutandis, what we have said about Firm A buying a man-hour of labour applies to any input it buys. If it buys an amount of steel costing $1, the above assumptions imply either an extra cost to society of $1 as a result of producing more steel, or the loss of a benefit of $1 as a result of using less steel elsewhere.

The discussion of this section has assumed that if the product of a firm sells for $1, then the firm receives $1. In reality it is true only if there are no indirect taxes or subsidies. In national income accounting terms output may be valued at 'market prices' (what the product sells for), or at 'factor cost' which is market price less indirect taxes plus indirect subsidies, i.e. what the firm receives. We return to this subject in 2.27.

2.23 *Marginality*

It should next be noticed that we have discussed small changes in production and resource use. It cannot be expected that a very large purchase of some input will give rise to a negligible change in profit elsewhere in the economy. If there is a significant change, the profit of Firm A cannot be a precise measure of society's benefit, although it may still be a good approximate measure.

2.24 *The Distribution of Wealth, and Government Consumption*

So much for costs. We turn now to the consideration of benefits. Why should it be supposed that a dollar's worth of a good sold represents a benefit to society of $1?

The good may be sold to the public, to another firm, or to the government. It may also be used for current purposes, or for investment. Consider, first, sales of consumption goods to the public.

Now consumption, including leisure, is normally taken as the ultimate end of economic activity. In other words, if some ordinary individual buys a good for $1, that is deemed to be a benefit of $1 (but see 2.27 and elsewhere for qualifications to this proposition). The problems associated with defining the end or ends of economic activity will be taken up again in Chapter IV. But one problem, that of income distribution, must be mentioned immediately. Surely a dollar's worth of consumption by a rich man, and a poor man, cannot both be reckoned as a benefit of $1 to society? Yet the view that profits are the best measure of benefit presupposes that it is so reckoned. We are now hard up against one of the basic theoretical and practical problems of economics. There will be further discussion of the problem later. Here we shall merely record that the profitability measure treats a dollar's worth of consumption as equally beneficial no matter who gets it. Consequently profitability will be a good measure of the net social benefit (i.e. the social profit) of a project only if, in the case under consideration, neglect of income distribution can be justified.

When a good is sold to another firm, given perfect competition (see 2.22), the sale must result in extra production of equal value, and, however long the intermediate chain, the case can therefore be identified with the sale of a final product—to consumers as before, or to the government. So far as government purchases of final goods are concerned, it is difficult to make any general assumption other than that governments act rationally on society's behalf (although we know it is not always true). This implies that a dollar's worth of one good is worth the same to society as a dollar's worth of any other good, whether bought collectively or individually (but see Chapters IX and XIII for further discussion and qualification of this point).

2.25 *Interest Rates, Risk, and Investment*
We have seen that there is a problem of comparing the consumption of different people. There is also a problem of comparing consumption at different periods. It is clear that a dollar's worth of consumption in 10 years' time may not be as valuable as a dollar's worth of consumption today (at constant prices, for we are not thinking here of changes in the value of money). For instance, a dollar's worth of consumption in 10 years' time might be thought to be no more valuable than half a dollar of consumption today. Now the profitability analysis described in 1.4 discounts future sales at an interest rate more or less close to the rate at which the firm could borrow (after allowing for risk). On this account, it follows that profitability is a good measure of social benefit only insofar as the rate at which the firm could borrow is the same as the rate at which

society ought to discount future consumption—this latter rate will be discussed in 2.48 and elsewhere. Here we need say only that it is questionable whether one can normally expect a close coincidence of the two rates. It should also be added that there may be no coincidence between the risks which any private profitability analysis must take into account, and the risks which society should allow for.

We have thus far written as if all goods and services produced were consumption goods. What is the benefit of a good or service used for investment, which yields no immediate satisfaction? The answer is that it must be valued in terms of the discounted consumption which it makes possible. In theory, under conditions of perfect competition (which implies also that firms do all the investment which pays), and assuming no difference between the rate of discount used by firms and the rate at which the future ought to be discounted, the value of an investment good will always be equal to the discounted value of the future extra consumption which it permits. Thus investment of an extra \$1 will produce a future consumption stream with the present value of \$1, which implies of course that the producer's good purchased with this extra dollar also has the same value as a present consumption good sold for \$1. Under these conditions society is indifferent as to whether it gets a little more consumption or a little more investment.

2.26 *External Effects*

It may happen that a firm's activities (and it should be recognized that by a 'firm' we really mean any individual or organization which both buys and sells goods and services) result in costs or benefits for society, which have no correspondence to its actual purchases or sales. A very traditional example, which has nevertheless only recently aroused much public attention, is pollution of the atmosphere. This is a cost to society, for which the firm does not have to pay—it does not compensate society for the damage it causes. On the benefit side, a good example is that a firm may both help to train its labour, and also has to pay a higher wage as a result, in order to retain it. In other words it 'produces' more fully trained people—but these it cannot sell (slavery having been outlawed). However, this example is watertight only if the firm has to pay the full market price for those whom it trains. In the case of trainees and apprentices, this is often not so. Also, football clubs are an exception (at least in the U.K.), for they 'sell', by means of a transfer fee, their players to other clubs.

Many, but not all, external economies and diseconomies can be ascribed to the non-fulfilment of the condition of perfect competition. A good example is when an extension of activity by one firm, or an increase in its purchases, would result in a lowering of cost per unit of output in another firm which supplies some of its inputs. This may happen when the latter firm's costs decline with increasing output—due, in the long run, to 'economies of scale'. But economies of scale which continue up to indefinitely large outputs are not consistent with perfect competition. This is because, in an industry where such economies of scale prevail, there will inevitably be so few firms that each must have an influence on the price at which it can sell its output.

But, since not all external benefits and costs can be ascribed to lack of perfect competition, it follows that such externalities must be assumed away if private profitability is to be an exact measure of net social benefit. External costs and benefits may arise in consumption as well as production, as noted in the next section.

2.27 *Consumers' Sovereignty and Public Goods*
It has been said that consumption is supposed to be the end of economic activity, and hence that everything can be valued in terms of its immediate or ultimate contribution to this end. This is part of what is meant by consumers' sovereignty. But the term usually implies rather more—that market prices, as determined by technical conditions of production and consumers' tastes, are the best measures of the relative benefit of different items of consumption. But where consumption itself has external benefits or costs, there is a clear case for denying this. If someone buys a handkerchief to sneeze into, he helps to keep his cold to himself.

Aside from such external effects, certain kinds of consumption expenditure are sometimes thought to be more or less worthy than their market valuation suggests. Thus a classical education is felt to be good, and alcohol bad. How far the government should be paternal is always a very open question. But it should be noted that 'bad' consumption is generally taxed so that the producer does not receive as much as the public pays, and consequently production and consumption is less than it otherwise would be. Similarly, 'good' consumption may be subsidized. Goods are also taxed and subsidized for income distribution reasons. This raises the question of the treatment of indirect taxes and subsidies. If consumers' sovereignty is taken very seriously, goods and services should be valued at market prices—what the consumer pays. But this has queer consequences. Thus project evaluation of cigarette factories would show large benefits, implying that more cigarettes should be made and sold, which could only be done if the tax were lowered. This would be futile, if it were long-standing government policy to tax cigarettes heavily.

The proper treatment of indirect taxes in project analysis is quite complicated, and a fuller discussion will be found in Chapters V and XII.

As already mentioned in 2.24, governments, both central and local, also buy consumption goods. Sometimes these goods (or their services when they are of a durable nature) are supplied free to individuals, and sometimes a charge is made. Other kinds of public goods (like bombs and tanks, which are not normally reckoned as investment) are more essentially collective, since their use cannot be a matter of individual choice. There is, of course, always room for argument as to whether the government's demands for such goods are sensible: whether it should spend so much on defence, whether it should buy more tanks and fewer aircraft, whether it should provide free meals and textbooks in schools. But these arguments do not often take place at the level of project selection although cost–benefit methods have been applied to defence and other sectors where benefits are very difficult to determine. But if textbooks are supplied free as a matter of policy, then the project evaluator must take the cost of supply as the measure of benefit (bearing in mind that it may be possible to supply the government's demand either from imports or from domestic production). To put the same point in another way, the benefit may have to be taken for granted at the project level, and the problem becomes one of assessing what is the socially cheapest way of meeting the government's demands.[1]

2.3 GOVERNMENT ACTION TO BRING ABOUT A COINCIDENCE OF PRIVATE AND SOCIAL PROFIT

The conditions which must be fulfilled if profits are to be a perfect measure of net social benefit have now been described (very briefly—

---

[1] Where the project evaluation is not called upon to assess the benefit of the output, cost–benefit analysis becomes what is sometimes called 'cost-effectiveness' analysis. But where the project under consideration produces traded goods we still value the output as a benefit in the normal way, even although the quantity required may be fixed solely by the government (as might be the case, e.g. with armaments). This is because the government has the alternative of importing the goods. Only if there is no such alternative, or it is ruled out as a matter of policy, does the analysis reduce to one of cost-effectiveness—that is, one assesses the socially cheapest way of supplying from domestic resources a given governmental demand.

one could stock a library with works on this subject). Of course, the real world does not correspond to these conditions. Nor could it ever be forced into this non-Procrustean bed, or heavenly strait-jacket.

2.31   *The Regulatory Framework*

In the great majority of countries by far the greater part of economic activity (even where public) is guided by the price mechanism activated, on the production side, by the profit motive. At the same time, government intervention, partly designed to improve the aggregate social benefit of the system, is quite widespread.

Firstly, and most important, governments usually take responsi-bility for seeing that large scale unemployment does not result from a deficiency of demand. Secondly, where competition plainly either does not, or cannot, work even approximately in line with the economic assumptions which ensure its social advantages, then certain controls are often introduced—e.g. price or profit controls over monopolistic production, regulations affecting wage-bargaining and employment conditions, etc. Thirdly, progressive taxation is used to help achieve a more equal income distribution than laissez faire might produce. Fourthly, governments often underwrite certain risks which private persons find it hard to estimate, or over-estimate, or cannot easily insure against—for example, the insurance of export credits. Lastly, there is always a tremendous amount of legislation designed to see that people's private activities do not impinge unfavourably on others (external diseconomies)—legislation on the siting of industrial activity, on harmful effluents, offensive architecture, infectious diseases, prostitution, drunken driving, etc., etc. Interference with the price mechanism, rather than legislation, also plays a part—for example, very heavy taxation in some countries on smoking and drinking. The positive encouragement of activities with beneficial external effects is less common, but not unknown. For instance, there are subsidized bathrooms in Britain. Some may consider education to be a more serious example.

Thus the profit motive and price mechanism operate within a regulatory framework—partly taking the form of legislative and other controls, and partly that of changing effective prices. It is thus important not to forget that governments never adopt the position that profits arising from uninhibited operation of the price mechanism are always a good measure of social benefit. The process of improving the system by piecemeal reform is an unending one. This is not to say that government intervention, however well intentioned, is always beneficial. Although, on balance, controls over the operation of the price mechanism are probably beneficial, sometimes they make matters worse.

The question to be asked therefore is whether profits, as affected by such government legislation and control, and by taxation, are a good measure of benefit—and whether, if the conclusion is 'not very', cost–benefit analysis can do any better. It is always much easier to think of reasons why a system falls short of an ideal, than it is to devise one which is better.

2.32 *The Use of Cost–Benefit Analysis in Developed Economies*
Since few Western industrialized countries exercise any direct control over investments in the private sector, the question of the use of cost–benefit analysis in the selection of investment arises only for the public sector. Since the public sector tends to include activities, which would be unlikely to serve the public interest very well under a régime of competition, and since this is often part of the reason for their inclusion in the public sector, it might have been thought that attempts to measure social benefits and costs would have gone further than has been the case.

Admittedly, it is not easy to draw a very clear distinction between 'ordinary' project analysis in the public sector, and cost–benefit analysis. But if either accounting prices are used, or if costs and benefits which do not arise from the purchases and sales of what are normally reckoned as inputs and outputs are quantified in money terms; and if the social value of the project is given a final quantitative expression, then we would say that cost–benefit analysis was used.

The practical use of cost–benefit analysis began with water resource development in the United States in the 1930s. Despite its intimate theoretical connection with parts of traditional economics, it was originated by engineers. Its use in this connection has become mandatory, and it is now spreading to other fields. Cost-effectiveness analysis has also been extensively used in defence planning, and elsewhere. In the United Kingdom the use of cost–benefit analysis came later, and has been used mainly in the field of transport—e.g. studies of a new underground railway line in London, and of motorways. Mention should be made of the Roskill Commission which reported on the site for a third London Airport.[1] The use of accounting prices has also begun to be acceptable for the analysis of other projects.

---

[1] *Commission on the Third London Airport,* 1971.

France can claim the intellectual father of cost–benefit analysis: Jules Dupuit discussed the subject as early as 1844.[1] His concept of consumers' surplus is used today in the analysis of, among other things, road investments. In this sphere, and also in water-resource investments, cost–benefit analysis has quite precise expression in France. For instance, the utility of road improvements to the consumers, as well as external benefits and costs, are estimated quantitatively. An accounting rate of discount is used (common to all departments), and the limitation of available funds for particular purposes is recognized by using a shadow price, or premium exchange rate, for such funds.

In our sense, until very recently, cost–benefit analysis was not used in the U.S.S.R. The planners were mainly interested in industrialization for its own sake, and were therefore concerned primarily with consistency, that is the interlocking of supply and demand by the method of 'commodity balances'. There was no decentralization whereby project decisions were based on the social value of a project as measured by accounting prices. Furthermore, the planners looked on foreign trade more as a means of correcting mistakes in planning, as a result of which physical surpluses and deficits of particular goods would arise, than as a systematic means of achieving a more efficient use of resources. In contrast, in the Eastern European communist countries there has been considerable project appraisal based on accounting prices. It is believed that the U.S.S.R. is now also beginning to move in this direction.

Part of the reason why cost–benefit analysis has not been carried further in developed countries in the West, and has met some criticism, is because it has been chiefly thought of in relation to economic activities where either (*a*) the price mechanism can offer virtually no guide to benefits at all, that is, in fields where the output of the activity either cannot be, or as a matter of policy is not in practice, sold to individuals—such fields including education, health, defence, roads; or (*b*) where the investment is so large that its costs and benefits cannot possibly be thought of as marginal, for which reason, as we have seen, it becomes clear that actual expenditure and receipts may offer a poor guide; or (*c*) where there is *prima facie* reason to believe that external costs and benefits are very large. In all these fields, it is rather difficult to apply. Nevertheless, its use is increasing rapidly.

In fields where new investments are not extremely large relative

---

[1] Dupuit, 1844.

to the existing system, and where the outputs are normally sold to individuals on a commercial basis, cost–benefit analysis is much easier to apply because receipts and expenditures offer a better basis for estimation. At the same time, if it is felt that market prices reflect social cost and benefits reasonably well, the same reasons that make cost–benefit analysis relatively easy also make it unnecessary.

2.4 THE CONDITIONS WHICH MAKE COST–BENEFIT ANALYSIS DESIRABLE IN DEVELOPING COUNTRIES

In offering guidelines for the use of cost–benefit analysis in developing countries we pay special attention to industry and agriculture, as well as to infrastructural projects where the output has a market price. Education, health, and defence are neglected. This is not meant to imply that useful work is not going on in these fields. Certainly, cost-effectiveness analysis can be applied. But it is still very controversial whether full cost–benefit analysis in such sectors, where benefits are particularly difficult to measure, is as yet sufficiently soundly based to be a good guide for policy makers.

Thus we are concerned with the application of cost–benefit analysis precisely in fields in which it is considered unnecessary in developed economies. The justification for this can only be that it is felt that within such sectors of more advanced economies the price mechanism works in such a way that profits are a reasonable measure of net benefit, but that this is not true of most developing countries.

Why should one start with the presupposition that actual prices are very much worse reflectors of social cost and benefit than is the case in advanced economies? The main reasons are briefly adumbrated below. Each of them will receive further attention throughout this book. Naturally not all of these reasons apply to all developing countries.

2.41 *Inflation*
Very rapid inflation is more common in developing countries, particularly in South America. This is no accident. The very urgency of the desire to develop rapidly results in a constant tendency for demand to outrun supply: furthermore, lagging supply in the sectors which are most resistant to change, particularly agriculture, results in sectoral price rises which tend to transmit themselves across the board, and may virtually force the monetary authority to increase total money demand if a recession of activity is to be avoided.

If inflation proceeded uniformly so that relative prices were unaffected, it would not be a reason for prices to be a poor measure of real costs and benefits. But this, for institutional and political reasons, is seldom the case. For example, governments in such circumstances will often use price controls in selected fields where they can in practice be operated. This makes activity in these fields relatively or absolutely unprofitable, without regard to the net benefit of such activities.

A particular case of such control concerns the price of foreign exchange, which brings us to the next reason.

2.42 *Currency Overvaluation*

In almost all countries, the government 'manages' the price of foreign exchange. With inflation, if the exchange rate is unaltered, domestic prices get out of line with world prices. This implies that on average, the rupee[1] prices of imports and exports are too low relative to those of goods which are not traded. So long as the currency is not devalued to rectify the situation, the demand for foreign exchange for imports and other purposes will exceed the supply, and the government will be forced to restrict imports, often in ways which open up gaps between the market prices of goods and the real cost of procuring them. But some governments faced with a price inflation do not resort to import controls in order to maintain the domestic currency overvaluation, but devalue more or less frequently. If inflation is rapid and the government devalues periodically but not very frequently, then it is inevitable that the currency will be alternately undervalued and overvalued. If the inflation is slow, the government usually tries to avoid devaluation, and long periods of overvaluation are likely.

2.43 *Wage Rates, and Underemployment*

It has been seen that the theory of competition requires that the marginal product of labour (the extra output resulting from the employment of a small extra amount of labour) be equal to the wage paid.

Because of monopoly power, and immobility, there are undoubtedly serious imperfections in the labour markets of many

---

[1] Throughout this book we use 'rupees' to stand for the domestic currency unit, and 'dollars' to stand for a unit of foreign exchange. This is solely because it is awkward not to have a short familiar expression for these units: forced to choose, we selected rupees and dollars as being the units of the largest non-communist developing and developed countries respectively.

industrialized countries. But these imperfections are not usually thought to cause major intersectoral distortions of the pattern of production (regional distortions may be an exception, and here wage subsidies have been used). On the other hand, it is often argued that this is the case in many developing countries.

In 'modern' sectors of the economy—including modern industry and commerce, government, and plantations—it is common to find that unskilled workers earn three or four times as much as casual rural labour, a difference far greater than can be accounted for by the difference in the cost of living; and therefore that the cost of employing people in these sectors is apparently much greater than the loss of rural production, assuming that such rural earnings are a fair measure of labour's marginal contribution to production. It has been argued that the earnings of casual labour overstate the marginal product of labour. This is because, in most developing countries, the greater part of rural labour is family labour. Since a dependent member of the family cannot be sacked, he may 'earn' (i.e. consume) as much as a hired man but yet have a lower marginal product. As against this, in some places it is probable that the marginal product of a hired man is greater than his earnings because the employing farmers exercise some monopsonistic power.

That men by working are unable to contribute as much to production as they consume is what is meant by underemployment. The extended family system permits underemployment in the towns as well as the countryside. If relief were given institutionally, via unemployment benefits, the very low productivity urban activities —petty trading, car-watching, etc.,—would largely disappear and more people would become openly and wholly unemployed, a circumstance which would, of course, imply that wages did not reflect the social cost of employment.

The real cost of employing a man in the modern sector is still a subject of controversy, mainly because insufficient is known about the effects on the traditional sectors including agriculture, and because these effects will vary widely from country to country, and perhaps from region to region, or even town to town. However, there is rather wide agreement that modern sector wages almost everywhere overstate, perhaps greatly overstate, the social cost of employment.

2.44 *Imperfect Capital Markets*
Where risks are equal, interest rates on loans should be equal, if profits are to measure net social benefits. Interest rates have such

an enormous range in many developing countries, that it is implausible to suggest that this is just a measure of differential risks. Other factors operate, such as government intervention, ignorance, and monopoly elements in the supply of capital, to widen the range from low to almost astronomical rates.

2.45 *Large Projects*

It is more common in developing countries—especially in small countries with, as yet, little development—that a project will be so large as to have important repercussions on profits elsewhere in the economy. In these circumstances, as we have seen, the profitability of the project itself cannot be regarded as a good measure of net social benefit.

2.46 *Inelasticity of Demand for Exports*

In a number of developing countries, a large part of export receipts is accounted for by one, two, or three export commodities. Where a country also accounts for a considerable part of total world production, then it can influence, within limits, the price it obtains by restricting sales—which is, of course, an abrogation of the conditions of perfect competition. The free market price cannot then correctly measure the benefit, because, like any monopolist, the country would gain if it exported less at a higher price.

This, in turn, implies that the country would gain by devoting rather less resources to producing these primary commodities, and rather more to others, or to industrialization. This situation can be best rectified by suitable export taxes on the commodities, together with other policies (including use of the revenue thus raised) which encourage the transfer of resources. Some countries recognize this situation and do in fact use export taxes. But the situation has also been used as an argument for encouraging industry by protection—which brings us to our next section.

2.47 *Protection—Import Quotas, Tariffs, Export Disincentives*

The protection of domestic industry may be a deliberate interference with the price mechanism designed to make it operate in a manner more conducive to society's benefit than would a laissez-faire commercial policy. A well-designed interference, in the shape of special encouragement of industrialization, may well make industrial profits a better guide to social advantage than they otherwise would be, either for the reasons given in 2.46 above, or for other reasons (protection is further discussed in Chapter V).

The main way in which industry is specially encouraged is by tariffs and import quotas. Thereby, the domestic price of the output is kept above the import price. But the outputs of one industry are often the inputs of another. Consequently, when an industry contemplates exporting, it finds that the very system which protects it in its home market puts it at a positive disadvantage in export markets; whereas reason suggests that if industrial production is worth special encouragement, then it is worth special encouragement, and not actual discouragement, in producing for export. Thus tariff protection, like currency overvaluation, implies that the rupee price obtainable for an export underestimates the social value of that export. Some developing countries have taken measures to offset this effect, but such measures are often insufficient, and not very scientifically devised in such a way as to make the rupee price measure the benefit to the country.

Apart from the fact that protection discourages exports of both industrial and agricultural products, it is also the case that different industries receive enormously different degrees of protection, usually for no apparently rational economic reason.[1] This situation has arisen partly because countries have selected industries or plants (or have agreed to protect private initiatives) without the kind of economic appraisal being advocated here. Protection has followed the establishment of industries, rather than itself being used as a screening device.

Another reason why the relative gap between domestic and world prices is highly divergent as between industries is the extensive use of import quotas. A country runs into balance of payments problems. The situation is brought under control by restricting imports and, naturally, the least essential goods are most restricted. The result may be a growth of domestic industry, behind protective quotas, which bears little relation to the long-run comparative advantage of the country. If a wrong industry gets established it handicaps any other industry which uses its output. For instance, steel-using industries will be handicapped by a high-cost local steel plant, unless the latter is subsidized so that it can supply at prices no higher than the import price. It is our belief that bad management of foreign trade or foreign exchange is one of the principal reasons why internal prices get highly distorted, and hence lead to industrial investments which are of little or no benefit to the country concerned.

We have now outlined seven important and fairly non-contro-

---

[1] See Balassa, 1971 and Little, Scitovsky and Scott, 1970.

versial reasons why the price mechanism and the profit motive may not work as closely for the social advantage as in developed countries. Other more general reasons could be adduced, such as ignorance of opportunities and techniques, inertia, short-sightedness, lack of a market economy, and greater fragmentation of markets leading to local monopoly power; but these have relatively little direct bearing on project evaluation especially in the public sector. We turn now to a further three reasons, which may be more controversial.

2.48 *Deficiency of Savings, and Government Income*

Two projects may have the same net profit, but a different effect on the relative amount of extra consumption, savings, and taxation.

As we saw in 2.25, economic theory often treats savings and investment as of equal value. This is really a facet of the principle of consumers' sovereignty. It is assumed that it can make no difference to benefit whether some extra income is consumed, or saved and hence made available for investment. This is reasonable for an individual who freely chooses whether to spend or not. For him, an extra dollar of savings is worth the same as an extra dollar of consumption. But is it true for society?

To cut a long story short, if the government believes that rather more savings and rather less current consumption would be good for society, there may be a conflict. The point is that savings can be transformed into investment, and investment can produce extra future consumption for a sacrifice of present consumption: and the government may put a relatively higher value on the consumption of people in the future than do private persons. Furthermore, private persons may be inhibited from saving by income and other taxes which have the effect of double-taxing savings. We have already referred to these problems in 2.25 above, where it was argued that the rate at which society ought to discount the future may differ from the rate at which a firm can borrow. Thus, if the government chooses a discount rate for projects which is lower than the market rate of interest,[1] this is in effect to say that it considers future consumption to be more valuable than is indicated by the aggregate choices of private individuals. If the public saved more, interest rates would be lower, and the government pleased. In other words, the government considers present savings to be more valuable than present consumption.

---

[1] 'The market rate of interest' may be quite a wide band in developing countries, even if we restrict the meaning of 'the market' to that for medium and large scale industrial borrowing. See 2.44.

Governments can reduce aggregate private consumption, and thus increase savings, by taxation. On the other hand, taxation has administrative and political costs. So perhaps it is money in the hands of the government which should be considered to be more valuable than private consumption: this view is strengthened by the fact that a rational government should see to it that the value of its expenditure at the margin is equal in all lines, whether it be defence, agricultural extension, education, or investing in industry. Many people will be rather unwilling to accept that money in the hands of the government is more useful than many kinds of private expenditure, especially when governments are seen to waste money and promote silly investments. But the project evaluator may in any case have to take a government view. This is a difficult and controversial matter, which will be taken up again.

Finally, it should be noted that although discussion of this problem has arisen mainly in the context of developing countries, it seems to us that it arises also in the case of rich countries.

2.49 *The Distribution of Wealth*
The preceding section was largely concerned with the distribution of benefits, as between the present and future. But there is also a problem of the distribution of benefits today—the problem of inequality, to which we have already referred. There is a dilemma here, for inequality tends to promote savings, and help future generations. This is especially true of corporations: company profits belong mainly to the rich, but are one of the main sources of saving. The dilemma can be made less acute insofar as public savings can, by increased taxation, take the place of the savings of the rich; but there is a limit to this, and some element of dilemma remains.

The extent to which project selection should concern itself with different kinds of inequality will come up again. There is the additional important question of how far a practicable criterion for project selection can take proper account of inequalities. Both of these matters are discussed below, especially in 4.2 and Chapter XIII.

2.410 *External Effects*
Some economists believe that external economies are of special importance in developing countries: that some industries have important beneficial effects on others in ways which cannot be, or anyway are not, reflected in the price obtainable for the output of the industry, or in the price it pays for its inputs. There has been

much speculation and debate on this subject. But there is very little positive evidence. Certainly there has been much naive wishful thinking—for instance, that the provision of electricity, steel, or transport, would somehow create its own demand.

In 1.1, it was already shown that many of the more obvious external effects can be allowed for by a suitable definition of the project to be considered. But others will remain. The subject is discussed at length in Chapter XVI.

2.5 SOCIAL OBJECTIVES AND THE NOTION OF ACCOUNTING PRICES

A rather strong case has now been presented for saying that a project's anticipated receipts and expenditures cannot be relied upon to measure social benefits and costs in most developing countries. It is believed that this is true also of more developed economies, but to a lesser extent. There is therefore a strong *prima facie* case for the use of cost–benefit analysis.

We have seen that the basic idea of such an analysis is to use hypothetical rather than predicted actual prices when evaluating a project. The rate of discount may also not correspond to any actual interest rate. These 'shadow' prices, as they are often called, are chosen so as to reflect better the real costs of inputs to society, and the real benefits of the outputs, than do actual prices.

The name 'shadow price' is perhaps unfortunate. It suggests to many, even to some economists, that an analysis based on them is remote from reality, and therefore academic and highbrow, and so is to be distrusted. Of course, shadow prices may be unreal in that they are not the current prices of goods in a market. But then no price in a project analysis can ever be an actual price—for every price assumed in such an analysis necessarily lies in the future. The whole point of a shadow price is indeed that it shall correspond more closely to the realities of economic scarcity and the strength of economic needs than will guesses as to what future prices will actually be. From now on we shall use the term 'accounting prices'.

It is worth emphasis that if any input or output is valued at a different price from that actually expected to be paid or received by the project, then, in our terminology, a social accounting price is being used. In this sense, most project appraisals have made use of accounting prices. For instance, it is widely accepted in project analysis that indirect taxes on inputs should not be counted as costs. Or again, for some years now, direct imports and exports of projects have often been valued at c.i.f. or f.o.b. prices (border prices, as we shall term them) by, among others, consultants working for the IBRD. Some evaluators may think that they are not using shadow prices when they make such adjustments. That is a matter of terminology. What we want to make clear is that, in our terminology, they are using accounting prices.

While accounting prices have been in use for some time, they have seldom been used in a comprehensive and systematic way, but rather haphazardly. This is dangerous. Once some important prices become badly distorted—e.g. the price of labour or foreign exchange—the repercussions are widespread. Every price is then liable to need adjustment. What we are primarily concerned with in this book is to show how a whole set of accounting prices can be systematically and logically estimated and applied, yielding a practical method of analysis which can be expected to measure net social benefit better than ordinary profitability analysis. Being practical precludes perfectionism. We make no claim that accounting prices can be exact reflections of social costs and benefits— merely much better reflections than actual prices for many projects in many countries. Nor, of course, is it claimed that the use of accounting prices is a very satisfactory method of dealing with distortions. Many of the distortions can be fully dealt with only by removing them—that is, by adopting policies which lead to proper correspondence of prices, and costs and benefits. There may be yet others which, because of the difficulty of measuring them in a reasonably objective way, cannot be satisfactorily allowed for in a usable and politically acceptable criterion. These have to be left to the judgment of the politician and his advisers.

CHAPTER THREE

Scarce Resources

It has been assumed so far that the reader has an intuitive idea of the meaning of social cost and benefit. For a more precise idea it is necessary to understand the general nature of what has been termed 'the economic problem', that is the maximization subject to certain constraints of some combination of social objectives: the way in which these objectives are combined is expressed by what is known as 'the objective function'. In Chapter IV we discuss the objective function, and in this chapter the constraints.

3.1 POLITICAL ECONOMY OR THE ECONOMIZING OF SCARCE RESOURCES

Any maximization problem involves a limitation, or constraint. If there were no limitation to the resources available, there would be no problem. In economics, the limitations are generally known as 'scarce resources'. The problem we are concerned with is how to use and combine these 'scarce resources' so as to maximize the objective function. In this chapter we shall simply assume that the objective is to maximize the 'social value of consumption', somehow defined. By 'resource' we mean anything 'scarce' which is not a consumption good.[1] Anything is 'scarce' if more of it would permit an increase in the value of consumption. In this general sense, all goods (other than consumption goods themselves) are scarce resources. So also are people.

Scarce resources, taken as a whole, are used not only to make consumption goods now or in the near future, but also to maintain, reproduce, improve, and multiply themselves, so that as many or more consumption goods can be made later on. This is the process of investment. It is important to note that investment consists not only of improving and adding to buildings, machinery, and the stock of goods; but also of improving the people and the land.

Scarce resources are usually bought and sold at a price. If they

---

[1] Consumption goods are, of course, scarce relative to the satisfaction of the individual. But we are not here concerned with the economics of individual choice.

were given away free (e.g. by the government) then the amount demanded would necessarily exceed the supply. In such circumstances, it is generally difficult to ensure that they go to those who can make best use of them (we refer below to methods of distributing goods other than by free market sales, such as rationing). Thus economists view the price mechanism as a way of 'allocating' scarce resources. If certain conditions hold, then the price mechanism can be shown to be the best way—that is, the goods go to those who will use them to maximum social advantage. It should be no surprise that these conditions are the same as those required to bring about a coincidence of private and society profitability, which were discussed in 2.2.

There are two essential features of a price mechanism if it is to work properly in society's interest. The first is that the prices of the final outputs of consumption goods should reflect the contribution of each to the social value of consumption. This is, by and large, a matter of consumers' sovereignty (as modified by the system of indirect taxes and subsidies) and of the distribution of consumption between individuals, and through time, as discussed in Sections 2.27, 4.1, and 4.2.

The second feature is that the prices of resources should reflect their scarcity. In the case of resources whose supply cannot be increased, e.g. unimproved land, this means only that the price should be high enough to equate the amount demanded with the fixed supply. But the supply of man-made resources, that is, of most resources, can be increased. In this case, what meaning do we attach to the statement that the price should reflect the scarcity? The statement that the price should equate the amounts demanded and supplied remains true: but it is inadequate since the amount to be supplied is a matter of choice. There is an additional requirement, which is that the amount supplied should be such that the social cost of supplying a little more (in economists' jargon this is the 'marginal social cost') is also equal to the price. If this condition is met, we have a situation in which it is both true that supply and demand are equal, and also true that the price equals the marginal social cost. This then is what we mean by saying that the price should reflect the the scarcity of the resources.

We still have to ask under what circumstances the price mechanism will operate so that the prices of reproducible resources *will* reflect their scarcity. Once again the conditions are the same as those required to bring about a coincidence of private and social profitability, since private entrepreneurs will, under such conditions, always expand output until the marginal cost (the extra cost of supplying a little more) equals the price. With a coincidence of private and social profitability, this also means that they will adjust the amount they supply until the marginal *social* cost equals the price.

We have stressed that prices should equate supply and demand. Otherwise, if there is excess demand, supplies have to be 'rationed' by queuing, bribery, official allocation, or even looting. There is then little reason to believe that the resource will make the same marginal contribution to the value of consumption when used for different purposes. On the other hand, if each producer can obtain a resource only at the same price as everyone else, a price which he cannot influence, there is then a presumption that each producer's use of the resource will result in the same value of output (and hence the same benefit), because each will tend to use the resource in such quantities that the cost of an extra amount to him is just equal to the value of the resulting extra product.

Rationing and government allocation of resources has often been justifiably resorted to. But, in general, this is because it is believed that, in some circumstances, the free market price of a good does *not* reflect the contribution of that good to the real value of consumption. For instance, if there is a crop failure, the rationing of cereals at a controlled price may be eminently justifiable. This is basically because the exceptionally high market price, which would otherwise result, would cause a shift in the distribution of real income (to the extent of starving the poor), and therefore reliance on market prices as a measure of social benefit breaks down. In such a case, it is also true that the market price would not reflect the *long-run* cost of supply. Therefore, in exceptional circumstances, a controlled price may well be a better measure of both scarcity and benefit than an ephemeral market price. This can be true of productive resources as well as final consumption goods; but it is usually for temporary reasons.

The above is an example where a free competitive price cannot for short-run reasons be taken as a reflection of real long-run scarcity or benefit. There are many other longer-run reasons why the prices of scarce resources often do not reflect their real costs to society, measured in terms either of their contribution to the objective function, or in terms of the cost of increasing their own availability. These many reasons why costs of production, paid out for the use of scarce resources, do not always reflect cost to society, especially in developing countries, have been outlined in Chapter II.

3.2 LAND, LABOUR, AND CAPITAL

Economists have in the past traditionally divided scarce resources into land, labour, and capital. The original idea behind this was that capital consisted of things accumulated as a result of past savings and their investment; while land, which includes mineral resources, was a gift of God; and labour, although it may indeed accumulate, was not accumulated as a matter of economic decision. This categorization of resources fails insofar as much investment goes not into accumulating capital goods, but into educating human beings and improving the land. Even so, the distinction can still be useful. But it has to be remembered that land and labour must (if the three categories are to be thought of as exclusive) be considered as unimproved or 'raw' land, and uneducated or 'raw' labour: while capital, in the above sense, includes not only those things which are usually thought of as capital goods (factories, railroads, machines, etc.) but also stocks of 'intermediate' goods (steel, oil, fertilizers, etc.), as well as that part of the value of land and human beings attributable to improvements and education.

Land, labour, and capital (in the senses defined above) are certainly all scarce in developed countries. But, as has been suggested in 2.4, the emphasis is rather different in many developing countries.

Unskilled labour has been thought not to be scarce at all in some developing countries: this implies that there is no alternative product lost, and no human cost involved, such as harder work, when labour is recruited for industry. This is an extreme view: but it is true in most developing countries that wages in the modern sectors are higher than is required to attract labour. Modern sector wages thus suggest that labour is scarcer than it really is, and so tend to exaggerate the real cost of using labour. For this reason it may be desirable to use an accounting, or 'shadow', price for labour.

In a few very underpopulated countries, land may be almost a free resource, from a social point of view. But, in some of these countries, the land tenure system, combined with the value placed by some individuals on mere ownership, may combine to give it an unreal value.

In all developing countries, capital is felt to be particularly scarce. But what exactly does this mean? Usually, it just means that developing countries have much less capital per head than developed countries. In this sense, it is a reflection of the poverty of these countries, and of their desire for development. More raw land is usually impossible to obtain, and in only a minority of countries might an increased population help to raise income per head: therefore more capital is the answer. To say that capital is particularly scarce may also be a plea for more domestic savings, or for more aid. Scarcity of capital in the above senses must be carefully distinguished from a scarcity of capital goods, in the sense that their price is too low, so that there is excess demand for them. This is quite a common phenomenon in developing countries, but it is by no means universal: moreover, it could arise in countries with the highest levels of capital per head.

One kind of capital shortage that is often singled out is the lack of skilled and educated human beings. This kind of capital may indeed be scarcer, in the least developed countries, than capital goods—in the sense that more capital goods cannot be effectively used if there are not enough people who know how to use them. But it is, as with capital goods, difficult to generalize about whether skilled human beings tend to be in excess demand—this will be the case only if they are paid less than their worth to employers. In some developing countries, the earnings of people with certain categories of skills which are in demand in the world at large seem to reflect fully their earning power on world markets: in other countries they may receive less than their contribution to the economy, as well as less than their earning power on world markets. This is a problem for some developing countries. If such people are allowed to earn their full world value, they earn an extremely high relative income for a poor country: if, for the sake of equality, they are not so allowed, then the 'brain drain' may be damaging. We shall see later that it is difficult to know how to value skilled labour in a social cost–benefit analysis. Only in a few developing countries is it so easy for unskilled labour to emigrate that this possibility has any effect on its price or its social value.

With the possible exception of unskilled labour, it is thus difficult to generalize about the manner in which prices reflect the 'scarcity' of all those people and things subsumed under such concepts as land, labour, and capital. Capital, in detail, consists of everything there is which is useful. It is the prices of individual goods and services that have to be scrutinized. These can, as seen in Chapter II, go wrong for a multitude of reasons. It is true that raw labour enters into everything, and therefore that no price will be right if that of labour is wrong. But this is only one of many reason why prices may fail to reflect scarcity for individual goods and services. So far as modern industry at least is concerned, it is not, moreover, one of the most important reasons.

3.3 FOREIGN EXCHANGE

We have, thus far, dealt with the scarcity of the real resources of the country in question—land, trained people, and things. But it is often said that two of the basic shortages facing developing countries are foreign exchange and savings. We shall deal with foreign exchange first, then savings, and then the two together.

If we take a snapshot picture of an economy at a given point of time, a reserve or stock of foreign exchange (including unspent loans) is an asset just as are the stocks of capital and intermediate goods which exist. Foreign exchange is, in this sense, a scarce resource like any other, because it can be very quickly transformed in real goods and services.

But this is not what is ordinarily meant by saying that there is a shortage of foreign exchange. What is meant is that the demand for it exceeds the supply: the demand for foreign goods and services is greater than the supply of foreign currency needed to pay for them; greater, that is, than the earnings from exports of goods and services plus any net foreign loans or gifts available. Such excess demand arises when, on balance, the rupee prices of foreign goods, and domestic goods which are or could be exported, are too low. It follows that foreign goods, and exportables, are on the average worth more to the economy than their rupee prices suggest: in other words they are undervalued relative to domestic resources. This is also often what is meant by saying that the exchange rate is overvalued.

But so far we have not said exactly what we mean by 'domestic resources'. It does *not* mean simply all goods and services purchased from domestic suppliers. Thus the purchase of an electric motor made at home may result in someone else importing an electric motor instead of buying it from a local source (if, for instance, the supply of domestically made electric motors cannot be quickly increased), or it may result in more imports of copper to make more motors.

The basic domestic resources are domestic labour and land, which cannot normally be traded. If their prices are inflexible then they can be too high relative to traded goods, whether these are actually imported or domestically supplied (the possibility of importing will, at least in the absence of rigid quotas, keep down the price of domestic goods which are in competition with imports). But land and labour are also, of course, inputs for other non-traded goods, like electricity, whose prices will also tend, therefore, to be relatively high.

It follows that, if the relative prices of foreign and domestic resources do not measure their relative scarcities, then a true evaluation of the social costs and benefits of a project can be made only by finding a way of separating out the *direct and indirect* use of, or savings of, foreign resources. Having made the separation, one has two sets of costs and benefits, one expressed in dollars (and this set includes much more than the direct expenditures or receipts of foreign exchange), and one in rupees (this set includes mainly domestic labour). The two sets must then be made comparable. This can be done by revaluing the final dollar total in terms of rupees (this is using a kind of 'accounting exchange rate'), or vice versa (by using a kind of 'accounting wage').

3.4 SAVINGS

Saving is not, of course, a real resource like human beings, land, and goods. 'Saving' means 'not consuming'. Provided the value of output is not thereby reduced, not-consuming implies that goods and services become available to help increase future production—which is 'investment'. It is thus not a means of production, but rather a means of accumulation and development. More saving now, which involves less consumption now, permits more investment; and hence more consumption later.

We have already discussed the meaning of a *long-run* scarcity of savings—the situation in which the government believes that society would benefit if there were more saving and hence more investment. It was said (in 2.48) that this was equivalent to maintaining that the public over-discounted the future, and that the market rate of interest was higher than the rate at which the future should be discounted. If the public were keener to save, there would be more saving and investment, and a lower rate of interest.

It is important to realize that this does not imply that the government should try to reduce rates of interest. This is appropriate action only if investors are not willing to invest as much as savers are willing to save. In the majority of developing countries, it seems that the government is willing and able to promote, whether by direct ownership or otherwise, sufficient investment to take up all the savings which people are willing to make. The problem of insufficient investment may arise, but we believe that it is more common for countries to be faced with the reverse problem—in which case a rise in market rates of interest is more likely to be the appropriate action. However, we cannot go into such questions of monetary policy, for any full discussion would take us far afield, and it is not essential for our purposes.

So long as a country can run a balance of payments deficit, as a result of a flow of aid or private capital, it can continue to operate with a level of domestic investment which exceeds the level of domestic savings. It is then drawing on foreign savings to the extent of the deficit. But if the government seeks to carry out, or get carried out, more investment than the total of domestic savings plus the balance of payments deficit, this implies that total demand (for investment, exports, and consumption) will be greater than the total supply that can become available from imports, and from domestic productive capacity which is, by definition, fixed in the short run. In this situation, inflationary price rises will occur, which will result, at least temporarily, in either less investment or more savings than was planned. This is the situation of a short-run scarcity of savings.

3.5 FOREIGN EXCHANGE AND SAVINGS

We saw above that foreign savings are a good substitute for domestic savings—except insofar, of course, as the deficit is covered by loans which constitute an external liability.

It is an interesting and important question how far the reverse is true. Are domestic savings a good substitute for a balance of payments deficit? An often asked and closely related question is, 'Is aid meant to supplement inadequate domestic savings, or to supplement inadequate earnings of foreign exchange?' To put it in yet another way, 'Can a developing country sustain, in the long run, any desired level of investment without a balance of payments deficit, provided it saves enough?' If a country can, by saving more, always cure a balance of payments deficit without causing domestic resources to be underemployed, then foreign exchange has no claim to be a separate and independent limitation or constraint. This is an important question, not only for aid-donors, but also in project analysis. We must therefore explore it further.

An increase in savings is synonymous with reduced consumption. The extent to which reduced consumption will affect the balance of payments and domestic output respectively will vary greatly from country to country, and also vary with the extent of excess demand. But it is clear that, if the steps taken serve only to reduce consumption, then part of the reduction will depress domestic output, even although imports will be reduced and exports may be increased.

But we are not concerned with the short run in project analysis. In the longer run, we must allow for other policy changes which will help to make the increase in savings cure the balance of payments deficit without affecting domestic production. The most notable is a change in the exchange rate, or substitutes such as higher tariffs, export subsidies, etc., which will make domestic goods cheaper relative to foreign goods, and so turn demand in their favour. Now, given this, there can be no doubt that *industrialized* countries could, within a year or two, substantially raise their investment rates (or sustain the same rate with a reduced inflow of capital) without balance of payments deficits or underemployment of resources, provided savings increased to the same extent. There is rather more doubt in the case of some developing countries. What are the reasons for this?

Investment can be increased, without affecting the level of aggregate domestic production, in the following ways:

(i) by switching domestic resources from making consumption goods to making investment goods;

(ii) by reducing imports of consumption goods, using the savings of foreign exchange to buy more investment goods;

(iii) by increasing exports of consumption goods, and of intermediate goods or materials which are released by lower consumption at home, using the proceeds to import more investment goods.

Now (i) may be difficult for a developing country, except in the rather long run, because it may lack the engineering and intermediate goods industries, such as cement and steel, which contribute largely to making investment goods. The second route (ii) is relatively easy, where there are large imports of final consumption goods: but some developing countries now import very little in this category. Finally, some developing countries' exports consist largely of food and materials which are not in very elastic world demand.

If a country is badly placed in all these respects, then investment can be significantly increased (without more foreign aid) only if the investment programme is itself made more labour intensive, and less intensive in the goods which can be obtained only from abroad. It is possible, though not always true, that this would make the investments less productive—and perhaps so much less productive that the desired increase in investment would be worthwhile only if the situation could be eased by more aid.

What does the above argument amount to? If a country is not in a position to make many capital goods itself, and if it cannot export more without considerably reducing its export prices, then as the level of domestic savings rises it becomes ever less worthwhile to try to increase savings and investment further. In these circumstances, foreign aid may be more valuable than a nominally equivalent increase in domestic savings. This is what is meant by saying that foreign exchange is 'more of a bottle-neck' than domestic savings. But it should also be added that a country which has got into the situation described has not pursued ideal policies in the past (given that the desire to raise investment was foreseen). Such a country should either have diversified its exports to a greater extent, or should have done less import substitution in consumption goods, and more in capital goods.

Our project selection criterion will, of course, make proper allowance for such difficulties in earning foreign exchange, and for a developing country's relative inability to switch production from making consumption goods to making investment goods. In the short run, and given the level of foreign aid, one must not attempt to raise savings and investment to unrealistic levels. In the longer run, by allowing for the difficulty of increasing export earnings from traditional products (which is done by appropriately low accounting prices for such products), the right degree of preference can be given to projects which substitute for imports and diversify exports. The more inelastic the export demand for traditional products, and the greater the difficulty of promoting new exports, and the fewer the consumption goods imported, the more likely is it to be socially advantageous for a country to begin to produce its own capital goods.

CHAPTER FOUR

Policy Objectives

In this chapter we shall look more closely into the objectives of economic policy, and the manner in which policy can help to ensure that the available resources are best used and adapted to satisfying those objectives. Project selection is, of course, only one of many policy weapons. Criteria for project selection can be properly defined only when one has placed project selection within a broader framework of economic policy and planning.

4.1 FUTURE AND PRESENT CONSUMPTION

Provisionally we assume that the ultimate object and intention of the government's economic activities is to provide a high standard of living (we return later on in 4.3 to the question whether other ends exist and are admissible). But we have already seen that consumption occurs through time. Consumption now and next year are competitive with each other. We therefore have not one but two objectives—indeed not two, but an indefinitely large number, since even a finite span of time can be split into as many periods as one chooses.

Now a useful way of reconciling many conflicting objectives is to attach a number or 'weight' to each, which is intended to measure the marginal importance to be attached to that particular one. By marginal importance we mean the importance to be attached to satisfying a particular objective a little more fully. By this method one weighs one objective against another in a systematic quantified manner.

Suppose we write $C_0, C_1, \ldots C_n$ for the anticipated values (at constant prices) of total consumption from year o to year n. Dividing by the anticipated population, we arrive at anticipated consumption per head $\dfrac{C_0}{P_0}, \dfrac{C_1}{P_1}, \ldots, \dfrac{Cn}{P_n}$. By policy changes the government can raise one of more of the Cs, but only at the cost of reducing one or more of the others (unless overall efficiency can be raised).

Now there is no presumption that it is just as important to increase say C_9 as C_0. For instance $\dfrac{C_9}{P_9}$ may anyway be higher than $\dfrac{C_0}{P_0}$. With consumption per head higher in year 9 than year 0 the urgency of raising consumption in year 9 is less than raising it in year 0. We therefore give a lower weight to consumption in year 9 than year 0, which reflects the lower importance we attach to increases of consumption in that year. We thus attach a weight to every year, which indicates the importance to be attached to increasing by a little (say \$1) the value of C in that particular year.[1]

The operational meaning of these weights, $W_0, W_1, W_2, \ldots W_n$ is that we would take a small change in consumption, from $(C_0, C_1, \ldots, C_n)$ to $(C_0', C_1', \ldots C_n')$ to be desirable if

$$W_0\,(C_0'-C_0) + W_1\,(C_1'-C_1) + \ldots W_n\,(C_n'-C_n)$$

were positive. It is worth giving up a unit of C_0 if that makes possible a big enough increase in C_9: the Ws tell us how big it would have to be. We can express the end of economic activity as bringing about changes that make the above expression positive.

Provided it can be expected that the outcome of economic activity will be rising consumption per head, there is a good case for saying that the Ws will fall over time—since the higher is consumption per head, the less important it becomes to increase it further. W_0 can be set equal to unity (which means that we take *present* consumption as the measuring rod), so that the Ws fall from unity and gradually approach zero. If it could be expected that income per head would grow faster in some future periods than others, there would be a good case for saying that the Ws should fall faster during those periods. But economic prediction is generally too inaccurate for it to be possible to produce any convincing argument against the simplifying assumption that the Ws fall at a constant rate—so that one can speak of *the* rate of fall of the Ws.

The rate of fall of the Ws, $\frac{1}{W}\frac{dW}{dt}$, is what some economists have termed the *social discount rate*. We prefer to call it the *consumption rate of interest*, this being the rate at which future consumption ought to be discounted to make it the equivalent in value of present consumption. This rate obviously embodies an ethical judgment about the importance of the welfare of different generations. We have

---

[1] Of course, the importance given to increasing consumption in a particular year should depend not merely on aggregate consumption per head, but also on who is going to get the consumption. Indeed, the distribution of consumption between contemporaries plays a role in our treatment of project appraisal. But in this section, we implicitly assume that the distribution of aggregate consumption between households remains more or less the same from year to year.

represented it as depending only on consumption per head.[1] Our discussion has implied that if consumption per head is expected to rise, then the *W*s should fall, and the consumption rate of interest be positive: and that the faster the expected rise, the higher should the rate be. Some may wish to deny even these propositions. A few might argue that a richer man of some future generation has no lesser claim to increased consumption than a poor man of today. Others might say 'Why should I do anything for the future? It has done nothing for me.'

But even if the above propositions are universally acceptable they amount to very little. Indeed, when a growth of consumption per head can be confidently expected, they tell us no more than that the consumption rate of interest should be positive. To get any further, one must be able to quantify the relation between the rate of growth of consumption per head and the rate of decline of the importance of further increases. Now this required quantity is once again a matter of ethical judgment. Furthermore, it is one about which people may disagree radically.

It is for the above sort of reason that many economists have said that it is for the government to decide what the consumption rate of interest is to be. This seems a rather ethereal sort of thing for a government to decide; and, indeed, no government has ever explicitly made such a decision. The reason why economists have made this demand is that they believe the consumption rate of interest should be used as the rate of discount in project analysis, and more generally that it is required to determine economic policy consistently: in an economy in which the government was in effective control of all investment, this rate of interest would then determine the level and kinds of investment, because all compatible projects with a positive PSV, when discounted at this rate of interest, would be accepted.

We agree that it is essential that the government set a rate of discount to be used in project analysis,[2] but we do not think this need be, or should be, identified with the consumption rate of interest. The reason in brief is that a project gives rise not merely to

---

[1] Economists have sometimes wanted to make the weight depend on total consumption and total population in some other way. But since the value of a unit of consumption is its value to the person who gets it, and the average person gets average consumption per head, it seems right to regard *W* as depending simply on consumption per head. The same view is taken in the UNIDO *Guidelines* (p. 164).

[2] It has increasingly been realized that the discount rate plays quite a powerful role in deciding which kinds of investment look best. For instance, it is well known

future consumption, but also to future savings and hence investment. As we have seen, consumption and investment may not be of equal social value: moreover, their relative social values may change as time goes on. Therefore a different treatment would need to be accorded to each of these different benefit streams. This, however, would be complicated, and it is simpler to revalue each year's consumption in terms of savings (or investment)—and then discount the single combined stream at a rate which is appropriate to investment, a rate which may differ from the rate appropriate to consumption and which we shall call the accounting rate of interest.[1]

It remains true that the government should take some responsibility for the level and kind of investment, these being the main ways of influencing the relative amounts of consumption in this and later generations. But we consider that the significance of the consumption rate of interest has been overestimated, especially for developing countries. For instance, a government may be quite convinced that it wishes to raise the rate of investment, and employ a lower accounting rate of interest, without being prepared to make the precise balancing of the relative value of consumption in different periods which the choice of a consumption rate of interest implies. In the above case, if the government's ability or willingness to tax is limited, then it may be important to shunt investment into projects the gains from which are likely to be saved and reinvested.

It may be asked whether a government can properly be regarded as wanting to raise the rate of investment at the expense of current consumption, if it does not raise taxation when it can, and if it does not take other steps to see that public savings, including those of public enterprises, are as high as reasonably possible. Of course, governments want to stay in power. There is a limit to the extent to which they will try to squeeze more savings from the public, even if it is believed on ethical grounds that a greater provision should be made for investment and growth, and thus for consumption in the

---

that the decision whether to have nuclear or conventional energy is sensitive to the rate of discount. Another example is electrification versus dieselization of railways. In each case, the former method uses more capital initially, but saves costs later, and so requires a relatively low rate of discount of the future to look better than the latter.

[1] In particular we shall discuss (in 14.21) the circumstances under which the accounting rate of interest may be expected to exceed the consumption rate of interest. Roughly speaking, this will be the case when the economy is undertaking investment projects with good returns, but investment is as yet insufficient to enable *per capita* consumption to grow rapidly.

future. This raises a very important point. The most important and normal way for a government to hold consumption in check, and so increase savings, is taxation; and taxation is notoriously unpopular.

The question therefore arises whether the government wishes to use project selection to help it increase savings and investment. This can be done by choosing relatively capital-intensive investments. With such investments, a given gross gain is reflected more in profits and depreciation allowances, which result in more re-investment, than in wages which result mainly in consumption. Thus capital-intensive projects tend to restrain both consumption and employment, but promote savings and growth.

A government faced with the above question may want to consider whether a low rate of growth of employment opportunities is not likely to be just as unpopular as more taxation. However, one cannot necessarily accuse a government of inconsistency which goes easy on taxation now, but opts for investments which result in only a small increase in consumption and employment in the next decade. The time pattern of the restraint is different. Taxation bites *now*. Moreover taxation tends to fall more upon the politically vocal. Anyway, in the last resort, the government itself must decide whether it is being consistent. Essentially, the designer of a system of project analysis needs to know whether the government (after the essence of the choice has been adequately explained) does or does not want to use project choice to promote savings (or, for that matter, employment—which by and large is the reverse case).

We turn away now from the difficult problem of the distribution of consumption through time, to another equally vexed question, but one which has received less attention in the context of project selection—that of the distribution of consumption between contemporaries.

4.2 EQUALITY: THE DISTRIBUTION OF CONSUMPTION BETWEEN CONTEMPORARIES

We implied in 4.1 that the main reason for discounting future consumption was the expectation that consumption per head would be higher in the future. But if one attaches less weight to the consumption of some average man in ten years' time, on the grounds that he will be richer, then it is clearly only logical to attach less weight to the consumption of a rich man today than to that of a poor man today.

So far we have taken the value of extra consumption in a particular year to depend simply on average consumption, i.e. consumption per head. But really we should have a weighted average of consumption per head for each year, because the importance of the consumption of each man differs (in precise analogy to the way in which the importance of consumption varies as between different time periods). Of course, such detail is unattainable. But one could approach what is required by attaching different weights to the consumption of different income groups.

The above can be said to be just what a government implicitly does when it tries to make the tax system progressive so that it bears more heavily on the rich; and when it subsidizes the consumption of the very poor in various ways.

It can also be argued that all instruments of economic policy should be geared to the same objective. Project selection is one such instrument. It follows from this that the consumption benefits of a project would need to be traced to different individuals (or at least different groups of individuals with roughly similar incomes), before the total weighted benefit could be assessed—in the same way that one assesses benefits through time, with an ever smaller weight as the future becomes more distant. Evidently, this is a great complication, and hard to carry out. Is there any good argument, which would make it unnecessary?

It would be unnecessary if it were true that other instruments of policy, such as progressive taxation, could achieve as much equality as was desirable, and achieve it more efficiently than if project choice were allowed to be influenced by considerations of equality and inequality. This is closely analogous to the problem presented in the previous section—the problem of whether project selection should be deliberately used to influence the distribution of consumption through time, by influencing the rate of saving. The argument that the project evaluator, if he be a civil servant, should take the existing distribution of income or wealth as ideal (implying that he need not 'weight' the consumption of different income groups differently), on the grounds that the government has the power to make it what it likes through other measures, principally taxation, does not hold water. We have already noted that taxation has administrative and political costs which may limit its use. Furthermore, increasing equality itself has costs in the form of reduced incentives. It thus seems that the marginal utility of different persons' consumption must remain unequal if production is not to suffer to the extent of making everyone worse off. Now the need for incentives will already be reflected in the costs of the project (e.g.

by recognizing that skilled managers and operatives must be well paid) : it follows that the differential value of the benefits, according to whom they accrue, should also be taken into account.

It seems to us to be very difficult to disagree with the above view. But it is equally difficult to give quantitative expression to it; the reason being, of course, that people will disagree very much as to the relative weights to be attached to marginal changes in the wealth of persons of different wealth—just as they would disagree about the importance to be attached to future generations. In these circumstances, the obvious thing to say is that the government must decide, and lay down a schedule of weights. (We saw, in the previous section, that it has been argued that the government should select a consumption rate of interest, which is analogous.) But it seems to us that it is unlikely that a government would do any such thing. Most governments would, in our opinion, desire that the distribution of income be taken into account. Many of their actions imply this. But to give quantitative expression to its preferences in this respect might be political dynamite.

A public airing was given to this question of weighting incomes in the evidence given before the Roskill Commission.[1] The case for weighting was strongly put by a number of economists (though, as usual, there was at least one who disagreed!), but it was rejected by the Chairman (who was a judge). He took the view that such matters could enter into the judgment of the Committee, but could not be quantified in the work of the research team which produced the cost–benefit analysis. So, as usual, the latter's figures presumed that a dollar was worth the same to everyone. In the event, the government rejected the findings of the Commission, primarily on environmental grounds (though these could, to some extent, be said to include consideration of the distribution of costs and benefits).

While the objections to quantification in this area are thus strong, it is also true that the disadvantages of non-quantification are great. It would very often be wrong that the results of a cost–benefit analysis, which neglected income distribution, should be simply accepted as pre-empting the final decision. But, bearing in mind that very many project analyses are conducted, and strongly influence and even pre-empt decisions, which are neither in the public eye nor come before any body which will exercise political judgment, it seems clear that income distribution will generally be neglected if not allowed for somehow in the figures. Even where

---

[1] *Commission on The Third London Airport*, 1971.

political judgment is exercised, the results are not likely to be very satisfactory. Different ministers, different departments, and other organs of government, will have varying views. The public attention may sometimes be caught, sometimes not. Often the income distribution argument will be used to support or oppose a project, which the proponent or opponent likes or dislikes on quite different grounds. Inconsistency and disharmony are likely to prevail, and rather little good may result for the poor. Also the relevant information about differential effects on different income groups will generally not be produced.

Are we then caught on the horns of an insoluble dilemma? We believe that is putting it too strongly, and that some progress can be made—although an element of dilemma will always remain. Our belief is that most governments would be happy if some quantified allowance for inequality were made. But many might prefer that it was done in a concealed manner, to that the weighting system did not become the subject of parliamentary or public debate. It may sometimes be politically expedient to do good by stealth.

To carry the argument further, let us consider how projects, especially industrial projects, affect the distribution of income. The main benefits come from employing labour which was hitherto unemployed or earning very little, and from profits. Much depends on the level of wages in the new employment. Modern industrial employment in developing countries often gains a man twice, in real terms, what he was earning or consuming before. In such new employment, he can enjoy a level of consumption well above the average for the country: as a result, inequality is actually increased. If the aim is to maximize welfare, one must give many people small increases in consumption, not large increases for a few.[1] The latter, it is true, relieves some people from poverty, but at the expense of increasing inequality: so that, with high wages, the more the employment, the more the inequality.

Provided the level of wages is not too high, so that the above effect does not arise, then it is clear that a project which gives low profits but high employment for low paid workers per unit of investment is better for equality now than a capital intensive project which may have high profits but gives very little employment. On the other

---

[1] It is often claimed that those finding new employment in the modern sector mitigate or even eliminate this disequalizing effect by themselves spreading the extra consumption around, by supporting relatives. No doubt this is partly true, but we have no evidence of how important and pervasive this kind of personal redistribution of income is.

hand, of course, the latter kind of project will result in more savings (since even in the private sector a large part of profit usually goes to the government in taxation or is saved), and more savings result in more investment; which will provide more income and employment later. There is thus a choice between giving more equality and employment now, and providing for more employment and equality later. Here it must be remarked that if the savings from capital intensive investments are in turn ploughed back into capital intensive investments, the promise of much future employment may never materialize. Nevertheless, it remains true that there is a dilemma as between employment and equality now and provision for the future, and it must not be forgotten that the rate of growth of the labour force in developing countries will continue to be rapid for many years.

It has now become clear that a government can if it wishes ensure that project selection works in the direction of equality now, by seeing that the system of evaluation and selection gives due weight to the employment of large numbers at low wages. One can give effect to this without any *explicit* weighting of different income levels. The method is to use accounting wage rates lower than the actual wage rates which would be paid, just how much lower depending on how much the government aims to promote equality on the one hand, or savings and growth on the other. The amount of such a shadow wage-subsidy would vary with the level of the actual wage: the lower the actual wage likely to be paid, the greater the percentage subsidy. A very low weight may also be attached to any increase in the consumption of the rich which is caused by a project. This subject is explored more fully in Chapter XIII.

It may be thought that much could be done by concentrating on the production of necessities, and abjuring the production of luxuries. But this is primarily a matter for the fiscal authorities, not the project evaluator. Certainly 'luxuries' should be heavily taxed: but when that has been done it is generally best to satisfy the demand, though often it will turn out to be better to allow imports than to embark on domestic production. For example, it may be quite a good idea to allow a rich man to import a Mercedes if there is, say, a 200% tax on it. So much of the money then goes to the government that alternative ways in which the rich man could have spent his money might well have cost the country more. If it is thought that certain items of conspicuous consumption, such as a Mercedes, create undesirable envy then it may be better to ban imports altogether (and, of course, domestic production). Turning to 'necessities', again the demand should of course be satisfied: but it may not be a very good idea to produce so much that the output can be sold only if subsidized; such subsidies are indiscriminate, helping the well off as well as the poor, so that better ways of promoting equality can probably be found—e.g. subsidizing low-wage employment.

All the differential effects of project selection on equality cannot be allowed for by the suggested means of using accounting wages. This is particularly true of non-industrial projects, and the already mentioned Roskill Commission provides an example. Here the claim was that much of the benefits went to the air-traveller and much of the cost, in terms of noise and loss of amenity, was borne by poorer people. This is an example of external costs on the one hand, and consumers' surplus as a benefit on the other. Where costs and benefits accrue in these forms, the fact that they accrue to people of different wealth cannot be allowed for by the suggested method.

A more serious problem concerns agricultural investments, where many of the poor who may benefit are not wage earners. If the benefits of two alternative schemes would accrue, for example, in different proportions to relatively wealthy and poor peasants, it may be impossible to find any quantified method of allowing for this other than by explicitly attaching different weights to the benefits depending on who gets them.

Thus, although the device of using an accounting wage makes an important contribution to the problem of how to deal with inequalities of wealth in project appraisal, it does not provide the whole answer. Part of the dilemma remains.

Another way in which projection selection may affect equality is by its location. If a given, relatively footloose, project is located in a poor area it may do more for equality than if put in a rich area. How would one in theory take quantifiable account of the different wealth of different parts of a country? Suppose there are two distinct States, one rich (R) and one poor (P); and that a project could be located in either. Suppose the unweighted net benefits for each year would be higher if it were located in R. The question is whether weighting the benefits according to the State in which they arise would make P the best choice.

The first problem would be to assess the net benefits by State. It would not be true that, because the project was in P, all the benefits would accrue to P, and vice versa. Having distributed the net benefits between P and R (for all future years), one would then have to weight them. How could the weights be determined? The central government would have to lay it down that, say, consumption generated in P was to count for 1·5 and that in R only for 1. It is a little difficult to imagine that agreement on such a fiat could be arrived at. Admittedly, the example given—that of a Federation— is a particularly difficult one. But even in a unified state it is not easy to imagine a government agreeing to such a bare-faced quantification of the regional problem, although governments are often willing to give subsidies to particularly poor regions, in one form or another. It should be noted, however, that this political problem might be eased if different consumption weights were attached to different classes of people of different wealth, for then there need be no explicit regional weight, since the region would acquire a high explicit weight simply because it contained a high proportion of poor people.

How does a project benefit a region? Once again, in the case of many projects, especially industrial ones, the answer is that it does so very largely by increasing the demand for unskilled labour. The other source of benefit, profit, is rather unlikely to be of much help to the region. Taxation out of profits goes back to the central government (and if it is a public project it all goes to the government). Any private savings may well be reinvested elsewhere. The profit receivers may well not live in the region—and even if they do, one must remember that the main point of helping a poor region is to help the poor in the region. It may be argued at this point that there are 'multiplier' effects, by which it is meant that there are second round and further benefits which result from the income-earners of the project spending their incomes in the region. This is true, but again it seems likely that such benefits will come mainly from the spending of labour incomes. Richer people associated with the project are likely to get their supplies, and their entertainment, very largely from outside any very poor area. Lastly there are externalities, the fact that a project may buy some of the inputs from the region and so increase employment in the supplying firms —but this indirect employment will normally be only a small fraction of the direct employment. We think it is legitimate to conclude that in the case of industrial projects a very large part of the regional benefits stem from direct employment. Granted the above argument, it follows that the subsidization of employment can play a very important part in the solution of problems of regional inequality: and if it could apply to all types of employment, even the indirect employment would be taken care of. This was at one time recognized in the United Kingdom, by the Labour Government of 1964, which instituted a system of 'employment premia'.[1]

So far as project analysis is concerned, if a regional wage subsidy were in question, the cost of labour would of course be reckoned to be reduced by the subsidy, which would have the effect of encouraging industry, and especially labour-intensive industry, to enter the area. If no regional wage subsidy is actually in operation, but the government has other means of steering enterprise to the region (including, of course, the location of government enterprise), then the use of a lower accounting wage for the poor region as compared with the rich, when using cost–benefit analysis to determine location, will have the same effect. The government can easily justify such wage subsidies in the name of employment without having to attach specific premia to benefits accruing to the region (although they may enter covertly into the calculation of the accounting wage, or amount of subsidization). Equality can, as it were, ride in on the back of employment.

It is not, of course, maintained that wage subsidies provide the whole answer to regional inequality. In a highly industrialized country, they might go most of the way to a solution. But in a developing country, agricultural and transport investments, for instance, may be much more important. We have already noted that a direct weighting of the benefits accruing to farmers of differing wealth still seems called for: and transport may have benefits in opening up a region to increased exploitation and trade with other areas which cannot be allowed for by the use of an accounting wage in project analysis.

It is not our purpose, nor are we competent, to go fully into the problem of regional inequality, and regional planning. Here we merely claim that with some kinds of investment, notably industrial projects, adequate allowance for the poverty of a region may be made in the analysis of net benefits by the use of an accounting wage. For other kinds of project this would be inadequate, or even irrelevant.

We are then still left with the problem of how to deal with inequality in our project analyses, when no explicit system of weighting

---

[1] This was a system under which a specific labour subsidy was given for manufacturing employment in development areas: it was originally financed by a general tax on employment in service industries (the so-called selective employment tax, abandoned in 1973). The discontinuation of the subsidy in 1974 has, however, been announced by the successor Conservative Government.

the benefits according to the wealth of the person or region has been laid down. We do our best to deal with this in 8.53 where we consider how a project appraisal should be presented when some of the important elements which may and should affect decisions are unquantified.

4.3   OTHER OBJECTIVES

It should first be said that many apparent short-term objectives of economic policy, such as preventing inflation and recession, correcting a balance of payments deficit, and so on, cannot be regarded as ultimate objectives. If rapid inflation is harmful to consumption, including the distribution of consumption, as it probably is in the long run, then it should be prevented. But the level of prices as such has no claim to consideration apart from its effect on the real standard of life of human beings. Again, a balance of payments surplus is no advantage in itself. No one would mind running a deficit for ever, if that were possible!

Having selected out all those apparent concerns of policy which are really means or constraints and not ends, is there anything but consumption left?

4.31   *Employment*

Until the last few years, employment was rather neglected in developing countries. The emphasis was on industrialization and growth. Many economists and politicians preached the virtues of capital-intensive industry, and most of the measures taken to encourage industry favoured capital-intensity. Few countries paid adequate attention to agriculture, which is the major labour-using sector in most developing countries. Many national plans did not even pretend to cater for a sufficient increase in the demand for labour. The conflict between growth and equality, of which we have written above, had been resolved too much in favour of expected growth which did not always materialize—partly because of bad projects. We say growth and *equality*, because equality and increased demand for labour are closely linked, especially in developing countries.

Despite the above it is questionable whether employment should be regarded as an end or objective of economic activity. We believe that the very welcome new concern with employment is largely a concern about poverty, although it must be admitted that social unrest, stemming partly from the unemployment of newly educated people, who are not extremely poor, is also an important factor. However, in our view, what is wrong is more that people are desperately poor, than that they have little work. Employment is an objective independent of consumption only if one believes that a man is better off working than if he manages to consume the same without working. This is a puritan belief. But whether it is acceptable or not has little importance if greater demand for unskilled labour is the best means to relieve poverty.

Given the difficulties involved in administering welfare payments fairly, and the dislike of most treasuries and governments of the idea of a 'dole', largely for incentive reasons, we believe that increasing the demand for labour is certainly the best way of relieving poverty; and that it is an important factor in promoting more equality, in that it directs a larger part of increases in output to the very poor. But, not only that: increasing the demand for labour should increase output itself (the truth of this proposition in no way conflicts with the reality of the choice between employment and the rate of growth, because more employment is likely to result in more output but less savings).

In contrast to what was said above, a few economists and others have introduced the idea that there is actually a conflict between employment and output. *Prima facie*, this is a bizarre notion. Why should more employment reduce output? How could it? The idea that it might stems from a variety of models, in which input co-efficients (including labour) per unit of output are fixed. With such models it is easy to set up an apparent conflict. Suppose that for 100 units of investment, one could in project A employ 100 men and get 100 units of output, or in project B employ 80 men and get 125 units of output. This is quite possible with sufficiently different techniques even in the same line of production. The conflict has apparently been established. But it is all appearance and no reality.

In the above example A is an inferior technique, for it uses more men to get less output, and yet saves no capital. To put it another way, if one's choice were really between two such techniques and one chose A, then one would be employing 20 extra men to reduce output by 25. The counter-argument is that in reality it is always possible to employ more men without reducing output.

One might take the following suggestions:

(i) Choose B, and employ the extra 20 men anyway—if necessary to make tea for the others.
(ii) Choose B, but cut out some of the equipment, and use some

of the 20 men to do the job by hand. This is virtually always possible, and the capital saving will permit the rest to be productively employed by investing elsewhere in the economy.
(iii) Put only 80 units of investment into B, thus employing only 64 men but getting the same output as if A were chosen. Use the savings of 20 units of investment to employ the 36 men in some other more labour-intensive activity.

The truth is that there are vast numbers of techniques and bases of production in any economy, and that labour input coefficients are never rigid. Consequently, unless we introduce some non-technological policy constraints, the conflict need never arise. If it does arise, it can only be because of wrong policies—which may or may not be due to some political constraint. How may this come about?

Let us suppose that most investment occurs in the private sector, and that the price mechanism favours undue capital-intensity, as is indeed the case in most developing countries. Then the government might try to reduce investment in the private sector, and use more capital in the public sector in certain conventional ways (not competing with the private sector) which were relatively labour-intensive but produced very little useful output. We do not know that his has actually happened. The common case which has certainly happened is that the government employs many redundant workers in the public sector—but this is employing people without using more capital. Unless the redundant workers actually get in the way, or reduce morale, so that output suffers, this would not be a case of negative marginal product.

What is the upshot? The answer is that a government might be led to reduce output in trying to promote employment. But it never need do this. In the above case what it should do, of course, is either to take steps to make investment more labour-intensive in the private sector by reforming or doctoring the price mechanism, or to take over some areas of private investment and plan them in a more labour-intensive manner. The chief political constraint which might lead to a conflict is the putative inviolability of high modern-sector wages together with unwillingness to use wage subsidies.

4.32 *Independence*
Another suggestion, which has to be taken seriously, is that 'economic independence' should be taken as a separate objective.

Economic independence can be given a number of meanings. The first to be considered is independence of foreign aid (excluding net private capital inflows). Although it is not the only reason why aid, especially bilateral aid, is disliked by some recipients even if accepted, it must be noted that non-grant aid leads to debt, and that excessive debt may be felt to be a form of dependence. Independence of aid is a stated objective of some countries' planning, most notably that of India. It implies that at some point in the future the country wishes to sacrifice some consumption to avoid indebtedness. There is no difficulty in dealing with this. It implies only that the level of investment almost certainly has to be lower than otherwise for some time, which will have some influence on project selection.

Aid is only one kind of contact with foreigners, even if it is a particularly sensitive one. Trade also results in many contacts, and a few countries have at times preferred to trade as little as possible. We are simply assuming in this book that pure autarky of this kind is not a relevant consideration.

But 'economic independence' is often given a more specific reference. It has been argued by different developing countries that they should aim at independence in food, other 'essential' consumer goods, capital goods, and armaments. The argument 'we should produce our own . . .' seems to have an intuitive appeal. Steel, oil products, airlines, and motor-cars, are particularly attractive. If all such demands for self-sufficiency were met, international trade would be extremely restricted with a forfeit of the very considerable economies which derive from producing things on an adequate scale, and from specialization. But the desire for autarky in one line or another seems so widespread that it is essential to discuss to what extent it appears to be a rational objective.

One point needs to be disposed of right away. It is often argued that countries must develop production of this or that, on long-run balance of payments grounds. We are not here concerned with that at all. Any good criterion for project selection will take proper account of the fact that a country cannot run a balance of payments deficit indefinitely. We are concerned only with valid reasons which would make domestic production desirable, over and above such production as would in any case be dictated by the scarcity of resources, including foreign exchange.

One reason which may lead a country to want to be relatively self-sufficient in some goods, is the risk that imports in general may sometimes have to fall sharply. While, in the end, any economy can accommodate itself efficiently to a change in its ability to import, nevertheless, in the short run, it can cause considerable havoc:

because when capital equipment has been laid down and methods of production established, it will be impossible quickly to re-orientate production so as to rely less on imports.

Such a sharp drop in the capacity to import could result from warfare dislocating world transport. Again, a few countries suffer from severe price fluctuations in their exports which at times will force a reduction in imports. In the latter case, foreign exchange reserves are, of course, the first and proper insurance against the risk; but it would be too expensive to insure in this way against every eventuality. In the former case financial reserves are useless: physical 'strategic' stocks of some goods may be kept, but this does not apply to perishables, and in any case may be very expensive.

If there is a severe risk of a general import shortage from time to time, the country should perhaps give some attention to seeing that its import bill does not contain a very high proportion of goods whose consumption cannot be postponed without severe damage to life, or to the country's own ability to produce. But it is questionable whether any developing country whose exports are liable to large fluctuations is in such a position.

It is curious that the present argument has been used in favour of producing capital goods. These together with consumer durables are the most postponable of all. It is better to delay investment than have people starving; and it is usually better to delay investment than have existing investments idle, with consequent unemployment for lack of materials (the exception would be if such investments had been badly misconceived in the first place).

There is also a reasonable fear of relying on one or a very few sources of foreign supply where either, first, the supply is liable to fluctuations so that exports might be discouraged or even forbidden; or where, secondly, exports might be stopped for political reasons. Certain foods might fall into the first category. Armaments and other 'strategic' goods may fall into the second. There is also the possibility of warfare, or near-warfare, with the supplying country. In these latter cases it may be preferable to foster a diversity of suppliers rather than give special priority to costly home production.

To sum up, it is the feeling of the authors that there is rather seldom a very good reason for making (relative or complete) self-sufficiency in particular goods a policy objective. But, of course, the government has to weigh this up. The consequences for project selection are relatively simple to deal with. If the priority given to self-sufficiency in a particular good is absolute—then cost mini-mization and the scale of production are the only problems left. But the priority is seldom absolute. In other words, the government will not be willing to create domestic production regardless of cost. In this latter case, the price obtainable for the output, given the competition of imports, is not taken as a sufficient measure of its value to the community. Of course all industry in a developing economy may be protected. But if there is a special argument for home production of a particular good, then it is logical to give it special encouragement—whether by subsidies, or by a tariff or quota.

4.33 *Power and Prestige*

Employment and economic independence apart, it would be naive not to recognize that many countries have aims which cannot reasonably be interpreted as themselves means towards the consumption objective. Expenditure on defence, police, law, etc., can all be regarded in this latter light. On the other hand, it is clear that expenditures for aggression and national prestige cannot normally be so regarded. If a government regards a super hotel, a steel works, an airline, as prestigious—then its value cannot be finally assessed merely in terms of its consumption potential. However, no politician would expect a project evaluator to apply a special numerical 'prestige weight'. He will do that himself in making the final decision.

Thus, in evaluating projects where such things as prestige enter in, one can sum up only the measurable aspects, and leave it to governments to go ahead despite the possibly low measurable return, or even loss. It needs emphasis, however, that an analysis of the (more or less) measurable aspects should always be carried out, even where non-quantifiable objectives may strongly enter in—for otherwise the government does not know how much it costs, in terms of the people's general standard of life, to pursue prestige or some other aim in that particular way.

CHAPTER FIVE

Towards a System of Accounting Prices

In this chapter we (*a*) summarize the progress made thus far; (*b*) give a sketch of the system of shadow prices whose elaboration is the subject of Part III, and of its rationale; and (*c*) discuss the implications of adopting such a system.

5.1 RECAPITULATION

It is obvious that an economy will, over the years, have a lower standard of living than it might if its individual investments or projects make little contribution to that standard, which is taken to be the main objective of economic activity.[1] Whether or not the profitability of any investment, whose output has a market, is a reliable measure of its contribution depends on how well prices reflect social costs and benefits. Where they do not do so, which is what we mean by saying they are 'distorted', then social or 'accounting' prices which better reflect social costs and benefits should be estimated—by making adjustments to market prices.[2] This is not an easy task, and it is the main purpose of this book to show how it can best be done.

In saying that accounting prices should be estimated, we are rejecting the view that 'the economic problem' can be better solved by the simultaneous solution of a model of hundreds or thousands of

---

[1] Of course we are not denying that society can have other important aims, such as freedom, and the promotion and preservation of individual participation in economic decisions and the processes of government. But the choice of investment projects in industry, agriculture, and the economic infrastructure, will seldom have any bearing on such aims or be affected by them. We steer clear of such large questions as the degree of public ownership, where these non-economic aims are significantly relevant.

[2] The output of some investments has no market price, and in this case the accounting value (or quantified benefit) cannot be assessed by adjusting market prices, but must be estimated directly if it can be estimated at all. Valuing outputs (including bad or negative outputs, like pollution) which have no market prices is a specialized task, which is widely discussed in the literature of cost-benefit analysis relating to particular investments, e.g. in roads, schools, and hospitals. In this book we have not found space or time to deal with this specialized literature, but some 'lead-in' references can be found in the bibliography.

equations expressing society's objective function, available techniques, and all the constraints.[1]

We saw in 2.4 that there is, in fact, reason to believe that prices are very distorted in many developing countries. Some of the worst distortions have arisen as a result of government policies and bad investment planning. It is ironical that, in the past, planning was advocated for developing countries largely because the prices thrown up by a laissez-faire system could not be trusted to reflect national costs and benefits; but it has been used in such a way as to make the distortions worse. This is particularly true of industrialization and trade policies,[2] so that the relative internal prices of many important tradeable goods are often, and for no good reason, far out of line with the rates at which they could be exchanged for each other through international trade. We also saw that modern sector wages usually overstate the social cost of employing labour; and that the price of foreign exchange understates its scarcity. As economies become more complicated and integrated, which is a concomitant of development, so do distorted prices in one sector or industry spread throughout the economy, often making it difficult to accept any price as a good measure of social cost or benefit.

5.2 OUTLINE OF THE SYSTEM ADVOCATED

Part III of this book, which is its core, consists of guidelines for the construction of a whole set of accounting prices, designed to be self-consistent, and to fill their function of being better guides to project selection than actual market prices. All those accounting prices relevant to a particular project cannot usually be efficiently, or even acceptably, estimated by the project evaluator himself: an institutional framework is required, and project analysis should be fitted into a rather comprehensive system of investment planning. This is discussed in Part II. But the reader may not easily understand Part II unless he has a rough idea of the system to be advocated: and some readers may not want to read Part III, which is addressed to the professional operator, but nevertheless feel they need to know the basic ideas in outline so that they can form a judgment about the system. The rest of this chapter is therefore devoted to a brief summary, and a discussion of the implications, of the system of accounting prices.

---

[1] Reasons are given in 6.23.
[2] See Little, Scitovsky, and Scott, 1970.

In any price system what matters is *relative* prices, for these relatives measure the rates at which real goods and services can be exchanged for each other. If one can find, in an otherwise chaotic system, some price relatives which reflect real opportunities open to the economy, then these can be used as sheet-anchors. In our system the border prices of traded goods fill this need. If a country can export 5 units of A at $1 f.o.b. each, and import 1 unit of B at $5 c.i.f., then the real opportunity cost of using a unit of B can be said to be 5 units of A, and the real cost of using a unit of A is $\frac{1}{5}$ unit of B. (If foreign demand or supply is not perfectly elastic, then the marginal export revenue from A and the marginal import cost of B need to be substituted for the f.o.b. and c.i.f. prices.) This relationship is unaffected by the monetary rate of exchange.[1] If a country produces and trades to its own best advantage, then the relative internal price of traded goods (near a port) will be equal to the relative border prices. Consequently border prices can be used as accounting prices for all traded goods, because they represent the correct social opportunity costs or benefits of using or producing a traded good. If the use or production of a good is likely to affect exports of it then one uses the f.o.b. price; and if imports, then the c.i.f. price.[2]

It is now necessary to discuss more closely the distinction between traded (and tradeable) and non-traded goods. Consider an economy which is using its resources to maximum advantage It will both import and export, but many things will not be traded at all. It follows from the definition of an accounting price (AP) that it is to its advantage to export anything where the cost measured in APs is equal to or less than the f.o.b. price, and to import anything where the local cost in APs is equal to or higher than the c.i.f. price.[3] It should trade up to the point where costs measured in APs are equal to border prices. Consequently the APs of all non-traded goods and services must lie between the import and export prices.

Some things, of course, could hardly be traded at all—and it is

---

[1] If marginal export revenue and marginal import cost need to be used, there might be some change in their values as a result of a change in the value of the currency, but any such change is likely to be small.

[2] It would be tedious to repeat every time that if foreign supply and demand is not perfectly elastic, then for c.i.f. or f.o.b. prices one should always substitute marginal import cost or marginal export revenue.

[3] This does not, of course, imply that it should not both produce and import the good. It implies only that extra demand should be satisfied from imports whenever the accounting cost is higher than the import price (the higher is domestic production, the higher may be the APs).

then reasonable to say that the good or service is untradeable: for instance, the Seychelles would find the c.i.f. price of electricity very high indeed (if it were feasible to lay a transmission line at all), and the f.o.b. price would surely be zero. There is then an enormous range, and the AP of electricity cannot be estimated from border prices (we shall outline our methods of estimation in such cases below). But some non-traded goods may be fairly readily tradeable, in which case the f.o.b. and c.i.f. prices (or rather, what the f.o.b. and c.i.f. prices would be if they were traded) may be fairly close together. In such a case the AP could be closely estimated as, say, the mean of the (hypothetical) import and export prices. Finally, it should be noted that some goods may be partially traded and partially non-traded, at the margin. For instance, it might be sensible to plan to sell some of a planned increase in production at home, and some abroad: this would be especially likely to happen if a larger volume of exports could be sold only by lowering the price. Similarly, it could be correct to plan to meet part of an increase in demand from domestic production and part from imports. But, in such cases, the project evaluator will not normally go far wrong in assuming that a commodity is either wholly non-traded or wholly traded. It is always essential to keep simplification in mind, and here, as we shall see, the bias must be in favour of treating goods as wholly traded, since the estimation of APs for traded goods is much simpler than for non-traded.

In the above paragraph we assumed that a country was trading to its own best advantage, everything considered. It could *never*, for example, be rational for it to import a good where the estimated cost in APs was lower than the c.i.f. price—because in principle APs take *all* real costs into account. Similarly, it could never be rational to make something when it would cost more to do so in terms of APs than it would cost to import it (naturally, APs take proper account of any shortage of foreign exchange). But, it may be objected, few countries trade altogether rationally! Many such imperfections of policy—e.g., a distorted tariff structure—leave the basic rules unchanged. But others, such as rigid quotas, may affect the estimation of APs.

Quota restrictions are common, and may result in a tradeable commodity becoming non-traded. For instance, if a country is *irrationally* restricting some import, the social value or AP of that good may be higher than the import price—but would, of course, be equal to it if the government permitted more imports. In these circumstances, a lot depends on whether or not the government can be induced to adopt more rational trading policies, at least for the inputs or outputs of the project under consideration. If the assumption is that the government wishes to choose its investments, and to trade, to the country's best advantage as defined by its own ends (and this is what we mean by 'rational') and that it will where necessary alter its policies, then any good which would be traded in such circumstances can be valued by reference to border prices. If, however, for one reason or another it is clear that production or use of a good will not in fact affect trade then it must be valued as non-traded in the manner discussed below.

When considering the use of a non-traded good whose output will be consequentially expanded, then the AP is equal to the marginal social cost of production. The social cost of production of non-traded goods clearly has to be expressed in terms which are directly comparable with traded goods: one must not have two standards of value. How is this done? Suppose we need to compare using locally made rubber (with a consequent need to increase its output) with imported rubber. The latter costs the country x rupees in foreign exchange per ton. We therefore need to ask what local production costs in terms also of foreign exchange. This can be done by input/output methods, which can be used to break down the cost of any non-traded good into foreign exchange and rewards to domestic factors of production. Taking unskilled labour as the domestic factor of production, the picture can be completed by valuing the earning power of labour in terms of foreign currency (in fact, we do not advocate always valuing unskilled labour by its earning power—see below).[1] This is done by applying a 'conversion factor' which is the equivalent of an exchange rate. This equivalence can be seen as follows. An exchange rate expresses the relative value to a country of foreign exchange and domestic output. If we assume that a rupee of hired labour produces a rupee's worth of output, then we can also say that the exchange rate expresses the relative value to a country of a dollar's worth of foreign goods, and a rupee's worth of domestic labour. Of course, actual exchange rates often get it wrong, which is why 'shadow' exchange rates are sometimes used. For instance, it may be said that the real value of a dollar is R. 10, not R. $7\frac{1}{2}$, which is the official rate. We express this slightly differently, by saying that 10 rupees spent on unskilled labour costs the economy the equivalent of only $1, not 1\frac{1}{3}$ as the official exchange rate suggests. We put it this way because we

---

[1] More primary domestic (i.e. non-traded) factors of production than unskilled labour may be distinguished: but the procedures are similar—see Part III.

advocate using border prices as 'sheet-anchors'; and since valuing goods in border prices implies the use of foreign exchange, it seems natural to value everything in terms of foreign exchange. The unit of account can be expressed as 'border rupees', which are the equivalent of 'dollars' at the official exchange rate.

The APs of non-traded goods or services often have to be estimated by reference to their value, rather than their costs. This is the case when an output is being considered, or when use of an input will not result in increased production (the services of unskilled labour is already a case in point). With the exception of labour, the AP in these cases is the earning power or 'marginal product' of the good or service in terms of border rupees (i.e. foreign currency). Usually, the marginal product cannot be identified in terms of particular goods, but only of domestic production in general. Therefore the value of 'domestic production in general' has to be expressed in foreign exchange by the use of a shadow exchange rate, or 'conversion factor' as we term it, in the manner already discussed. This conversion factor will be some average of conversion factors for particular goods and services. The appropriate average may be different depending on what non-traded goods are being valued— so that several different conversion factors may be used. The reader must seek further detail and explanation in Part III.

It was remarked earlier that we did not always advocate setting the AP of labour—which, following convention, we term the shadow wage rate—equal to its marginal product at border prices. The reason for this is that employing labour often implies, in developing countries, an increased commitment to providing consumption goods. If the government wants to use its choice of investments to help raise overall savings at the expense of current consumption (as already discussed in 4.1) then one has to attribute a higher social cost to employing people (at all except very low wage levels) than the alternative or marginal product of that labour. Formulae for estimating shadow wages (corresponding to different levels of actual wages) which take account of the above consideration are given in Chapter XIV.

It is not merely consumption and savings which may have different social values. Further subdivision seems necessary. Thus government consumption, government savings, private consumption, and private savings may all be considered to have different social values. In these circumstances it is necessary to select some category of income or expenditure as being the yardstick in terms of which the values of the others are measured (just as it was necessary, as we saw above, to select either domestic or foreign currency as the yardstick when they could not be considered to be equally valuable at the official exchange rate). We select in fact uncommitted government (or social) income as the yardstick, or numéraire: so that a full description of the numéraire used is 'uncommitted government income measured in terms of foreign exchange'.

Equality was discussed in 4.2. As already adumbrated there, we put considerable weight on the use of shadow wages as a means of allowing for the effects of a project on equality: the system of shadow wages which we advocate gives greater encouragement to employment, the lower is the wage. The profits from a project are, of course, weighted according to whom they accrue. Other possible ways of allowing for the distributional effects of a project are discussed in 8.53 and Chapter XIII.

The flow of social income predicted to arise from a project will usually have a different time profile depending on the choice of numéraire. At the same time, it is a logical requirement that the choice of numéraire must make no difference to the relative present social values of different projects. From these two statements it can be seen that the choice of numéraire affects the discount rate to be used. Indeed, the proper discount rate to use (the ARI) is the expected rate of fall, as seen from the present, of the value of the numéraire. As with all systems of project analysis, the ARI also acts as a cut-off, rationing the amount of investment to funds available. The manner in which it satisfies both these requirements is complicated, and the reader is referred to 9.13.

This completes our formal sketch of the investment planning system proposed.

5.3 RATIONALE OF THE SYSTEM

The rationale of the system described is that of estimating those prices which would prevail in the economy if it were to operate so as to maximize society's ends, this maximization being constrained by the available resources, and by the possibilities of the tax system. But the maximization may also be constrained by the fact that certain indicated reforms are very unlikely to be made, whether because of sectional interests, inertia, or sheer irrationality. This may make it harder to estimate reliable accounting prices. It is a matter of nice judgment as to how far such additional constraints should be assumed. If they have to be assumed, then a new and lower level of satisfaction of ends is all that is attainable, and this will most probably result in different APs.

The emphasis we have given to border prices arises from the belief that many developing countries are very far away from optimizing their foreign trade. The more a country is willing to let new investments be chosen in the light of foreign trade possibilities, the more extensive can be the justifiable use of border prices as APs. The greater is the tendency to want to make certain things for their own sake—treating such manufacture as an end not a means—the more things have to be treated as non-traded. This makes it harder and more laborious to estimate correct APs, because in principle the cost structure of each non-traded input has to be investigated. An extreme case would be an economy which cut itself off from trade altogether. Formally speaking our system would not be changed, everything becoming non-traded: but clearly we would not have written the book the way we have unless we believed that many countries would be willing to move in the direction of choosing investment in the light of foreign trade possibilities. Rather similar remarks apply to direct taxation, and to pricing policy in nationalized industries. The use of APs may sometimes imply that a tax or price should be changed, and the analysis may be invalid unless it is changed.

5.4 POLICY IMPLICATIONS

What then are the policy implications of adopting our system of APs? We cannot make any statement about this without (a) specifying the political constraints which the evaluator builds into his estimates (normally the more political constraints he accepts, the fewer will be the policy implications), and (b) without specifying how extensively project evaluation is used. For the sake of the following argument we shall assume, so far as (a) is concerned, that there are no important political constraints preventing reform of the price system (although others, especially concerning the imposition of direct taxes, may remain). So far as (b) is concerned, we shall discuss a limited and tentative use of the system, as well as a thorough-going use.

Very limited use of the system would be to reject projects which did not show a positive PSV using a low ARI, and to accept projects only if they both passed the above test and showed an acceptable rate of return at market prices. Then there are no further policy implications. The investment programme will have been improved by weeding out some very bad projects. Knowing that in many developing countries more than a few very bad projects have been built, we think that even such limited use would be well worth while. But the full potential of the system would be far from being realized: in particular it would have little effect on employment, and one of the aims of the system is to encourage labour-intensity (and hence, we believe, equality).

More extensive use implies the acceptance of projects which would not be financially profitable. Unprofitable but socially desirable projects arise for various reasons: equipment or material inputs may be over-priced, because some mistakenly established industry is trying to earn a profit or reduce its losses, or because it has been excessively protected: an imported material may bear an irrationally high tariff, or some domestic component a high excise tax: exporting may be insufficiently profitable because the exchange rate is overvalued: or the level of wages which has to be paid over-states the real cost of labour. When some unprofitable project is accepted, it is highly desirable for both managerial and political reasons that it should be able to make a profit, at least after allowing for possible subsidies on particular inputs and outputs—open-ended subsidies or losses are to be avoided. This in turn may imply any one or more of a number of policy decisions, e.g. reducing import prices by increasing a quota, reducing or waiving a tariff or excise tax, changing the price policy of another public industry (possibly by writing down the book value of its assets), giving an export or labour subsidy. Some such things can be *ad hoc*, i.e. specific to the project; others could hardly be introduced in such a partial way. But the point to remember is that these changes would not be arbitrary (similar decisions have often been made in developing countries to suit particular investments, but often arbitrarily because the investments were not chosen in the light of shadow prices); they would be making prices equal to accounting prices.

It is clear that if a great many investments were selected which implied such changes, then one would be well on the road to a reform of the price mechanism. The better the price mechanism becomes, the less necessary, and the easier, is the task of estimating the APs (though the need for project evaluation would not, of course, be eliminated). It would indeed be good if actual producer prices were equal to APs. Since the main means open to governments to achieve a socially desirable set of prices are taxation and subsidization, together with management of the exchange rate, we now turn to a discussion of their role.

5.5 THE EXCHANGE RATE AND THE OPTIMUM USE OF TAXES AND SUBSIDIES

If a country were suddenly to remove quotas and tariffs so as to bring the domestic prices of traded goods in line with border prices, it would surely run into crippling balance of payments problems. Indeed, just this argument is used to support the conventional wisdom that developing countries must control the use of foreign exchange. But, broadly speaking, the best way of controlling foreign exchange is to keep its price high enough. Aligning domestic prices with world prices need not mean that the country is flooded with imports it cannot afford. If some prices come down, others should go up, and the way to ensure that is to devalue at the same time as tariffs are reformed. Of course, price increases—and some are implied by such a policy—may be politically very unpopular. If only for this reason, it will normally be prudent to plan a gradual transition from one system to another, especially when the changes which need to be made are large. It must also be said that, if tariffs were removed, some of them should be replaced by taxes on sales to consumers.

It may well be desirable to control some uses of foreign exchange (e.g. capital exports), but general control usually leads to increasing divergence between actual and accounting prices. In recent years, a number of developing countries have reduced controls over imports and foreign exchange, and taken steps to raise the price of foreign exchange, and hence imports, to a level at which such decontrol is possible. We believe these changes, such as have occurred in Brazil, Taiwan, South Korea, and the Philippines, are in the right direction.[1] In the remainder of this chapter we shall work on the assumption that the exchange rate is, when necessary, adjusted to keep international payments in balance and therefore that there is no extensive use of import controls for balance of payments reasons.

Taxation has two main purposes. One is to reduce private consumption, and thus free resources for investment and government consumption. The other, and here we include negative taxes or subsidies, is to correct distortions which arise from the free operation of the price mechanism: excessive inequality, although not normally referred to as a 'distortion', may be regarded by some people as one

---

[1] The subject of these paragraphs is treated at length in Little, Scitovsky, and Scott, 1970.

of the most important. At the same time, taxation (and subsidization) can, as an unwanted by-product, create new distortions. Taxes and subsidies also have administrative costs.

Every tax contains within itself some conflict. In reducing private consumption and in removing distortions, it almost inevitably creates other distortions. For instance, heavy taxation of luxuries will reduce private consumption and help to reduce inequality, but it means that more resources are required to keep the rich at any particular real income level than would otherwise have been needed, and it is liable to reduce incentives to work hard and take risks. Taxation may be said to be optimal when a good, rational, and benevolent government has carefully weighed all such effects. In practice, of course, many bad taxes exist because governments do not understand the workings of the economic system, or because special interests are preferred to the common weal.

We are not very much concerned with direct taxes in this book. But a brief discussion of how the above principles affect indirect taxation will be useful.

First, the primary intention of taxation being, normally, to restrain private consumption, indirect taxes are best imposed on the sales of final consumers' goods. Where possible the taxation of intermediate goods should be avoided. The only point of taxing intermediates is really to raise the price of those consumers' goods which use them. It is much better to tax these latter goods directly, for this does not result in producers trying to minimize the use of those inputs which happen to be taxed.[1] There can admittedly be administrative reasons for taxing the input of a material into a consumption good: this arises, for instance, when the producers of the input are relatively few and large, while those of the consumption good are small and many. But before doing so, the end-uses of the intermediate, and the possibilities open to producers to use other inputs instead, should be carefully considered. Thus a tax on steel is unlikely to be a very good tax, since much of it is bought by the government itself, or goes into investment which one does not normally want to tax; while consumer goods which use steel, like cars and refrigerators, can easily be taxed.

Many goods are both producer and consumer goods—coal, oil, electricity, passenger cars, typewriters, etc. There are many minor items which are unimportant for industrial costs, and it can hardly

---

[1] This does not apply when a value-added tax is used, because any purchaser of the taxed good who pays value-added tax can set off the tax paid against his own liability. The burden of the tax thus falls ultimately on the final product.

matter if they are taxed as consumer goods. Power is the most important, but in this case it is very easy to separate industrial and domestic consumption, and tax only the latter. Passenger cars and petrol are the most important items where a separation of markets is difficult or impossible. If they are taxed as consumer goods, care should be taken to see that close substitutes, even if mainly producers' goods, are equally taxed (failure to appreciate this has led, for example, to an uneconomic shift to diesel engines in some countries).

Exports are intermediate goods from the point of view of the exporting country—their function is to 'produce' imports. They should not therefore normally be taxed. There are two exceptions to this. The first is when the price can be raised by restricting supply: then the price received by the exporting country is not the marginal revenue obtained, and a corrective tax is desirable. The second exception arises when the price of an export is liable to severe fluctuations. A sliding-scale export tax (which becomes zero when the price is 'normal', and a subsidy where lower still) may then be a good way of smoothing private income and expenditure (a marketing board may also adopt policies which come to the same thing).

Tariffs, by which we shall mean any tax levied on imports, often account for quite a high proportion of the revenue of developing countries. Tariffs are not necessarily protective in intention or effect. If the tariff is not expected to encourage, and does not result in, domestic production of the taxed good or a substitute, then it is purely a revenue tariff. One can often ensure that there is no protective effect by having an excise tax on domestic production equal to the tariff. These primarily revenue taxes should not normally be levied on intermediate goods.

But tariffs are much associated with protection. Tariff protection means having a lower tax on domestic production than on imports. Suppose it is a consumption good which is in question, and that, protection apart, the government considers the ideal rate of tax to be $x\%$. Then protection implies having either a local production tax of less than $x\%$, or a tariff of more than $x\%$. Compared with the ideal tax, protection may thus either lose or gain revenue. Since the ideal tax on producers' goods is normally zero, a tariff on them will raise revenue, so long as it is not too high.

The *intention* has been that protective tariffs should be corrective: for it is widely believed that industry needs more encouragement than it would get if indirect taxation did not favour domestic production. But, in practice, tariffs have been highly distorting.

Their protective effect varies enormously from industry to industry, for no logical reason. Often the protective effect is negative, as when the tariff system raises the price of inputs but not outputs: this is always the case for exports.

The corrective intention of protection can usually be better realized in other ways. The reason why some industries need special encouragement in developing countries can almost always be expressed as a divergence of actual and accounting prices. Sometimes the corrective device will be a tax (the taxation of agricultural or mining exports for which the world demand is inelastic indirectly encourages industrialization). More usually it will consist of the subsidization of inputs, especially labour which, we have seen, is often overpriced in the modern sectors of developing countries. Sufficient subsidization is often thought to be impossible, because other taxes are required to pay the subsidies. We cannot go fully into this objection here, and will give only a hint as to why we think it is of only very limited validity.[1] Protection is itself a sort of subsidization. The consumer pays the 'subsidy' directly in the form of a higher price. This is true even of a protected producer's good for the higher price will ultimately be passed on to consumers (to some extent of course it will be the prices of government purchases which are raised by protection: the government could to this extent subsidize the producers in other ways). If domestic production for the home market is taxed as heavily as imports, the resultant increase in revenues can be paid back to industry in the form of subsidies which correct the distortions whose presence makes the special encouragement of industry desirable. The consumer, of course, ultimately pays either way. In the one case industry is subsidized by getting a high price for domestic sales. In the other, the consumer pays the same, the producer gets less by way of sales revenue, and receives the difference in the form of subsidies to those factors of production which are overpriced. Sometimes, for administrative reasons, domestic production is harder to tax than imports (though not where smuggling is easy): and, again for administrative reasons, subsidies may be hard to administer without inviting corruption. This applies especially to very small-scale industry. In such cases, an element of protection may be desirable and will arise naturally if competing products, whether they are imported or made by local large scale industry, are taxed.[2]

---

[1] For further discussion of this point, see Little, 1971.
[2] The subjects of this and the preceding paragraph are discussed at length in Little, Scitovsky, and Scott, 1970.

Turning to agriculture, taxes and subsidies are already extensively used. Here it is mainly commodity prices, both for inputs and outputs, that are in question. The chief difficulty arises when it is desired to subsidize some production for income-distribution reasons (usually because it is important for small farmers or poor regions), with the result that too much gets produced. There is also the problem of how to tax richer farmers without wantonly interfering with productive efficiency. But it would take us too far afield to explore how the difficulties can best be overcome. In the more capitalized parts of agriculture in developing countries—plantations —the subsidization of labour may be desirable.

In the main non-traded sectors, no new problems arise. There is here no question of whether to export, produce for the domestic market only, or produce for export as well—a question which makes the subject of protection versus subsidization so important. But there is still the problem that wage rates may be wrong in relation to output and other input prices; and there is also the problem of pricing the output, which is linked to producing the right amount. This is described in detail in 12.3.

5.6 SUMMARY

We may now conclude with a sketch of what the economy might look like if our system of shadow-pricing and investment selection had been comprehensively used for many years, or if the government irrespective of the process of investment selection deliberately tried to reform the price mechanism to bring about equality of prices and accounting prices. Only the broadest sketch is possible, because, of course, the detail would vary from country to country.

The most important and difficult change for a number of countries would be managing trade predominantly, though not necessarily entirely, by prices rather than quantitative controls: many already do this. Although this could be achieved by a combination of tariffs and export subsidies, such methods are very unlikely to be as satisfactory as changing the exchange rate whenever required (as is now done in Brazil), or permitting it to float. In the rest of this sketch a flexible exchange rate is assumed, tariffs not being used as a substitute. But there would be tariffs (and possibly some export taxes) for various reasons. Firstly, there might be some tariffs because it was thought that foreign supply of some goods was inelastic. Secondly, there might be a low uniform tariff to allow for some general inelasticity of world demand or supply. Thirdly, there would, of course, be tariffs on most consumption goods (all, perhaps, except a few very basic necessities) as part of the general tax system: but this latter variety of tariff would be matched, whenever administratively possible, by excise duties on domestic production so that this major component of the tariff system would not be protective. The main vehicle to encourage domestic industrial production would be subsidies, especially on labour:[1] besides this, improved capital markets, and a cheap supply of advice and information are also of importance.

If this sketch seems too radical for some, this does not at all imply that our advocated system of APs should not be embarked upon. It is merely the '*augmentum ad optimum*' of the system. Indeed it can be said that if such reforms are not to be envisaged in the near future, then a system of accounting prices is all the more essential, although rather harder to apply.

---

[1] This sketch can be found, enlarged, in Little, Scitovsky, and Scott, 1970—together with a discussion of the problems of transition.

Part Two

PROJECT ANALYSIS AND PLANNING

CHAPTER SIX

Plans, Project Choice, and Project Design

In this chapter we turn to a consideration of the relationship between project planning and macroeconomic and sectoral planning: we also consider the institutional structure required to integrate project planning into overall investment planning, and the roles of different types of evaluating agencies, including the foreign aid agencies.

6.1 PUBLIC OWNERSHIP AND PLANNING

The degree of public ownership and planning varies very greatly in developing countries. The two are not the same.

A large public sector does not by any means imply much centralized planning. Different departments may make their own investment plans, with little attempt made by a central department or planning office to relate these to the future of the economy, or to assess priorities. Nor, where some such attempt is made, is it necessarily made within the framework of a plan which seeks to predict, or to influence or control, the movement of the main economic magnitudes (such as consumption, savings and investment, or the balance of payments), as well as their breakdown by major sectors. Where there is such a 'macroeconomic' plan (which may or may not be published), the extent to which it is supposed to be operational, indicative, or only predictive, in turn varies widely; as also does its possibility of achievement, and in general its relation to reality.

On the other hand, a small public sector, more or less limited to traditional activities, is consistent with the government having a major deliberate influence on project selection: but, where it exercises such influence, it does not follow that it exercises it according to any established or discernible principles.

Despite the great range of circumstances, it is necessary to relate project selection to planning. Ideally at least, the two are intimately connected, as will appear below. In this chapter the public sector is considered alone, neglecting the private sector and relations between the two, which are dealt with in Chapter VII. A government is no exception to the rule that every agent of rational intent must plan his expenditure. This is not to say that investment expenditure, with which we are primarily concerned, need be centrally planned. A lot can be delegated to departments, municipalities, and public companies. But large projects must be centrally scrutinized, decided upon, and fitted into an investment programme, if government planning is to have any meaning.

6.2 PLANS AND PROJECTS

6.21 *Plans Require Projects*

A sound plan requires a great deal of knowledge about existing and potential projects. This is obvious enough for a short-term operational plan (1–5 years) which should, among other things, contain firm and realizable plans for expenditure in different sectors. But it is just as true for a 'perspective' plan, by which we mean a medium-term sketch of economic developments in quantitative form, covering a period of, say, 10 to 15 years.

Such a perspective plan will lay down target rates of growth for gross national product, consumption, and also for investment and its financing by both domestic and foreign savings. For this to be done, it is clear that realistic assumptions must be made as to the amount of investment that can be achieved in each year, about the lags between investment and output, and finally about the amount of output which will flow when capacity operation is achieved (the capital–output ratio). Only then can one establish a well-worked-out relationship between investment and the growth rate—for the relationship between the two is not simple, and varies greatly from time to time, and country to country.

Realistic assumptions about the level of investment which can be effectively carried out, and the connection between this investment and output, presuppose a knowledge of the rate at which good projects can be planned, designed, built, and brought to capacity operation. One also needs to know the capital–output ratios which can be expected in different sectors of the economy. It is important to note that this kind of knowledge cannot be sufficiently accurately obtained either through the study of investment and output trends in other economies, or from project data, derived from other, especially fully industrialized, economies. However, lacking any-thing better, it may be necessary to use such sources. If so, allowance should be made for the fact that costs are usually higher than expected, and outputs lower, in developing countries than they are in industrialized countries. Further to this, the capacity to develop sound projects is often overestimated, while the time-period required for their planning, their construction, and for bringing them to full production, is underestimated. In short, if a plan is to be consistent and feasible, a lot of self-knowledge is required. If this self-knowledge is to be gained, the critical appraisal of projects which have already been constructed should not be neglected.

But one cannot be satisfied with a plan which is merely consistent and feasible. In principle, there are an infinite number of such plans, many of them bad, and only one of which is the best of all. One can never hope to arrive at this optimum plan. But unless a government strives continuously to direct investment to those sectors where it will yield the most benefits to the economy, and within sectors to projects which yield most, it will certainly end up with a plan which is very far short of what could be achieved. Thus, if the division of investment between different sectors of the economy is to be rational, it is essential that the costs and benefits of many different projects in each sector should be assessed on a comparable basis.

Here, one must admit that there are severe limits to what economic analysis can achieve. No matter the sector of activity, costs are relatively easy to estimate on a comparable basis. But this is not true of benefits. The difficulty of estimating benefits increases as one moves from industry, agriculture, and the economic infrastructure, on the one hand, to such activities as education, health, and birth control, on the other. We are concerned in this book only with the former areas. This is not to say that SCB analysis is valueless in the latter. The difference is that in the former measurement is often sufficiently soundly based for it to be reasonable to let it determine decisions; while in the latter measurement is still experimental, and SCB analysis can be regarded as no better than a guide who has some familiarity with a region that has not been fully mapped.

While hunch must play a part in the above-mentioned sectors where benefits are hard to measure, it is often carried much too far, and usurps the place of economic analysis, even where the latter can be well applied. Such hunches often carry the misapplied and euphemistic name of 'strategies'. A list of some of the hunches, dogmas, doctrines, or 'strategies', which have played a role, suggests that they can have no general validity. They include the following:

   (i) Priority must be given to industry.
  (ii) Self-sufficiency in food is a first consideration.
 (iii) Heavy or basic industry must be established first.

   (iv) Light and consumer goods industries are usually, and should be, established first.

   (v) Labour-intensive industries must have priority.

   (vi) There is a lot to be said for capital-intensive industries.

  (vii) Preference must be given to industries which process indigenous materials, especially those which are exported.

 (viii) Import substitution is the best road to progress.

Countries differ a lot in their natural endowment, their acquired skills, their location and trading opportunities, and their institutional development. The best direction of advance of a particular economy can be determined only by close analysis of that economy. Furthermore, non-quantitative analysis, even if shrewd, is dangerous. It tends to lead to exaggeration. Excessive emphasis on one sector and neglect of another is not uncommon. The best balance between sectors can be achieved only by applying quantitative analysis whenever possible. All the arguments which lead some to advocate more for agriculture, and others more for light, or for heavy, industry, can be given due weight. The arguments on both sides usually have some validity: in practice, though, everything depends on how much validity—and this can be determined only by a proper system of cost–benefit analysis.

The point has been made that good realistic plans can hardly be formulated in the absence of a great deal of project planning, and without proper economic appraisal of projects. This should be obvious: in fact it has been almost everywhere neglected. It is widely accepted that one of the main reasons why planning is required is that market prices are misleading. It is ironical that most planning at the project level has nevertheless been done in the light of market prices.

6·22 *Projects Require Plans*

But it is also true that the best economic appraisal of projects cannot be made without a plan. To choose the right projects, one must have an estimate of the demand for the product. But how can one estimate the domestic demand for any product unless one has some idea of how the economy will develop? And how the economy develops in turn depends on the long-range plans and policies of the government. For instance, one can go very wrong in estimating future demand if one bases the estimate solely on past trends. This is particularly true of intermediate goods and capital goods. In these spheres especially, the government's plans for industrialization and capital development must play a large role in any demand analysis. This sounds obvious indeed, but even so there are examples of its neglect.

However, it must always be remembered that the total demand (including sometimes export demand) for many goods may be met either by imports or by domestic production. The extent to which one or the other of these sources of supply will be dominant depends very much on government policies with respect to tariffs, exchange rates, and import controls. These in turn will depend on estimates of how the overall supply and demand for foreign exchange is likely to develop.

Turning to the supply side, any analysis of the real cost of a project requires a knowledge of the strength of the scarcities which are operating and will operate in the economy. It is most usual to take the actual prices of scarce resources, reigning at the time, as adequate measures of the real scarcities. But scarcities change as development proceeds: and projects last 10 or 20 years or more. In theory, at least, future prices thus need to be predicted, and used for the estimation of those costs and benefits which occur in the future. In particular, the relative scarcity of domestic and foreign resources may change, involving a change in the exchange rate. Furthermore, some scarcities, or present bottlenecks, may be broken in a few years' time. If this can be foreseen, it would be wrong to use the existing price as a measure of scarcity throughout the life of the project. A likely future change in a price may be taken as a reason for using an accounting price now—as an approximation to the insertion of a predicted price for each future year.[1]

Part, at least, of the point of perspective planning should be to help the planner to guess how scarcities will change. Will disguised or actual unemployment rise or fall? Will the balance of payments position become easier? Will the population growth continue to accelerate, with its implications for educational expenditure? And so on! Thus the look into the future—and it can be somewhat better founded than mere crystal-gazing—which perspective planning in particular entails is necessary in order to produce informed guesses as to future scarcities.

It is not only in matters of supply and demand that perspective planning should help. Economic planning consists of juggling with

---

[1] For example, Israel is said to have used a shadow rate of exchange in project analysis because the reasonable expectation was that foreign exchange would get scarcer. See Bruno, 1967.

resources to produce the best outcome: this can be achieved only if the planner has some values to steer by. We have assumed that consumption is the ultimate objective. But we have also seen that the project planners and evaluators cannot aim for this target without being given (or assuming for themselves) some value judgments concerning the distribution of consumption between people of both today and the future. To be more concrete, in our system they need to know at least an accounting rate of interest (ARI), and a shadow wage rate[1] (SWR—we retain the word 'shadow' rather than 'accounting' for the wage rate because it has become a familiar concept), these two project planning parameters being, as we have seen, determined in the light of distributional value judgments.

Clearly, it is desirable that the political authorities should lay down, in consultation with project and other planners, these parameters. This implies close contact with some planning division —whose existence is now assumed. Let us call it the Central Office of Project Evaluation (COPE), which will be part of the ministry or commission responsible for planning and coordinating public investment. But ministers will not be able to make sound judgments about such matters unless they can form, in broad outline, some idea about the future course of the economy. For instance, one cannot make a sensible judgment about shadow wage rates without knowing how fast the working population is likely to grow. Again, informed guesses about many aspects of the future of the economy are useful when deciding on the discount rate (this is discussed in more detail in 14.4). Thus an Office of Perspective Planning (OPP) should also be in close contact with ministers, and take part in discussions concerning project planning. (The COPE and the OPP could conceivably be one.)

The above description may seem a little idealistic to some. But it is not really so. The basic elements of such a planning framework exist in many countries.[2] Moreover the idea that a rate of discount is an important planning parameter, which must be arrived at by consultation between planners, economists, and politicians, is certainly not unpractical. It is recognized and used in a number of countries. For developing countries, we are urging the addition of a

---

[1] This would in practice be expressed as an accounting discount to be applied to actual wages. It could vary with the level of wages, and by region.

[2] Recently a COPE has been instituted in the Planning Commission in India (known as PAD—Project Appraisal Division). An OPP (known in India as the PPD—Perspective Planning Division) has existed for many years.

second such policy instrument which would be a formula expressing the accounting or shadow wage to be used in project evaluation as a function of the actual wage, and also, possibly, as a function of the region in which the project was to be established. This is analogous to the 'employment premium' used for development areas in the U.K., (see 4.2).

However, project planning and evaluation will continue to be done in many countries without the benefit of the kind of planning framework sketched above. Whereas it is beyond argument that good plans require good projects, the argument that a proper analysis of projects itself requires good plans can be overemphasized. It is true that analysis within the framework of an overall plan for the economy should produce a better estimate of the costs and benefits of a project than can be the case if no plan exists. But this does not at all imply that cost–benefit analysis is useless if it has to be done without the benefit of knowledge of the central government's guesses as to the future development of the economy. It will probably be less good insofar as guesses have to be made about the government's own investment intentions. But, in general, one can make some guess as to the real scarcities which face the economy in its development, and put a price on them, even without the help of any attempt at overall planning. The difference is that the guess will be less enlightened without such planning (although less enlightened it may sometimes be better—unrealistic planning has on occasion made demand estimates worse than they otherwise would have been, with the consequence of wasted investment).

Finally, social cost–benefit analysis can proceed without the analyst having explicit guidance on values. In that event he has to be guided partly by his own sense of morality, while also interpreting government policy in a broad sense so that he does not feed in values that are at variance with it. He may also feel bound to leave more things open and unquantified when he presents his analysis. We discuss this again in 8.53.

6.23 *The Interaction of Project Analysis and Plan Formulation*
In presenting the twin propositions that 'plans require projects' and 'projects require plans', it may seem that an insoluble chicken-and-egg dilemma has been posed. If good plans cannot be formulated without a proper economic appraisal of projects, and if the real value of projects cannot be properly ascertained, except within the framework of a plan, where does one start? But the chicken-and-egg analogy is false, as one is never totally devoid of knowledge.

Inadequate or inaccurate plans may be first formulated with little knowledge of the contribution to growth made by individual projects. These in turn should permit improvements in project analysis and appraisals, and so on. Macroeconomic planning, in terms of figures aggregated for the whole economy, can then be gradually improved in the light of improvements in micro-economic planning, i.e. planning at the sectoral and project levels; and vice versa. By such iteration and reiteration, one gradually tries to come nearer to an optimum plan.

There are a few economists who reject the kind of feed-back process described and deny that the cost–benefit analysis of projects can play a valid role in optimal planning. They see the plan as the solution of an optimum programming model of the economy. The objective function might be specified in much the same way as we have described, that is, as the weighted sum of everyone's consumption from now to eternity; and the constraints might also be similar, being specified in terms of quantities of resources. Information on the inputs and outputs of all existing production processes, and the inputs and outputs appertaining to all future possible projects, are also in principle required, for these constitute the technological possibilities of transforming resources into consumption. The solution of the model (assuming it were soluble) would yield the optimum quantities of all goods to be produced at all periods: as a by-product it would also yield the optimum prices, these being the very accounting prices whose estimation is discussed in Part III of this book. But these prices would be redundant, for the model would already have selected the processes and projects to be used, together with their inputs and outputs. These economists point out that prices are signposts, and if one has already reached one's destination one has no need of signposts. Thus the argument is that correct accounting prices cannot be established without 'solving' the whole economy, or, what comes to the same thing, that a project can be correctly selected or rejected only simultaneously with the selection and rejection of all other projects.

One might think that the unworldliness of the above line of argument was obvious enough. But it is an argument which is often repeated, and has had some influence, and it is therefore necessary at least to give brief reasons why we find it entirely unconvincing.

(i) Technological information neither is, nor soon will be, available in an accessible form for the computerization and solution of models of a whole economy in sufficient detail for deciding on particular processes and projects. Such information is always more or less aggregated, and even if one can envisage compiling and solving input/output matrices with many hundreds of rows and columns, one would still find mentioned only a tiny fraction of the numbers of separately identifiable things which are produced by all but the simplest economies.

(ii) Despite the aggregation, technological matrices require so much work for their assembly that they are invariably many years out of date.

(iii) One can feed only known technologies into such a model. But virtually every project contains technology, in the form of the input/output mix, which is new for that economy. Simultaneity could not therefore be achieved, and the model would in principle need to be re-solved for every new project. Since projects in reality come up for decision *seriatim*, and increased knowledge of the possibilities is a continuous process, so too should amendments of both operational and perspective plans be a continuous process.

The above are the more practical difficulties. But there are also theoretical reasons why such models usually give implausible results (until one has tinkered with them so that they are constrained to produce answers which one already finds sensible on grounds of general economic reasoning). Firstly, economic relationships have to be assumed to be linear when they are certainly not (and consequently arbitrary constraints have to be inserted to prevent ridiculous solutions): when a model manifestly fails to reflect the workings of the real world, it is absurd to suppose that it can produce an optimum solution of anything but itself. Secondly, such models can handle only a very limited range of techniques so that coefficients are fixed for most sectors, and there is no response to price changes. There is an enormous amount of evidence suggesting that people not only respond to prices within a given framework of technical knowledge, but also that they make innovations and inventions in order to economize in the use of scarce resources. Consequently the 'solution' of any model, based on a fixed technological matrix, will immediately falsify itself by changing that matrix.

We do not, however, want to deride research on such models, or to maintain that they can play no part in planning. Given the degree of aggregation it seems that their role is limited to perspective planning. Here they may, if very carefully handled so as to avoid their worst failings, give some insight as to the likely desirable development of the economy on a broad sectoral basis.[1] When it comes to filling in the sectors, they are useless.

It remains only to deal with the question whether the simultaneous solution of an ideal model of the whole system is nevertheless needed to throw up correct accounting prices. Since no such model or solution is possible, the answer is that one must find indirect ways of guessing the accounting prices that would hold for an optimal solution. In so doing one starts with actual prices, for the market mechanism does provide a 'solution' to the actual economy, and indeed a new solution every minute. But, as we have seen, there are good reasons to believe that these solutions are not optimal. By allowing for these reasons, one can make good guesses about how to amend actual prices to approach nearer to those prices which would be likely to reign if the economy were operating in a properly efficient manner in pursuit of the objectives demanded of it.

We have now dealt with the mutual 'feedback' between project analysis on the one hand and the formulation of economic plans in terms of rather broad macroeconomic aggregates on the other hand. In summary, one can say (*a*) that reasonable economic plans are not likely to be achieved without an assessment of the productivity of investment in various sectors—which requires project knowledge, and (*b*) that a good assessment of the productivity of investments itself requires a knowledge of scarcities and benefits which can, in principle, be properly made only if a long-run plan has been constructed on the basis of choosing the most productive investments. Everything thus hangs together, and planning must proceed on this understanding.

6.3 THE SELECTION OF PROJECTS, AND THE INVESTMENT PROGRAMME

Most countries, whether they formally have plans or not, are now alive to the fact that a single year, the traditional period for budgeting, is too short a time over which to plan government expenditure, especially investment expenditure. Those planning to spend public money on investments, which once decided may commit capital expenditure for five or more years ahead, need to be guided by estimates of how much is likely to be available for such expendi-

---

[1] See Khan and Mirrlees, 1973. For a valuable survey of programming models see Manne, 1972.

tures for several future years. Of course it is true that the further ahead, the less firm will such estimates be, but it is probably worth trying to look five years ahead, which is what most plans do. In principle any such five-year forward look should be revised as often as possible—the 'rolling plan' as it is sometimes termed: experience has shown that constructing a new plan only quinquennially can lead to uneven investment.

The investment programme will then be phased so as to secure expenditures of about the right amount, this year, next year, and so on. For the current year, the estimates should be very firm. In subsequent years, they cannot be so firm, for they will be based to some extent on projects which are not yet approved, and for which plans may not have been finalized or evaluated. The main purpose of looking further ahead is to see, on the one hand, that projects already approved and beginning to be implemented do not already add up to an excessive commitment in some future year, and, on the other hand, that a sufficient number of projects likely to be approved (or having received provisional approval at the 'feasibility' stage) are in a sufficiently far advanced state of preparation for enough expenditure to be capable of being efficiently made in future years.

Ideally, at any one time, there will be more projects on which money could be spent than there is money available, so that the least good can be abandoned, sent back for redesign, or simply postponed to a time when more funds are available and better projects are not forthcoming. There will, ideally, also be sufficient project planning to ensure that this state of affairs normally continues. Of course, it is wasteful if many projects, which have been brought to an advanced stage of preparation, are abandoned: but this should seldom happen, for decisions in principle can be taken on the basis of engineering cost estimates which are made before the most expensive process of detailed design is undertaken. That there should always be an excess supply of projects at any one time need not imply that a lot of design work never comes to fruition.

In a number of developing countries there is a deficiency of projects in a sufficiently advanced state of preparation for sensible decision to be taken. This implies that the country has failed or been unable to find sufficient skilled people, at home or from abroad, to devote to this work. Sometimes there is also a deficiency because decision-makers, who often include aid agencies as well as the local government, procrastinate.

For the above reason, some people are suspicious of the idea of setting up any complicated system of project evaluation. They fear it may delay decision-making even further, and hence reduce the level of investment below what it might be. As against this, a proper economic evaluation requires resources which are very small compared to those required anyway at the engineering level, and it can reduce the amount of decision-making time necessary at the highest levels. Moreover it must be emphasized that selection is still required even if there is a deficiency of projects. This is because it can very well be better to do nothing and save (or not borrow) the money than embark on some projects. There is no doubt that there have been many investments in developing countries which have actually reduced the national income and been a burden on the people. Delay is not always bad. The general problem is then to formulate a criterion which will either permit a just sufficient number of projects to be approved to fill up the investment pro-gramme from year to year,[1] or admit all projects such that it is better to proceed than do nothing.

The basic formal criterion is to accept all projects with positive present social value (PSV). We have seen that the estimate of this PSV will vary with two policy instruments which should ideally be the subject of decision by the central government. These are the shadow wage rates used in the project evaluations, and the account-ing rate of interest These two are mutually dependent: if the SWRs are low then a high ARI is likely to be required to ensure that there are not too many projects with positive PSV; this is simply because lowering the SWR reduces accounting costs, and hence raises the PSV. Only if there is a bottleneck in project preparation, or if some country has little possibility of development and a lot of money, are both SWR and ARI likely to be low. Some oil-producing countries are a case in point: here the ARI is likely to be no more than the real rate of interest which can be earned on foreign portfolio invest-ment, say 4%.

The formal inter-relationship of these instruments is rather intricate, and the factors affecting their estimation complicated: discussion of this is reserved for 14.15 and 14.4. At this point in the argument it is necessary only to understand their *modus operandi*. Of

---

[1] There is an ancillary problem of phasing expenditure on the projects so that not only the average amount of expenditure over a number of years is about right, but so that it does not fluctuate unduly. This is not in principle too difficult, first because considerable fluctuation is permissible (any estimate of the amount of public investment desirable in a single year, or even shorter period, on macro-economic grounds is subject to quite wide error), and secondly because it should be possible to advance or delay the implementation of many projects at fairly short notice.

the two, the SWR will, presumably, be chosen with rather long-term considerations in mind—such considerations including, as we have seen, the desired demand for labour and the supply of savings. This implies that the shorter-term regulator, which serves the function of rationing acceptable projects, must be the ARI.[1]

Up to this point the argument has proceeded as if the government had a single investment budget. Before making any further observations about the use of the ARI it is necessary to approach reality more closely. Investment proposals may come up from many different sources, from the different ministries or departments, possibly from quasi-independent government agencies, and from nationalized industries or public companies. Some of these departments or agencies, including those responsible for health, education, defence, and law and order, will be responsible for investment proposals whose expected social benefit can hardly be expressed in quantifiable terms: for such investments the present value criterion is not operable. This is not to say that projects need not be submitted, nor that project analysis plays no role: on the contrary, certain objectives can be decided on as a matter of policy (e.g. the size of the secondary school intake, or number of hospital beds), in which case the departmental programmes can be considered from the point of view of cost-effectiveness. But the criterion of present value cannot determine the level of investment permitted for that department.

There must therefore be separate budgets for the non-quantifiable sectors. The total size of these should depend on the marginal rate of social profit resulting from a change in the size of the quantifiable investment budget. The smaller the latter the more reasonable it will seem to spend money on education and health which, apart from making some contribution to development, are desirable in themselves. But there is a limit to this, for investment in education and health results in the need for recurrent expenditure in future years, which will limit investment in industry, etc., just when more socially profitable investments in these fields may be coming forward. There can thus come a point when it may be better to raise less taxation for a few years rather than to invest as much as possible— or else to invest abroad. This is all the more true insofar as domestic

---

[1] In principle, any revision of the ARI implies also recalculating the SWRs. But there is reason to believe that the latter may not be very sensitive to changes in the former. We would envisage that in practice revisions to the ARI might not require recalculation of the SWRs, especially if they were thought of as provisional or temporary.

investment is also a drain on foreign exchange reserves which might have been put to better use later.

For the purposes of this book, we effectively limit ourselves to the sectors or sub-sectors which together comprise the quantifiable 'area'; and we here assume that the investment budget for this area has been decided. When we speak of the investment budget, we henceforward mean the total budget for quantifiable investments. But this budget, which need not be thought of as rigid except for a short period ahead, is itself split up between departments. The problem is to see that the departmental totals add up to about the right amount.

There are two basic ways of solving this problem. The first is to allocate departmental budgets, as in the case of the non-quantifiable sectors. The second is to succeed in setting the ARI at such a level that the total of acceptable proposals emanating from the spending agencies adds up to about the right figure. This second method is undoubtedly the most rational, for it is in principle the way of maximizing the present value of the investment programme. There are two main objections. The first objection is that departments will be too easily able to grind their own axes by slanting their analyses in an undetectable manner. The second objection is that it may be too difficult to keep adequate control over the total volume of government investment if there is no quantitative budgetary control: this is especially likely to be true in the early stages of any attempt to plan in this manner, for there will then be little experience of setting the ARI at the right level.

The first method has the obvious objection that any more or less arbitrarily selected amount of investment expenditure for particular agencies or ministries is bound to result in one agency producing more socially profitable investments than another. This disadvantage can be mitigated provided a careful watch is kept on the situation, and budgets can be flexibly adjusted in favour of the most socially productive sectors. However, it is easier to suggest such flexibility than achieve it. Departments acquire a vested interest in their budget, and fight for it; consequently, the objection that departments can too easily produce biased investment analyses is an objection to the budgetary method also, if it is to operate with reasonable overall efficiency. Another disadvantage of the budget method is that it institutes an added, and basically artificial, planning problem for the department, which now has to maximize the present value per rupee of its budget. This may be difficult especially if it cannot foresee changes in the size of its budget.

We believe that control by means of the ARI should be the intention, and that it should be achievable as the normal method within a few years of trying to operate it.[1] In advocating this we have in mind two safeguards: first, that if total investment seems at any time to be becoming excessive, a reversion to the budgetary method can be instituted as a temporary measure; second, that in the case of very large projects the centre can retain control over the timing of the investment. There may also occasionally be some desirable exceptions to the rule. An example could be some agency which typically invested in a large number of small projects, too large a number to be vetted centrally: if there was not perfect trust in the agency, then it might be desirable to make it operate within a budget ceiling.

It should be noted that there is nothing novel about allowing most public investment to be normally delegated under the control only of achieving positive PSV at a 'test' rate of discount, i.e. the ARI. This is, for instance, the system in U.K. nationalized industries which account for the bulk of the 'quantifiable' public investment. At the same time, of course, they submit to the responsible ministry, and through it to the Treasury, forward estimates of the amount of investment they expect to achieve. In some cases these forward estimates may be part of a comprehensive plan for the industry or sector. From time to time, however, more or less arbitrary cuts may be made (rather than trusting to a rise in the ARI) if the Government wishes to effect a reduction in total public investment expenditure in the fairly near future.

6.4 Sectoral Planning

Sectoral investment planning may be said to consist of the simultaneous appraisal and selection by one responsible authority of a set of projects extending over time.[2] The selection should not, of course,

---

[1] Guidelines as to how the ARI may initially be estimated, the circumstances in which it may require to be changed, and in general how it may be used as effectively as possible in its role of rationing projects, are all discussed in 14.4.

[2] This definition excludes the case when a project-by-project approach is adequate, but where each project evaluation requires an analysis of the operation of an integrated system. For instance, even if power plants were small and quickly built, any new plant would nevertheless alter the mode of operation of the others. The optimum age structure of the plants, and their technical characteristics, requires such analysis. Such inter-relatedness occurs in all industries, but it can usually be ignored since the price mechanism can be expected to solve the problem quite well. This is not the case for electricity because of the peculiarity of the market for the product.

be immutable. Circumstances change and plans have to be, or should be, frequently revised. In theory, whenever work on an individual project is about to begin, the question should be asked as to whether it is still part of the best plan that can be envisaged.

The question that must be asked is 'When is such planning desirable?'—or, what comes to the same thing, 'When is it inadequate to proceed project by project, *seriatim*?' A possible answer might be 'Whenever one investment decision affects others': but this is unacceptable, because all investment decisions affect to some degree many others. This answer is therefore saying 'Forget about sectoral planning: the only possible sector is the whole economy'. We have already discussed and rejected the feasibility of such a solution in 6.23. Common sense tells one that it is not really necessary to make decisions about all individual investment projects for a decade ahead when planning, say, electricity supply: but that it is necessary when planning a port whether some other important port will be enlarged or not.

Where two or more projects are large, take a long time to build, and are strongly competitive either for resources or in their outputs, there is a case for considering them together. It might be foolish to do both, at least without modification. Similarly where they are complementary, the output of one being an input of the other, it may be foolish to plan only one. Size and time lags are both important. If projects are large relative to demand, there is a danger of producing more or less than the best amount at any one time. Therefore the time phasing becomes important, and such investments should be planned together. Even if projects are small, future planning may be important if time lags are long. Thus in a developed economy power plants are quite small relative to total supply—but, being absolutely large, the planning or gestation period is long. Therefore it would be quite easy to start too few or too many, if the number is not carefully planned in anticipation of demand. There is a theoretical case for sectoral planning in the above circumstances; but it must not be thought that such planning in practice always improves on laissez-faire.

Tradeability, as well as size and gestation periods, is very important. It breaks the interconnectedness of investment decisions. If too little is produced, there is no great disaster. Imports can come in. A good investment opportunity may have been missed, but that is all. If too much is produced, then perhaps more is sold abroad at a lower price than one would ideally have planned, and the investment is not as profitable as hoped—but, again, no disaster.

In contrast, it is a disaster if much too little power or transport is produced, for a lot of other production is held back. Of course, this is a good reason to err a little on the side of excess supply so far as non-tradeable goods and services are concerned.

Thus the sectors where sectoral planning seems most desirable are those non-traded sectors where economies of scale are important so that plants tend to be large, and consequently gestation periods tend to be long. Ports, airports, railways, trunk roads, power, and large-scale irrigation and river control, most clearly fall into this category.[1] But it may also be desirable in some tradeable sectors, where it is reasonably clear that the industry concerned is one which the country should have, and where foreign demand, and possibly supply, is likely to be imperfectly elastic. Steel and nitrogenous fertilizers in large developing countries like India or Brazil may be examples. Where such an industry is also nationalized, or predominantly nationalized, the case is clear. The top management of the industry should consider a set of projects spread over time, possibly for as long ahead as 10 years, since any one project will affect others for whose planning it is also responsible.

Appraisal of a set of projects, i.e. a plan, raises no new issues of principle so far as accounting prices are concerned. The important thing is to consider a number of alternatives: the number, being probably limited only by the research work which can be done, may amount to as many as a dozen if a sophisticated research organization is in being. Each such alternative comprises a system which should, of course, be assumed itself to operate in as near an optimal manner as is feasible (for instance the levels of operation of a plant common to two systems may be different in each system—as is, for example, the case with power generation). This implies that existing plants will be included in each such alternative system, unless or until it is optimal to scrap them. (The calculation of the optimal mode of operation of each system may involve quite difficult programming techniques, and will certainly be very demanding of information.) The PSV of each alternative system can then be calculated, and the best selected. This best alternative should then finally be compared with doing nothing—which implies in this case continuing with the existing plants (and maybe making small replacement investments to maximize the PSV of doing next to nothing). If the PSV of thus 'doing nothing' is

---

[1] Planning is also, of course, required in such fields as education and public health: but we are not, in this book, concerned with these sectors.

subtracted from the PSV of the best programme of investment analysed, and the remainder is positive, then the plan is viable.

If a project forms part of a central plan which has been made up, and appraised, in the manner discussed above then no further evaluation is required: indeed it can in theory be appraised only by comparing the plan of which it is a part with the best plan which does not include it. This will probably have already been done in the process of selecting the best plan from among the alternatives envisaged.

6.5 THE ROLE OF THE CENTRAL OFFICE OF PROJECT EVALUATION

The administrative system through which and by means of which properly evaluated projects are assembled into a coherent and productive investment programme is relatively easy (it is, of course, never easy) to operate in a country in which the price mechanism is trusted more or less adequately to reflect social costs and benefits. This is because only one accounting price, the ARI, is used. But in most developing countries it is desirable, as we have argued (in 2.5), to institute a wide-ranging system of accounting prices. This is a complication which naturally gives rise to quite serious administrative problems. It is this complication and these problems which necessitate the institution of a COPE, an organization whose more limited functions may be adequately exercised by a less specialized division of the finance ministry or planning ministry in a developed country. The possible role and functions of COPE will now be further discussed.

It has already been envisaged that COPE would be the body which would consult closely with the government in the choice of the two main policy instruments, the ARI and the SWR—since these presuppose not only economic estimation but also basic value and policy judgments. We have also seen that the exchange rate in many developing countries under-values foreign currency. Although the setting of an accounting rate of exchange is not something we envisage as a major policy instrument involving a value judgment, nevertheless the manner in which this disequilibrium is handled in project analysis probably needs to be understood and affirmed by economic ministers. Again, a decision from ministers is likely to be required as to how regional issues should be handled in project evaluation. Most other accounting prices stem from, and are implied by, decisions on the above matters (there may be exceptions, as we shall see). This then is the first task of COPE—to propose, explain, and get approved by ministers, a system of social cost–benefit analysis.

The next problem is how large a role COPE itself plays in the evaluation of individual projects. In principle it could carry out the social cost–benefit part of the analyses. This would imply that initiating or sponsoring departments would submit analyses in the conventional manner, based on market prices. COPE would have to see only that these were submitted in a manner which permitted a transformation to APs: in the main this would mean requiring that inputs and outputs were specified both by quantity and value whenever possible, and that the 'format' was that of a DCF analysis.

While it is possible that the above might be a useful early stage when COPE was newly formed it would be far from satisfactory as a permanent arrangement. First, there would be a conflict between COPE and the departments, which would be operating on different principles. Second, it would fail to get accounting prices used in the design of projects: this seems so important that the next section is devoted to the question of design. Third, as we saw in the previous section, some projects may be part of sectoral plans which should themselves have been drawn up in the light of accounting prices. Fourth, COPE would either be able to evaluate only a few large projects, or there would be a wasteful duplication of expertise. Fifth, as we shall see, many accounting prices can be better estimated by someone with intimate knowledge of the industry concerned.

For these reasons it is clear that the social–cost benefit analysis, or 'economic evaluation' as it is sometimes termed, should be done by the initiating agency, let us say a ministry.[1] Consequently, the ministry should have a small staff versed in the methods which COPE lays down. The second role of COPE is therefore that of a general staff which sees to it that the ministry planning staffs, as well as those of public industries, work along the right lines in assessing the social profit of the projects or plans which they formulate and propose. This can be done in various complementary ways: by issuing a guidelines document or manual (and amending

---

[1] There will often be a three-tiered structure. The project will be initiated by a public agency or company, for which a ministry is responsible and which will sponsor the project. The same reasons which lead us to argue that a ministry should do the evaluation when it initiates the project, also support the view that the initiating agency or company should do it in the case of a three-tiered structure. Naturally the responsible ministry could also append its comments and amendments, as can COPE in its turn.

'codicils'), by secondment and exchange of staff, by giving advice, and by arranging training programmes. In some cases COPE will itself lay down conversion factors (the factor by which an actual price is multiplied to give the accounting price). It should do this for the main non-traded goods and services which are used in almost all projects, e.g. electricity, transport, construction, banking, etc. It would be very wasteful and inefficient if every different project designer or evaluator calculated these for himself. We have earlier noted the tendency of departments to believe their ducks are geese, and dress them up accordingly. This tendency should one hopes be reduced by the staff arrangements suggested. But it should be noted that the dressing-up is not limited to the economic variables of the project.[1] If the engineers or agronomists give, consciously or unconsciously, biased estimates, the economist is relatively helpless. For this reason it is almost certainly desirable that COPE should have an engineering staff, and possibly also experts in other fields, to act as watchdogs. Although the whole range of possibly desirable expertise can hardly be covered, even in a very large country where COPE might have a professional staff of 50 people or more, nevertheless in time the experience gained from past investments should help in spotting exaggerations or dubiously feasible solutions, and in general permit appropriately searching questions to be asked.

Another function which seems to be desirable, if not essential, for good planning is that of systematically monitoring the progress of at least large projects, after the decision that they should be implemented has been taken. It seems that there is often too little knowledge at the centre of how projects are progressing. Such monitoring is of importance for several reasons: (*a*) if there is undue delay, to set in motion 'trouble-shooting' action to break the bottlenecks, (*b*) to reschedule planned expenditure, which may have effects on the desirable timing of other investments, (*c*) to warn any linked project that there will be delays in the supply of the output, (*d*) to learn lessons which may make future planning more realistic, (*e*) because it is sometimes correct to reverse the original decision, even at this stage, if prospects have changed, and the earlier the warning that this might be advisable the better, and finally (*f*) to discipline the project appraisers who have to make predictions.

---

[1] Unfortunately it is true that some consultant firms employ economists primarily to justify projects which they want to sell, or which they believe some politician wants to 'buy' anyway, rather than to give as objective an appraisal as is within their powers. The resultant sort of social cost–benefit analysis has been aptly termed 'social cosmetic' analysis.

The last three reasons given clearly makes it desirable to compare the progress of planned social costs and benefits with those actually attained by the project. The consequent desirability of monitoring projects in the same format as the original DCF analysis (so that, ideally, for every projected figure in the original analysis at a given date a realized figure is ascertained) suggests that this should be a function of the originator of the analysis, normally a ministry or protégé agency of the ministry. But in order that COPE can learn from this monitoring, as well as initiating any action which may be appropriate to it (including making a submission that the project should be stopped), it should receive, study, and store such progress reports.

The process of monitoring progress shades into that of conducting 'post-mortems'. This is a misnomer, since one should not wait until the project is dead to make a reappraisal, which can perhaps be best done when the project has been operating for several years. Since a lot can surely be learned about the actual and potential social profitability of both industrial and agricultural projects in this manner, it is remarkable that even impressionistic reappraisals are seldom made, and no full-scale partially ex-post-facto cost–benefit analysis had, so far as we are aware, ever been made or anyway published until one of us started a research project to do this.[1] Especially in the case of agricultural projects it is uncommon to find any records kept which permit such an analysis. Public investors in fact show an amazing lack of interest in the question of whether their investments were worth while. We would suggest that COPE ensures that sufficient records are kept to be able to conduct reappraisals, and that it either carries out regular studies of this kind itself or commissions some research institute to do them.

The highest level function of COPE has been left to the end. It is, of course, to receive feasibility reports, discuss them with the originators, agree amendments, append their comments, submit them for decision to the appropriate body, and assist in the integration of such projects into a planned investment programme. Where sectoral plans are made, COPE should fill the same role.

In the above paragraph we have assumed that a feasibility report gives a full analysis of projected inputs and outputs, but does not go into details of the design. A provisional decision to go ahead with detailed planning is assumed to be taken on the basis of the feasi-

---

[1] For publications so far see the bibliography.

bility report. Of course, if in this later planning stage it is found that inputs will be significantly greater or outputs less than were previously predicted an amended feasibility report should be submitted. It is notorious that projects are almost never turned down at the full project report stage. This is as it should be. It also happens, of course, that costs escalate or market prospects shrink during the implementation stage. Sometimes, after making due allowance for sunk costs, it is right to reverse the original decision even at this stage. This is seldom done, but it happens occasionally. For instance, the U.S.A. stopped its supersonic transport project after a lot of work had been done.

The account given above of the role of COPE and its relation to other government organs may well be unrealistic for the immediate future in the case of many developing countries. Some lack the trained people who could efficiently man such an office. Technical assistance could be given in such cases, but sometimes countries would be unwilling to have foreigners in these key positions. Nevertheless it should normally be possible to overcome this difficulty within a few years. An increasing number of training courses in project analysis are being instituted in various universities and development institutes. We believe that improving the social profitability of investments and designing them with the possibilities of developing countries more in mind is of such importance that good project analysis is a very high priority area for the use of even the scarcest skilled people.

It is true that, in some developing countries, public expenditure on the sort of project whose benefits are reasonably easily quantifiable is very limited. Much of the planning and design of such projects as there are may also be done by foreign consultants. In these cases, the government's project analysis staff would be more skeletal than has been suggested here, and might not extend to any ministries or public companies. Nevertheless, a central staff, even if it consists only of a small handful of people, is still almost certainly desirable in every country if only to deal with the private sector—which is discussed in Chapter VII.

6.6 PROJECT DESIGN AND DECENTRALIZED EVALUATION

It was already pointed out in 1.1 that the final version of a project as presented in a feasibility report, together with an economic appraisal, will generally have been arrived at only after the rejection of many alternatives by the planners and designers in the initiating agency. The same planning department will, it is assumed, also be responsible for the economic appraisal. Because of the need to make many planning and design decisions without reference to higher authority, it is not very useful to distinguish the planner and the evaluator at this level. The planners and designers should, as it were, evaluate as they go along.

In industry, the range of alternatives is often large. This is because production usually consists of many, more or less separate, processes. The generation of electrical power is relatively unusual, as is the production of steel, in that the main part of production is a single process, which may be of one kind or another, but is an indivisible whole for any particular technique of production. More frequently, each different part of the production process presents its own, independent, alternatives. In the production of textiles, for example, storing, handling, and moving materials around the factory are quite separate activities from the main business of operating the looms. It may be desirable to use advanced power-driven looms, each with many automatic devices for controlling the output, and yet use relatively 'primitive' labour-intensive methods for moving the material to the looms and away from it, for controlling the finances of the undertaking, for dyeing the cloth, and so on. The chemical industry is another in which there are usually many separate production processes involved in any particular project, and the same is true of the building of most kinds of machinery, and of construction. In agriculture, the alternatives which the planner, of agricultural settlements say, has to consider are at least equally large in number: and decision between them may well involve judgments which are more obviously ethical than is common in industrial planning. Such considerations may include the kind of family to settle, the size of plot and its layout, the amount of land preparation, the amount and kind of irrigation, the quality of housing and its siting, the availability and proximity of agricultural and social services, and so on. Some policy guidance may come from on high, such as the level of farm income to aim at, but there will inevitably remain a host of possible solutions within any policy framework laid down.

Agricultural planners and industrial engineers are generally also economists. But they are not usually the kind of economists who are trained to look at matters from the point of view of the economy as a whole. They will have either profitability, or the least-cost achievement of certain planning objectives (e.g. family income in the case of land settlement) in mind. But they will, of course, arrive at their solutions in the light of actual prices, unless instructed otherwise.

Let us therefore now look at the problem of using accounting prices from the point of view of this 'decentralized' planner. Initially, it will be assumed that the kind of planning set-up, sketched in the previous section, is in operation. COPE will have laid down an ARI: the planner/evaluator cannot operate efficiently without this, for all his alternative solutions are incompatible projects. It will also have laid down a rather precise formula by which he can calculate the real cost of labour, that is the shadow wage (or implicit shadow wage in the case of unpaid family labour). It may also have told him what conversion factors or APs to use for such things as electricity, water, road and rail transport, etc. But many other APs will remain to be determined—those which the specialized agency or the man on the spot is in a better position to determine than COPE. Here he will have the guidance of a manual prepared by COPE, but this will certainly leave him uncertain in some cases just what valuation he should put on some input or output of the project.

The dilemma in which a designer/evaluator may find himself will be discussed at greater length in Part III, but the following example is sketched here in order to bring out the political nature of some of the decisions that may have to be made, even by someone remote from the corridors of power.

Suppose that some fertilizer is to be used in an agricultural scheme, but that it forms a small part of the costs (at market prices). How is a social valuation to be put on this fertilizer? Fertilizers are all imported, but there is an import quota, and the domestic price is consequently higher than the 'border' or c.i.f. price. The COPE manual says 'value traded goods at border prices (plus something for inland transport)'. But are fertilizers really traded goods in these circumstances? If the government does not change the quota as demand increases, no more fertilizers will be imported, the c.i.f. valuation becomes irrelevant, and some other method of valuation would be appropriate. So the evaluator ideally has to know how the government is going to operate the control. Or, perhaps the present government will fall, and one that favours a different approach to international trade will take its place. It may seem clear in such circumstances that COPE should do any guessing about government policy that is necessary, and give sufficiently precise instructions to cover such cases. But if it does not, the evaluator has to resolve the dilemma himself. Since the input is a small part of the project it may not matter very much exactly how it is valued, and the simplest treatment may well be the best even if it is founded on a wrong assumption (the right assumption might not have led to a very different value anyway).

But now suppose the project is to build a fertilizer factory in this same country. The valuation of the fertilizer will then be crucial. But similar problems arise. If the government reduces the quota as more domestic output becomes available, then the fertilizer is an import substitute. If government policy for the future were to have no import restriction on fertilizers, and the quota was going to be removed anyway, then the output of the new factory will still be an import substitute. But if the government retains the quota at the previous level, then the new factory will cause more fertilizers to be available than otherwise would have been the case. Then a different value has to be put on fertilizers. Since the value of fertilizers is supposedly crucial, the evaluator would in such a case ask COPE for guidance.

But COPE may not itself know what government policy will be. In that event, it might well want two or more valuations to be put on fertilizers, depending on government import policy. It could then present the resultant alternative PSVs of the project to the government, and point out that the project's acceptance or rejection depended on the manner in which the government was going to restrict imports, if at all. It is reasonable to suppose that the government would then expect COPE also to advise on the best import policy (in the light of the government's more fundamental objectives), which would then determine the PSV to be placed on the fertilizer project. If a COPE did not exist, the evaluator in such a case would still be well advised to present alternative valuations, although he might have to be more circumspect in advising the government on its import policies (or might not feel competent to do so).

We shall revert to the problems which arise from uncertainty as to the basis of valuation in Chapter VIII, which discusses some of the devices which can be used to assist in the process of communication with the decision-making authorities. In the next section it is convenient to comment on the role of the foreign evaluator.

6.7 THE SPECIAL CASE OF THE AID AGENCY

A very large number of projects are evaluated by aid donors. Sometimes this will be the only evaluation, as when consultants of the IBRD are responsible for the formulation of the project, and for submission of the report to the IBRD and the host government alike. In other cases a country will itself have initiated the project (with or without foreign consultants), and, having decided it wants it, hawk it around possible aid-donors in the expectation of getting one of them to accept it.

There are those who believe that donors should not ask any questions about how aid is spent. We believe this is unrealistic, and that donor governments must feel responsible to those who provide the money for seeing that it is well spent. What, however, can 'well spent' mean in this case? May there not be conflicting aims on the part of the donor country, or international agency, and the recipient? If so, what is the evaluator's task and how can he proceed?

The donor has two kinds of interest which could give rise to conflict at the project level. The first is in the economic development of the recipient, which raises the question of what 'economic development' means. The second kind includes all the more direct donor interests, such as favouring its exporters.

We do not believe that the second kind of interest gives rise to any problems for the evaluator He can base his valuations on the assumption that it is either the recipient's objectives, or the donor's interpretation of what constitutes economic development in the recipient country, that matters. This is because no aid agency that we know of, which relies to some extent on project evaluations using APs,[1] would expect the economic evaluation or SCB analysis to take the more direct interests of the donor into account To give an example from British aid, the appraisals produced by the economic staff of the ODA would take no account of the fact that the U.K. government may want to use aid to help exporters. This is not to say that such considerations do not enter into the final judgment. They do, but not at the level of the economic appraisal. A project which the host country wants, but the economic staff believes to be a poor project on the basis of its economic appraisal, may well be approved either for the political reason that it is desired to please the host government, or for reasons of favouring British business interests, or both.

Turning back to the first kind of interest—the development of the recipient country—there can of course be two views of what constitutes development. If the views diverge too widely—for instance if the donor believes the potential recipient is really more

---

[1] This description now includes the IBRD and IFC, the USAID, the British ODA, the Kreditanstalt für Wiederaufbau (which advises the West German Aid Ministry on projects), and the EDF—agencies which account for the bulk of aid.

interested in aggression or expelling people of other races than in development—then there may well be no aid. But aid combined with a more moderate divergence of view is not uncommon. Now in 4.1, we assumed that the objective which defines development is a weighted sum of the consumption of individuals from now to eternity. If this is the case, a divergence of view as to what constitutes development is a matter of the weighting. In less technical language, it will be a divergence of view as to how much stress is to be put on equality, or on savings and investment for the future (the U.S.A., for instance, under the Alliance for Progress, put more stress on reform leading to equality than many of the recipient governments—though we are not aware that this was in fact reflected in any conflict over projects). Such a divergence could imply, for instance, the use by the donor of a low AP for labour, which the recipient government might not agree with. We are not aware that such conflict has in fact arisen, but it could do so in the future.

In the last resort, the donor government is entitled to use its own weighting. It is sovereign so far as the use of its citizen's money is concerned. Equally the IBRD must, one imagines, take the view that money contributed to it, or raised by it, for development is given or subscribed with the understanding that it itself must judge what constitutes development. This is not to say that a recipient's own views would not be taken very fully into account. If a recipient sets up a COPE which establishes any well-thought-out system of APs, its hand will be strengthened: by making its objectives rather precise in this way, a recipient government would give donors less room for manoeuvre in the use of their own values, and disagreement would have to be rather extreme for a donor not to accept the system.

Lastly, there is the problem that a donor agency may not always be able to take the point of view of a particular developing country because it is right that it should also have the interests of other countries in mind. Thus, for instance, the world demand for tea is inelastic: but it may well be elastic for Kenyan tea which is a small proportion of the total. The expansion of tea production in Africa may be good for Africa, but hurt Asia. There is no solution to this dilemma short of some international agreement.

So much for ends. There can also be some disagreement about means. This is likely to be more common. Many industrial projects have been manifest failures in developing countries. Often this has not been owing to a failure of economic apprisal, but for technological, managerial, or marketing reasons. Often again it has been because of over-optimistic predictions of domestic demand. But many industries and plants have also been set up which would contribute little or nothing to the countries' own policy objectives even if they operated as expected. Some developing countries would now agree that their industrialization, and related trade policies, had been at fault; and that they were disappointed from the point of view both of the value of output and of employment. In these circumstances it seems unreasonable to take the view that if the government of a developing country wants a project, then that project must be a good one from its own point of view. Governments makes mistakes, and adopt mistaken policies.

However, it remains true that a project may be good from the point of view of a host country, only if it is assumed that certain irrational policies will inevitably continue. We have already seen an example in 6.6. It might be in a country's best interests to import fertilizers freely. But if the government insists on restricting fertilizer imports, then it should have a fertilizer factory. The donor is then in a dilemma. We have considerable sympathy with the view that donors should assume that rational policies will prevail. It is, for one thing, very hard to predict irrationalities (policies on particular tariffs and quotas are seldom immutable). For another thing, analysis along fully rational lines may have an educational effect in improving policies. The situation, however, remains different from when it is a COPE in the developing country which lays down the guidelines for the analysis. A COPE is in a stronger position to influence policy, and it is hardly likely to have been set up unless the government wanted to rationalize its project selection procedures. But if a COPE tries and fails to influence policy, then it has to accept this situation—unlike a donor government.

6.8 THE OPERATION OF PUBLIC SECTOR PROJECTS

Projects which have been selected in the light of accounting prices might show a loss if operated at actual prices. In this event, automatic subsidies equal to the public company's loss should be avoided, although this may be impossible, for a time, if a mistake has been made. The reason for this is that managers get careless if they think that losses are acceptable. Instead, the subsidies should be given in respect of the inputs or outputs whose actual prices fail to reflect social costs or benefits—and thus are the cause of the unprofitability of a well-chosen project.[1] For instance, labour-intensive projects may be initiated in the public sector as a result of using an accounting price for labour which is less than the actual price. In this event, the labour employed should be subsidized, and the project thereafter be expected to be profitable in terms of the ARI. To take another example, a public sector project may have to use an input from another such project, although it costs more than the import price. The use of that particular input should then be subsidized. In general, steps should be taken to make APs be reflected in the accounts of public sector enterprise. Despite the above, some readers may worry that the selection of public sector projects by our principles would imply that many unprofitable projects would be selected in the public sector, and that this would bring the public sector into further disrepute (since so many people are indoctrinated with the idea that profitability, at least for industrial projects, is the only measure of success).

It is true that losses, and hence subsidies, are very common in public sector industry in developing countries. We believe that these losses arise mainly from three causes. First, the government tends to require the project to sell its output for less than people would be willing to pay (especially where the output is a 'welfare' good), or to employ too much labour often at rather high wages. It is very doubtful whether these social reasons justify the subsidization of public industry; for there are usually better ways of pursuing the social ends. For instance, if more employment is needed, it is surely better to design and choose relatively labour-intensive projects than employ redundant men in capital-intensive ones. A second reason why public sector enterprises often make a loss stems from inflation. Governments are wont to try, in vain, to stem inflation by refusing to permit price increases in the public sector. The third, and perhaps the main, reason why losses occur is that the project was a mistake, and never should have been chosen. Many such projects would certainly have been weeded out on our principles. We therefore believe that the adoption of these principles would be very unlikely to make the problem of losses and subsidies to public sector industry worse. Certainly, projects might sometimes need to receive some form of subsidy, but this should be more than offset by a reduction in the number of bad projects started, and by a reduction in the employment of redundant labour in the public sector.

We turn now to another, albeit related, problem. If projects are

---

[1] This does not cover the case when losses arise because of economies of scale. Treatment of this case would take us too far into a much discussed field.

designed, as is hoped, in the light of accounting prices, but are operated in the light of market prices, then the managers will have an incentive to depart from the input or output mix which the project designers intended. This conflict may or may not be serious. The design may fix the use of inputs rather rigidly, in which case there is no problem. For instance, if labour-saving materials handling equipment is not provided, then the manager will have no choice but to shift materials by the use of labour. On the other hand, managers, and even more the boards of public companies, will normally have some discretion over relatively minor items of investment; and they may use this freedom to save labour, or make other changes which seem profitable in the light of actual prices. This is, of course, another argument for using taxes and subsidies on particular inputs (or sometimes to give tax rebates, e.g. of import duties) in order to bring the prices facing the producer into line with the accounting prices used in the project analysis. Sometimes, however, this counsel of perfection may be difficult to achieve. Then certain controls, or direct instructions may be in order. Agriculture provides a good example of a case where the design does not do much to fix the inputs and outputs. Agricultural projects are also a good lead-in to the next chapter, for projects are often planned in the public sector, but operated in the private sector by farmers who respond to the actual prices they receive.

Agricultural planners, when designing an irrigation or settlement scheme, will usually need to make assumptions about the crops to be grown. In order to optimize the crop mix, they must use accounting prices. But if these differ from actual prices, the lay-out of the land and buildings, and even the irrigation system, will do rather little to restrict the farmers' possibilities of substitution. They will then grow a non-optimal set of crops: and the lay-out chosen by these ill-advised planners will not be ideal for these crops which are actually grown. Farmers' incomes also will differ from those envisaged by the planners.

A plant intended to produce steel cannot be switched to aluminium: but it is easy to switch from rice to sugar, or from vegetables to flowers. Because of these easy possibilities of substitution, it is particularly desirable that accounting and market prices should coincide in agriculture. In most countries, many agricultural prices are subject to 'control' or 'doctoring' by the government. Outputs are often taxed or subsidised, and minimum guaranteed prices used. Attempts are also made to prevent high price peaks by sales from buffer stocks: or they are prevented from reaching the grower by sliding-scale taxation. Thus price interference is widely practised, usually for good reasons (though, in practice, the results are quite often unhappy). Inputs as well are often taxed or subsidised. Costly water is, for instance, often provided free.

In the circumstances described it is worse than useless for agricultural planners to do anything but predict inputs and outputs on the basis of the prices that the farmer is actually likely to receive, taking full account of the interference of the authorities, except where controls can and will take the place of prices. Thus irrigation water can be rationed if the price is too low (but this does not prevent excessive use in many areas by those lucky enough to get it): or, if some crop is too profitable (the price is higher than the accounting price), restrictions on planting may be used. But these are clumsy devices, and the possibilities of optimal planning are still severely restricted.

The moral is obvious. First, the agricultural planners, and the authorities that influence agricultural prices, must work in close coordination. The latter should be fully aware of the need for social prices in agriculture, both for inputs and outputs, prices which should among other things (including the need to help poor farmers) reflect the trading possibilities for the country. Secondly, the evaluator must evaluate what will probably happen, not what he would like to happen.

CHAPTER SEVEN

Private Sector Projects

7.1 THE NEED FOR PUBLIC EVALUATION OF PRIVATE PROJECTS

At the end of Chapter VI we saw that agricultural projects are often planned by public authorities, and then sold or leased for private operation. The same thing happens to a lesser extent in industry. The public authorities may build industrial estates, and occasionally factories have been initiated in the public sector and later sold to the private sector, as in Japan and Pakistan. But nationalization has been more common in recent decades than denationalization.

This chapter, however, is concerned with projects which are planned in, and initially owned by, the private sector. Although a government cannot directly select projects in the private sector, it has much influence in most developing countries over large projects and those involving foreign finance. There is often import or investment licensing, so that the government has to approve the investment. Still more important, private entrepreneurs will not pursue projects unless they promise to be profitable. For this reason, the government is frequently asked for favours. Such favours include quotas and tariffs on competitive imports, relief from quotas and tariffs on imported inputs, export subsidies, finance (often on very favourable terms) from government owned or controlled development banks, and direct tax relief.

Finally, the government quite often promotes particular industries in the private sector. It decides that it would be good to have, for example, a motor-car assembly industry. It then canvasses the fact, promising favours to potential entrepreneurs whether domestic or foreign. This virtually amounts to selection of projects in the private sector, although the planning and design normally remain the prerogative of the private owners. Such ways of creating plants or industries, usually proceeding with little or no analysis of social profitability, can lead and have led to a pattern of industrial development of little or no advantage to the country—though, doubtless, of advantage to the promoters.

It is useful to divide private sector projects into two categories:

(i) those which are expected to be profitable without particular adjustments of the price mechanism, or fiscal favours;

(ii) those where favours are offered or demanded in order to make the project sufficiently attractive to the private entrepreneur.

Category (i) may come up for approval if there is import or industrial licensing, or if money is required from public sources (but not on concessionary terms, which would constitute a 'favour'). Category (ii), of course, must always receive government approval. Countries vary from those where almost no industrial projects would be considered by the government, e.g. Hong Kong, to those where all above a certain size are considered, even if in the most cursory manner, e.g. India.

Category (i) are profitable anyway. But where the price mechanism is significantly distorted, it will often happen that they would not be sufficiently socially profitable. It is clearly to the national advantage that such projects should be turned down. This could be done either by the licensing authorities, or those which approve the financing. These authorities are usually quite distinct. Which should take the lead depends on the circumstances and administrative set-up of the country in question. Usually, we would think, the financial authority is the more appropriate: for it is more likely to start with some knowledge of project appraisal. Financial approval is often delegated to a development bank, except perhaps where much foreign finance is involved. In Mexico, for example, some analysis of private investment projects is carried out by Nacional Financiera, using SCB methods. As against the above argument many of the smaller projects may not require either government or foreign finance. That they should slip through the net may be unavoidable and relatively unimportant.

While category (i) projects are privately profitable, but may be socially unprofitable, it is also true that with a distorted price mechanism there will be many potential projects which would have been socially profitable but never see the light of day because they promise to be privately unprofitable. Although some of these may find their way into category (ii), it is quite likely that most projects in this category will be both privately and socially unprofitable. Furthermore, although rejection of projects may sometimes lead to redesign, there might well be variants of rejected projects which would be socially profitable but will not be submitted because they would not be privately profitable. For these reasons, and where the planning of projects is in the light of a different set of prices to those used by the appraisers, e.g. the development banks, a system which operates only by rejection is unsatisfactory, although better than nothing.

It is clear that SCB analysis of category (ii) projects should be carried out, whether it is government or private industry, domestic or foreign, which makes the initiative. The last thing a government should want to do is to doctor the price mechanism so as to create private profits and social disadvantage, although there is no doubt that this has occurred. On the other hand, if a project passes some test of social profitability, then it is right to doctor the price mechanism in order to make the project privately profitable, and so permit it to proceed. It should be noted here that if some change in the price mechanism (e.g. the institution of a tariff) or in controls is part and parcel of the project, then the package, consisting of the project plus the policy change, is what has to be evaluated: this complicates the project analysis because the indirect effects of the price changes accompanying the policy change should be allowed for (see 12.5 and 12.6).

Doctoring of the price mechanism will generally reduce the distortions which made a socially desirable project unprofitable. But one can go further, and say that the best way of making it profitable is to make actual and accounting prices, including the price of labour, coincide as far as possible. To give an example, a socially beneficial industry may not have got started because the country's protective system of tariffs and quotas raised the prices of its inputs above world levels, while it did not protect the industry's output from foreign competition.[1] It is then much better to start it by subsidising the over-priced inputs, rather than by creating protection for the output which, while perhaps securing the home market, not only hurts other industries which use the output, but also does nothing for exports, and hence is likely to lead to an operation which is on too small a scale.

Thus, once again, as with the agricultural example given earlier, the best way of proceeding is to try to make market prices equal to accounting prices. While true of the public sector (as was noted in 6.8), this is even more true for the private sector. It is a refrain which keeps on recurring. The fiscal means which may be used for the purpose have been discussed in 5.5.

Finally, it should be noted that 'post-mortem' evaluations of private sector investments can be enlightening. The government should find it very useful to know what lines of investment seem to

---

[1] An example of this was Case Study No. 2 in the OECD Manual—of a Mexican Machine Tool project. Little and Mirrlees, 1969.

have been socially most valuable, since it can by no means be taken for granted that private and social profitability coincide. There is always the difficulty of obtaining information from private companies. But the government should be able to exert pressure if it sponsored a programme of such analyses at a research institute.

7.2 THE METHOD OF EVALUATION OF PRIVATE PROJECTS

Meanwhile it is necessary to examine briefly the methods of doing SCB analysis for private sector projects, which we initially assume to be wholly domestically financed. Basically, the method differs in only two respects from that which we advocate for public sector projects.

The first difference concerns the opportunity cost of capital. If a public sector project is not carried out, it is reasonable to assume, as we have, that some other (marginal) public investment would instead be made. But if a private sector project is not carried out, it is much less obvious what the alternative use of the funds will be. There is a range of possibilities. The government may borrow more, increasing its own investment. The private capitalists might start some other project, which could be either inside or outside the area requiring government approval. The money might find its way abroad, whether legally or illegally, and there be used either for investment or consumption. Finally, the alternative might be an increase in domestic consumption.

In developed countries it is a traditional Keynesian assumption that savings and investment are done by different people, so that investment decisions do not affect savings decisions. This is not entirely true for a developed economy, and is certainly far from accurate for LDCs. Here, however, it needs to be borne in mind that only large private sector projects, normally carried out by a firm, are ever likely to be the subject of public evaluation. The Keynesian adage might be thought to remain reasonably true in this area. This may be the case, but equally it can be doubted, and we know of no evidence. It is worth noting that an increase in consumption resulting from non-investment does not have to be direct. If some investment is frustrated, then a rich family may buy land instead of putting more money into their business: and those who sell the land may increase their consumption.

All these possibilities affect the social valuation of the potential capital expenditure. If, at one extreme, the alternative is a government project, then private investment funds are worth no less than money in the hands of the government.[1] At the other extreme, the funds might have no social value, or almost none. This would be the case if the alternative use was for a rich family to send the money abroad, remit nothing, and use it to create a splash in Miami or Monte Carlo. This all raises difficult problems for the evaluator, and some further advice on how to make the best assumptions is given in 11.2.

The second difference concerns the treatment of profits. With a public sector project, the extra private consumption which will result from initiating the project comes about entirely as a result of paying wages and salaries. But profits arising in the private sector induce extra consumption; moreover it is extra consumption on the part of the relatively wealthy, which is clearly less of a social benefit than extra consumption by poor wage earners. Admittedly quite a lot of private profit may be paid in taxes, or be saved: nevertheless private profit will not be worth as much as profit accruing to the government.

It should be noted that private profit also accrues to relatively indigent peasants and traders, as well as to wealthy capitalists. Clearly, therefore, all profits cannot be treated on a par: some profits are closer to wages than they are to those of a large corporation or rich family business. The valuation of private profits is examined in some detail in 11.5.

Some people may well object to the statement that private profits, especially perhaps those accruing to peasants and small businessmen, are worth less, from a social point of view, than profits going to the government. In some countries there is no doubt that a convincing case can be made against our contention. The objector can point to corruption and waste, to disastrous public projects, to the President's palace, and so on; and he can contrast this with high savings and productive investment on the part of progressive budding entrepreneurs in small-scale industry, or indeed with the private consumption of poor people.

We do not claim that money in the hands of the government is always in reality worth more than in the hands of private capitalists, let alone salary earners or the higher paid industrial workers. This must depend on the goodness of the government, and the uses to which individuals would have put the money. We make two claims (a) that it would be worth more if the government were rational and benevolent; and, what is possibly more to the point, (b) that the

---

[1] The fact that the lender gets some interest, which is a cost to society, is allowed for in estimating the benefit of the project. See 11.11.

government-employed project evaluator may find it difficult to assume otherwise even where he doubts its truth. A foreign aid evaluator can take a different view though some conflict with the host government could result (see 6.7).

7.3 PRIVATE FOREIGN INVESTMENT

7.31 *General Considerations*
If all the capital comes from abroad, and all the net of tax profits are remitted abroad, then a foreign investment is much easier to evaluate than a similar one which is domestically financed. This is because there is usually little doubt in this case about the social cost of the investment and of profits. If a foreign project is turned down, the foreign company will not normally invest in anything else, so that the opportunity cost of the funds is nil: whereas, of course, profits remitted abroad are, dollar for dollar, a cost to the host country. Usually, however, profits are not wholly remitted, and some doubt then arises as to their treatment. It may be argued that they belong to the foreigner, and that any further profits resulting from ploughing back these profits, also belong to him: however, despite this, such further investment yields benefits or costs for the host country, as did the original investment; moreover this further investment would not have taken place without the original investment. Unfortunately, the project report will not normally tell the evaluator either how much will be ploughed back, or into what. Nevertheless, some attention should be paid to this point, and suggestions as to how to pay it are given in 11.3.[1]

Private foreign investment is widely encouraged by governments of developing countries, although it often causes passionate fear and resentment. This passion has its roots in colonialism and theories of historical determination. It is aroused and sustained by easily found examples of the behaviour of foreign corporations which appear to have economic consequences at variance with the interests of the host country. It is seldom asked whether such behaviour has anything to do with the foreignness of the corporation; whether the

---

[1] A much fuller guide-line for such appraisal than we feel is necessary to give here is contained in Part IV of Bos, Sanders and Secchi, 1973. It is based essentially on the methods proposed in the OECD Manual and in this book: but it differs importantly so far as shadow wage rates are concerned. It also suggests (6.2) that unremitted profits should be counted wholly as a cost. This we believe to be strictly incorrect, though in practice it may not matter very much if they are so treated. Another study of private foreign investment, with numerous case studies, again essentially using OECD Manual methods, is Lal, 1974.

behaviour is not caused by the host government's own policies; or whether the economic consequences were not inevitable. Claims of damage caused by foreign businessmen go beyond what can apparently be supported by economic facts, and refer to malign influence over the host country's own government or its institutions, and on the people's culture and spending habits. It would be out of place to examine such claims in this book, except insofar as they can be linked to the expected net social cost or benefit to the host country of a particular foreign investment.

A few governments may fear that armed intervention by the foreign investor's own government is not a thing of the past. Almost all feel they have less control over foreign than domestic firms, and so want them to come in only if there is local participation, even voting control. Some make demands concerning the employment of local managers, or insist on other special requirements. It is not our purpose to say whether these rules are sensible. They are taken as part of the legal or quasi-legal framework. If, having made laws which govern it, an LDC still wants to limit the amount of foreign investment, but yet maximize the PSV resulting from it, it can (as it gains experience) seek to maximize the ratio $\frac{PSV}{Capital\ Inflow}$ (a rule of thumb which applies whenever a budgetary constraint is in force.)

We have already indicated in the first paragraph of this section that the PSV of a foreign private investment is estimated in much the same way as any private investment. Given the emotion surrounding the subject, this will be felt by some to be wrong. Let us therefore look at the contentions which have been made to suggest that there should be something special about the evaluation of a foreign project.

7.32 *Foreign Investment and the Balance of Payments*
There is a feeling that foreign investments put a special strain on the balance of payments. The point is often made that more money eventually goes out by way of interest and dividends than ever came in. This is certainly to be expected, and no foreign investment would ever take place if it was not expected by the investors. But the effect on the balance of payments cannot be measured in this way, for all investments affect imports and exports, both directly and indirectly, as well as financial flows. In fact the method of appraisal advocated in this book ensures that no *acceptable* foreign investment would put any undesirable strain on the balance of payments. In fact if the extra domestic consumption induced by the project (and this

extra consumption is at least in part desirable—see 9.5) is left out of account, the estimated social profit in any year is equal to the estimated *improvement* in the balance of payments caused by the project, after all direct and indirect effects on financial flows and the balance of trade have been accounted for.[1] Only bad projects put a strain on the balance of payments.

7.33 *Alternatives to and Participation in Foreign-Owned Investments*
It has been argued that it is especially important to look at 'alternatives' in the case of foreign investment. At first sight, this seems strange, for it is always important to look at alternatives, by which in general one means projects which are incompatible with the project under examination. A final project report should always have already rejected variations which have a lower PSV. If one is thus examining a finalized project, after such rejection, then the 'alternative' is simply not to do it. In the case of a public sector domestic project, some other marginal public investment gets carried out; in the case of a foreign investment nothing gets done.

But there is a list of conceivable alternatives which arise in the case of a contemplated foreign investment, but not in the case of a domestic investment. These may range from some element of local participation, to the country doing the same thing, or nearly the same thing, itself—although this is usually impossible without the participation of the foreign firm, which provides a package of investment, know-how, and management that cannot be easily unscrambled. (A different agreement with the foreign firm on finance and tax liabilities, etc., might also be considered to be an 'alternative': this is considered under the subject of bargaining below.) It is clear that all such alternatives should, if possible, be examined, and that with the highest PSV form the subject of the final examination. This is in principle no different from any project whether foreign or domestic.

Is there any simple rule which determines whether (questions of control apart) it pays the host country to get in on the act? Suppose the alternatives are (*a*) accepting a wholly foreign investment, and (*b*) the host doing it itself. We assume (unrealistically, but for the sake of argument) that the host could produce exactly the same outputs with the same inputs by hiring directly the same amount of foreign management—so that the SCB analysis will look

---

[1] See Chapter XVII; and also, for a discussion of the macroeconomic assumptions required for a coincidence of income and balance of payments effects, Little, 1972.

identical apart from capital, interest, dividends, and taxes. Now under alternative (*a*), if the investment is worth contemplating by both parties at all, there will be a certain division of the total social profits between the investor and the host country—some positive amount going to both parties. If the country instead finances the project itself, what it will get out of its investment is not the total social profit but that part which accrues, under alternative (*a*), to the foreigner. The host country will have a target ARI for its investments. So the crucial question is whether the profitability for the foreigner (after payment of taxes) is greater or less than the ARI. If it is greater then the country should get in on the act to the greatest extent it can, provided that its participation does not tend to reduce the level of the profits (see 7.36 and 7.37). This is common sense. The greater its investment opportunities and the scarcer are a country's own funds, the less sense it makes to try to participate— and vice versa. An alternative to participation is to try to reduce the return to the foreigner by striking a harder bargain. This may be the better solution in some cases.

Although nationalization, or forced private foreign disinvestment, is strictly speaking a public 'project', the economics are closely akin to the subjects of participation or going it alone, which have been discussed in this section. The reasons are often, of course, highly political—and careful economic analysis may be rather unlikely to play a large role in the decision (economics may enter more into the determination of compensation). So far as we can see, however, no new problems would present themselves in trying to work out the PSV with and without the planned take-over.

7.34 *Bargaining over the Terms of Foreign Investment*
A long process of bargaining often precedes a foreign private investment. The investor tries to maximize tax and other concessions, and the host country gives way as little as possible, and may make special demands concerning exports, employment, and profit repatriation. All too often the host government appears to have little awareness of the real social cost of the concessions it offers, or the real social benefit of the basic investment. No doubt developing countries could often in the past have made better bargains than they did. It is certainly not enough to know that a project is beneficial, if it might have been more beneficial still. Yet it is a loss if a project is rejected in the hope of a better alternative which does not materialize.

In principle all these alternatives, which arise and vanish during the bargaining process, should be appraised. If some basic proposal, e.g. the foreign companies' original proposal, has been properly evaluated, it can be quickly seen what differences various concessions make to the host country's PSV, and therefore whether they are worth making or insisting on as the case may be. In general a country can bargain better if it knows how much it wants, or should want from the project. Bargaining, however, in no way affects the methods of appraisal proposed in this book.

7.35 *The Externalities of Private Foreign Investment*
Externalities are often thought to be particularly important with foreign investments. On the negative side there is the malign political and social influence in which some people believe. We do not think that a host government would want the evaluator to attempt to assess such matters. Quite likely they are too vague or uncertain to attach to a particular project: but if the decision-maker thinks collaboration with some particular foreign company, or country, is particularly undesirable he would no doubt prefer to make his own allowance for this.

On the positive side, it is often claimed that foreign investments have beneficial effects in spreading knowledge and in training. Wherever possible such effects should be quantified, but this is difficult. Externalities are discussed in general in Chapter XVI. On the negative side it is sometimes claimed that foreign investments are particularly liable to knock out domestic production. It is always as well to look out for this possibility, although it is not obvious that a modern foreign investment is more dangerous in this respect than a modern domestic investment. In a certain limited number of lines of production, modern methods in general may hurt cottage or handicraft industry. It is also claimed that foreign enterprise inhibits the development of modern indigenous business and entrepreneurship; or, as seems to be required by the infant industry argument, that it encourages it.

7.36 *The Waywardness of the 'Multi-National' Corporation*
It is feared that the few giant corporations which produce in many countries and sell in world markets will, in arranging their operations with global profits in mind, make production decisions which are not in the interests of some particular host country. Certainly this may be so. If, for example, production in one oil-producing country becomes relatively unprofitable (usually as a result of action by the host government itself), an integrated oil company will try to

produce more elsewhere, whenever it has any spare capacity. This may or may not be prevented by an organization such as OPEC.

It is also sometimes suggested that a multinational corporation is more likely than others to cease operations altogether in a particular country. This seems more doubtful and we know of no evidence to support it. Its original investment is largely sunk costs, and there seems little reason why it should be more prone to write it off altogether than any other kind of investor. For any kind of foreign investor, the fact that costs are incurred which cannot be recovered if the host country changes the rules of the game gives the latter the whip hand.

The question arises as to what difference, if any, such considerations make to project analysis. In considering alternatives, the element of international flexibility which belongs to a few multinational corporations may make it less attractive for a host country to consider participation. The multinational corporation cares less about local profits than global profits. If it is in its interest to reduce output and profits in country X, which is a participant, then country X's return on its investment suffers. If country X merely receives taxes or royalties, then it receives less—but the PSV of the project will suffer much less than if it had put in some of its own capital originally.[1] The control of local operations, which a 51% participation would give it, might be of little value, for the local company is liable to find difficulty in selling except to its parent in whose policy it still has no say.

As against the above, however, the reason why operations in a particular country become relatively unattractive to a multinational corporation usually stems from a change of policy on the part of the host government. If the host government participates, it will be less likely to make the environment unattractive for the multinational corporation. Alternatively if it becomes less attractive for reasons outside the control of the host government, the latter can offset this by lower taxes or royalty charges.

---

[1] Suppose that actual and accounting prices coincide, and that a wholly owned foreign investment of 100 produces a profit of 20 per annum for ever, of which the host government gets one quarter, i.e. 5 per annum. With an ARI of 10% this is a PSV for the host of 50. If profits are halved, the PSV becomes 25. Now if there was a 50/50 participation, the PSV of the host government would be 75 (it receives 5 in tax and $7\frac{1}{2}$ in profits: this stream has a PV of 125 from which its investment of 50 must be subtracted). Participation is beneficial because the net of tax return of 15% exceeds the ARI of 10%. But now suppose profits are halved. It is easily seen that the PSV reduces to $12\frac{1}{2}$, half what it would have been without participation. Participation greatly increases the sensitivity of PSV to changes in profits. There is no getting away from the fact that equity participation involves risk.

Once participation, or perhaps another alternative, has been decided, it probably makes little difference to the project analysis that it may be slightly more likely that the predicted scale of operations will be deliberately varied in the case of a corporation with far flung production possibilities, than in the case of a smaller company. The risk may for this reason be a little higher, but even this may have been limited in the agreement, by minimum royalty payments or other forms of insurance. It is also to be noted that the multi-national corporation may greatly reduce risks for the host country in other ways, e.g. by providing a secure market.

7·37 *Profit-Shifting*

Corporation and profit taxes, dividend taxes, and royalties on natural resource utilization are among the ways in which the host country obtains its benefit.

It is relatively easy for a foreign investor to shift profits from a subsidiary to the parent company, by charging the subsidiary high prices for goods or services provided, or (in the case of projects which make goods for export to the parent), by paying low prices to the subsidiary for its exports. This is very hard to check when such goods or services have no established market price. Provided that the foreign investor is confident that post-tax profits, and capital, can be transferred abroad when desired, it would seem that the shifting of profits by unjustifiable and unrealistic transfer pricing, is not very often in the interest of the foreign investor, because the tax payable in the country in which the parent is registered is seldom less than in the developing country, and because tax paid by the branch or subsidiary producing in the host country could (in 1964) be wholly offset against the parent's tax liability in the case of the U.S.A., U.K., and Canada; while profits earned abroad were not liable in the case of France, the Netherlands, and Switzerland.[1] Thus, in the case of most foreign investors, profit-shifting for tax reasons is likely to occur only if the investor is making losses elsewhere, or if he is able to move the profits to a tax-haven thus evading tax in the country of the parent also (and still be able to use them). There may also sometimes be a political reason for profit-shifting—if, for example, high profits in the host country would attract hostility.

The incentive to shift profits is stronger if there is local equity participation, for then the profits accrue wholly to the foreigner if they are shifted, and only partly if not. As against this, the transfer

---

[1] See OECD 1965, and 1972.

prices cannot easily be hidden from the local partners: but this is a sure safeguard only if there is a reasonably objective test of the fairness of such prices, and if the local partners are incorruptible. This may clearly make participation by the host country undesirable if sales to or from the parent are important, and if there is no good open market in the commodities or services transferred.

There is little hard evidence concerning profit-shifting.[1] It is in any case often conceptually difficult to determine. For instance, if a firm finds it cheaper to make a component abroad there is, within fairly wide limits, no objective way of splitting the gain between the parent and subsidiary, which is why we have used vague words like fair and reasonable. It should also be noted that developing country governments often do not base taxation of an overseas subsidiary on its actual accounting profits. The oil countries provide the most obvious example. But there are other cases in which a specified minimum profit level, expressed as a percentage of capital invested for the purposes of taxation, is agreed.[2] The growth of such practices should reduce the importance of the subject.

7.4 SUMMARY

It has been seen that the social evaluation of private investments is more difficult than in the case of public investments, because the social value of the funds invested and the private profits which result are both harder to estimate. Nevertheless the social evaluation of large private sector projects, which seek public funds or favours, is both feasible and important.

Private foreign investment is a particular case. The host government may want to consider the possibility of participation, whether on its own part or on the part of private local investors. It may want to consider carrying out a similar and incompatible investment without any partnership with a foreign company. The PSV of any such alternatives can always be compared with the 'straight' foreign investment: this does not make it different from any other project, except insofar as the kind of alternative considered is different. Bargaining over terms and concessions produces in effect a number of alternatives, quite apart from any question of partici-

---

[1] In Vernon, 1971, the evidence is summarized as follows: 'Multinational enterprises, therefore, transfer goods and services among affiliates at prices that are often at variance with the results that independent buyers and sellers would reach. But cases so far uncovered do not create the basis for assuming that there is a systematic bias in favor of assigning the largest profit to the parent' (p. 139).

[2] See Reuber, 1973.

pation. Their PSVs all, ideally, need to be estimated. The host country's bargaining can be much more purposeful if it is aware of the social value of the proposal, and possible alternatives.

The possible existence of viable alternatives in no way affects the appraisal of the foreign project itself. Each such possibility or alternative, including the proposal itself, is examined against the hypothetical alternative of doing nothing. Once the best of these incompatible investments is singled out, then the hypothetical alternative of doing nothing becomes the real alternative. All this is common form and has nothing special to do with foreign investments: it is emphasized in this context only because debate about alternatives has centred on foreign investment for the reason that those who are suspicious of foreign private investment want to put special emphasis on alternatives which reduce foreign investment. Where developing countries are not especially suspicious of foreign private investment, it is equally reasonable to insist that alternatives involving foreign participation should always be examined when any purely domestic investment proposal is made.

Provided (and in some cases it may be a serious proviso) that profitability is not affected by participation, there is a simple rule to show whether participation is economically beneficial. If the foreigners' rate of return *at accounting prices* exceeds the country's ARI it should try to participate. Going it alone can be considered as an extreme case of participation.

Apart from alternatives, various of the special considerations relevant to private foreign investment have been briefly alluded to—briefly because we do not think that a host government would want any attempt to be made to quantify the primarily political aspects in what purports to be an economic appraisal. Of course, if it is thought that some special risk, whether of an economic or political character, attaches to a particular proposal, then this can be referred to.

It seems to us that the emotions aroused by private foreign investment make it of central importance to ascertain whether a foreign investment is socially profitable for the host. Countries have not concentrated on this issue. As a result we believe that there have been many foreign investments which are a net social cost to the host country: this has nothing special to do with the behaviour of the investor, which may be impeccable; it has most to do with distortions in the price mechanism of the host country, and with sometimes excessive financial inducements offered to him.

At the risk of anticipating ourselves we may say that, in the case of the simplest foreign investment (no local participation and all profits remitted), ignoring unquantifiable externalities, the social profit of the host country in any year consists of (*a*) the direct tax paid, plus (*b*) the accounting value of the output minus the actual receipts, plus (*c*) the actual value of its expenditure minus the accounting value. Thus if a foreign project sells its output for an amount greater than the cost of imports would have been (which will be the case with any protected project), that is a social loss for the host country. On the other hand, to the extent that it employs labour at a wage greater than its social cost (which is almost invariably the case), that is a social benefit. It is clear that the foreign investments most likely to be beneficial are those which are unprotected—e.g. export projects—and those which are labour-intensive, and pay as much direct tax as possible. Heavily protected, capital-intensive projects which receive large tax concessions are all too likely to cause social loss for the host country.

CHAPTER EIGHT

Presentation of the Analysis

8.1 SCB Analysis as Part of a Feasibility Report

The SCB analysis will normally form part of a feasibility report or project report, which should of course detail and justify the assumptions made about inputs and outputs, and the appropriate market prices. It will, in the case of a public sector project, generally also give some indication of what alternatives have been considered and rejected. Attention should be drawn to any special risks, and to any required developments or changes elsewhere in the economy on which success or failure may depend. It should discuss such matters as management and marketing, where relevant. It should also indicate the financial requirements over time—that is, the ordinary cash flows—and the sources of the finance required to meet the outflows.

8.2 The Simplest Form of an SCB Analysis

The simplest possible full SCB analysis will put a social price on everything; add up for each year, thus reaching a net social profit or loss for that year; and discount these totals by the ARI to give the PSV. It will say how each social price has been arrived at, probably in an appendix: these notes may range from 'given by COPE', or 'c.i.f. value assumed', to a fairly lengthy explanation where there seems to be doubt, and therefore some justification is required. The difference between PV (at market prices) and PSV (at social prices) should be analysed. Possible externalities, which have not been covered by counting them as inputs and outputs and putting a value on them, should always be mentioned; but in the simplest case the comment will be 'nothing known which is particular to this project and has not been allowed for'.

8.3 Complications

We turn now to the complications. These can be grouped under (i) distribution of income (including location), (ii) other unquantified variables, (iii) doubtful assumptions about government policy, and (iv) uncertainty.

(i) We have seen that if the system of accounting wages is appropriate and is used, and if there is no problem of location, then the distribution effects of the project have been largely looked after. This is likely to be the case with many industrial projects.

But these 'ifs' are not always substantiated, as was seen in 6.5 and 6.6. In that case (unless the government lays it down that distribution should always be ignored in project analysis—which is unlikely) it may be necessary to allocate the benefits and costs to different income groups or social classes, and strike a balance for each group for each year.[1] The PSV can then also be divided between the groups. This can be a little complicated, and the methods are discussed in Chapter XIII. [2]

The question then arises as to what to do next. It is unenlightening for the decision-maker if he merely sees that, say, x rupees goes to the government, y to relatively well-off peasants and z to relatively poor peasants. What can he infer merely from that? We deal with this problem after discussing considerations (ii) and (iii). But, before that, it is worth mentioning that attention should always be drawn to any groups which may actually be damaged by the project. Sometimes, the 'project' may be to close down an existing project; or it may involve closing an existing project without any possibility of transferring the workers; or the output of the project may eliminate other producers, as when a textile mill puts hand weavers out of work. The government, if it accepts the project, may want to look into possible ways of compensating some or all of those who lose by it.

(ii) Apart from income distribution there may be other un-quantified items. These may include some externalities for which the evaluator can think of no method of quantification. The method of dealing with any such unquantified item,

---

[1] We discussed in 4.2 the conditions under which it may seem necessary to deal explicitly with income distribution. It will always be a matter of political judgment whether these conditions are fulfilled—a political judgment, however, which has to be taken at sub-political or para-political levels.

[2] Examples are also contained in Stern, 1972, and in Scott, MacArthur and Newbery, 1974.

whether or not it is an ethical variable, is the same.

(iii) This has already been discussed, and it remains to be seen only how the presentation of the report is affected, which is considered below.

(iv) Uncertainty is a difficult subject discussed in Chapter XV. It is mentioned here only because of the relevance of sensitivity analysis, which is the general method of dealing with unquantified variables whether ethical or not, and to which we now turn.

8.4 The Definition of Sensitivity Analysis, and Switching Values

Sensitivity analysis shows how the value of the criterion (normally PSV, but possibly the IRR) changes with changes in the value of any variable in the DCF analysis. It may be expressed either as the absolute change in PSV (or the IRR) divided by a given percentage or a given absolute change in the variable, whichever seems more appropriate. Usually a percentage change will be chosen. Thus the sensitivity will most often be expressed as $X \frac{dPSV}{dX}$ where X is the chosen value of the variable. The variable might be the price of the output; and the sensitivity analysis would then record that a 10% change in the assumed price would make a difference of, say, 1 million rupees to the PSV; or, if the IRR is being used as a criterion, it would record that a 10% change in the assumed price would make a difference of, say, 1 percentage point to the IRR. One can record the sensitivity to any single figure (e.g. the price of the output in year 1), or any part of a row of figures (e.g. the price from year 5 to year 25), or a whole row of figures. It may finally be useful to give the sensitivity of PSV to delays in bringing the project to fruition.

The most useful way for the reader of giving the results of the sensitivity analysis is often to record what absolute or percentage change is required in any figure, or sets of figures, to make the PSV zero. Thus we may say 'It would take a halving of the price to make the PSV zero', or 'A change of only 10 rupees in the price assumed would make the PSV zero'.

The absolute assumed value of a variable which makes the PSV zero is known as a 'switching value'. As the assumed value of the variable passes through this absolute value, the decision (if it depends solely on the chosen criterion) is switched from 'Yes' to

'No', or vice versa. It may be noted that it follows from this definition that the IRR is the switching value of the ARI.[1]

8.5 THE USES OF SENSITIVITY ANALYSIS

8.51 *In showing how marginal a project is*
Sensitivity analysis is useful for an ordinary profitability analysis, as well as for SCB analysis. If one gives the decision-maker merely the fact that the PSV of a project is 1 million rupees, he has no idea whether this represents a relatively large positive balance between small costs and benefits, or a relatively tiny balance between very large costs and benefits. This is one reason why it is desirable to give also the IRR of the project, because, by comparison with the ARI, this shows how near it is to the margin. Sensitivity analysis is another way of showing this. If a very small percentage change in the quantity or price of an input or output wipes out the positive PSV then the project is clearly marginal.

In theory it does not matter that a project is marginal if there is no uncertainty. But even if the project's costs and benefits were known with certainty (which is impossible), there would still probably be some doubt about the ARI, and this alone makes it useful to indicate the marginality of a project even when it is particularly risk-free.

8.52 *In indicating risk, and the need for further work*
Sensitivity analysis can also be used to illustrate the riskiness of a project. Thus if the value put on some variable is known to be very much of a guess, and the true value could fall within a wide range, then it is worth looking at the sensitivity of PSV to values of the variable within this range. If the PSV is sensitive the project is clearly risky. This does not necessarily mean that the estimated PSV should be reduced to allow for the uncertainty (see Chapter XV). Only if it is the sort of project where some allowance for uncertainty ought to be made, need the evaluator attempt to give any illustration or quantification of the risks in his report. A project may also have such a high IRR, given best guesses as to the values of the variables, that it is clear that no reasonable allowance for uncertainty would bring it below the margin.

Sensitivity analysis may be useful in suggesting how much care

---

[1] We have taken this brief discussion of switching values from the UNIDO *Guidelines* (Sections 12-6 and 13-5), which advocates much more extensive use of them than we do.

should be devoted to making estimates. If the PSV is insensitive to the value of some particular input or output, there is little point in being perfectionist about trying to estimate that value. However, what is important is fairly obvious without formal analysis. The larger the value, and the nearer in time it is, the more sensitive will the result be to any percentage variation in the estimate.

8.53 *In dealing with unquantified values*
We turn now to the social value variables which are used in estimating the accounting prices. If these are firmly laid down, such as we advocate should be the case with the ARI and the shadow wage rates, there is no need for sensitivity analysis in this area. But we have seen that it is quite unlikely to be laid down what differing weights, if any, should be attached to the benefits going to different groups of persons or different regions.

Suppose first that there are only two such groups, and that two variants of a project (which can include the same project in two locations) are under consideration. The two variants differ in the amount of benefit going to each group. If we weight the present value of the richer group A by 1, then we can vary the weight attached to group B from 1 to any higher number, and see how this affects the PSVs of the two variants. We may suppose that with equal weighting variant X has the higher PSV. The difference in the PSVs can be said to be the cost of favouring group B by choosing variant Y, and it is always a useful number to give. Now suppose the difference between the two reduces as the weight attached to group B increases, until it is eliminated at a value of, let us say, 2 which is then the switching value. In principle if the decision-maker attaches more than twice the weight to group B that he attaches to group A, he will opt for Y. He may also like to know the sensitivity of the difference between the weighted PSVs to changes in the weights. Thus he may be quite unsure as to what weight he would attach to group B. If it makes rather little difference (as would be the case if the ratio of group B to group A beneficiaries was not very different for the two variants), then he may not want to bother to make up his mind on this score, and would prefer to think harder about some other aspect of the two variants.

If there are more than two groups, and in matters of income distribution this is likely to be the case, then the matter becomes more complicated. The economist might then want to use a utility function, which relates the weight (equal to 'marginal utility') to the level of income. He can show the sensitivities, and the switching value, as a function of the parameter of the utility function which expresses the weight put on equality (this parameter is the elasticity of marginal utility with respect to income). But it is highly unlikely that any decision-maker would find this helpful. The report writer should probably resort to a table giving some illustrative combinations of weights which would together be switching values (each one is also a switching value given the levels of the others).

The device of a switching value is essentially an attempt to get the decision-maker to put a value on something (or at least to say the value is greater, or less, than a given value) in the context of a project, which he is not willing to value in a void. That he should be more willing in the context of a project is very reasonable, for he knows what follows from his decision: whereas no one can easily say what the consequences would be of making some general rule to follow in matters of income distribution. However, consistent valuations are unlikely to be achieved in this manner. This is for several reasons. First, the same person may make inconsistent decisions on different occasions (he would probably need some rule to keep him consistent). Second, many different decision-makers are likely to be involved. There is also a third reason, which may rather generally reduce the usefulness of sensitivity analysis and switching values, to which we now turn.

There will all too often be more than one aspect of a project which has not been firmly quantified. In this case the project analyst will be tempted to submit a range of values not just for one but for several variables (which may be either social value variables, or other more 'objective' but uncertain ones). Suppose there are just two such aspects, say income distribution and environmental amenity. Then one can give the switching value for one variable only if one knows it for the other. For instance, in the above example 2 would remain the switching value for the distributional weight only if the (unknown) difference in environmental harm were implicitly valued by the decision-maker at zero. If variant Y were judged by him to be superior on environmental grounds by 1 million rupees one might be able to tell him that his distributional switching value was 1·75, or if by 2 million rupees then 1·5, etc. He might or might not find this enlightening. We think one can certainly say that trying to treat two variables in this way is the limit. It should also be noted that if there is more than one thing in doubt then a single project decision tells one nothing about the decision-maker's valuation of any particular aspect.

If only for these reasons, we think that as much as possible should be quantified by rule. A programme of 'discovering' decision-makers' valuations by analysing actual investment decisions is probably a wild goose chase. It is claimed as a great advantage for our advocated system that distributional considerations are, as already argued, largely taken care of by using a system of shadow wages.

8·54 *The IRR as a function of the Shadow Wage*

Nevertheless we have to consider the situation when no shadow wage rates have been laid down. In this case, one cannot very sensibly investigate the effect of different levels of shadow wages on PSV—the reason being that a different ARI would be appropriate to each such level.[1] (The exception to this is when two variants of a project have the same or nearly the same time profile: in this case, the analysis might be legitimately used to convince a decision-maker that either a more labour-intensive or a more capital-intensive solution was preferable.) One can instead give the IRRs corresponding to levels of shadow wages within some sensible range. This may suffice to show, for example, that the lowest shadow wage that might be contemplated would still not result in a reasonable rate of return by any standard. The trouble with this, however, is that decision-makers are likely to have some more or less conventional rate of return in mind—but one that is appropriate to the actual wage level. The combination of a low shadow wage and a conventional rate of return will rule out relatively few projects. Even so, it is better to have a net with a wide mesh than no net at all. In the initial stages of setting up a project analysis system it may indeed be no bad thing to have a lenient criterion. Our experience suggests that many capital-intensive industrial projects would have shown returns of less than 10% even at a zero shadow wage; and quite a few would have shown returns of less than zero.

---

[1] Any weighting system for benefits according to the wealth of the recipient will in principle alter the ARI. In the discussion of such weighting earlier in this section we considered only incompatible projects (i.e. variants of the 'same' project). If, having decided on the variant by this means, the PSV of the chosen variant is kept at what it would have been under equal weighting then the ARI would not be changed—since the IRR of the marginal project would then be unaltered.

8.6 ABUSE OF SENSITIVITY ANALYSIS

Sensitivity analysis is abused if

(i) The evaluator uses it as an excuse not to try to quantify things that might have been quantified.

(ii) If the report presents merely a complicated set of interrelated switching values, and fails to give a lead.

The evaluator must normally be taken to be an economic adviser, as well as a technician. Even if he uses sensitivity analysis it should usually be in an appendix, from which he selects the values of the variables he believes to be most appropriate. The project should be recommended for acceptance or rejection. The sensitivity analysis may then be used to select illustrative sets of values which would have made the decision go the other way. If the selection is honest, this is usually enough to alert the decision-maker (who will not usually read more than a few pages anyway) to a possibly serious divergence of view.

It needs to be remembered that the good decision-maker normally wants his mind to be made up for him by people who have studied the project, and its social costs and benefits, far more deeply than he can; and who are in tune with his own way of thinking and with government policy. It is not that he can make better decisions, or that his values are more sacrosanct: but that he takes the ultimate responsibility.

Sometimes it is the case that the political decision-maker is unduly swayed by relatively ephemeral considerations, or by considerations that have nothing to do with social costs or benefits. With this sort of decision-maker, the less room for manoeuvre the analysis gives him the better. Also the more authoritative it is, the better. The greater the extent to which certain value variables and the method of analysis have been agreed by the government the more authoritative it will be. For this reason also a COPE, backed by strong political support, is desirable.

If a COPE is in existence it is less essential that the original evaluator should himself fill the role of an economic adviser: for COPE can do this in its own comments on the report. Even so it is probably a good thing that he should in effect make a recommendation. COPE can always disagree, especially if it comes to learn that a particular department tends to suit its figures to its recommendations, rather than the other way round.

8.7 DEALING WITH DOUBTFUL ASSUMPTIONS ABOUT GOVERNMENT POLICY

This is primarily a matter of high-lighting the assumptions made, and saying why it is thought best to assume that the government is going to behave in a particular way. This should be done only if the analyst has assured himself that his assumption is crucial, that is, likely to make the decision go the other way if it were wrong. Where the doubt is very great, it will be necessary to evaluate the project on alternative assumptions, and present both. The evaluator, as we have already seen, may or may not be in a position to recommend that his assumption about government policy be validated.

Part Three

THE ESTIMATION OF ACCOUNTING PRICES

CHAPTER NINE

The Principles of Accounting Prices

In this chapter we present our criterion for project selection in some detail, and the reasons for using that criterion. At this stage, we establish the principles: practical methods of estimation are described in Chapters XI–XIV. To keep things simple, we here ignore the private sector, economies of scale, externalities, uncertainty, and other complications. These important items of our agenda are reintroduced into the discussion in later chapters.

9.1 What Happens when a Project is Undertaken

If a project is accepted, the economy is committed to using certain things in certain ways. It has to be decided whether, comparing the good consequences of this commitment with the bad, it is better that things should be used in the ways proposed rather than in other possible ways.

This remark, though trite, is a useful guide through the complexities of project evaluation. It suggests at once that the task can usefully be divided into two: first one has to estimate what kind of changes in the economy a particular investment project will lead to; then one must consider what these changes are worth to the country by, implicitly, comparing them with other changes that might have happened instead. As foreshadowed in Chapter I, we take up the story at the second stage; that is, we take it that the physical inputs and outputs of the project, and any other important direct consequences for the rest of the economy, have been estimated.

In the first year or two of its life, and in some cases for much longer, a project draws resources from the rest of the economy, while apparently giving little or nothing in return. The site is cleared, buildings are built, machinery purchased and installed, production lines laid down. Only when this gestation period is over will the economy gain more from the outputs of the project than it loses by providing current inputs of materials, components, labour, power, and transport.

Both in the gestation period and the operating period, some of the inputs will be purchased directly from abroad. But domestic purchases of inputs will also have an import content. If there is no domestic excess capacity in a supplying industry, then a purchase from it will either cause some previous customer of that industry to import from abroad instead, or else he will be starved of materials with a resultant loss of production. If this does not happen, because output can be expanded, there will still be a foreign exchange cost because the input will itself use some imported inputs. Even the use of unskilled domestic labour has an effect on the balance of payments. If not employed on this project, it would normally have produced something—however little—in some other occupation: and the lack of this production, say of cereals, will mean that more cereals must be imported (even if total consumption were not increased as a result of the extra employment).

In the operating period, the most important item will be the output (unless the project is a failure!). This may be for export. If not, it may be a domestic consumption good, or an intermediate or capital good destined for use in some other branch of industry. Usually, if none of the output is exported, it will replace goods in the domestic market that would otherwise have been imported. If it does not have a direct effect on the foreign exchange balance in one of the above ways, it will be used as an input in the production of other goods, which in turn may be exported or substituted for imports—and so on.

It is a common practice, but a bad one, when considering projects in developing countries to separate *direct* foreign exchange costs and receipts (i.e. purchases and sales from abroad) from the rest— because foreign exchange often appears to be especially scarce. The result is often claimed to be the balance of payments effect of the project. But the above account should have made it clear that the balance of payments effect of a project cannot be estimated in this simple direct way. Indeed, it is positively misleading to try to do so. It is nearer the truth to say that *every* output of the project is a gain of foreign exchange, and that *every* input implies a use of foreign exchange. If more electricity is produced, that will enable some other producer to use the electricity to make goods for export, or goods that would otherwise have been imported; or if not, then that producer's output can be used in one or other of these ways. Following the chain of production around, one must eventually end at commodities that are exported or are substituted for imports. For, even if the goods produced are consumed in the country, some kind of consumer goods would have had to be imported if they had not been available, in order to provide an equivalent benefit. Exactly the same argument applies to costs.

All we are saying is that, in principle, everything can be compared with everything else. Given time to plan production so as to avoid unnecessary bottlenecks, society can have a little more electricity if it is willing to do without a sufficiently large quantity of steel; it can have a little more food by giving up a quantity of clothes. Because of these possibilities of substitution, we can compare one thing with another; and in particular, if it is convenient, compare any particular commodity with foreign exchange. This is why it is not sensible to isolate a few of the inputs and outputs of the project, and regard their foreign exchange value as indicating the balance of payments contribution (or burden) of the project. The only things one can leave out of account are the inputs that have no use elsewhere, and the outputs that are of no use to anyone.

The accounting price for clothes in terms of rice is, then, the quantity of clothing the economy could obtain by giving up a unit of rice (at the date in question). Obviously, just as it is a great convenience to express market prices in terms of money, so it will be best to measure accounting prices all in terms of a single 'good', which is called the *numéraire*. We shall explain exactly what we propose to use as numéraire in 9.12, but for the moment the reader may think of it as convertible foreign exchange. One could use other things—labour, say—but what we have already said suggests that foreign exchange may be a rather convenient numéraire.

9.11 *Social Income and Social Profit*
Using these accounting prices, we can calculate the value of the increases in supply less the value of the increases in demand, for each year of the project's life. We shall call this number the *social income* of the project in that year. It is the income imputed to the project, as a measure of the net increase in the output of the economy which it brings about. In the early years of its life, the social income of a project will usually be negative—just as the actual financial outlay exceeds receipts when the project is being set up. But we hope that social income will be positive later on, to offset the initial costs.

The social income generated by the project is not the measure of its value to society in that year. To construct such a measure, we must consider the use to which the social income is put. If a million rupees of social income could always be used in the same way, whatever the kind of project that provided it, there would be no need to ask how the social income of the project would be used. But some projects may commit the economy to large increases in consumption by particular groups, whereas others commit a much smaller part of the social income to the consumption of these groups, leaving the government free to do what it likes with the remainder.

Now, as between two projects that generate the same social income, a government would normally not wish to choose the one that *commits* it to a greater increase in the consumption of a particular group, if that increase in consumption could have been obtained in other ways. The government could always devote an equal amount of the social income arising from the second project (involving a smaller commitment) to consumption; but might well prefer to see the income ploughed back into further capital investment instead of being consumed at once, or spent in ways that would benefit more deserving social groups.

Why should the government be committed to allowing a certain increase in consumption in the economy if it decides to go ahead with the project? The reason, in general, is that governments are never in a position to control completely the distribution of incomes arising in the economy; nor, in particular, the pattern of incomes created by a project. Politics and administrative considerations may set a limit to possible taxation. As a result, the government cannot ensure that the social income of the project is used in the way that seems best: its choice is restricted, often severely, by the nature of the project, especially by the extent of the new employment it provides. For example, industrial projects often employ workers who would, in the absence of that employment, have enjoyed a much lower standard of living. Or an irrigation project may provide those fortunate in the location of their farms with increased incomes which will largely escape the tax net. In many other cases it may be possible to reduce such commitments to consumption by the introduction of new taxes or charges. Nevertheless unavoidable commitments do arise and are sometimes very important. A government would usually believe they reduced the value of the project.

We visualize the project as a certain pattern of *social income* over time, having associated with it levels of *committed consumption* in each year. The social income will be corrected to allow for the disadvantages of being committed to consumption by particular income groups: when this correction, for a given year, is subtracted from the social income, we have our measure of *social profit*. *The social profit in a year is the definitive measure of the value to society of the project's activities during that year.*

Lest there be any misunderstanding, we should emphasize that, in the end, all social income ought to give rise to someone's consumption. But there is no reason why it should be consumed at once, except insofar, perhaps, as it goes to the poorest people. On the contrary, part of social income will be ploughed back into the creation of new capital equipment: this possibility is called 'reinvestment'. The reason for reinvestment is that the increases in future consumption that can be expected to result more than compensate for the present consumption sacrificed.

In principle, one might think that it would be best to evaluate a project by estimating the consumption it makes possible, at all times, both directly, and indirectly as a result of the expenditure of uncommitted social income. But a moment's thought shows that this would be extremely complicated, for many other projects and acts of government policy would have to be considered when calculating the streams of consumption over time. Since there is usually no reason to think that the uncommitted social income of one project will be used in ways different from another, it is best to provide rules for evaluating uncommitted social income that can be applied generally, without the necessity of tracing out all that is done with that income for each particular case. It is our aim to provide such rules.

9.12 *The Numéraire*

We shall measure all commodities in terms of *uncommitted social income, measured in terms of convertible foreign exchange.* The units of foreign exchange need not be dollars, or any other foreign unit of account: we shall normally use the rupee equivalent of any convertible foreign currency after application of the official exchange rate. Suppose a country is given 1 million pounds sterling, as a gift, to be spent without restriction. If the official exchange rate is 20 rupees to the pound, we shall say that it has received 20 million units of the numéraire—that is, 20 million rupees at accounting prices. Any project which is, all things considered, as good as but no better than that gift is worth 20 million accounting rupees (at the date of consideration). We shall refer, in this sense, to 'accounting rupees' or 'border rupees'.

We have already seen in general terms that an item might seem to be worth 20 million rupees, yet not be regarded as worth 20 million accounting rupees. Rupees and accounting rupees may differ because market and accounting prices differ; or because an item may be committed to some use less valuable than the use to which the government would put an equal amount of uncommitted social income. We shall later have plenty of specific examples of how the numéraire is used. There is no great difficulty about it.

What may be a little confusing, however, is that different parts of the uncommitted social income available to government may come to be used in ways that have different social value. This is particularly apparent if we look with the benefit of hindsight at what governments have done in the past. It may actually be foreseeable, as we shall see in Chapter XIII. But this need not trouble us in our choice of numéraire, for the reason that the various conventions, commitments, and imperfections that govern the use of public funds do not in any way distinguish the uncommitted social income generated by one project from that generated by another. In each case, the unit is an average unit of uncommitted social income. The fact that the average unit cannot be supposed used for one particular purpose is a nuisance when we come to consider how to allow for commitments to consumption: but it is an unavoidable nuisance, representing a genuine difficulty in project evaluation. A visual guide as to which money flows are in terms of the numeraire and which not may be found in Chart I and Table I on pages 148 and 149.

The choice of a numéraire cannot, from a formal point of view, make any difference whatever to project selection: if a number of projects are analysed, using two different numéraires, then the ranking of those projects will remain the same, provided the same economic assumptions and judgments are made.[1] The choice of a numéraire depends on conceptual and computational convenience: a more convenient numéraire from these points of view may help to reduce error, bias, and muddled thinking.

The numéraire used in this book—uncommitted social income—is an innovation, but one we believe to be justified. Uncommitted social income accrues to public authorities. Since social cost–benefit analysis is essentially addressed to governments, to help them solve problems of public expenditure in general and investment in particular, it seems natural to use as numéraire something in terms of which they must think and operate. Ideally, all units of a numéraire are equally valuable: which is why currency is a convenient numéraire for a private individual or firm. We have seen that governments will not in fact commit all their expenditures to things which are equally valuable: nor will an individual do so either.

Among possible alternative numéraires, government investment funds might be suggested. But that would seem to imply some firm division between funds which may be used for public investment and

---

[1] In the methods of project appraisal recommended by the authors of the UNIDO *Guidelines*, a different numéraire is used. The *formal* correspondence of the UNIDO *Guidelines* and the system developed in this book is demonstrated in 18.1.

public consumption: not only is there no such firm division, but also whether some particular item of expenditure should count as consumption or investment is often debatable. Investment in total, public and private, is still more objectionable; because public and private investment have different objectives, and it begs too many questions to assume that in fact the results will be, on average, equally beneficial from a social point of view.

Finally, in the UNIDO *Guidelines*, aggregate consumption is used as numéraire. It seems to us that this choice is open to serious objections. It is not the case that aggregate consumption is the ultimate objective, which might make it a good numéraire. On the contrary, the authors emphasize that the consumption of different economic groups should be given different weights. This conflicts with the principle that different units of the numéraire should be, in prospect at least, equally valuable. Yet no particular group is singled out to have its consumption treated as numéraire. Moreover, if proper emphasis is to be given to these different weights that ought to be attached to different consumer groups, then it is more convenient that the numéraire be something neutral in this respect, just as money is not something that people eat: without this neutrality consistent treatment becomes quite difficult, and bias is more likely to creep in.

The numéraire we have selected is not fully described as 'uncommitted social income': this is because social income will accrue both in a form which can be spent abroad (foreign currency), and in a form which cannot (domestic currency). Since the two forms are seldom equally valuable, a choice has to be made. Our choice of foreign currency seemed the better alternative for the following reasons. First, foreign aid and loans account for a large part of new fixed public investment in many LDCs: the use of our numéraire makes the accounting rate of interest directly comparable with interest on loans payable in foreign currency, or with lending abroad. Secondly, border prices expressible in convertible foreign currency or 'accounting rupees' play an important role in the system of accounting prices which is formulated in this book.

Uncommitted social income in the future is not as valuable as uncommitted social income today. The future has to be discounted (see 9.13). Therefore, since every unit of the numéraire should be equally valuable, a still closer definition of it is '*present* uncommitted social income measured in convertible foreign currency'.

The reader may at this point begin to worry because the prices of different convertible foreign currencies change from time to time,

CHART I

THE SOCIAL INCOME AND SOCIAL PROFIT OF
A PUBLIC SECTOR PROJECT

(The numbers are those of the arithmetical
example corresponding to the chart)

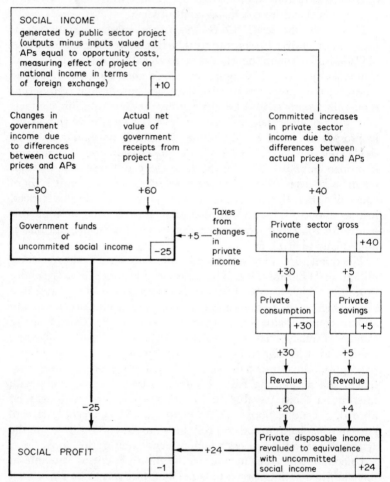

Notes

(i) The boxes and lines in thick type represent flows that are deemed to be equally valuable: these therefore are the numéraire.

(ii) It is recognized that some government funds arising from the project might themselves get committed to uses which are less valuable than others: but the view is taken that projects cannot normally be distinguished from each other in this respect. The increase in government funds is therefore assumed to be uncommitted.

(iii) The revaluation boxes represent the application of conversion factors to prospective uses of resources so as to make their values after revaluation equivalent to uncommitted social income.

TABLE I

ARITHMETICAL EXAMPLE CORRESPONDING TO CHART I

(The figures in boxes correspond to chart I.
The figures in bold type are in terms of
the numéraire)

	Public project accounts (actual prices)	+	Indirect effects on government revenue	+	Effects of total private income	=	Social income in APs
Output value[1]	+200		−100 (loss of import duty)			=	+100
Use of imported[1] inputs	− 30		+ 10 (gain of import duty)			=	− 20
Use of local[2] commodity inputs	− 30				+ 10	=	− 20
Use of labour[2]	− 80				+ 30	=	− 50
	+ 60		− 90		+40	=	+10
Direct tax from changes in private income or expenditure			+ 5		− 5		
Social income	**−25**				+ 35	=	+10

Consumption   Saving

+ 30   + 5

revalued[3] to

+ 20   + 4

SOCIAL PROFIT	**−1**	=	**−25**	+	**+24**

---

1. Traded commodity outputs and inputs are assumed to be sold and bought at c.i.f. prices plus duty.
2. The effects of the project's commodity and labour purchases on total private income are further discussed in Chapters XII and XIV.
3. The revaluation of private consumption and savings is further discussed in Chapters XI and XIII.

and in recent years even from day to day. It is certainly important if possible to predict future changes in the relative value of particular currencies. For instance, if sterling is going to be devalued relative to the yen, it is better to incur liabilities in sterling. Again if *future* earnings of yen are anticipated from a project, it might also be right to anticipate that they will be worth, say, more dollars than the same number of yen today.

It is hard to foresee changes in currency values, and their timing, but no formal difficulty is involved. In practice we express the numéraire in present 'border rupees', consisting of any convertible foreign exchange, converted at present official (or actual) rates of exchange. If it is expected that the yen will be revalued next year, then next year's earnings of yen must be converted to next year's border rupees at the new rate.

Finally, there is the problem of inflation. While movements in particular prices, such as those of copper, coffee, or sterling, should be allowed for, we do not advocate the same when it is a matter of prices in general. Thus we advocate working in terms of 'constant (average) prices', or, more precisely, 'border (or accounting) rupees of constant purchasing power'. Thus in an inflationary economy one would not try to anticipate future changes in the country's own prices and its exchange rate: that would be pointless insofar as it affected all prices equally.[1]

Inflation is mainly a problem for the project analyst if he is looking backwards, not forwards: if he is trying to establish the historical social rate of return on an investment, or to interpret past movements of prices for a particular product to see if there was any trend independent of general inflation. It is only in such cases that it may be desirable to have a still more precise definition of what is meant by 'border rupees of constant purchasing power'. This more precise definition is given in the footnote.[2]

---

[1] In reality, inflation tends not to affect all prices equally. If the differential effects of inflation on particular prices, especially those of non-traded goods and services, can be anticipated then they should be allowed for: but, in 'constant (average) price' terms, this would imply anticipating some price falls as well as some rises.

[2] Since domestic consumption is the objective of economic activity, we require that the numéraire, expressed in foreign exchange, retain constant purchasing power over domestic consumption. Thus the correct deflator is the price index of consumption multiplied by an index of the consumption conversion factor, the latter being described in 12.35. This deflator is consistent with the definition of the consumption rate of interest in 13.32, on which are based estimates of the shadow wage rates. The way in which one can form a view about the consumption rate of interest is explained in 13.43, and its relationship with shadow wage rates and the accounting rate of interest in 14.21.

To sum up, we can restate our definition of the numéraire. It is 'present uncommitted social income measured in terms of convertible foreign exchange of constant purchasing power'. To which we may add the riders that (*a*) in practice we use 'accounting rupees' which are the equivalent of convertible foreign exchange at official exchange rates, and (*b*) that if there is no official exchange rate, then any exchange rate will do as well, provided the same one is used for all conversions.

9.13 *Present Social Value*

Having calculated the net social profit in each year of a project's life, we must tie these profits and losses together to form a single measure by which the project can be judged. This is done by discounting each year's social profit back to the present and adding up, as explained in 1.4. Just as discounting actual profits, and adding up, yields the present (commercial) value, so discounting social profits yields the present social value: this is the final yardstick.

The question remains 'What rates of interest should be used for discounting social profits?' How one sets about answering this question in practice may well depend upon the extent to which cost–benefit evaluations are expected to apply elsewhere in the economy. If a social cost–benefit analysis of a project were a unique event, the only way the evaluator, or anyone else, could determine the appropriate interest rates would be to estimate how the investment funds required by the project might have been used elsewhere, and consider directly whether a greater social profit could have been generated each year in these alternative uses. But cost–benefit methods are most advantageous when quite widely applied. When this is so, the principles to be followed can be explained quite simply.

Suppose we have a project for which all the investment cost comes in the first year, all the output in later years:

Year	Social profit (thousand rupees)
1	−8,000
2	1,000
.	.
.	.
.	.
21	1,000

We must strive to satisfy the following two principles:

(i) Whatever a million rupees in, say, three years' time is worth to the economy now certainly does not depend upon the particular project under consideration. If another project promised the same social profit in three years' time, that would be equivalent to the same quantity of foreign exchange available to be used for any purpose. So the value now—the 'present value'—must be the same. Therefore, *future social profit must be discounted in exactly same way for all projects.*

(ii) A million rupees in three years' time is therefore worth a precise amount now—say 750 thousand rupees. If, by spending 749 thousand rupees now on a particular project, the economy could obtain a return of a million rupees in three years' time, it should do it; but it should reject a project costing 751 thousand rupees for the same result. This argument can be applied to social profits throughout the life of the project, discounting each year's profit by the interest appropriate to that year. *The rates of interest must ensure that all mutually compatible projects whose present social value is positive, and only those, can be undertaken.*

Suppose, for instance, that the accounting rate of interest were 10% per year, and expected to remain constant. For the project described above, we should calculate:

$$\text{PSV} = -8{,}000 + \frac{1{,}000}{1 \cdot 1} + \frac{1{,}000}{(1 \cdot 1)^2} + \cdots + \frac{1{,}000}{(1 \cdot 1)^{20}}$$
$$= 514 \text{ thousand rupees.}$$

This implies that the project should be undertaken. (The IRR is 11%, so it is rather marginal.) At the same time, many other projects will yield a positive PSV with an interest rate of 10%: they all ought to be undertaken too. If, as a result of using this interest rate, too many projects were accepted, with too great a total call on investment resources, there would be a balance of payments deficit and a tendency to inflation. If too few projects were undertaken, there would be unused resources. In either case, we should know that the interest rate used was wrong.

Given the government's other expenditure, and the levels of activity in the economy generally, there is at any time a certain level of investment funds that the government can allow for those projects to which cost–benefit analysis is applicable. Ideally, the rate of interest should be such that just this amount is used. Other means of rationing the funds should, if possible, be used only as temporary expedients. It is possible that the funds available for investment projects may vary with the rate of interest used: if the interest rates are higher, the government may, for example, be more willing to divert funds from public consumption. But that is a minor issue which does not affect the principles. The two rules enunciated above tell us how to discover whether the *accounting rate of interest* (ARI) has been correctly estimated.[1]

Having indicated the lines on which a project evaluation proceeds, we shall explain in the remainder of this chapter how social incomes and social profit should be calculated.

9.2 SIMPLIFICATIONS

In order to simplify the explanation of accounting prices we leave aside a number of considerations for the moment.

(i) We assume that the project will be in the public sector, so that any profit it makes accrues to public funds; and that the investment cost has to be met out of public funds. The commitment to consumption that arises with private profits will be discussed in 11.1. So also will the problem of encouraging desirable private investment, and discouraging undesirable private investment.

(ii) We neglect all *indirect effects* of our project. These might be of several kinds. Firstly, there are pure external effects (such as industrial pollution) which are discussed in Chapter XVI. Secondly, the operation of the project, by altering supplies and demands, may change the market price of various goods. This might encourage some producers—for example private producers who are not guided by cost–benefit analysis—to change their production plans in a way that could be important. Thirdly, in the same sort of way, the project might raise or reduce the consumption of people working in other parts of the economy. These second and third kinds of indirect effect will be explained in more detail in 12.6 and 12.7. It is probably not seriously misleading to neglect them at first.

(iii) We assume that there are no *economies of scale*. These arise when the cost of production—that is, the cost of inputs— per

---

[1] The subject of this paragraph has been discussed more fully in Chapter VI.

unit of output, is less when the size of the project is greater. For example, until the scale of production is very large, more cars of a particular model are cheaper to produce than fewer. Similarly, large power stations produce electricity at a lower cost per kilowatt-hour than do smaller ones. As a result, the accounting price for the output may change if a decision to undertake the project in question is taken. In such a case, it is a little more difficult to estimate the contribution of the output to social income. We therefore postpone consideration of large-scale projects until Chapter X.

(iv) We assume there is no uncertainty about the results of the project. This simplification will be removed in Chapter XV.

9.3 ACCOUNTING PRICES FOR TRADED GOODS

In this section, and the succeeding ones, we discuss the principles that should govern the estimation of the various accounting prices. Accounting prices, like ordinary market prices, may vary from year to year: we are always looking ahead, and estimating what they will be in future years.

The title of this section indicates that a rather sharp distinction is drawn between traded and non-traded goods, probably sharper than corresponds to reality in at least the more sophisticated economies. The most general assumption one can make is that increased demand or supply will affect imports, exports, production, and consumption of the commodity in question. Only if domestic production (if there is any) and consumption is unaffected, can one strictly say that the commodity is *wholly traded*; and similarly a good is *wholly non-traded* only if imports and exports (if any) are unaffected. All other commodities can be said to be *partially traded*.

However, in most cases it would be quite impracticable to predict the exact repercussions of changes in the demand or supply of a partially traded good. One must in project analysis limit the amount of research to be done. For this reason, and because more research may often not produce a better answer, we categorize goods as either traded or non-traded in many cases where neither category is likely to be exactly correct. We advocate doing this except in those few cases where all of the three following provisos hold: (*a*) the value of the input or output is clearly important for the PSV of the project, (*b*) there is real doubt as to whether trade or the domestic economy will be mostly affected, and (*c*) where a change in the classification would be likely to affect the value significantly.

In general we shall say that if some of the demand for a commodity will be satisfied from imports, or some of the supply exported, it is a *traded good*. Other goods and services are referred to as *non-traded*. Whether or not a particular commodity will be a traded good or a non-traded good, an import or an export, in some future period, depends on how it is thought that the economy is going to develop between now and then. But, in many cases, it will be quite obvious how a commodity has to be classified. Among cases that may not be so obvious are the following:

(i) There is no domestic production of some commodity—say, fertilizers—nor is there likely to be in the foreseeable future, but fertilizer imports have for some time been subject to a quota, which is occasionally revised, but is likely to continue for some time. If the quota were absolutely fixed, additional use of fertilizers could only be at the expense of some other domestic user. There would be no change in trade as a result of setting up a fertilizer-using project, and the commodity would have to be treated as a non-traded good. But the project report could contain a specific recommendation that the project be assigned a special fertilizer quota (or quota extension), which would make the commodity a traded good. And even without such formal arrangements, quotas can change and disappear in response to changed demands and supplies. If fertilizer were very important, this might be a case in which it would be worth assuming that it was a partially traded good.

(ii) There exists domestic production capacity for a project input, which is not being traded, but there are grounds for thinking this domestic production actually undesirable, or at least any expansion of the domestic capacity undesirable. Here we have the standard problem, whether the government will be pursuing rational policies or not. As we have already said in 6.6, the right procedure depends on the standing and confidence of the evaluator, and on the extent of the government's commitment to cost–benefit methods. But at least we can say with emphasis that it ought not to be assumed merely because the commodity is now non-traded, that it will continue to be non-traded in the future. That belief might well deprive an economy of many good projects.

(iii) There is no current domestic production of the project input, but the evaluator suspects that the commodity might be a good one for the country to produce. In such a case, it is generally best to regard the commodity as a traded good. Domestic production might make the commodity available at a lower accounting price than is implied by the assumption that it is traded, but the evaluator is unlikely, without a great deal of work, to be able to verify that with sufficient certainty. COPE, however, may well be in a rather different position, and able to estimate better accounting prices for some commodities by assuming that they will be non-traded goods.

(iv) The project input is agricultural, and is both exported and consumed at home. Increased production may result in greater exports, which will, of course, be valued in accordance with the effect on foreign exchange earnings. But if export prices fall a little as a result, then domestic prices will also fall and result in increased domestic consumption. If the domestic demand were thought to be elastic, and foreign demand inelastic, this effect might be considerable and the good would have to be treated as partially traded, the benefits of the increased exports and the increased domestic consumption being separately evaluated.

Generally speaking, we think it right to urge some bias in the direction of regarding commodities that are readily available in world markets, or for which a ready and well-defined export market exists, as traded goods; especially if it would be optimal for the country to trade them. Evaluations then form part of a consistent system that urges the government towards optimal policies, and evaluators are saved from undertaking usually very uncertain guesswork about the impact of a new project on import quotas, domestic production capacity, taxes, and so on. The more sophisticated project evaluations become, the more they will be able to treat commodities as partially traded goods (it will become apparent below that this involves more research and calculation). But there is no point in striving for undue sophistication.

9.31 *Imported Goods*
Suppose that raw cotton can be purchased from the world market at a definite price, which is virtually independent of the amount bought. If the project is going to use some raw cotton, we shall charge it the amount of foreign exchange that has to be spent to buy the raw cotton. This is the *border price* (or c.i.f. price). If a bale

of cotton costs $x and the official exchange rate is 7 rupees to the dollar, we shall take the accounting price to be 7x rupees. A charge must also be made for the cost of transporting the goods from boat to factory, including insurance and trading costs; the details of this will be discussed later.

What is the justification for the above rule? The answer is that it ensures that the use of, say, 1,000 accounting rupees in buying any one imported commodity is deemed to cost the economy the same as its use in buying any other imported commodity. For instance, if instead of using raw cotton that costs 1,000 rupees of foreign exchange (say $133 worth), raw jute costing 1,000 rupees is used (bought from another country that happens to use rupees as currency), that in itself makes absolutely no difference to the economy. These two inputs cost the economy exactly the same. Thus purchase taxes and import duties are excluded from accounting prices; for the project should not be encouraged to use inputs that happen to have low tariffs or taxes on them, since that might lead the country to spend more foreign exchange to no advantage.

The rule that one should ignore duties and purchase taxes would not be a good one if the government was using these duties deliberately as a means of discouraging one import as compared to another, for reasons that demanded respect in project evaluation. Indeed, governments should, when considering changes in the tariff structure, keep very much in mind the possible effects of tariffs on production decisions. But, in reality, one cannot pretend that the structure of tariffs, as we find it in any country, is designed to provide just the influence on imports and hence internal production decisions, that the government would now deliberately choose to exert.

The structure of tariffs in most countries is far more the result of a series of historical accidents than of a deliberate attempt to influence production decisions so as to get more of this used and less of that. The import duty might be higher on one commodity compared to others because it is an important import and therefore a useful source of revenue; or because of past programmes to encourage domestic production of the commodity; or because negotiated tariff reductions had involved the second commodity but not the first. Usually, the reasons for tariffs are irrelevant to the decision whether to use one input or another in production.

There is, however, one exception. The rule that the accounting price should be the foreign exchange cost of a unit of the commodity is correct only if the price the country pays for the commodity is independent of the amount it wants to buy. If this is not true, there is a case, at any rate in terms of purely national interest, for discouraging use of that commodity. The reason is that an increase in demand will increase the foreign exchange cost of what is already being bought; so that the actual foreign exchange cost is more than the price of the extra amount demanded. In this case, one might well want to have a tariff on imports, and this is a tariff one would want to include in the accounting price. This might happen either because the country's demand for the commodity was a very important part of total world demand, or because any expansion in demand would force the country to resort to more expensive suppliers. The first reason for having an accounting price above the world price is applicable only rarely to the case of a developing economy. The second reason arises more frequently. Actual tariffs are rarely, if ever, put on for the above reasons. Therefore rather than include any actual tariff, it is better to make a direct estimate of the amount by which the foreign exchange cost exceeds the price paid. Thus the general rule is that the accounting price for an imported commodity is the total foreign exchange cost, including any increase in the cost of existing purchases, of increasing imports by one unit. The technical term for this quantity is the *marginal import cost*. It will seldom be easy to tell just how much higher the marginal cost is than the border price.[1] Probably there are few cases where the difference would matter very much. But a similar point arises in connection with exports; and there it is liable to be more important.

The border price of the imported commodity is the price to use whether it is an input or being produced as an output. The same accounting price should be used for a commodity whatever its role in the economy. It is just as useful to the rest of the economy for a project to make 10,000 rupees worth of steel, as it is for it to save 10,000 rupees worth of steel; we want to encourage both to exactly the same extent, and therefore assign the same price to each.

It should also be emphasized that a good is normally considered as an imported good even if it is actually purchased for the project from a domestic supplier, provided that some of the total supply would in any case be imported. The justification is that someone else will have to import instead of buying from this domestic supplier. But, in some particular year, a commodity that would normally be imported may in fact be available from a domestic

---

[1] Marginal cost = price $[1 + (1/\eta_s)]$ where η_s is the elasticity of supply.

producer with excess capacity. This is hard to predict far ahead, but might be known to apply to a piece of capital equipment to be bought early in the life of the project. The accounting price can then be less than the price of imports. It becomes, effectively, a non-traded good whose price is to be estimated by the methods of 12.3 and 12.4.

9.32 *Exported Goods*
We can now compare a commodity that is exported with a commodity that is imported. If the exported commodity can be sold at a fixed *border price* (in terms of foreign exchange—i.e. neglecting taxes and subsidies, special exchange rates, etc.), that price is the accounting price for the commodity. It is as valuable to obtain 1,000 rupees by exporting cotton piece goods as to save 1,000 rupees by reducing the import demand for tin. Similarly, when comparing two commodities that are both exported, it is obvious that what the projects provide the economy with is the foreign exchange earned; in comparing the two commodities, one should look only at the prices they will fetch in world markets.

Thus, if the project produces a commodity that is being exported, it must be credited with the foreign exchange equivalent (less the appropriate transport and distribution costs). This is correct even if the output of the project will not itself be exported, but used in some other domestic industry. For, given the demands of this domestic industry, the output of the project still has the effect of increasing exports, as compared to what they would otherwise have been. (Some indirect effects are here neglected, which might occasionally be important. They will be taken up later.)

The above description of an exported commodity may sound rather unrealistic to some readers. Countries seldom feel that they can export as much as they choose of any specified commodity, without significantly affecting the price they can hope to receive. Perhaps the developing countries are apt to exaggerate the difficulties of selling goods abroad; often the problem is not so much that of finding markets as of maintaining adequate quality on a sufficient volume of production. But sometimes countries face, or feel seriously threatened by, the prospect of impenetrable trade barriers erected by the more industrialized countries.

If, on reflection, project planners decide that the limit on the export of bicycles is the rate at which good quality production can be expanded, then no special problems arise in evaluating particular production proposals (once they are reckoned to be genuinely feasible). If, however, increased production will have to be sold in less and less favourable markets, it may be necessary to reduce prices to all purchasers if exports are to be expanded. This is certainly the position in many of the markets for primary commodities; if cocoa producers try to increase production too rapidly, the price is forced down. In that case the extra foreign exchange, which will be earned by producing more, is less than the actual foreign exchange receipts from the new sales, since the price reduces the earnings of existing production.

In such a case, it is a good idea to discourage production by crediting the project with rather less than the ruling price for the commodity; this is the reason for the export taxes discussed in 5.5. This lower price, which is the increase in foreign exchange earnings per unit of extra exports, is called the *marginal export revenue*. It is analogous to the marginal import cost discussed in the previous section.[1] The general rule for determining the accounting price of a commodity that is being exported is that the accounting price is equal to the marginal export revenue.

In fact, most commodities are produced by a number of countries, and one country acting on its own cannot usually get a significantly better price for its production by restricting its own output. For this reason there are sometimes agreements among the producers of primary commodities to reduce overall production, in order to keep prices from falling too far. In such cases—the International Coffee Agreement is an example—the various producing countries are given quotas which limit the amount of the commodity that they should export. The accounting price for a commodity which is exported under a quota of this kind should not be very different from the border price (for quota exports), provided domestic demand for the commodity is small. But if the country's own demand for the commodity in question is large, and the level of exports is given, the commodity should be regarded for the purposes of project analysis as a non-traded good. The accounting price must, of course, be less than the border price (otherwise it would not be worth exporting at all).

It may be thought that we have still not covered all possibilities. It often seems that the exports of some particular commodity are given in *both* quantity *and* price. What is the project planner supposed to do then? In fact, the planner may be too quick to suppose that both quantity and price are fixed. He is, after all, planning for

---

[1] Thus, marginal revenue = price $[1 - (1/\eta_d)]$ where η_d is the elasticity of demand.

the future, and not for today. There is time to try to expand markets by offering lower prices, and mounting selling campaigns (these latter are costs to be included in the project). Occasionally, export contracts—e.g. for bilateral trade—may be fixed well in advance, specifying both quantities and prices, and productive capacity is established precisely for this purpose. In such a case it is obvious what the foreign exchange earnings of the outputs are! But we suspect that, in general, it is merely a matter of statistical convenience to suppose that future export demand is a given quantity, which cannot be expanded except with the most expensive difficulty; and not an accurate statement of export possibilities.

However, sales of new exports often require the gradual development of markets, as agencies are built up, designs developed, reputations established, the characteristics of different markets learned, and so on. It may then be sensible to act as though exports could be expanded easily up to a certain point, without prices being much affected. This point will be changing through time, and may well not be where the planners think it is going to be. While planning production within these limits, the expected prices may be used as the accounting prices in evaluating projects, at any rate when uncertainty about probable markets is not too great. It would be better if one knew how much one could expand sales by spending still more on selling efforts, so that rational decisions could be taken about export promotion: but that is difficult to know.

9.33 *Summary*

The general rule for traded goods is as follows: the accounting price is the border price, or, in cases where the border price is believed to vary significantly with the amount bought or sold, the marginal import cost, or marginal export revenue, as appropriate.

Particular problems and exceptions should not blind us to the essential point of the argument. Border prices are used, not because it is thought that they are, in any sense, necessarily more 'rational' than domestic prices, but simply because they represent a set of opportunities open to a country, and the actual terms on which it can trade. If the commodity in question is going to be exported or imported in the year under discussion, planners have to decide the accounting price by studying the foreign markets from which the country buys or to which it sells. Often, it will be enough to forecast the price at the port. But the planners should not look to domestic market prices at all.

9.4 Accounting Prices for Non-Traded Goods and Services

We do not discuss labour here, since it is a special case, which is best treated in a special way. We take it that the shadow wage rate, and the accounting rate of interest, are known parameters, which the evaluator or COPE can make use of when working out other accounting prices.

The general principles for non-traded goods (9.41) may seem a little complicated, but many of the most important cases can be dealt with in a relatively straightforward way, namely those commodities that are supplied at constant cost (9.42). Commodities in fixed supply, such as some natural resources and goods subject to fixed quota, also deserve special attention (9.43).

9.41 *Marginal Social Cost and Marginal Social Benefit*

The same accounting price should be applied to a commodity in all its uses (apart from the differences that must arise because of transport or transmission costs). If a project uses a hundred thousand kilowatts of electricity, the purpose for which it is used does not alter the sacrifice which society must make in allowing the project to use electricity at that rate. Similarly, the value of an extra unit of electricity to the nation is the same whatever means are used to produce the electricity, or even if the extra electricity is made available by using less electricity in other projects.

Yet, if a project is to use a quantity of some non-traded commodity, that quantity may be obtained by diversions from various other uses, and also by increasing production. These various losses to the rest of the economy may not all have the same social value. If a thousand tons of raw jute are required (actually that is likely to be a traded good, but let us suppose it is not), farmers may be induced, by a price rise, to supply the jute, in part by diverting resources from rice production. The rice price will also be greater, and many families will consequently reduce their consumption. Thus the farmers incur costs, and so also do the consumers who have less rice. Some consumers and producers are poor, others are better off; losses and gains to the poor should count for more than losses and gains to the rich.

It is difficult to trace the various effects of a new demand for a non-traded good in the way just sketched (and we have left out many further effects). But we can bring some order into the analysis by defining the *marginal social cost* (MSC) and *marginal social benefit* (MSB) of a commodity. The marginal social cost is the value, in terms of accounting prices, of the resources required to produce an extra unit of the commodity. For example, if a man puts soap powder into cartons, both the soap powder and the cartons being imported, the MSC of the packaged soap powder is the cost of the soap (at border price) plus the cost of the carton (at border price) plus the cost of the labour (at the shadow wage rate). The marginal social benefit is, similarly, the benefit, evaluated in social terms, derived from supplying to the economy an extra unit of the commodity. For example, if the commodity is untaxed and consumed by only one income-group, with no other effects, the marginal social benefit is what that income-group spends to obtain an extra unit of the commodity (i.e. its market price), multiplied by a fraction, which is the weight assigned to an increase in the income of that group as compared with an equal increase in uncommitted social income.[1]

In general, the MSC and MSB will vary with the total amount of

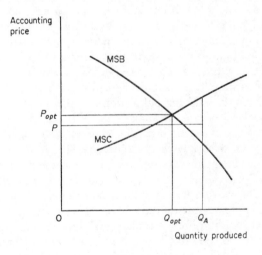

Figure 1
Marginal Social Cost and Marginal Social Benefit

---

[1] Cf. 13.1, below.

the commodity that is produced. This is illustrated in Figure 1, where the MSC is assumed to increase, and the MSB to diminish, with the amount supplied. The actual quantity produced in the economy (OQ_A) is not necessarily such that the MSC is equal to the MSB (the amount OQ_{opt}), although the government ought to make it so, by appropriate taxation. Equality of untaxed supply and demand brought about by an uncontrolled price is not in itself sufficient to ensure the right output, because private costs and benefits may differ from their social counterparts.

To find the accounting price of a non-traded input, one should estimate the proportions in which extra demand for a unit of the commodity will increase production and reduce consumption elsewhere. Suppose the increase in production is twice the reduction of consumption. Then the accounting price is two-thirds of the MSC plus one-third of the MSB—since that is the social cost sustained by the economy in providing the supply to the project. If the commodity is bought and sold in a free market, the increase in production and reduction in consumption are brought about by an increase in the price of the commodity. Therefore the proportions in which the MSC and MSB are averaged to obtain the accounting price are the proportion of supply response to demand response for the necessary price change. In any event, we may take it that the AP is an average of the MSC and the MSB—as represented by, say, OP in Figure 1.

The estimation of the MSC and MSB poses problems, which we shall discuss in the following subsections. Of the two, the MSC is the more important, because in many cases it is reasonable to assume that the MSC is constant over the relevant range of output. This implies that extra supply can be obtained without there being any reason for a change in consumption. There is then no reason why the market price should change, and no new reason why government policies with respect to consumption should change. We will be most likely to assume that the MSC is approximately constant if the commodity is required in some years' time, so that new production capacity can be established to meet the new demand. In the shorter run, when capacity is more or less fixed, the accounting price may well be greater than or less than the long run MSC.

It is generally easier to estimate the MSC than the MSB, and a government able and willing to operate optimal taxation policies would ensure that the two were equal. It is therefore tempting to proceed as if the government's policies were optimal, and use the MSC as an estimate of the AP. This is a temptation that should be avoided only for good reason.

The alternative is to estimate the MSB, which implies checking the optimality of the government's policies. The nature of such optimal fiscal policies has been sketched in 5.5, and is referred to again in 12.5. It will frequently be sensible to assume that things which one does not have time or resources to examine and criticise are the way they are for good reasons. This does not imply that the government's policies should never be criticised, merely that one may be wise to concentrate on other matters, especially if they are more important in the final evaluation.

It should also be noted that, if production in the public sector can be expanded or contracted fairly freely, it ought to be brought to a point where the MSC is equal to the MSB (even if the government's tax policies are not optimal). If cost–benefit methods are being widely applied in the public sector, the AP some years ahead may be taken to be the MSC at the point where MSC and MSB are equal —the price represented by OP_{opt} in Figure 1. Thus, ideally, the MSB curve is needed by those planning the growth of the industry which produces the non-traded commodity. All this may seem hard. But another way of putting the rule in this case is that the accounting price is the MSC at that level of production which it is desirable to attain. Put that way, it is clear what has to be thought about.

9.42 *Commodities Producible at Constant Cost*
Consider a commodity which is produced in the public sector, for which the MSC is relatively independent of the amount supplied. In that case one can speak simply of *the* cost of production, since each unit produced costs about the same, and the *accounting price is equal to the cost of production, measured at accounting prices.* To show more clearly why in such a case it is not necessary to worry about the level of demand, and the MSB, we shall discuss the particular case of electricity.

Except for hydro-electricity, most of the inputs (oil or coal, and equipment) are traded goods, and will, therefore, be valued at border prices. Let us suppose that the shadow wage rate has also been determined, so that the accounting prices for all inputs are known. Further, suppose that supplying any amount of electricity is simply a matter of building more or fewer coal-burning generating stations of the same type (of course, we are simplifying!). Now there will be a minimum accounting price for electricity below which it would be socially unprofitable to build any power station—so that, if the accounting price were less than this, the project selection procedures would not permit the production of electricity at all.

But if the accounting price were significantly higher than the minimum, there would be good reason to build a limitless number of power stations. So, in this case, there is an unambiguous accounting price, which is equal to the MSC, and which is independent of the amount of electricity demanded and supplied. There is thus no need, in estimating the accounting price, to worry about the prices that householders ought to pay, nor about such things as the licensing arrangements which should govern private producers of electricity, nor anything else that affects the demands made upon the public supply. Needless to say, the electricity authorities must still worry; for they have to estimate the actual future level of demand (as affected by the accounting price, together with any regulations or rationing the government may impose), in order to decide how many power stations to build.

There are many ways of making electricity. The accounting price for electricity should be the cost of production with the particular method of production that is expected to be used at the date in question. If the electricity-generating industry were operating optimally, the method of production would be such as to make the cost of production as small as possible. In that case, the accounting price would be so low that only the best technique would be used. For instance, it might permit coal-fired stations but disallow oil-fired ones—or vice versa. But this may be too perfectionist, and in practice (especially when risk is allowed for) a somewhat higher AP is desirable which permits alternative techniques when their pre-dicted social cost is only a little higher than that predicted for the apparently best technique.

When the MSC varies with production, it may on the one hand still be justifiable to neglect demand elsewhere in the economy, provided it does not vary very much; for then the additional demand of one particular project will not have a significant effect on what other users do. On the other hand, it may become necessary to predict total demand to get a sufficiently accurate estimate of the MSC: for instance, total demand might grow very substantially over a period of ten years, and so render current costs quite out of date.

The discussion so far has been in terms of a single non-traded commodity. The accounting prices of all inputs into the production of the commodity were assumed to be already known. For instance, in discussing inputs into electricity, the non-traded input of con-struction was used without saying how it was arrived at. Is that not cheating? In fact it is not, for we are providing ourselves with an equation corresponding to each non-traded commodity—in the general case, its AP is related to other APs through its MSC and MSB. Some of these equations depend on several of the accounting prices we want to calculate. But there are as many equations as prices. It can be confidently asserted that these equations have a solution. It is theoretically possible that they might have more than one solution: but we will take it, when we come to discuss the estimation of the accounting prices in Chapter XII, that this particular problem is much less troubling in practice than in theory.

9.43 *Commodities in Fixed Supply*

It is convenient to discuss the determination of the MSB in relation to commodities that happen to be in fixed supply (except, possibly, for new output from the project), because the case of fixed quotas has often been taken to be characteristic of developing economies. In our view, the project planner should accept the claim that a quota is rigidly fixed only with reluctance and under protest; but it is certainly important to know how to calculate the MSB of a commodity subject to quota, and important to emphasize that it is not at all likely to be the market price of the commodity.[1]

The theoretical problem in estimating the MSB is to determine who gets, directly or indirectly, the benefit of the new project output. In practice this may be a difficult problem in what economists call general equilibrium analysis (for many prices may change when the supply of a single commodity is altered). At this stage, we shall do no more than point out what has to be looked for and expected, by examining a very simple case.

10,000 units of a commodity (X) are imported and sold by the government, which makes a monopoly profit. There is now a project to produce 1,000 units. Supposing that the import quota is not changed, the price must be reduced from Rs. 1·0 to Rs. 0·95, to sell the larger quantity. Now a change in one price generally causes changes in demands for other things, and hence further changes in prices. To avoid all the effects on social value which might arise from these complications it is necessary to assume that only demands for goods traded at fixed prices change, and that there are no taxes, subsidies, or monopoly rents, in respect of these goods (alternatively one can simply suppose that these effects are negligible).

The social benefit can now be calculated, taking into account both consumers and the government. Consumers have an extra 1,000

---

[1] We emphasize this because the UNIDO *Guidelines* tend to support the use of market prices.

units of X, worth somewhere between Rs. 1000 and Rs. 950 to them (say Rs. 975). As against this, they are spending Rs. 450 extra on X, which implies a reduction in (we suppose) purchases of traded goods of Rs. 450. So total consumers' gain is Rs. 525—a little more than half what the new output sells for. The government gains the extra Rs. 450 spent on commodity X. This is also a social gain of Rs. 450 in terms of accounting prices—but this equality is valid only because we have arbitrarily assumed that there were no taxes on the traded goods which consumers no longer buy as a result of their increased consumption of X. If they had been taxed at 100%, the government's gain, and the corresponding gain of social income, would have been halved.

So far we have a governmental gain in accounting prices of Rs. 450, and a consumption gain of Rs. 525. In general the latter is valued at less than the government gain, which is the numéraire. Suppose that consumers' income is on average worth only about 70% of government income: then the consumers' gain is reduced to about Rs. 367 in accounting rupees, and the total social benefit of the output is Rs. 817. This simple example makes it clear that the social gain from the output can easily be less than the actual amount for which the output of the project is sold (Rs. 950). It would have been still less if the traded goods no longer bought had been taxed. For instance, if the average rate of duty on the traded goods which consumers no longer buy had been one-third, then the governmental gain would have been reduced to Rs. 300, and the total benefit from the output would have been Rs. 667. On the other hand, if the rental income, or excess profits, arising out of the quota accrued to private traders, then the apparent social benefit from the government project would have been much larger. The government's Rs. 450 gain would be transformed into a governmental gain of Rs. 950 and a private trader's loss of Rs. 500, the latter being worth, rupee for rupee, very much less than the former in terms of accounting prices. But, in this case, it is highly questionable whether this added benefit should be attributed to the project, because the government could have got its hands on the private monopoly profit created by the quota in several other ways than by producing the commodity itself—by a tariff, by auctioning import licences, or by multiple exchange rates. It could also, of course, have reduced or eliminated the monopoly profit by allowing more imports, a possibility we assumed away.

The estimated social benefit of the project could possibly have been increased in another way. Since it makes consumers better off, one might assume that the government could increase direct taxes as a result, thereby shifting more of the gain to the government. Indeed, the possible complications are almost endless. However, the general principle should be clear. The evaluator has to estimate the gains and losses to various social groups which occur directly and indirectly as a result of the project, and which could not be assumed to have occurred without the project, and then weight them according to some assessment of the social value of marginal changes in their incomes; and, often most important, he has to estimate the change in the government's uncommitted social income, as measured by quantities of goods released from consumption, evaluated at accounting prices. In Chapter XIII, we shall suggest how all this may conveniently be done—or avoided—with sufficient accuracy in practice.

The above was the first case examined where the distinction between social income committed to the consumption of particular groups, and uncommitted social income freely available to the government, has been allowed to influence evaluations. This distinction is particularly important in the evaluation of labour, to which the next section is devoted.

The reader may feel at this stage, that it may be rather hard to estimate accounting prices. It is easy to get the difficulties out of proportion. How far one should go in worrying about the proper classification of a commodity—traded, non-traded, or partially traded—depends, as does the amount of work that should be devoted to estimating the accounting price, on the importance of the commodity for the project in question. In project analysis, troubles tend to come singly. Most of the inputs and outputs of a project will be quite easily dealt with.

9.5 The Treatment of Labour

Some labour can be regarded as traded. But normally labour inputs have to be treated as non-traded goods. In most cases, the accounting prices for labour can be estimated as the MSC, since actual real wage rates are probably not very sensitive to changes in the demand for labour. The MSC is not, however, easy to estimate, even in the case of unskilled labour. The various categories of unskilled labour deserve special attention, not least because it is the consumption of those who engage in or hope to engage in unskilled work that is the chief object of development. To emphasize the special role of these inputs, we shall follow tradition by calling their accounting prices *shadow wage rates*. The case of skilled labour presents special difficulties, which will be discussed in Chapter XIII.

Various categories of unskilled labour need to be distinguished. Urban and rural labour is paid at different rates, and contributes different amounts to production. Within the urban sector, labour in small enterprises generally receives a much lower wage than in the large plants of 'organized industry'; and, within the rural sector, increased labour provided within a family farm may have to be treated differently from increased employment of wage-labour in agriculture or in rural works. But, in all these cases, the first question to consider is how much the labour would have contributed to production if it had not been employed in the project. This may have a rather direct and straightforward answer in the case of rural labour, but may require some guesswork about indirect consequences in the case of urban workers.

To take an extreme case (which is probably not true anywhere, yet), if there were always, every day, unemployed people in rural areas, ready and willing to work if jobs were available, one could probably assume that new employment in these rural areas, say on road-making, would bring about no reduction in agricultural production. Then the employment of this unskilled labour would not reduce the social income of the project. If, more realistically, labour is scarce for part of the year, that scarcity will normally be increased by the project and, as a result, the production of agricultural commodities will be reduced; and also some people will probably work harder than previously. An estimate of the loss of agricultural production is needed, each item being measured at its accounting price.

By the MPL, we shall mean the loss of production which would arise by withdrawing a man from agriculture, or any other sector of the economy, if the rest did not work harder. We say 'if the rest did not work harder', because more manual labour is a real cost to the individual. If, as a matter of fact, others would work harder to make up some of the production loss caused by the withdrawal of a man, that does not on our view significantly reduce the social cost below the cost as estimated in the manner explained, unless a rise in the level of consumption of those remaining in the sector has such an effect on their physique or outlook on life that they can work harder without real cost to themselves.

Normally, the MPL is estimated as the direct contribution of the man to production. It could be less, if a reduction in the rural labour force caused some consolidation of holdings (or prevented fragmentation), or caused any other change in land tenure with a costless and beneficial effect on production. There is, however, no evidence which would permit an evaluation of such an effect, if it exists, and we believe it can be neglected at least when marginal changes are being considered.

The loss of production must be measured at accounting prices: and throughout this book 'the marginal product' should be understood to mean 'the marginal product measured at accounting prices'. It will be appreciated that, in principle, the value of the loss of production depends on the pattern and nature of an average individual's work throughout the year, and may include such items as harvesting at peak periods, carrying grain, serving tea in a café, working on the roads, and so on. However, in practice, it will often be necessary to estimate it by looking at the most obvious and typical employment only (see 14.13).

In the case of new urban employment, workers may be drawn from many places. Typically, perhaps, they will be drawn from the families of workers already living in the towns and cities, who would otherwise have been unemployed, or found occupation in small workshops or by squeezing into service industries already suffering from overemployment. But in many developing countries, there is a steady flow of workers and families into urban areas, a flow that is likely to be speeded up as employment opportunities in the towns improve (unless there is a corresponding improvement in rural areas). One might think—correctly in some countries—that an extra job in a public sector urban industry simply implies one less unemployed man, or one boot-black fewer with no loss in service quality. If that is the only effect, the relevant MPL is zero. But it is possible to take the other extreme case that the extra job increases the attractiveness of the city so much (by increasing the income that a newcomer can on average aspire to) as to draw perhaps two more potential workers to the city.[1] In our view neither of these extreme possibilities is plausible for most of the countries we know. If we had to select a typical case, we would probably assume that the new urban job draws one more man from rural areas. The newcomer might get the job. More probably the job is secured by someone already in the town whose less attractive position is taken by another, who is again replaced by another, and so on. But somewhere a position is created—perhaps only as a regular frequenter of factory gates—which had been thought worth

---

[1] Harris and Todaro, 1970.

filling, and which will now be filled by the newcomer. In this case, the relevant MPL would be the rural MPL, plus whatever annual expenditure of resources is required to compensate a man for living in an urban rather than a rural area.

Unfortunately, the above simple model probably does not fit the facts with any precision anywhere. One can find good *a priori* arguments for suggesting either that an extra urban job draws in less than one man from the countryside, or that it draws in more than one.[1] A lot depends on the employment situation in both urban and rural areas in the country concerned. If sufficient information is available, and that will often not be the case, a more realistic model of the employment changes consequential on the creation of a job may be used.

Whatever the average direct consequences of creating an extra job, the general principle remains the same. One should try to estimate in what proportions labour is drawn from other sectors including the wholly unemployed sector, and then estimate the resultant loss of production there. To that one adds the annual cost of compensating a worker for moving from rural to urban areas, and an allowance for the human cost, if any, of any increase in the total amount of work done. The result is the relevant (net) MPL.

The MPL is an essential component of the MSC of employing labour, but the two are not in general the same. This is because a developing country can seldom afford to commit so much of its production to consumption as would be implied by a shadow wage rate equal to the MPL (given that actual wage rates are higher). In many countries it cannot be expected that all those who would like more work should actually be given it in the near future. The number of jobs it would be worth creating if the MPL were universally taken as the shadow wage rate is quite often so great that the economy would be committed to more consumption than it could supply from the resources available to it. The difficulty is that, very often, unskilled labourers are paid wages that allow the worker and his household to consume, despite taxes, goods whose value is considerably greater than the MPL. There are many reasons for this, among them the following:

(i) Since market prices are not the same as accounting prices, even if the actual wage rate were equal to the MPL at market prices, workers' consumption may still exceed the MPL at accounting prices.

---

[1] Scott, MacArthur, and Newbery, 1974.

(ii) Workers often come from alternative occupations in which their consumption is greater than the MPL (because of charity, family ties, government relief arrangements, or the overstaffing of public services), and they have to be paid accordingly.

(iii) Union bargaining power, the political strength of the urban proletariat, minimum-wages legislation, and custom, often create wage levels that exceed the opportunity cost of labour.

(iv) In certain sectors, higher wages may bring about a more than proportionate improvement in labour productivity, either for physiological reasons, or because they result in a more contented labour force with lower turnover; this increased productivity will be allowed for in the project analysis—but the high wages which this may justify imply also a rise in consumption which has to be taken into account.

(v) High wages may be necessary to induce rural labour to migrate to the urban sector, even though when they arrive they find themselves substantially better off.

Some economists prefer explanations like (iv) and (v), which offer some kind of internal economic logic. Others note that the factors referred to in (iii) are obviously present. In some ways, the precise reasons for the phenomenon matter little: the question is whether it happens, and in most of the developing countries it certainly does. The only appropriate test in any particular case is to look and see.

An example will help to show how the commitment to consumption might be estimated. Suppose that the value of output in a project, which is thought to draw its labour predominantly from the agricultural sector, has been calculated; and that the value of commodity inputs has been subtracted from it: the result is 1 million rupees. The wage bill is 300,000 rupees. It is estimated that the loss in the value of agricultural production as a result of removing this labour force from agriculture is only 50,000 rupees, and that no allowance for harder work by others in the rural sector need be made. Let us suppose that average consumption per head in the agricultural sector is equal to the net value of production there, and that the wage earners consume all their income. (Private savings, and taxes, are neglected: the example is not meant to be particularly realistic, and these details will be dealt with later.) We now have the following situation (valuing all quantities at accounting prices):

The project provides	: Rs. 1,000,000 (excluding labour costs)
The wage earners would otherwise have produced	: Rs. 50,000
Agricultural output is reduced by	: Rs. 50,000
The wage earners consume	: Rs. 300,000

Thus the net surplus over consumption requirements is Rs. 700,000. But it is impossible to justify subtracting the whole of the wage bill (equal to workers' consumption) from the net value of production of the project. People are consuming commodities which they could not otherwise have consumed: they are therefore better off, and this is a benefit for which the project can take credit. As against this, more people could be provided with consumption later if it were possible to use the Rs. 300,000 for investment in extra projects. The question is whether it would be better to postpone consumption in this way: alternatively, we might want to build hospitals, or finance famine relief schemes with the resources.

The answer depends upon how fast the economy will be growing anyway, and what could be done if it were possible to undertake more investment projects. The value of other government expenditure programmes should also be considered. We shall go into this in detail in Chapters XIII and XIV. What must be clear already is that we shall not advocate subtracting the whole of the wage bill from the net value of production, only a part of it. To determine what part, we multiply the number of people employed by a number that is (usually) less than the actual wage rate. We shall call this number the *shadow wage rate* (SWR). There will, of course, be many different SWRs in an economy; but for grammatical simplicity we shall speak of 'the SWR' as if there were but one.

Since the two quantities that are needed when we estimate the shadow wage rate (the MPL and the additional consumption generated by new employment) are both measured at accounting prices, and some of the relevant accounting prices are usually prices of non-traded goods, it seems that we need to know the shadow wage rate before we know these accounting prices. What this means is that the SWR and some APs have to be estimated together. But we shall see in 14.1 that this is not a serious problem, unless we aim at great precision, for the APs can be based on initial rough estimates of the SWR, and, within a few years, there is plenty of time to improve accuracy by feeding into the calculation subsequent estimates of the SWR.

Clearly the SWR should be different for different kinds of labour employed on different projects in different locations, and may not be the same proportion of the actual wage rate under all circumstances. For example, the way in which the consumption provided through wage payments is distributed among different consumer groups will be very different in the case of a rural works programme from what it would have been in a busy seaport relatively isolated from the rest of the country. In particular, the government may want to give special weight to the needs of the inhabitants in certain regions by assigning a lower shadow wage rate for projects located in them. The case of new employment generated by agricultural improvement schemes, such as irrigation projects, requires special consideration, since much of the additional labour might be provided within families. In such cases, there may be a substantial commitment to additional consumption by poor peasant families, this being regarded as of at least equal value to uncommitted social income—it may be that these peasants can be effectively helped only through agricultural and other rural development schemes. In such cases, of course, the whole of the additional social income counts as social profit, despite the commitment.

It is also necessary to consider how to allow for changes in wage rates over time. In developed economies, the more far-sighted employers allow for a rising cost of labour. Similarly, we must consider whether, in a developing country, the SWR will rise; it would hardly be safe to assume that it will be constant. Nevertheless, as we shall see in 14.2, there is some reason to think that (in the circumstances of many developing countries) the *ratio* of the SWR to the actual wage rate may remain roughly constant, at any rate for a decade or so. Naturally, this depends upon the country; and no doubt one should allow for changes in the ratio in some cases. But it is unlikely that the changes will be big enough to make very much difference to investment decisions. This is one of the complications that project evaluators can usually afford to ignore.

For a country setting up a system of project evaluation, the magnitude of the SWR is one of the most important questions that has to be settled. We have seen that it may be the marginal product of labour (always measured at accounting prices), but only if the extra employment causes no extra consumption (at accounting prices) in the economy as a whole, or if there is no reason to regret the commitment to consumption that is generally involved. In order to decide how much greater than the MPL the SWR should be, it is necessary to consider the value of the uses to which uncommitted social income can be put, as compared to the value of the committed consumption. In Chapters XIII and XIV, we shall suggest how this may be done. The SWR can be estimated very accurately only by calling upon rather sophisticated economic analysis, if at all. We shall try to indicate ways of making rough, but generally adequate, assessments.

9.6 THE FINANCING OF PROJECTS

So far in this chapter, finance has been ignored. This is correct for a public sector project whenever the finance required could have been used for some other public project. Leaving foreign financing on one side for the moment, it is our general assumption that one public sector project is indeed at the expense of another. But this might not be perfectly accurate in some cases. One can, for instance, envisage a project which itself induced the government to raise taxes. In that case, the project would be at the expense partly of private consumption and partly of private investment: the social cost of the invested funds might be very similar to those of a private investment, and would in any case be lower than if the project was at the expense of another public project (see 11.2). Alternatively, the project might cause the government to increase its total borrowing from the public: again the project would be at the expense of private consumption and investment, though in different and less favourable proportions; but there would be a further effect of increasing payments on the national debt which would raise the government's commitment to consumption in the future, and this effect would somewhat reduce the desirability of the project. However, we think it would be rare for the project evaluator to have to worry about these complications, because we think it can be reasonably assumed in almost all cases that one particular project will not affect total taxation or borrowing.

Foreign finance raises quite different questions. If a loan is available, by way of foreign assistance, to finance part of the costs of a project, *but is not otherwise available to the country*, it should be brought into consideration from the beginning. Thus, if the generators for a hydro-electric scheme are being provided under a credit which could not otherwise be drawn on, then the foreign exchange cost to the country is not the purchase price of the generators now, but the interest on and repayments of the loan, which will arise only later. The project, with its associated loans, can be evaluated by ignoring the initial cost of items provided under the loan arrangements, and entering in the list of input costs the servicing costs of the loan. In the case of foreign aid it may not always be easy for a recipient country to know whether the aid money would be available for other projects: the clearest case of when it would not be is that of suppliers' credits.

Further difficulties arise. Often a project may have to be evaluated before it is known what the source of the finance will be. This is probably typical of a country receiving aid from many sources. There are then two possibilities: (*a*) to produce as many estimates of PSV as there are potential donors, and (*b*) to evaluate it as if it were to be financed using the country's own reserves; in other words, finance is ignored, and it is assumed that inputs can be purchased in the cheapest market. The former is probably impracticable, since it requires establishing the cost of the inputs from every one of the potential aid-supplying countries. In the latter case, the question arises as to what modifications have to be made, when it becomes allotted to, say, a line of U.S. tied credit. Given that such allotment is definite then the evaluator has to make two adjustments: (*a*) allow for the increased cost (if any) of the equipment which now has to be bought in the U.S.A., and (*b*) incorporate the loan as part of the project in the manner already described.

The latter procedure presumes that those responsible for matching aid to particular uses have done a good job—or anyway that this particular decision to allot the project to U.S. aid is irreversible (unless, of course, the adjustments (*a*) and (*b*) have made the PSV negative, which would be likely only if the aid were on rather unfavourable terms and the particular items of equipment were exceptionally expensive in the U.S.A.).

The task facing those responsible for the best use of aid is an exceptionally difficult one for several reasons: (*a*) projects come up *seriatim*; (*b*) it is probably impracticable, as we have seen, for the project evaluator to produce a whole list of PSVs for every potential donor; and (*c*) it is far from certain that the project in question would be acceptable to all donors.

This difficult process of the optimization of the use of aid may be rendered slightly easier if the present value of loans of various kinds are separately established. It is then quicker and easier to see the implications of attaching them to different projects. This is an easy exercise except in the case of those loans from socialist countries where repayment is accepted in rupees, these rupees being cashed by the export of goods under some barter arrangement. The convertible currency values of these exports then require to be established (see 12.2).

The upshot seems to be that full optimization of the use of foreign credits is outside the bounds of possibility. But rough attempts can be made, if project evaluators indicate at an early stage which projects are likely to be much more desirable if financed by donor A, or much less desirable if financed by B, and which are likely to be comparatively unaffected by the line of credit, and the source of equipment to which they are allotted. If only all aid were untied!

9.7 Some Further Remarks

9.71 *Alternative Techniques and Industrial Expansion*

In this chapter we have been talking about the decision whether or not to undertake a particular project, proposed in a particular form. But often there are a number of alternative projects, i.e. different ways of producing the same product. Then the PSV for each proposal needs to be worked out, and the one with the largest PSV chosen. As was pointed out in Chapter I, there is often a considerable range of choices available, but a detailed cost–benefit calculation can be done for only a few.

If the different ways of making a product—say, cotton textiles—are not mutually exclusive, it is rather odd if several of them come out with a positive PSV. A positive PSV implies that the project ought to be undertaken. What can it mean if highly capital-intensive methods of producing the textiles have a positive PSV, while a rather less capital-intensive method gives a larger PSV per unit of planned output? Obviously, in this case, we can always get a larger PSV by using the less capital-intensive methods, so our calculations ought not to tell us to undertake the more capital-intensive production as well. This might have happened because the ARI was set too low, so that projects which should not be undertaken nevertheless look acceptable. If this is not the case, it follows that the accounting price for cotton textiles is too high. Indeed, the present social value of producing them, *by the best method*, should be very small—only just positive. If cotton textiles are exported, the accounting price is equal to the marginal export revenue. This can be reduced by producing and exporting sufficiently more. If this were done, only one method would be the best. In anticipation of this, the accounting price can be reduced until only one method is acceptable.

Thus, the cost–benefit methods described can be used to decide what kinds of technology to employ. This leaves the problem of what quantity to produce. The above argument shows that production should be planned so that the accounting price will be just high enough to give a positive PSV for the best method of production. So the cost–benefit rules can be used to suggest, for example, just how far exporting in any particular line should be pushed.[1]

The above is one example of how a particular project analysis might properly lead COPE and other branches of government to consider the whole development of an industry. Any project that looks very good when evaluated at the current ARI, and other accounting prices, should lead civil servants and politicians to ask what more of the same kind can be done (and whether competing countries might start doing the same kind of thing!). There is much to be said for planning a carefully scheduled expansion of an industry through a sequence of projects, the whole programme being evaluated together (and revised as time goes on). This kind of sectoral planning is also discussed in 6.3, 6.4 and 10.2.

9.72   *The Operation of Projects*

Another by-product of the arguments of the present chapter is the set of rules for operating projects once they are in commission. We have seen what principles govern the calculation of social profit. Obviously projects should be operated so as to yield as high a social profit in each year as possible. If accounting prices turn out to be different from what was expected, a response may be made to these changed circumstances in the way that the project is used. Lorries might be equipped with tyres made of artificial rather than natural rubber; replacements of parts of an assembly line might be of new design; means might be found for economizing in the use of labour if the shadow wage rate should be higher than expected. Such adaptations will, however, usually depend on market prices being made equal to accounting prices so that the project manager reacts appropriately (see 6.8).

In particular, rules can be derived for deciding when the project should be closed down, or particular pieces of equipment scrapped.

---

[1] This works perfectly satisfactorily only if we exclude one (theoretical) possibility, by assuming that the *accounting price for the product decreases as the amount exported is increased*. The fact that eventually the actual price for the exports will be lower if more are exported, does not prove that the marginal export revenue will also be lower: and it is the marginal export revenue to which the AP is equated. We believe however that a rising AP as more is exported would be exceptional.

Certainly the project should be shut down if the social profit has fallen to zero, and will continue to be negative. Indeed, the project should most probably be closed down before that time, since parts of the plant may have a second-hand or scrap value sufficiently high to make further operation too expensive an 'investment'. In principle, calculations to check whether the operation of the project should continue should be carried out fairly frequently.

It is likely to be easier to carry out cost–benefit calculations for the purposes of investment planning in terms of accounting prices, than to have the day-to-day or even year-to-year operation of the project governed by the same prices.[1] Even so, it may often be useful to know what the correct rules are. And sometimes changes in the operation of a particular project may involve expenditures comparable to those required for the establishment of some new projects, and may therefore be of comparable importance.

9.8 SUMMARY

In this chapter we have attempted to justify certain general principles on which project evaluations can be based. We have shown how commodity accounting prices, the shadow wage rates, and the ARI should be used, and explained what they are and what kind of thing one should be trying to estimate. The reader whose main concern is with the public sector, and who is prepared to neglect the problems of economies of scale, may now want to go straight to Chapters XII and XIV, where we discuss methods that may be used in practice to put numbers to the various accounting prices.

It should be emphasized that the simplifying assumptions that have been made in this chapter can be quite important, though not by any means for all projects or industries.

---

[1] See also 6.8.

CHAPTER TEN

Large-scale Production

10.1 THE BENEFITS OF A LARGE PROJECT
If accounting prices would be much the same whether or not the project was set up, then it is legitimate to measure the social value of production by multiplying the levels of the various inputs and outputs by the corresponding APs. The accounting price for cotton cloth is supposed to tell us the value, in terms of foreign exchange, of producing an extra unit of cloth; if we intend to produce a million units, and the extra foreign exchange earned will be the same for each successive unit, the total gain in foreign exchange is indeed the quantity produced times the AP (in this case, the export price).

For many small projects, this is a reasonable assumption. And even with quite large plants, any effect on APs can usually be neglected when choosing the best means of production: e.g., the choice between nuclear and thermal power stations. In this latter case, as explained in 9.42, the choice of the best method (or, if the best method is unlikely to be adopted, the most likely method) will also give the AP for the output, and the only task remaining is to estimate the demand that should be supplied at that price. However, we still have to consider cases where the whole of domestic production might be done in one or two plants, not necessarily large enough to make full use of all possible economies of scale; or where a new good (such as piped water, or radio transmission) is introduced to a new locality.

10.11 *A Traded Good with Economies of Scale*
There are a number of industries where, subject to the provision of a reasonable variety of products, one usually wants to produce on as large a scale as possible. Aircraft, automobiles, computers, and railways, are all examples where large 'overhead' costs must be incurred if any production is to take place (at a reasonable cost). The greater is production, the greater is the number of units of output over which these overhead costs are spread. The reason why a production plant in these industries is not always of enormous size, is that the limited market and the presence of other firms make production on too large a scale unprofitable. Naturally, this may be an extremely important problem for small countries. Often

large-scale production would commit them to attempting to export, possibly in very risky markets.[1]

We shall not deal with all the problems of deciding whether, when, where, and to what extent it is worth venturing into large-scale production. We shall limit ourselves to explaining how a particular proposal for a large-scale plant can be evaluated, and indicate briefly the nature of the alternative plants that might have to be considered, and the extension of our methods that might be used to choose amongst them.

We are presented with plans for a very large project: large in the sense that whether or not it is undertaken makes a substantial difference to the price of at least one of its outputs or inputs; but not so large that it enjoys all possible economies of scale. Let us suppose that the problem is whether or not to establish a steel foundry. We recall that the first principle is to examine and attempt to quantify the benefits and costs resulting from the actual changes in the economy that the establishment of the project will lead to. Since these changes are measured in terms of the foreign exchange they earn or use, we examine the effect on the foreign exchange balance if a large-scale steel foundry is set up. To bring all the main points out at once, let us suppose that at present the country is importing all its steel, but that the proposed foundry is so large that a substantial part of its output will be available for export if the scheme is accepted.

Let us take it that the changes in inputs required are not so large as to lead to any significant change in their accounting prices. This might not be realistic if the country had to change from being an iron ore exporter into an importer, or if it had to go further afield for imports of coking coal, but it is easier to see what is going on if we concentrate on the output, and anyway the same principles apply when further complications are introduced.

The value of the output can be divided into three parts:

(i) the foreign exchange saved by not importing. This is equal to the total foreign exchange that would be spent on the relevant kind of steel imports, if the project were not undertaken;

(ii) the earnings of foreign exchange as a result of exporting some of the production if the foundry is established. This would

---

[1] It may be very advantageous for several countries to cooperate in large-scale investment so that they do not all try to make automobiles, for instance, but benefit from having all their requirements produced in a single plant.

be estimated by multiplying the excess of production over domestic demand by the expected average export price. Domestic demand is the amount of steel that will be used if the accounting price is the export price of steel (less a possible allowance for some price sensitivity of export demand);

(iii) the benefit to the country of using more steel than it otherwise would have done. More steel will be used because the accounting price for steel is lower when it is being exported instead of imported.

The part of the benefit that is most difficult to estimate is the last. It is *less* than could have been obtained from the foreign exchange required to import the extra steel that will be used if the project is set up; for, in fact, the country would have chosen *not* to import more steel: on the other hand, it is *more* than could be obtained from the foreign exchange that could be earned by exporting the extra steel consumed; since, in fact, the choice will be not to export so much. If the import and export prices of steel are fairly similar, or if the change in the domestic use of steel would not be very large, one could take the average of the two figures without fear of seriously distorting the assessment. Only exceptionally would this rough means of approximating to the benefit of using more steel be misleading. Since it is very troublesome to make any more accurate assessment, it is as well to use this simple method. As it happens, most of the products that enjoy important economies of scale are easily traded.[1]

The diagram in Figure 2 may be a convenient way of remembering the various elements in this calculation. The quantity of domestic production is measured on the horizontal axis, marginal import cost and marginal export revenue on the vertical axis. The falling continuous lines show the way in which the price paid for imports, or received for exports, depends upon the planned scale of production. The dotted line represents the 'averaging' method of estimating the value of the increased domestic use of steel. It is the total area under the curve—shown shaded in the diagram—that measures the estimated benefit of the planned output, in terms of foreign exchange.

Notice that, in this case, the accounting price at each level of possible production is the marginal social benefit. We can therefore refer to the curve drawn in Figure 2 as the MSB curve. If we were

---

[1] An important exception is railway transport, which we do not discuss in this book. The methods indicated in 10.13 would normally need to be used.

considering a large project using an input whose accounting price varied significantly within the scale of use contemplated (e.g. an agricultural raw material obtained by replacing production of an alternative crop on successively less favourable land), we should have to use an MSC curve, defined in a similar way.

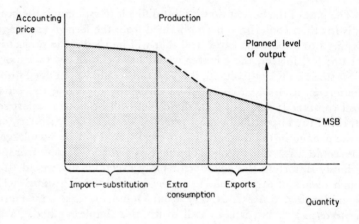

Figure 2

By calculating the value of production as described, one can estimate the benefit of the project in each year: after allowing for the cost of inputs, this gives the social profit, which can then be discounted in the usual way to obtain the PSV. If it is positive, there is a gain from undertaking the project, as compared to using the investment funds for some other project in a different sector of the economy.

It must be recognized that such a calculation will normally require a great deal of research and careful guesswork, not least because the MSB curve will change from year to year. This is no small matter, for it is just in such cases as steel, transport equipment, etc., that the market, particularly the domestic market, for the commodity is likely to grow rapidly. The quantity that would have been imported had there been no domestic production might double in five to ten years. For this reason it is important to calculate the foreign exchange gains with some care for a number of different years of the plant's probable life.

10.2 SCALE AND TIMING

There is yet another aspect to be considered when estimating the value of the plant's output. As the market grows, and technology improves, it is to be expected that, at some date in the future, a new, and probably much improved, plant will be established; and later, while the original plant is still operating, yet more new plants may be built. The existence of these later plants will affect the value of the first plant. For, when we are considering how valuable this first plant is, we must consider what it will add to the economy, *assuming that the later plants will be built anyway.*

The above situation is illustrated in Figure 3, where MSB curves are drawn for Year 1, the first year of full capacity output by the

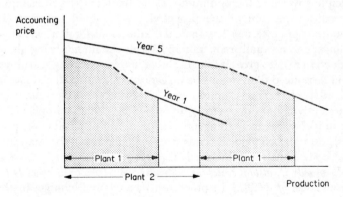

Figure 3

initial plant, and for Year 5, when a new plant has just come into full capacity operation. It is assumed that the new plant is larger than the old. (This need not be true, and would require special consideration in each case.) The MSB in Year 5 is shown as greater than in Year 1: this is mainly for convenience, and does not affect the argument. The shaded areas show the estimated benefit of planned output from the first plant in Years 1 and 5. It is clear from the diagram that the value of production in Year 5 is less than would have been thought if no allowance had been made for the building of a new plant in the interim. (It would then have been the area under the Year 5 curve corresponding to the position of plant 1 in Year 1.)

This analysis forces us to consider how big the second plant will be (and later plants as well). It should be assumed that the second and subsequent plants will be chosen on the basis of cost–benefit calculations too. However, we have not yet discussed the principles that should govern the choice of scale for a large investment project. To this issue we now turn.

In the previous sub-section, so as to establish principles clearly, we concentrated on the case where the project evaluator is presented with a fully determined production plan, and has only to consider whether it is worth having or not. But decisions about scale and timing ought also to be taken on the basis of accounting prices. The principle governing the optimum scale of the plant is quite simple. A (small) expansion of the proposed plant should not cost (in accounting price terms) less than the additional foreign exchange earnings; and a (small) reduction in its scale should not bring about a reduction in costs greater than the loss of foreign exchange earnings. It will be noticed that, so long as we concentrate on small changes in the basic project plan—and to save extensive work, project planners are well advised to do so—the gain or loss in benefit is simply given (per unit) by the accounting price at the level of production proposed, and the changes in costs are just (per unit) the marginal social cost. Thus the principle is that *the proposed scale of production is optimal only if, at that scale, the discounted sum of MSCs is equal to the discounted sum of MSBs.*[1] In other words, any small change in the scale of the plant would leave its PSV virtually unchanged.

The question of timing is not quite so readily dealt with. Even if

---

[1] As economists know, this condition is *necessary* for optimum scale, but not *sufficient*. It might be satisfied, and yet a greater or smaller scale be better. But we doubt whether most project evaluators need worry too much about this point.

the project would yield a positive PSV if started at some proposed date, it should not necessarily be started then; for once it is started, it precludes starting up newer projects, at least for a time. It might have been better to wait for a year or two, either because the value of production will be much greater in a few years than in the immediate future; or because there is a good prospect that the costs or performance of new plant for the industry will improve in the near future. As a rough guide, one can say that *it is best to postpone building the plant if the sum of the probable rate of technical improvement (measured by cost reductions brought about by new plant), and the rate of increase of the value of production, is greater than the ARI.* If this is the case, a project evaluation of the postponed project, with social profits discounted back to the present, will yield a greater PSV than would the unpostponed project. Generally speaking, however, a more precise way to determine whether postponement is desirable is to do a separate cost–benefit calculation for the project postponed by a year or two (always discounting back to the same date as is used for the original project), in order to determine whether the PSV is thereby increased.

It is thus not particularly hard, though it may take a lot of work, to make a good choice of scale and timing for a particular project, provided one can take the future development of the industry as known. But now we return to the considerations brought up at the beginning of this sub-section, where we pointed out that the decision about the initial project actually depends upon choices of scale and timing for future plant in the same industry.[1] In other words, if the analysis is to be done thoroughly, it will be necessary to work out a development plan simultaneously for the whole future of the industry. As more information becomes available in future, the industry will not actually follow that plan, but this calculation is the only way of making coherent predictions of future development.

This requirement raises mathematical and computational difficulties of some severity, which could, however, be overcome in most particular cases. Necessarily, however, considerable technical expertise in the field of operational research, particularly dynamic programming, would be required.[2] It is not the purpose of this book to go into techniques of that kind. We simply point to their value in a case such as this. Ideally, where industries with important economies of scale are concerned, planners should seek well-worked-

---

[1] And perhaps, in some cases, also in related industries.

[2] Some problems of this kind are discussed, with particular reference to a developing economy, in Manne, 1967.

out development plans for the industries, rather than cost–benefit evaluations of single projects. Having said this, there are two points we want to make. The first is that such technical studies will be worse than useless if they do not use the same basic procedure—involving accounting prices and so on—as other economic planning. The second point is that something can be done if the more sophisticated analysis we have referred to is deemed impracticable.

What can be done is to make an intelligent guess as to the probable future development of the industry, and evaluate the initial plant (or whatever plant is to be evaluated) against the background of that guessed development. This is a possible procedure because, very often, there will be good grounds for assuming a particular rate of growth for the industry, and for assuming—perhaps on the basis of experience in other countries—the scale on which future plant will be built. With a certain amount of back-of-envelope calculation, one can then make sensible assumptions about the timing of future projects. True, one is probably not making very good assumptions about the future development. But it is unlikely that the present investment decision will be *very* sensitive to assumptions about future development. Furthermore, if the result of the cost–benefit analysis suggests that the future development initially assumed is badly wrong (e.g. because it suggests considerable postponement of the initial development, or a much larger initial scale), one can revise the initial guess. And it is always possible to work decisions out on the basis of one or two alternative pictures of future developments in the industry. If a really good and careful technical analysis cannot be obtained, we certainly think that these more rough and ready procedures should be used. But it must always be remembered that large-scale projects can involve the economy in enormous social gains or losses, and for that reason they deserve rather large expenditure of research resources.

It is for this reason, as well as for the reasons indicated above, that we think it important, when large-scale projects are under consideration, to work out the PSV of a number of well-researched variants, involving different scales, and different timing of the initial developments.

10.3 PRODUCTION OF A NON-TRADED CONSUMER GOOD

Another circumstance in which the project itself may have a significant effect on the relevant accounting price (or accounting prices) is that in which a new good or service is introduced into a

town or village, or, more generally, where transport costs are so high that a small local project has a large effect on total supply and demand in the locality. To see how these cases may be treated, we discuss two examples—a local water-supply project, and a telephone system.

We consider a water-supply project first, because it may not involve any charges to users. We suppose that its cost, in terms of accounting prices, is known, and the question is how great are the benefits. The benefits accrue to the households that get, or use, the water supply. We must assess the benefit to each of the households and add up all these household benefits. The case is particularly awkward in practice because—in the absence of water charges— the commodity has no price. However, a sample of households can be taken, and each one asked what it would be willing to pay for access to the water supply. How much a household would be willing to pay[1] measures the value of the water supply to that household, relative to other things the household consumes.

If we can find out the willingness-to-pay of each household, we must convert that money amount to accounting-price terms by multiplying by the weight attached to that household's income,[2] relative to the numéraire (uncommitted social income). Broadly speaking, the weight will be lower, the richer the household: we shall say more about all this in Chapter XIII. The value of the commodity is then the weighted sum of the estimated willingness-to-pay. There are two steps in this procedure, and they are both awkward: the weighting step we are postponing for the moment; the other step is the estimation of willingness-to-pay.

There are two particular difficulties about estimating willingness-to-pay. The first is that, in practice, households which have seldom had much experience of the kind of water supply proposed, nor of expressing that kind of want in monetary terms, will probably find it hard to predict how much they would be willing to pay even if they knew just what difference it would make to them. The second difficulty is that, even if the consumer understood perfectly the nature of the charge and what was being asked of him, it would not be in his interest to answer honestly, since he would not actually be

---

[1] This is one definition of what economists call 'consumer surplus'.

[2] The weight might actually depend on much more than income—family size, age, environment, and access to economic opportunities might all be relevant. Also, it is conceivable that the project would so change the economic status of the household as to change the appropriate weight. Something will be said about all these issues in 13.13.

paying what he said he was willing to pay. Nevertheless, whatever the difficulties, willingness-to-pay is what has to be estimated. Fortunately, many consumers try to be honest, and most understand the uses of money. Also, there will usually be some possibility of studying earlier projects of the same kind. No one would pretend that evaluations in such circumstances are easy, but it is as well to know what one is trying to estimate.

Before leaving this particular case, it should be remarked that, even if no charges for the use of water are levied, an improvement in the standard of living brought about by such a development may make possible increased local taxation. Whether this is so should always be considered, and if it is thought possible, an estimate of such increased government revenue should be included in the project evaluation, just as in the case of other non-traded goods discussed in 9.43 and 12.3.

The other imaginary project we want to discuss is that of a new telephone service. The same general principles apply, but this time there is a price for the commodity, which gives us some information about the value that consumers put on the service. However, if a man makes 100 local telephone calls a year when the price is 10 cents a call, we cannot deduce that the existence of the telephone service is worth 1,000 cents a year to him. Obviously it is worth more. Perhaps if the price were 20 cents, he would make 30 calls—so these calls are worth at least 600 cents to him; and if he is then charged 10 cents per call for any further calls, he will still make the other 70 (assuming none of this has any significant effect on his total income), spending 1,300 cents in all. So his willingness-to-pay is at least 1,300 cents; and we might by more complicated charging systems discover that it was much more. It is clear that the consumer's behaviour as the price of the service varies is very relevant to estimating his willingness-to-pay. We shall explain how this might be used to get reasonable estimates in 12.41.

In the case of the new telephone service, the calculation of benefits would, once willingness-to-pay had been estimated, go as follows. Each consumer is better off to the extent of his willingness-to-pay, less what he actually pays. These amounts are to be weighted and added as before. In addition, the total payments made constitute a gain of uncommitted income for the state (assuming the telephone service is provided by the public sector). This gain is equal to the value of other goods and services which the consumer now does without: since some of these will be taxed (or subsidized), it is necessary to convert this income to accounting prices in order to derive uncommitted social income, which then goes on to the benefit side unweighted. This adjustment is done by means of a conversion factor which is discussed in 12.35.

Although it is not at this point our main concern, it is worth remarking that the above calculation would underestimate the benefits of the telephone service, since each user would be willing to pay for other users to be connected (so that he could communicate with them). In particular, a widely connected telephone system may be of considerable value to productive enterprises and to government. Thus the chief items on the benefit side when appraising a telephone system are likely to be, not the consumers' surpluses of the householders (who are likely to be rather well off), but the gains to producers, and the gain in government revenue.

CHAPTER ELEVEN

Private Sector Investment

A private sector investment project is, like a public sector project, a user of inputs and producer of outputs, which can therefore be evaluated using accounting prices, by the methods suggested in Chapter IX. But the sources of the investment funds, and the uses to which the profits are put, require us to make further adjustments.

11.1 CAPITALIST INCOME AND CONSUMPTION

11.11 *Estimating Consumption*

What distinguishes a private project from a public, apart from any difference that private incentives may make to performance—a difference that should in principle be reflected in the estimates of social income generated—is that part of the profit is available to owners of capital for their own uses, and part at least of the finance of investment comes from private funds. The part of profits that accrues to the capitalists may all be consumed, or part may be saved (for the sake of future consumption, presumably): the extra savings, if any, would augment the private funds available for private investment. In order to evaluate a private sector project, therefore, we must have methods for measuring the value of capitalist consumption, and the value of private investment funds. These methods are discussed in 11.12 and 11.2. But first, it is necessary to say something about estimating the increase in capitalist consumption that the project makes possible.

Private capitalists must get some reward—some increase in wealth—if they are to be willing to undertake investments. On the face of it, more wealth is a reason for consuming more. If the investors can borrow readily at reasonable rates of interest, on the security of the approved project, or by abandoning other less profitable activities, they can start consuming more as soon as the project is approved.

We need to estimate how much more the private capitalists will consume. No general rule can be expected to apply perfectly everywhere, but the following method may be sufficiently accurate. First, estimate the increased income the capitalist gains from the project. This is the excess of total capitalist income from the project over what the funds invested might be expected to have earned for him in another use. The capitalists *could* consume this amount extra, as a result of being able to undertake the project, and they may well do so, particularly if approving one project makes them more optimistic about the approval of similar investments later. But it may be more likely that they will save part of this increase in income, and we allow for that possibility.

To show in detail how the estimation can be done, it is a help to have some notation:

I = the capital cost, to private capitalists, of the project.

r = the rate of return, after tax, at which the investors would on average have invested their funds elsewhere: this return may often most realistically be regarded as the average rate of return expected for direct investment in the private sector, rather than the rate of interest on bonds: but it may be some mixture of the two.

P_t = the gross profit of the project in year t, *less* company and personal tax liability arising from that profit,[1] *less* an allowance for depreciation sufficient to leave the investors with wealth I (in real terms) at the end of the project's life.

σ = the proportion of capitalist income that is saved (i.e. not consumed).

Then we estimate that, in year t,

Capitalist consumption = $(1 - \sigma)\ (P_t - rI)$

Capitalist saving = $\sigma\ (P_t - rI)$.

Because capital gains are subject to considerable fluctuations, we recommend basing the estimate on the actual profit made by the project, rather than upon dividends paid to shareholders plus capital gains on the shares in that year. Of course, it is also much easier to base the estimate on profits to the company.

Both capitalist consumption and capitalist saving (which is a way of postponing consumption on the part of the capitalists) represent costs to the economy, since they involve a commitment of social income to purposes that are likely to be less valuable than the uses

---

[1] In calculating liability for company taxation, allowable depreciation deductions must be made. Personal liability to income and similar taxes may be hard to estimate if the project is managed by a limited company, especially when dividends may be taxed at one rate and capital gains at another. In the latter case, capital gains tax should be assumed equal to a tax on retained profits at the personal income tax rate appropriate to the income of the average shareholder.

to which the government would put uncommitted social income. Both should be measured in APs, and that will normally require conversion from market prices. In the remainder of this section, we discuss the social cost of the consumption, assuming it is measured in APs. The saving represents an increase in the total investment funds of private capitalists, and we shall discuss the evaluation of these investment funds in 11.2.

11.12 *The Value of Capitalist Consumption*
In order to decide what capitalist consumption is worth, we have to face again the problem of weighing one man's consumption against another's. This problem is discussed in 13.1, and we rely to some extent on that discussion now. But the general idea will be clear without it: one can often deal with capitalist consumption very easily. We argue as follows.

For most private *industrial* projects, it can reasonably be assumed (unless there is evidence to the contrary) that those who will receive the profits, be they shareholders, partners, or owners, are wealthy, with annual consumption expenditure ten, twenty, or even a hundred times as great as an average peasant farmer or urban labourer. For this reason, we think, and we think that most governments would agree, that an increase in the consumption of such people deserves only a very small weight in comparison with the average consumer, and even less in comparison with uncommitted social income. Thus the whole of the consumption of rich capitalists (evaluated at accounting prices, of course) may be counted as a cost of the project, since the direct value of the additional consumption—though perhaps a positive good—is not sufficiently important to be worth including in the calculation.[1] We are not denying that there is a social need to allow capitalists to consume: if private investment has advantages, they have to be paid for, by allowing this consumption.

Private investment by small enterprises, or small farmers, may

---

[1] There is an old argument that the consumption of the rich *is* socially valuable insofar as it provides employment for the poor—e.g. by employing domestic servants, tailors, hotel and restaurant staff, and so on. We have allowed for whatever is valid in this argument when we say that the cost of the capitalist's consumption is to be evaluated at accounting prices. If the shadow wage of domestic servants is low, the accounting cost of capitalist consumption is reduced accordingly. But there is still some cost, and it may be quite large. It would be wrong to regard the employment provided by capitalist consumption as positively valuable, thus justifying that consumption, when the government could have made better use of the labour if it had itself had the social income to spend.

have to be treated rather differently. Firstly, the investors' normal level of consumption expenditure may be rather small, so that increases deserve a significant weight in measuring the benefits of the project: therefore the whole of the investors' consumption will not count as a cost, only the difference between its value as uncommitted social income and its value as their own consumption. Secondly, these investors may not be able to borrow easily for new investment, and may therefore have to finance part of it out of consumption.

To see how this last possibility should be treated, consider an extreme case, in which an investment is financed entirely by foregoing consumption. In such a case the whole of profits P_t might be consumed as they accrue. If that is expected to happen, the profits count as benefit to the extent appropriate to the investing group, and that proportion is added to the rest of social profit (which equals social income, less the committed consumption of the investors and others, plus the value of this committed consumption). Similarly, since the investment cost is not met out of uncommitted social income, but out of consumption, which is less valuable, the cost is counted simply as the social value of the loss of consumption by the group in question.

The general rule is, however, to subtract from apparent social profit (i.e. what would be social profit, if the project were in the public sector) the consumption of the capitalists; this is conveniently estimated as profit after tax, less the income that would have accrued at the average *real* rate of interest (i.e. the money rate of interest less the expected rate of inflation) on investments normally available to capitalists.

11.2 THE COST OF PRIVATE INVESTMENT

The way to value privately financed investment is easily stated: find the PSV of the same resources used as they would be if the project were not approved. The difficulty is that there are a number of different possible uses, which could well have quite different social values (the social value being different from the value to the private investor). For example,

(i) the investment funds might have been lent to the government, by purchasing government bonds (at a real rate of interest r). This case is easy: by approving the private project, the government is deprived of investment funds it could have used itself. The real counterpart of this is that the opportunity cost of the private investment is a public investment using an equivalent amount of real resources. The cost is therefore precisely what it would have been if the project had been in the public sector. But we doubt whether this is normally an alternative for businessmen and those accustomed to hold industrial shares.

(ii) The funds might have been sent abroad. Then their value is the present value, discounted at the ARI, of any tax that may be due on remitted dividends, etc. That might be equal to the unadjusted social cost of the investment, but would generally be less. In extreme cases, where the taxes are zero, or nothing is remitted, perhaps because the transaction is illegal, the value in this alternative use is zero.

(iii) The funds might be lent to private individuals to finance consumption. This might happen directly or indirectly. A common example of the indirect effect is where land or some other fixed asset is purchased, and the seller uses his receipts for his own consumption and to pay off debts, thus financing consumption by his debtors. Then the value of the investment is the social value of the consumption that the lending allows—which will probably be much less than the apparent social cost of the investment.

(iv) The resources might have been used for other private business ventures not requiring government approval. The value is then the PSV of these alternative productive activities, with proper allowance made for any private consumption arising. It is plausible, but not certain, that this value too will be less than the value of the investment funds as uncommitted social income.

(v) The resources might have been used for other private projects requiring government approval. If private savings have to be used largely in projects requiring government approval, it is possible that the government will feel committed to allowing enough projects to use all the available saving. In that case, the problem is solved by finding the accounting price for privately financed investment which will lead to the right volume of private investment being approved.

Which of the above possibilities is most important must be considered specially for each country. We tie the whole exercise together by introducing an *accounting price for private investment*

(APPI), which is a number, normally less than one. *It is defined as the value of a unit of social income (measured in APs, of course) which is devoted to investment by the private sector.* Then the investment costs of a private sector project are evaluated for the purpose of a cost–benefit analysis by working out the cost of the inputs used, at accounting prices, and multiplying that figure by the APPI.

Although circumstances vary, we think that the main alternative use of the funds is usually (iv). A rough guess at the kind of use to which the funds might be put under (iv) will be needed: some imaginary, but realistic, project can then be evaluated with accounting prices so as to estimate the value of a typical non-approved use of funds. An appropriately weighted average of the cost in the different alternative uses (i)–(v) will then complete the required estimate of the APPI.

The APPI should be used to evaluate the worth of the capitalist saving arising out of project profits, estimated above as $\sigma(P_t - rI)$, as well as for costing the initial finance of the project. Since the APPI will normally be assumed constant, the fact that the value of the typical private project itself depends on the APPI will cause no difficulty in calculating it by the method just suggested.[1]

There may sometimes be several different sources of private funds, with only imperfect connections between them—for example, different racial groups or different regions may have to be thought of as providing different pools of investment funds. In that case, different APPIs would be required. Also, as we have seen, programmes involving investment by small enterprises and farmers may be evaluated in quite a different way, when investment is financed by foregoing consumption.

11.3 Foreign Investment

Funds that come from abroad are a somewhat different matter, but very easily dealt with (see 7.3), except for one consideration. The accounting price of the investment in this case is zero, since the funds are normally of no use to the country in question if they are used in some other part of the world. Capitalist income from the project is profit after tax. If it is all remitted abroad at once, it

---

[1] For instance, if the investment of capitalist savings of 100 now produces a stream of future social profit (neglecting future capitalist savings) with a PSV of 70, plus future capitalist savings with a PV of 10 when discounted at the ARI, then the APPI is $\dfrac{70}{100-10} = \dfrac{7}{9}$.

naturally all counts as cost: these remittances are the cost of foreign investment, and the question is whether social returns to the country justify that cost. However, part of after-tax profits will generally be ploughed back within the country: there may even be a requirement that this be done when the project (or industry) is approved. How should these ploughed-back profits be valued?

The answer is quite easy if the relevant accounting prices are not expected to change much, and if one can presume that the retained profits will be ploughed back into projects of much the same kind as the one now under consideration. If it can be assumed that such projects would also have the same value in the future as they have today, then we may as well evaluate the project as though the retained profits were actually remitted at once. For, if our evaluation gives a positive PSV on this assumption, then allowing for ploughed-back profits would add to the value of the project, which should therefore be approved; while, on the other hand, a negative PSV, on the assumption that all profits are remitted at once, would actually be further reduced when the negative value of ploughing-back was allowed for.

However, at least in the case of important projects, it should not be assumed too readily that accounting prices will stay constant. Furthermore, it is quite likely that profits will be ploughed back into somewhat different kinds of production (as when the profits of automobile assembly are ploughed back into, say, engine manufacture). In principle, the social value of the uses to which ploughed-back profits will be put should be estimated right into the whole future—which is clearly rather a difficult exercise. We would suggest that the project evaluator consider what kind of projects retained profits are likely to be used for, half-way through the (initial) project's life, and evaluate that use, on the assumption that still later retentions will all be used in the same kind of use, with similar accounting prices. This sounds complicated, but it is actually quite easy to calculate the value of putting funds into a particular use when a proportion of the profits is ploughed back into the same use: one simply discounts, not at the ARI, but at a discount rate equal to the ARI minus the rate of plough-back (i.e. the amount ploughed back per unit invested).[1]

---

[1] This proposition rests on the assumption, which is reasonable in practice, that capital recently ploughed back will earn the same social profit as capital ploughed back some time ago. The proof runs as follows:

Let A_s be the social profit in year s on a unit of capital invested, not counting any ploughed-back profits. That is, A is the social income of the project, less the

Finally, we remind the reader that many projects involve a combination of two, or even all three, of the various kinds of financing we have considered: public investment, private domestic investment, and private investment from abroad. Now that we have shown how to evaluate the costs and benefits for each particular method, it is easy to do the same for any mixture of the methods.

11.4 THE EVALUATION PROCEDURE SUMMARIZED BY AN EXAMPLE

We have discussed the principles that should guide evaluation of a private sector project. We have pointed out that projects involving many small firms or other small enterprises may need to be treated somewhat differently from, say, large urban industrial projects. We now summarize the procedure for the latter case, in terms of an example.

Take the simple example discussed in 9.13, but suppose it to be a private project. Eight million accounting rupees is spent on capital equipment (bought from abroad, and valued at c.i.f. prices, or built at home and valued by using the shadow wage rate, and other accounting prices as required), and as a result a social profit of 1 million rupees per year for twenty years is obtained. The calculation consists of the following steps:

(i) *Estimate private profit.* We shall suppose that a typical year's activity can be summarized as follows (for convenience we write everything in thousands of rupees):

	At market prices	At accounting prices
Output	3,000	1,800
Material inputs	1,000	400
Labour	500	400
Profit	1,500	1,000

We now deduct profit and income taxes, and make an allowance for

after-tax profits accruing to the owners. Let v_t be the value (then) of a unit of capital ploughed into the business in year t. Let R be the ARI, and p the ploughback rate, both supposed constant. Then, using integrals for convenience,

$$v_t = \int_t^\infty e^{-R(s-t)}(A_s + pv_s)ds.$$

Therefore, differentiating with respect to t.

$$v = Rv_t - A_t - pv_t = (R-p)v_t - A_t.$$

Integration of this equation gives

$$v_t = \int_t^\infty e^{-(R-p)(s-t)}A_s ds,$$

verifying the proposition stated in the text.

depreciation. The calculation might go:

Depreciation	−300
Net profit	1,200
Corporation tax	
(30% of net profit)	−360
Net profit after tax	840
Income tax on dividends	−168
Capitalist income after tax	672

(ii) *Estimate the real rate of interest* for private capitalists. Let us assume that a direct (non-portfolio) investor can earn 9% on his capital after tax without undue trouble or especially good luck. The current rate of inflation, which is expected to continue, is 4%. Therefore the real rate of interest on this class of investment is 5%. Other possible uses of private money are government bonds, and moneylending (see (vi), below). The former have a lower and the latter a higher real yield. Since they are also among the minor uses of capitalist money, 5% can stand as an estimate of the real rate of interest (r).

(iii) *Estimate increased capitalist income.* This is done by subtracting interest from the estimate of capitalist income obtained in (i). The initial capital cost of the project at market prices is 10 million rupees. Therefore we must deduct 500,000 rupees:

$$\text{Income increase} = P - rI = 172.$$

(iv) *Estimate capitalist consumption and saving.* We suppose that enquiries have shown that typical shareholders in the kind of firm undertaking the project save about 20% of income (including capital gains). This is one of the figures that will generally have to be guessed on fairly inadequate evidence. It must be remembered that some of the shareholders may actually be dissaving—i.e. running down their wealth—because they are retired, for example. Thus we estimate

Extra Capitalist consumption	=	137·5
Extra Capitalist saving	=	34·5

(v) *Convert to Accounting Prices.* If one knew exactly what this consumption and saving would be used to purchase, one would evaluate it by using APs instead of market prices for the various goods and services. Usually one will not have such detailed information and shortcuts will be needed: this will be discussed in the next chapter. In the present case, we shall take it that information, including some intelligent guesswork, about the consumption expenditure of rich families, has suggested that the market prices for consumption are on average 30% above the accounting prices (largely because of taxes, but also because the shadow wage rate for labour employed in personal services is quite low). Therefore

Extra Consumption at APs = 106.

Conversion of the saving figure is trickier because the uses to which the saving can be put are so diverse. But the figure is in any case not large, so that something quite crude will do. In general the prices of investment goods are guessed to be 20% above APs, and alternative investment is thought to be the major use of private savings, so we estimate

Saving at APs = 29.

(vi) *Find the Accounting Price of Private Investment (APPI)*. Suppose that a research institute has obtained evidence that about a fifth of private capital is held in government bonds (this part has a weight of unity), a fifth in private lending most probably for consumption, or in land which may also be thought of as financing consumption. The remainder is held in shares, partnerships, etc. The consumption financed by the saving is judged to be by relatively wealthy groups. By using the Census of Manufacturing Industry, it is estimated that, in the past, social income devoted to private investment has earned a social rate of return of 6% (the evaluation of capitalist saving has a negligible effect on this figure). Some improvement is expected, to an extent that ought to bring the average up to around 8%. The ARI is 10%. Thus the APPI is obtained as follows:

APPI = $\frac{1}{5}$ × value in consumption lending + $\frac{1}{5}$ × value in government bonds + $\frac{3}{5}$ × value in private investment

$= \frac{1}{5} \times 0 + \frac{1}{5} \times 1 + \frac{3}{5} \times \frac{8}{10}$

$= 0.68$.

(vii) *Estimate Social Profit*. We subtract consumption and saving, both at accounting prices, from the original figure for profits at accounting prices in (i). But we have to add on a figure for the social value of the saving, which is the amount of saving times the APPI.

Profit at APs	1,000	
Less consumption		106
Less saving		29
Plus saving × APPI		20
Social Profit	885	

(viii) *Finally, compute Present Social Value.*

$$PSV = -0.68 \times 8,000 + \left[\frac{1}{1 \cdot 1} + \frac{1}{(1 \cdot 1)^2} + \cdots \frac{1}{(1 \cdot 1)^{20}} \right] \times 885$$

$$= +2,080, \text{ approx.}$$

The result is that this project is socially more profitable as a private sector than as a public sector project. The reason is worth some discussion.

In the formula for the PSV given above the transition from a public to a private sector evaluation is made by multiplying the capital cost by the APPI, and the stream of net benefits by the proportion which the social value of the private profit bears to the profit at accounting prices.

The APPI plays only a small role in this latter adjustment, which can be neglected. If the project has zero PSV in the public sector, which is the most interesting case, then its PSV considered as a private sector project will be positive or negative depending on whether the APPI is smaller or larger than the proportionate adjustment factor for private profits (in the above case these were respectively 0·680 and 0·885). We may also note that the net allowance for private savings is likely to be very small, so that the adjustment can be thought of primarily as an adjustment for capitalists' consumption. Given the tax system, the adjustment for private capitalists' consumption depends largely on the divergence between private and social profitability. If a project would have, say, zero PSV with 10% ARI in the public sector, but is extremely profitable in the private sector, then the adjustment for capitalists' consumption is relatively large (in our example the private IRR was not very much greater than the public). The fiercer and more effective the tax system, however, the lower will be the adjustment for consumption.

The APPI is probably harder to estimate than the adjustment for consumption. It can also have a much larger range, from 0 to 1. It may also vary markedly with the type of investor, who has different opportunities open. In the above example the figure of 0.68 was perhaps fairly low, because as much as 20% of the funds were assumed to flow into consumption. It seems clear that it is worth doing a lot of work on the problem of estimating the APPI in countries where domestic private capital is an important source of funds, and private projects can be and are evaluated from a social point of view.

It will probably have surprised the reader that a project in the private sector can be worth more than the same project in the public sector, when we have emphasized that public profit must normally be considered to be more valuable than private profit. The reason is that public investible resources are also more valuable than private investible resources.

Finally, we should say that our example (or any other similar construct) throws little or no light on the relative merits of public and private ownership, even at the margin in a mixed economy: this is because it assumes no difference in the inputs and outputs, which is to assume away a large part of any controversy. Even less does it throw any light on the merits of a large shift: this is because the opportunities open to private savers would be very different in a predominantly capitalist and in a predominantly socialist economy.

11.5   THE SOCIAL COST AND VALUE OF PRIVATE PROFITS
It may be useful in some analyses and calculations to have a weight for private profit which can be applied to a change occurring as a result of a change in wages (see 13.42); or, indeed, to any change in the total of private profits.

The previous example suffices to show how this calculation can be made. The net private profit after tax was 672 (thousand rupees). This was divided as to 538 of consumption (80%) and 134 of savings (20%). The latter two figures are transformed into accounting prices, and become 414 and 112 respectively. The social cost of the consumption remains at 414. The social cost of the savings is arrived at by multiplying by $(1-\text{APPI})$, and becomes 36. Thus the total social cost becomes 450, while the gross social income in APs was 1,000. Therefore the social profit is 550, and the weight is 0·55. In other words, private profit in APs is worth 0·55 of public profit. If this weight is combined with the conversion factor which reduced a profit of 1,500 at market prices to one of 1,000 at APs, we also have it that social profit in APs is 37% of private profit at market prices.

The figures given are, of course, purely illustrative. They should be worked out, not from a particular project, but using average levels of taxation and conversion factors for the private sector as a whole, or relevant parts of it.

CHAPTER TWELVE

Commodity Accounting Prices

In this and the following chapters we show how the principles we have described can be put into practice. In so doing, we shall not only carry the reader to the point where he could use the method to evaluate particular projects; we shall also tie up a few loose ends that have been left earlier on.

The accounting prices of commodities, it will be remembered, are based, directly or indirectly, on border prices. The problems can be quite different from one commodity to another. Fortunately, only a few commodities will be of the first importance in any particular project: many of the inputs and outputs can be dealt with very crudely, without fear of seriously distorting the final decision. Therefore, rough and easily used methods are wanted; as well as accurate, but complicated, ones.

12.1 PREDICTION

When evaluating investment projects, one is looking into the future. Since the kind of project dealt with is often expected to have a life of several decades, it is necessary to look rather a long way into the future, and prices could change greatly. There may be no particular reason to think that the price is more likely to move up than down, even when one can be sure it will change. The way in which this uncertainty about price movements should influence the result is a topic reserved for 15.4 and 15.5.

Risk apart, if there is no good reason to think that a price will probably change more in one direction than the other, the calculations must be made on the assumption that it will remain constant. It saves a lot of time and trouble to decide quickly that one is ignorant, when one *is* ignorant. But first one must try to learn about the probable changes in the most important prices. Bad mistakes may sometimes be avoided by noticing that there is good reason to think that some particular price will be higher or lower in the future.

Any of the following reasons might justify planners in thinking that a price will probably rise or fall:

    (i) In the past behaviour of the price of some important raw material, or of the output, there may be clear evidence of an upward or downward trend. (This applies also to inputs other than materials, but insofar as machinery is installed early in the life of the project its price can usually be predicted quite accurately.) Many people are much too quick to see a trend in figures for two or three years; on the other hand, some people never see a trend in *any* series of figures! Clear evidence of a trend can be had only from quite a long series of years—at least ten, and preferably much more. After all, this trend is going to be extrapolated for two or three decades in the calculations. If fluctuations in the price have been large in relation to any plausible trend during the years for which evidence is available, one should be wary of drawing conclusions. If the input is really important, it may be advisable to call in the help of a trained statistician. But one should not assume that the price will most probably remain constant just because the evidence of a trend is weak. Nor is it better to assume wrongly that the price will be rising by, say, 2% per annum. If the immediately available evidence is uninformative, one ought to look for more— if not more data on past prices, then evidence of the kind discussed below.

(ii) Statistics of past prices are not the only information that can help in forecasting the future behaviour of prices. For example, it may be known that, as a result of recent improvements in technique, it is likely that steel will soon be much cheaper; or recent increases in steel-producing capacity may have outrun demand, so that prices are likely to fall in the immediate future; or it may be known that some raw material is likely to be in increasingly short supply (with consequent rising price), because new techniques are leading to an increased demand for it. Reasons of this kind, which have to do with general knowledge about the changing conditions of supply and demand, can also give useful support to forecasts of prices based on statistics from the past, or a valuable warning not to be guided by what has happened in the past. For example, if prices of raw materials of importance in armaments have been rising, but the conflicts that have given rise to the special demand have recently been much reduced, one will want to use the past data with caution.

(iii) We know also that the price that will have to be paid for an import, and the price that will be received for an export, may sometimes depend upon the quantity the country is importing or exporting. Certainly, the accounting price will change if a commodity that was being imported is no longer going to be imported (because of the expansion of domestic capacity), or one that has previously been sold only in the domestic market will begin to be sold abroad. It must also be assumed that when the quantity of a commodity produced domestically changes substantially, the accounting price will often change too. It follows that forecasts of at least some of the accounting prices that are required for evaluating a project will depend upon the changes in production that are expected in this and other sectors of the economy. For example, if the country is going to adopt a special programme of expansion in the cultivation of raw cotton, hoping soon to be an exporter, even although most of the cotton required by the textile mills is currently imported, then the accounting price for cotton should probably be predicted to fall. (Of course, if there were in any case a tendency for the world price of raw cotton to rise this would have to be balanced against the effects of developments within the home country. And in that case, the prices of cotton textiles would be expected to rise also.)

(iv) The likelihood of a change in the relative value of some particular foreign currency might be a reason for predicting a change in the AP of a traded good. But caution is necessary. For instance, if pumps are sold to Germany, and a 10% revaluation of the mark in relation to other convertible currencies is confidently expected, it may still be unwise to assume that the border value of pumps will rise a full 10%, for it may be necessary to reduce the mark price to maintain sales. Similarly, a 10% devaluation of the dirham is unlikely to result in India getting supplies of phosphate rock any cheaper. On balance, we think it likely that the project evaluator would do well not to attempt to allow for the possible effects of changes in the relative value of foreign currencies.

These different kinds of information are progressively harder to quantify. Since one cannot meaningfully compare one consideration with another, unless they have been quantified, it is necessary at least to make intelligent guesses. As experience of using these techniques to make forecasts of accounting prices accumulates, the guesses can become more intelligent. What is of the first importance is that the possibility of changing prices should be kept in mind, and that it should never be assumed that the price of an important input or output will remain constant unless there really is, on balance, no good reason to think the contrary.

12.2 TRADED GOODS

The previous section provided a necessary prologue to the business of making actual estimates. In the remaining sections of this chapter we suggest how, in many particular cases, the actual estimating should be done, beginning with the simplest commodities. First, it is as well to remind ourselves how information about the project is likely to be presented to the evaluator.

The essential information is the quantification of inputs and outputs. At some point in the preparation of estimates, the amounts of the main inputs and outputs must be given in physical terms—so many tons of a particular kind of steel, so many machines of a certain specification, and so on; but some parts of the costs are likely to be estimated in money terms, the estimate being based on the con-tractors' or surveyors' experience. These rough estimates in money terms will sometimes refer to quite specific items—collections of tools, say, or small items of construction. It will then be fairly easy to see whether the actual goods and services concerned are traded goods and services, or not. But there are bound to be some miscel-laneous items which cannot be so assigned.[1] These last items must be adjusted to fit the calculations in a fairly rough-and-ready way, increasing or reducing them by an appropriate factor. Since a number of non-traded commodities have to be treated in exactly the same way, the details are left until the next section.

Consider, now, an imported commodity, such as a piece of machinery. For a definite item like this, one can find out what has to be paid for it at the port: this is the c.i.f. (cost, insurance, freight) price, the one that is used for customs purposes and the like.[2] The

---

[1] A typical miscellaneous item is 'contingencies'. Contingencies may be a genuine allowance for unexpected costs based on past experience. But sometimes it is more in the nature of an administrative device, permitting the project to proceed without further reference to the decision-making body provided the 'contingency' allowance is not exceeded. In the latter case it is not a genuine cost allowance at all, and should be left out altogether.

[2] Using the c.i.f. price without adjustment strictly implies that freight and in-surance are traded services. This may not always be true of insurance, though it usually is. India for instance uses a 'c. and f.' valuation, leaving out insurance, which should then be accounted for separately, probably as a non-traded service.

further cost of getting the machinery off the ship at the port and to the site of the plant, is known as the port-to-user margin. The service of getting commodities from port to user is a non-traded good, consisting partly of transport costs, partly of handling charges, partly of the services of traders, agents, insurance, etc. The method used here is to divide the port-to-user margin into two parts, one the transport cost, the other all the rest. The actual cost of each of these two parts then has to be adjusted so that transport and services are valued, as near as possible, at their accounting prices. It is best to keep all these transport and trade or port-to-user margins separate from the c.i.f. costs of the inputs, and add them up separately. One can later value these sub-totals by using the appropriate accounting prices. (We deal with the accounting prices for transport and trade in the next section, since they are non-traded commodities.)

A similar procedure applies in the case of an exported good. The commodity—cotton textiles, say—is valued at its f.o.b. (free on board) price—the price that is received for delivering it on board ship at the port. It may be important in such a case to estimate the marginal revenue from exporting instead of the price. To do that, one has to estimate the effect of a further increase in exports on the price received, and then deduct the net effect of this on export earnings. In either case, the cost of the transport and trade services involved in getting the commodity from the plant to the ship is converted to accounting price terms and entered into the calculation as a cost. In none of these cases are taxes or subsidies included.

A brief word on more complicated cases may be useful. If the input is imported, or the output exported, it is obvious what the transport margin is. It is not so clear if the input comes from a home producer, although some users of the same input may import their requirements. When transport costs are small, the costing can be done as though the equipment was actually imported; but if transport costs are large, one must be more careful.

Users near the port of entry will use imports; users near the domestic factory will use home production. One has to guess how far imports will penetrate into the country. At the furthest point, the prices of imported and home-produced versions, including transport costs, must be the same. Therefore:

price at factory = price at port *plus* transport cost to furthest point to which imports penetrate *minus* transport cost between that point and the factory.

Finally, the price to the user of the home-produced version is the price at the domestic factory, plus the transport cost from there to the user. Usually one would work out the factory price by using the normal route from port to factory. The dividing point along this route between users of imports and users of domestic production will depend upon the proportion of total use provided by domestic production.

Another complication arises when the home-produced commodity is of a different kind or quality from those that are being imported. This is very common. For example, domestic cotton may be used for some purposes, but certain kinds of cloth (perhaps for export) require a long staple cotton, which is imported. Similarly, heavy-duty electric motors may be imported, while smaller ones are made in the country.

In such cases, it is wrong to look up the average c.i.f. price of cotton or electric motors, and use that to value the domestic production. Theoretically, the correct price is then the export or f.o.b. price, if, for example, the light electric motors are in fact exported; or, if export is a very unlikely possibility, they should be valued as non-traded (see the next section). But if it is a small item, or if the commodity in question could in some uses be substituted for imports, even if not in all, then one would not go far wrong in taking the c.i.f. price of the imported variety and multiplying it by the ratio of the domestic market price of the home variety to the domestic market price of the imported variety.

A slightly different case arises with final consumer goods, which have the same basic uses, but where the quality is different, or where consumers' preferences are such that the imported and home-produced varieties sell at different prices. A good example is American wheat, which sells at a discount compared to indigenous wheat in India and other countries.

Let us suppose the discount is 20%, and ask what happens if some extra quantity of wheat is produced, and hence decide how to value it. Let us take it that the extra quantity saves an equal tonnage of imported wheat costing 1 million rupees of foreign exchange. But the extra quantity of domestic wheat will actually sell for $1\frac{1}{4}$ million rupees (this assumes that the government previously made no profit or loss on the imported wheat—and also, for simplicity, ignores transport costs). People pay an extra $\frac{1}{4}$ million rupees, because they prefer the domestic variety. This will reduce their consumption of other things by roughly the same amount. This in turn will save some more foreign exchange, how much depending on the foreign exchange cost of consumption in general (this may be estimated by applying the standard conversion factor—see 12.34).

Suppose the foreign exchange cost of consumption is $\frac{2}{3}$ of its domestic value, then the extra foreign exchange saving is $\frac{1}{4} \times \frac{2}{3} = \frac{1}{6}$. Consequently the accounting value of the extra quantity of domestic wheat is $1\frac{1}{6}$ million rupees.

The above was an agricultural example, and makes assumptions which may not be true even in this case, and would surely not be true in other cases. First, it assumes that if people consume an extra ton of more expensive domestic wheat, they will consume just one ton less of imported wheat, and that they will reduce other expenditures in an average sort of way. If it was thought more probable that expenditure on wheat, domestic and foreign, would remain constant, then the whole $1\frac{1}{4}$ million rupees of extra expenditure on domestic wheat would save foreign exchange. Secondly, the example assumes that there is no tariff on wheat, but considerable tariffs or quotas on other consumption goods; and this is not likely to be generally true. In fact, each case has to be treated on its merits, remembering that the crucial question is, always, how much foreign exchange is saved (or earned).

For industrial goods, it is more often the home product which sells at a discount. Thus a domestic car may be worth less than an imported one, although both claim to be the same model. The accounting price of the home product is then less than the foreign exchange value of the imported model, the difference being calculated in the same sort of manner as in the previous example.

Another, rather different, puzzle arises when the project evaluator finds, as he sometimes will, that there is quite a wide range of import prices for a particular product. This could be because of a difference of quality, or differences in the size of the consignment, or because the goods were not bought at the same time. It could also be simply irrational—someone has paid more than he need have done. The project evaluator should always try to estimate the lowest price at which imports of a given quality are likely to be actually obtainable at the relevant times. This will not always be the same as the lowest price at which a good has been recently imported: sometimes, for instance, foreign firms may make sales at abnormally low prices (perhaps because of excess capacity), or because of some subsidy scheme of a foreign government which cannot be relied upon to last. But, equally, it is easy to imagine circumstances in which some recent import prices are higher than can reasonably be relied upon in the future. Again, an aid or a trade agreement may cause the lowest price at which an import could be obtained to become irrelevant. In the simplest case of a loan which is tied to the project in question, the price of imported capital goods is irrelevant. The cost becomes the cost of servicing the loan. There are, however, more difficult intermediate cases about which we cannot generalize. Common sense, allied to the principle that it is the saving or earning of freely usable foreign exchange which matters, should provide a guide in difficult cases. All this is inevitably a matter of well-informed opinion and nice judgment, about which it is impossible to generalize. Much the same considerations apply to exports— except, of course, that it is the highest price which one can expect to obtain which is relevant.

The final complication mainly concerns trade under bilateral trade agreements with the centrally planned economies. In recent years it has been possible to settle balances arising from such agreements in convertible currency. But the convertibility of earnings from such trade is still only notional, because there is an obligation on both sides to balance: and if balance is not achieved pressures will be exerted when the next agreement is negotiated. In these circumstances an import or export valued at so many roubles (or 'accounting dollars') cannot necessarily be translated into accounting rupees at the official rouble/rupee rate (or dollar/rupee rate). Our recommendation is that COPE works out a shadow exchange rate (for accounting dollars to accounting rupees) for its trade with each of these countries, having regard to (*a*) the convertible foreign exchange which its marginal exports to the country in question might have earned, and (*b*) the expenditure in convertible currency which would have been necessary to obtain imports of similar quality from countries with convertible currencies. In this connection it is worth noting that there is a regular trade in switching goods obtained from centrally planned economics for sale in countries with convertible currencies, and that a 'switch premium' for convertible currency arises out of these transactions.

12.3   The Marginal Social Cost of Non-Traded Goods

We have seen in 9.4 that, in many cases, the AP of a non-traded good can be calculated by estimating its MSC. Clearly, it will not always be possible to estimate the MSC with great accuracy. The exact inputs required in the production of a non-traded good will not be known to the project analyst without a great deal of research. Except in the case of a very important input or output, the amount of work involved in calculating the MSC makes it impossible to consider doing so. For that reason, it is very important to have available conversion factors, which will provide a convenient and satisfactory short-cut. The idea is that the cost of an input as reported to the project evaluator can be converted to accounting price terms by multiplication by the conversion factor. If there is a conversion factor for construction, say, there is no need (unless, it should be emphasized, the construction input is large, and of special character) to work out the construction cost directly: the estimates of actual construction cost are simply multiplied by the construction conversion factor.

In describing how to estimate the MSC, we shall therefore bear in mind that it is generally most useful to apply the methods to representative production methods—a typical railroad, or coal mine, for instance—and deduce a conversion factor that can then be applied in many particular instances. This, ideally, is work for the COPE. But, if necessary, it could be done in a rough and ready way by those evaluating a particular project, when the same conversion factor can be applied to a variety of different cost figures (e.g. trade margins, transportation, commercial services, and so on). Just how wide a range of commodities a particular conversion factor has to be applied to must depend on circumstances.

Among the most important non-traded goods whose APs will be estimated from the MSC are construction and civil engineering, electricity, and transportation. We shall say something about each of these, by way of example. Similar methods can be applied to services (in trade, banking, insurance, etc.), commodities produced by industries with temporary excess capacity, and indeed most industrial products which are expected to be non-traded.

12.31 *Example 1: Construction*

The case of construction is, in principle, one of the easiest. We have to estimate the accounting cost of the inputs required for doing the construction—the labour, the raw materials, and the services of the various bits of machinery. Labour we shall come to in due course. Raw materials are usually traded goods, and if not, can be treated by one or other of the methods we are discussing. Machinery requires rather careful treatment. A bulldozer may be used on a project for a number of years, but will not be worn out at the end of that time. We must therefore evaluate the services it provides each year. The price of these services should be just high enough to justify the initial expenditure on the bulldozer. One can estimate the number of hours a bulldozer should work in a year, and how many years it will last. The price per bulldozer-hour should be falling from year to year at the same rate as the prices of bulldozers themselves may be expected to fall. Then the price of a bulldozer-hour is set at such a level that the PSV of the services of the bulldozer will just equal its cost (import cost, most probably).[1]

We should emphasize that the above method is correct only if there are no spare bulldozers that would otherwise be idle. Since construction work is normally a rapidly expanding activity, we should hardly expect construction machinery to have no other use. But, sometimes, an earlier mistake may have left the economy with a temporary glut of one particular kind of machinery, which commands no second-hand market abroad. In that case, using the machinery does not involve any cost to the economy (apart from the cost of operating and maintaining it, of course).

Thus, if the major construction work associated with a project can be costed in detail, then the labour used can be regarded as labour used by the project, and so can the services of the machinery used, and the raw materials. The cost in terms of accounting prices can then be calculated using the methods indicated. If the construction is supplied by the private sector one should also make allowance, as will be explained in 14.2, for the consumption out of profits by engineering contractors, labour agents, and so on.

But when construction costs are small, or are not available broken down into various parts, it will be useful to have a *construction conversion factor*, which can be used to revalue the actual money cost of construction work to its cost in accounting-price terms. The conversion factor should be estimated by costing, at APs, one or more typical construction programmes. These might be imaginary, but realistic, construction projects, formulated in consultation with firms in the construction industry, or the relevant government departments; or they could be based on the actual construction work done for a number of public-sector projects, for which detailed information is available.

Sometimes, information on construction costs will be available only in the usual accounting form, where the characteristics of

---

[1] Suppose that bulldozers can be expected to provide $h_1, h_2, h_3, \ldots h_\tau$ hours of useful work in the successive years of their lives, and that the price of new bulldozers is expected to fall by $100g\%$ per year. If a new bulldozer today costs C rupees, and the ARI is $100R\%$ per year, today's accounting price for a bulldozer-hour, p, is given by

$$C = p \left[\frac{h_1}{(1+g)(1+R)} + \frac{h_2}{(1+g)^2(1+R)^2} + \cdots + \frac{h_\tau}{(1+g)^\tau(1+R)^\tau} \right].$$

capital equipment are not given in detail, and are merely reflected in figures for depreciation. Depreciation *plus* interest charges on the book value of capital should, ideally, give the cost of the services of the capital equipment for a year. But tax laws and accountants' conventions have a considerable effect on the figures for depreciation. This is not, therefore, a very satisfactory means of estimating the value of the equipment's services. One may nevertheless have to shut one's eyes to the unsatisfactory nature of the figures, and calculate the normal annual cost of providing a million rupees of construction work on the basis of data for current inputs, labour costs, depreciation, and the value of fixed and working capital. The accounting-price value of the million rupees of construction work would then be obtained as follows:

> raw material and miscellaneous inputs, converted to accounting prices;
> labour costs, measured at the shadow wage rate;
> value of consumption out of profits, measured at accounting prices;
> annual depreciation, converted to accounting-price terms by using the ratio of the accounting-price cost of the machinery to its actual costs;
> interest cost, evaluated by charging the ARI on the value of the fixed and working capital stock, converted to accounting-price terms.

The sum of these items is an estimate of the social cost of the million rupees of construction work, and the conversion factor is obtained by dividing by a million.

12.32 *Example 2: Electricity*
Electricity generation and transmission is a more complicated case than construction, because it costs more to supply electricity at peak times than at others, and the older or less efficient methods of producing electricity may be used only at peak hours. Also, when hydro-electric and thermal power stations form part of a single grid, it may be quite a complex matter to identify the cost of making electricity available in a certain place at a certain time.

If the input of electricity is an extremely important item, as in the case of the manufacture of some non-ferrous metals, then more expert calculations than can be dealt with here should be carried out. But, in the case of a large number of projects, where electricity is neither extremely important nor negligible, the following crude method should be adequate.

First, make some convenient division of the day, and the week, into peak hours and off-peak hours. The normal practice of charging by the electricity authority may give some guidance. Then it can be assumed that the accounting price for off-peak electricity is given by the accounting cost of the current inputs on the least efficient plant that has to be used—neglecting the capital equipment, that is. Although this neglects some costs such as wear and tear, it is not likely to be seriously inaccurate. Next, a typical power station can be costed. To do this one must estimate for how many years of its life it will be providing off-peak electricity; and one must estimate the rate at which the peak and off-peak prices of electricity will be falling over time. For simplicity, it is assumed that both fall at the same rate (this is not a very good assumption, but then the method is admittedly crude). Finally, today's price for peak-hour electricity is determined by the requirement that this typical power station should just break even, that is, have a zero PSV. The details of how the peak-hour accounting price (p), and the off-peak accounting price (q) can be calculated are given in the following paragraph.

Assume C = cost of the plant at commissioning date, interest at the accounting rate of interest being charged on earlier expenditures.

h = number of peak hours operated per annum (this will not in reality be constant: an average, weighted towards the present, should be taken).

T = number of years the plant is expected to be in use at peak hours.

t = number of years for which the plant will operate during off-peak hours.

k = number of off-peak hours per annum that will be worked during the period t (this, like h, may also vary with time—a similar average can be taken).

g = annual rate at which accounting prices are expected to fall.

R = ARI per annum.

a = running cost at the time of commissioning.

p = accounting price per kwh of peak electricity at the time of commissioning.

q = accounting price per kwh of off-peak electricity at the time of commissioning.

Since, by assumption, q is equal to the running cost of a plant t years old, it follows that:

$$q = a(1+g)^t. \tag{1}$$

Up to time t, the social profit of the plant in the year ending at time n is

$$ph(1+g)^{-n} + qk(1+g)^{-n} - a(h+k)$$
$$= ph(1+g)^{-n} + ak(1+g)^{t-n} - a(h+k).$$

After t and up to T, the social profit is

$$ph(1+g)^{-n} - ah.$$

Summing, discounting, and setting the result equal to C, we have

$$C = ph \sum_{n=1}^{T} (1+g)^{-n}(1+R)^{-n} - ah \sum_{n=1}^{T} (1+R)^{-n}$$

$$+ ak \sum_{n=1}^{t} \left[(1+g)^{t-n} - 1 \right] (1+R)^{-n}. \tag{2}$$

q is estimated from equation (1), and p from equation (2).

Since we are estimating future accounting prices, calculations of the kind described must, in principle, be made on the basis of the techniques expected to be in use at the relevant date. If current techniques are not the best available, there will be time to change; the estimates should be based on the lowest-cost techniques for the industry, provided there is reason to think that they will get used. In practice, when the system of project planning in terms of social cost–benefit analysis is just beginning, it is hardly worth while to do a very detailed analysis of alternative methods of production when estimating accounting prices. The business of project evaluation can begin by using accounting prices based on the techniques currently used in these industries. The accounting prices can be revised later, if it is found that other methods of production are better.

12.33 *Example 3: Transportation*
It is not true in all industries that expanded production involves no change in the cost per unit of output. It is not true in railway transport, for instance. (Indeed, it is not exactly true in the cases already examined, and special treatment is needed when this convenient assumption is too unrealistic.) Thus, what we really want to know, when estimating the accounting price for railway transport on a particular route, is what it would cost to provide the extra transportation that will be required if the project we are interested in should be undertaken. But transportation will often be

too unimportant a part of costs to justify a very careful analysis of this point. So, for many cases, a conversion factor for transportation, as for construction, is a useful tool. It should be estimated by applying to the railways and other modes of transport the same kind of calculations as discussed in the cases of construction and electricity: that is to say, transportation costs on a few typical routes should be costed at accounting prices, and the ratio of accounting cost to revenue calculated.

But, sometimes, there would be a difference. The kind of situation we have in mind is one where a railway line is relatively under-utilized, so that traffic on the line could be expanded quite easily, without the necessity of laying new track, rearranging signalling, expanding handling facilities, and the like. In that case, the accounting price for railway transport should be just the price that is necessary to cover the additional costs of new inputs—new loco-motives, workers, rolling stock, and so on. However, one has to be rather careful when doing this kind of calculation, as it is easy to miss out some quite important costs: for instance, an expansion in traffic as a result of carrying raw materials to a new factory may result in slowing down deliveries to other factories on the line. Similarly, new traffic on a road may greatly increase the cost of maintaining it to an adequate standard.

We cannot go any further into the details of estimating accounting prices in particular cases where costs of production are available. Each case has its own peculiarities. Usually, quite rough overall calculations will do. But it must be emphasized that project appraisal is much easier when good conversion factors are available.

12.34   *A Further Short-Cut: the Standard Conversion Factor*
When a particular input (or output) is likely to be rather un-important in the overall evaluation of the project, or when—as in the case of many trade and other services—it is difficult to get hard information about the methods of production, one has to resort to cruder methods. In such a case, one may be able to estimate the actual cost (at market prices) of the input, but one wants to make a correction for the extent to which the actual prices are overstating or understating the social cost.

The actual prices paid cover the cost of imported inputs, including import duties, the market cost of various other inputs, the cost of labour at the ruling wage rates, profit, and tax payments. To get the accounting price of the inputs, we would like to subtract import duties and other indirect taxes, the excess of actual wages over shadow wages, the excess of profits over that required to cover the accounting rate of interest, and to add on some allowance for the consumption out of profits by those involved in providing the services. This is hard work. It might be worth doing for a few commodities, but certainly not for all.

Instead, one can take some average of the ratios of accounting prices to market prices (these ratios can be termed 'conversion factors', whether the reference is to a particular commodity or a sectoral average). It has already been seen that a number of conversion factors for non-traded sectors should have been worked out: these will enter into the average.[1] But so will traded goods in general. Conversion factors for these are ratios of border prices, plus the AP of internal transport and trade margins, to market prices. COPE should have available a large number of such ratios, and it should be COPE's responsibility to establish the average which we call the *standard conversion factor* (SCF).

What sort of an average do we have in mind? Of course, some commodities or non-traded sectors are more important than others. So a weighted average is in principle called for, and the most appropriate weights would seem to be total available supply (production plus imports) measured at market prices. Thus the average would be of the form

$$SCF = \frac{\Sigma Q \cdot AP}{\Sigma Q \cdot MP}$$

where MP = market price, AP = accounting price, and Q is supply. However, this would take a lot of work, and the required figures may not be easily ascertainable. Another less demanding approach is to plot the distribution of conversion factors. If they cluster round a particular value, then it is safe to take this value (i.e. the mode), unless some important sectoral or other conversion factors lie far from the mode.

It is obviously useful to have an SCF: but, at the same time, it should be remembered that it is very much of a short-cut which should in principle be used as little as possible. It is the inverse of a shadow exchange rate (the latter being appropriate when expenditure at market prices is used as numéraire): consequently the same warning applies to the use of shadow exchange rates. For further discussion of this point see Chapter XVIII.

---

[1] In practice, though not in theory, the conversion factors for non-traded sectors may themselves include use of a standard conversion factor. In theory simultaneous determination is then required. In practice, it should not be difficult to achieve sufficient consistency.

It may also happen that the relatively unimportant items, whose accounting prices cannot be estimated in detail, can be guessed to come mainly from a few particular sectors of the economy—rather than being regarded as a microcosm of the supplies available to the economy at large, which would be implied by use of the SCF as described above. In that case a more appropriate weighted average of conversion factors should be struck.

12.35 *Consumption Conversion Factors*
We have already seen in 9.43 and 9.5 that it is frequently necessary to revalue the consumption of different groups in terms of accounting prices.

Budget studies must form the basis for decomposing the expenditure of different types of consumers into particular items. One then adopts the same procedure as for the SCF, except, of course, that the weights attached to the different items will be the consumers' expenditure on them.

The number of different consumption conversion factors worth calculating will vary with the country and with available information. Rural and urban consumers should, if possible, be separated—and two or three divisions by wealth would be desirable.

It is worth noting that the inverse of a conversion factor for aggregate consumers' expenditure is identical to the shadow exchange rate which should be used if, as stated in the UNIDO *Guidelines*, aggregate consumption is used as numéraire: but the method we propose for its calculation is not that actually advocated in the UNIDO *Guidelines* (see Chapter XVIII).

12.4 Using Marginal Social Benefit to Estimate Accounting Prices

The principles were discussed in 9.4, and an example given in 9.43.

It is necessary to use the MSB for outputs of non-traded goods and services, and also for inputs when, for some reason, supply cannot be expected to expand: or when it is not worth calculating the MSC. Thus the use of the SCF is often in effect a crude estimate of MSB. We now give a number of other examples of the use of MSB. The first is a generalization of the arithmetic example of 9.43.

12.41 *Example 1: A Non-Traded Consumer Good*
With a non-traded good it has to be expected that the price will fall (at least below what it would have otherwise been) as the supply is

increased (by a public sector project). Sometimes a *prima-facie* traded good will fall into this category. An example might be wheat or maize produced far inland. Although there is trade, nevertheless the main effect may be to reduce local prices and increase consumption, rather than save imports or raise exports.

Assuming that only a small addition to output (call it one unit) is in question, then the value of this to the consumer can be taken to be the price he is willing to pay: in the absence of rationing, this will be very close to the price he actually pays (p); and thus he neither gains nor loses so far as this unit is concerned. But since the price falls a little, he does gain a sum equal to the previous consumption (q) multiplied by the difference in price (dp). Thus, consumers' gain $= - qdp$.

The social value of this consumer's gain is found by multiplying by the relevant consumption conversion factor (γ) to express it in terms of our numéraire, and by the social value of a unit of consumption relative to government expenditure (v). Therefore,

The Social Value of the Consumption Gain $= - \gamma v q dp$.

Now we turn to the government, whose change in revenue is $d(pq) = p + qdp$. Although the government gains the market value of the extra unit (p), it loses the amount—qdp—which the consumer gains. The effect of this change in government revenue is that an equal value at market prices of other consumption goods will no longer be bought (or an equal extra value will be bought if $p + qdp$ is negative). This amount must be converted to border prices by using the consumption conversion factor. Thus:

The Social Value of the Change in Government Revenue
$$= \gamma(p + qdp).$$

Adding consumers and government together, we have

Social Value of a One Unit Increase in Supply
$$= \gamma[-vqdp + p + qdp]$$
$$= \gamma p\left[1 + \frac{qdp}{p}(1-v)\right].$$

Elasticity of Demand is defined as
$$\eta = \frac{-pdq}{qdp}, \text{ or } \eta = -\frac{p}{qdp}$$

where $dq = 1$, as in our example.

Hence,

Social Value of a Unit Change in Supply $= \gamma p\left[1 - \frac{1}{\eta}(1-v)\right].$

It should be noted that the expression in square brackets measures the social effect of changes in distribution between the government and the consumer. Thus if $v = 1$, the expression is unity and has no effect on the social value, and similarly if $\eta = \infty$: in the former case the redistribution does not matter, and in the latter case there is no redistribution.

It is also important to note that when extra supply of some consumption good involves a redistribution, but this can be compensated for by a change in taxation which would otherwise not have taken place, then there is effectively no redistribution and the social value is simply γp. An example would be if an improved water supply permitted an increase in property tax.

The above analysis assumes that prices of other consumption goods are unchanged. Although in general this will not be exactly true, it will usually be safe to assume that the social value of such changes is negligible: they will often involve mainly some redistribution as between people of very similar wealth. It also assumes that the change in output was quite small. Where it is large, the effects of the change had better be spelt out arithmetically as in the example of 9.43.

Finally, although a particular consumption good is non-traded, it may sometimes be justifiable to assume that it is such a good substitute for another traded consumption good that the main effect will be that the quantity of consumption of the latter is reduced by $p_1 dq/p_2$, where p_1 and p_2 are the prices of the good and its substitute respectively. One can then proceed as for a traded good.

12.42 *Example 2: The Production of a Non-Traded Producer's Good— e.g. Irrigation*

Often the value of a non-traded producer's good is easier to assess than a consumption good. Thus an increase in electricity supply to industry can usually be treated as marginal, implying that the price which producers will pay per unit is a good measure of the value (in domestic rupees) of the increase in industrial output caused by the use of an extra unit of electricity. This latter value can then be translated into APs by multiplying by the SCF. If the right amount of electricity is being produced, the MSB thus estimated will be equal to the marginal social cost: this implies that private industry is charged the MSC divided by the SCF.[1]

---

[1] Thus MSC = MSB = marginal product in domestic rupees × SCF = price in domestic rupees × SCF; whence price in domestic rupees = MSC/SCF.

But things are not always so easy. A large irrigation scheme, for instance, raises a number of problems.

(i) The output cannot be easily valued on the basis of what the buyers would be willing to pay. If, for instance, irrigation water has been provided free or at a nominal charge the market gives no indication.

(ii) Quite often the change will be a large one, at least in relation to farmers' incomes in the area. The size of the change may also make it necessary to consider the effects on employment.

If the value of water in terms of other goods (many of which will be traded) cannot be estimated by what the user would pay, then it may be necessary to estimate its marginal product by direct research into production functions.[1] If we can establish the productivity of water in producing more rice, wheat, etc., then its social value can be established by this route. It is worth noting that in valuing electricity we would assume that its marginal product was, say, industrial output in general—and an appropriate conversion factor would be used to translate domestic values into border rupees. But, in some cases, such as irrigation water in a particular area, the marginal product is likely to be expressible in terms of a small mix of outputs—or even one only, say rice. These specific outputs can then often be valued directly at border prices.

The second difficulty to which we made allusion was that the provision of water would sometimes represent a large change for a particular region. In that case, there would be little point in trying to sum up all the effects of the irrigation scheme into an accounting price for water. The effects on different farmers' incomes, on casual labour, and on government revenue would have to be separately assessed: the effect on the output of some crops might be great enough to result in a change in their price; changes in the use of complementary inputs—fertilizers, extension services, etc.—would probably have to be allowed for. In short, the value of the immediate output—water—might be submerged in a full scale cost–benefit analysis of the effects of a 'package' deal.

12.43 Land
The cost of land is what it would have been worth in alternative uses. Quite often, this can be estimated as the amount that other

---

[1] This method was adopted in Lal, 1972.

producers would have been willing to pay for it, multiplied by a conversion factor (to convert from market to accounting prices). This conversion factor should relate to the inputs and outputs of producers who might otherwise have used the land, but normally a standard conversion factor would be adequate. If the accounting price of land is estimated in this way, we are neglecting adverse effects on income distribution that may be caused by the general increase in land prices that any increase in demand will bring about. (Similar considerations apply to skilled labour, which is discussed in 12.8.) If land is privately owned, and landowners are relatively wealthy, we would recommend adding a premium to the AP calculated above.[1]

In the case of agricultural projects, where there is no very good market in land, it may be necessary to estimate the MSB directly by working about the PSV of alternative uses (using APs for fertilizer, seed, labour, etc.). Fortunately, this is not always necessary, since the land used in agricultural schemes may not have to be valued explicitly. The 'package deal' of the previous section was an example. In practice, difficulties arise because there is no sufficiently reliable record of previous inputs and outputs that could be used to estimate the average net product.

12.5 THE TREATMENT OF INDIRECT TAXES

Indirect taxes (sales taxes, value-added taxes, purchase taxes, tariffs, excise duties, and so on) have not played a prominent part in our discussion of accounting prices. In many cases, the rules for estimating APs ignore such taxes—as in the simplest case of imported traded goods where the tariff, if there is one, is omitted from the AP.[2] This corresponds to the usual rule in cost–benefit analysis of regarding taxes as transfers to the government, and therefore not costs. On the other hand, taxes do affect the estimates of MSB, as we saw in 9.43. One could leave it at that, but it is worth considering whether one would usually get a better approximation to the AP

---

[1] Assuming the elasticity of demand for land is unity, a proportion equal to the ratio of landlord income after direct and indirect taxes to total landlord income would be near enough.

[2] We have explained above (9.31 and 9.32) that we advocate direct estimation of elasticities of foreign supply (or demand) rather than assuming that tariffs (or export taxes) are intended to correct prices for any inelasticity. Another exception to the use of border prices might arise if some externality (such as pollution) attached to the use of a traded good, and was reflected in a tax imposed for that reason. In such a case the tax should be added to the border price to give the AP.

by subtracting indirect taxes from the market price to buyers, or by using that market price without adjustment. A general rule-of-thumb here, though not perfect, could be very convenient.

12.51 *Taxes on Sales to Consumers*

In general, we would regard taxes on goods sold to final consumers as 'corrective': meaning by this that the net-of-tax price is a better measure of the social value of the good than the market price. Some economists, who are inclined to think that the price consumers are willing to pay is the best measure of the social value of the good, may find this strange. The reason we take a different view is that a government should, and often does, put on indirect taxes after full consideration of the effects on the welfare of the people as a whole. There may sometimes be doubts about the *level* of the tax, but normally one can see that there should be one. Thus considerations of paternalism, income distribution, and consumption externalities, may all be taken into account. If this is how taxes arise, then, in the eyes of the authorities, the market price of, say, cigarettes, clearly does not measure their welfare-value. The same is true of heavily taxed luxuries. A mink coat may be relatively very valuable to its user. But its user is rich, and her marginal utility counts for little. It would be different if some other form of taxation could be used to achieve all the revenue and income redistribution the government wanted—but when luxuries are heavily taxed, plainly the government does not believe it.

It is true that an economist might be able to show that some feature of the tax-system was distorting—effectively different rates to similar classes of consumers that have gone unnoticed when the tax regulations were being drafted, for instance; or he might be able to provide evidence that the government had made empirically false assumptions—e.g., that a tobacco tax would reduce smoking, or that an increased tax on luxuries would increase revenue. But he cannot argue that consumer taxes are *in general* distorting. On the contrary, taxation, and subsidization, of consumer purchases is a useful and socially desirable weapon of policy. Project planners and economic advisers have no general warrant to attempt to nullify the effects of that tax system: that is what reckoning the value of the output of a taxed consumption good at its full market price would amount to.

The principle can be further illustrated by considering a sales tax on domestic consumption of electricity. If one included the tax as a benefit one would tend to promote the production of electricity to the point where it could be sold only at a price which, net of tax, would show a loss. Private producers would obviously not do this, so one is here considering a public supply. We feel that it must obviously be presumed that the government, in designing the tax system, would not want the tax on consumers to be offset by what is in effect a negative tax (the difference between marginal cost and price) by the public undertaking. Of course, a project evaluator may himself consider a tax on final consumption to be distorting. But our view is that he ought to take it to be corrective, unless there is evidence that the government regards the tax as only a temporary measure (sometimes indirect taxation is used to prevent excessive profits when there is a temporary shortage of supply). If there is any doubt, he should take steps to see that the fiscal authorities are consulted.

12.52 *Taxes on Producer Goods*

Matters may not be so clear in the case of non-traded producer goods. On the one hand, and in general, taxes on transactions between producers are undesirable.[1] Thus, taxes on producer goods are 'distorting', and should not exist. For the purposes of project evaluation, the AP should be the same, whether the commodity is an output or an input. For example, if the commodity is produced under constant costs in the public sector, and there is a tax on it, the AP is the price received by the seller and in an appraisal would not need to be altered. For a buyer of the commodity, the tax has to be subtracted from the price paid to obtain the AP. In other cases, it is possible that a price intermediate between buyers' and sellers' price, or even the tax-inclusive price, would be a better estimate of the AP.

On the other hand, and in practice, some taxes on producer goods exist for reasons which the project evaluator should respect, so that the tax is corrective. As a first example, consider a commodity that is produced by a public sector undertaking. The government may require the undertaking to charge a particularly high price, or make an exceptionally high return on capital, in lieu of an indirect tax: or vice versa. We saw in 12.42 that usually the proper price to charge for sales of non-traded producers' goods to the private sector is the MSC divided by the SCF—normally a higher price than MSC. Since the public sector should obtain its inputs at APs, an undertaking whose sales were predominantly to the private

---

[1] This has been shown—making certain assumptions—in Diamond and Mirrlees, 1971. The argument is discussed in Chapter XIX.

sector would, given this criterion, make exceptional profits. These might or might not be eliminated by a suitable tax (equal to $100 \left(\dfrac{1}{\text{SCF}} - 1 \right) \%$). If there were such a tax then it should, of course, be regarded as corrective—since it has to be subtracted to arrive at the correct AP. A number of other possibilities where the tax should be treated as corrective come to mind:

(i) The use of the good may give rise to external diseconomies, and the tax be levied for that reason: this is, in practice, rare.

(ii) The tax might be intended to reduce the monopoly profit of a private firm using the good: if this case ever arises in practice then it is clear that the government wants to restrict output, and that therefore the benefit should be measured using the net-of-tax price.

(iii) The producer's good in question may be an important component in the production of consumers' goods which should ideally be taxed instead, but are administratively too difficult to tax. Cloth in India if produced by the public sector would be a good example, being virtually a final consumers' good.

Commodities which are both consumers' and producers' goods present difficulties if the two markets cannot be separated. For instance, a tax on petrol, cars, furniture, or typewriters, might be regarded as corrective when sold to households but distorting (in most cases) when sold to firms. Where a distinction cannot be made (since firms could too easily pass the goods on to households) then—remembering that we are here concerned only with valuing outputs—such taxes should generally be regarded as corrective when the outputs are sold to the private sector.

In all these cases taxes should be subtracted. Exceptionally, when the tax is regarded as temporary, one has to guess what the price will be when the tax is removed, and that may be higher than the current net-of-tax price.

We next take public sector inputs. If these also come from the public sector, any tax should be subtracted unless it has been imposed because of external diseconomies: with this exception, intra-public sector taxes are always distorting. Inputs from the private sector are more difficult. The key question to ask is whether there can be any reason to want to curb *public sector* use of the private output in question. For instance, there may be a tax on (non-traded) cloth for the good reason that it is a near-consumption good: but that does not imply that the government wishes to restrict its own use of cloth for, say, uniforms. The tax should be subtracted. (It may be better to estimate the AP directly on the basis of costs.) However, there could be cases where the government should, as it were, pay attention to its own tax and curb its use of the commodity in question accordingly: apart from the usual case of external diseconomies, an example might be if a private producer had a monopoly of some material, and the government wished to encourage the use of substitutes whether in the public or private sector (admittedly, taking over the private monopoly would seem to be a better solution!). A more important example might be the employment of salaried staff if there are taxes on the employment of categories in particularly short supply.

Do different considerations apply to the private sector? Its non-traded outputs, if sold also to the private sector, are valued no differently from public sector outputs: any tax will be corrective if it is to control external diseconomies or monopoly profits, or if it is in effect a substitute for, or an unavoidable by-product of, a tax on consumption goods. Private sector outputs sold to the public sector will be valued in all cases net of tax. Private non-traded inputs from the public sector are generally valued net of tax, except where the tax is there because of external diseconomies. For instance, in an evaluation of a private firm producing steel there would be no reason to include any indirect tax paid on typewriters as a social cost: the tax may be there because private individuals use type-writers, but that is irrelevant.

We are talking about a good whose price is more or less determined by supply and demand. If the supply is predominantly from the public sector, we would expect the selling price net of tax to be nearest the AP. If the demand is predominantly by the public sector, we would take the buying price, including the tax. If private and public sectors are intermingled in the market in a more complicated way, the tax is large, and the commodity important for the project evaluation, the planners should forget about market prices and taxes, and find some way of estimating the AP directly, by the methods of the earlier sections in this chapter.

It should be emphasized that even after adjusting market prices for taxes in the way we have been discussing, one can often further improve the estimates of APs. If, for example, the public sector industry under consideration is paying tariffs on its traded inputs, we would expect the net-of-tax output prices still to be too high: it should be reduced by a conversion factor based on the general level of indirect taxation to which this part of the public sector is subject.

This section has been written in terms of taxes. If a subsidy is in question, the same general ideas may be applied: a subsidy is just a negative tax, and should be treated as such.

12.6 OUTPUTS WHICH AFFECT PRODUCTION ELSEWHERE

As we saw in 9.3, it may sometimes happen that an output must be considered to be partly non-traded. For instance, output from a new textile or shoe factory may partly displace imports, but partly displace local production of hand-made cloth or shoes. If it is suspected that the latter effect may be considerable, then that part of the output should be considered as non-traded. A precise analysis of the possible effects would be complicated, and we suggest a rough method. First value the non-traded part of the output as if no loss of domestic production was involved, e.g. as in 12.41, above. Then allow for the loss of domestic production by subtracting the difference this is likely to make to the earnings of handicraftsmen, some of whom will have to switch occupations or even become wholly unemployed: this difference will be multiplied both by a conversion factor and the appropriate consumption weight.

It is also possible that an increase in the output of a non-traded commodity will reduce profits, and employment in factories elsewhere. If this can be predicted, then there is no problem in making the appropriate adjustments. More generally, the changes in availability brought about by a project can affect private investment and production decisions. For instance, more cement may cause a fall in its price, thus encouraging its use by other producers; or the project may raise the wages of certain scarce categories of skilled labour, and so discourage other firms from employing them. The effects of all this on other project choices in the public sector can safely be ignored: they will be influenced by such small price changes only if the project in question has a very small PSV anyway. But this may not be true of producers who use different criteria— for example, private profit, which, as we have seen, may be very different from social profit. The project might, as a sort of by-product, encourage investment projects that are socially desirable, but which private businessmen had not previously thought profitable enough to be worth the effort. For instance, railways are often seen as a valuable source of encouragement to private businessmen who would not be accessible to theoretically better forms of promotion.

Alternatively, the project might make profitable other investments of low, or even negative, social value. For example, the domestic production of aluminium might encourage wasteful domestic production of kitchen utensils, if there is a tariff on them.

However, the above argument is usually more tempting than convincing. If we have no reason to think that there will be a balance of desirable (or undesirable) effects on private production decisions, we are right to ignore the theoretical problem. Yet it is a question that someone should ask. As and when economists have available a more thorough quantitative record of the developing economies, it may become possible to identify particular relationships of this kind. At present, it is important not to allow ignorance to generate unwarranted optimism or pessimism about these indirect effects of public investment.

12.7 Outputs which Affect Consumption Elsewhere

It is also possible that consumption elsewhere will be affected by a project, even though output and employment is unaffected. Suppose that a project will increase cocoa output in a country which is such an important world supplier that the demand for exports is inelastic. Then the added output is valued at the marginal export revenue: this properly reflects the loss of export earnings by existing producers in the country. But it does not allow for a possible reduction in consumption by those other producers. Insofar as their consumption is reduced, and is valued at less than uncommitted social income, this is an offset to the extra committed consumption on the part of those employed by the new project.

12.8 Skilled Labour

We shall come to unskilled labour in the next chapter, and in that category we can also include many grades of semi-skilled labour, and even skilled labour where the skills required are easily and quickly learned on the job.

In the case of many projects skilled labour will be so small a proportion of costs that it would be folly to take a lot of trouble. In that case the SCF can be applied to these expenditures, and the following discussion be regarded as of only academic interest.

There is at present considerable unemployment among educated people with unspecialized skills in many developing countries, and even some unemployment of people with special skills. If there is unemployment, the application of our principles suggests that the

social cost of employing them is the implied increase in consumption'
suitably weighted (as discussed in 13.1). However, it may be argued
that the government, by providing the education, has already willed
the increase in consumption which skilled people come to expect: in
other words the increase in consumption is committed by the education not by the act of employment. This is an argument which is a
little difficult to accept, since the government pays them no unemployment benefit: but if it were accepted, the cost of employing
them would be nil—so long as serious unemployment could be
expected to last.

But if in the longer run it were not the intention of the government
to provide education beyond that needed for the productive processes of the economy, and if a balance has been reached so that
there is no more than frictional and temporary unemployment of
skilled people, then in principle the MSC of skilled people can be
calculated in the following manner.

There are three cost elements. The first is that of the education
itself. Here a lot depends on who pays. If the state pays, then that
is entirely a social cost. If private people pay then that represents a
reduction in consumption, or other private investment. The social
cost could in principle be estimated by valuing the private consumption foregone along the lines of 13.1, and the investment
according to the principles proposed in 11.2 To the extent that
private people pay the social cost is likely to be small.

The second element is the increase in consumption occasioned
by employing such people. By analogy with private profits this can
be regarded as almost entirely a social cost (admittedly salary
earners do not often have incomes comparable to capitalists, but
they are nevertheless likely to have a very low consumption weight
compared to people the social value of whose consumption is
reckoned as equal to that of money in the hands of the government
—i.e. compared to people with a level of consumption of b—see
13.13).

The third element is the production lost as a result of diverting
these people from work to training and education. This is likely to
be a small part of the cost.

We do not imagine that many developing countries in the near
future could produce a reliable estimate of the MSC of producing
skilled people. But the indications given above suggest that the
social cost may typically be a lot higher than the consumption level
(we here neglect the conversion factors which may need to be
applied). Unless direct taxation is rather heavy so that consumption

is reduced well below the salary paid, the social cost may also be higher than the gross salary.

If there is a shortage of skilled people (and for many categories of skills this is true and likely to remain true for some time in the case of many developing countries) then, as usual, the MSB is the more appropriate accounting price to use. In this case one cannot do better than ask what employers are willing to pay for the relevant skills. This suggests that the AP should be at the level which would eliminate any excess demand for such skills.

We have thus far neglected the fact that some skilled people are traded. They may be imported—and, in reverse, a brain drain may be open. The social cost of an imported man is relatively easy to calculate: it consists of the remittances he makes plus the social cost of his consumption within the country; even if no budget studies exist, a little guesswork should provide an accurate enough estimate of the conversion factor to apply to an expatriate's consumption. Finally, what is the social cost of retaining a potential emigrant? It is, with sufficient accuracy, the salary (net of tax) he has to be paid.[1] Even if still regarded as a national after emigration, any higher earnings he might have abroad would have a negligible consumption weight. Even if he were only temporarily an emigré the case would not be greatly altered, since any repatriation of funds would normally benefit mainly himself and his relatives.

To sum up, it does not seem to us that very much time should normally be spent on contemplating the problems raised in this section. It will usually be sufficiently accurate to take, say, the man's gross salary, after applying the usual conversion factor, as his accounting price. This is what most project analysts would tend to do anyway.

12.9 NON-TRADED GOODS: THE GENERAL RULE AND ITS EXCEPTIONS

The general rule for the production of non-traded *producer* goods in the public sector is that the price actually charged should equal (*a*) the MSC for sales within the public sector, or (*b*) the MSC divided by the SCF for outside sales, and that the demand resulting from these prices should be satisfied. A general rule can be stated because, as argued in 12.5, producers' goods should not normally be subject to tax: but there may well be exceptions to part (*b*) of the rule. Thus, if necessary for the profitable operation of an approved private project, the price of the government-supplied producer good should

---

[1] The fact that the social cost of retaining a man within the country is likely to be less than the social cost of educating him, is the essence of the problem of the brain drain.

be reduced to the MSC. But, exceptions or not, the demand should be satisfied.

There is no such general rule for consumers' goods, precisely because many will be taxed. But, subject to the tax, and possibly a rationing scheme, the demand should be satisfied.

Nevertheless it may happen that, within the framework of the above pricing rules, there will be excess demand. This implies that too little, say, electricity, is being produced. It also implies that, so long as this condition of inadequate supply holds, the social value of electricity is higher than the estimated marginal social cost of supplying it: indeed, the social value becomes the price which equates the existing inadequate supply to the demand. As we have seen, there may sometimes be a case for restrictions on use, or rationing: if, despite this, there is still excess demand, then the social value is equal to the MSC at the level of output which meets the rationed demand.

There may also be a deficiency of demand. This implies that too much electricity capacity has been installed, and that electricity is worth less than the long-run marginal social cost: while such conditions hold, its social value is no more than the accounting cost of the current inputs of fuel and labour required to make it (capital costs become irrelevant as there is already too much capacity).

The above paragraphs strongly suggest not merely that actual prices should be adjusted so that supply equals demand (provided the price falls no lower than the social cost of current inputs), but also that accounting prices should vary, and therefore that supply and demand should be used as guides for the revision of accounting prices which were initially based on the methods discussed in 12.3 and 12.4 above. But before coming to this conclusion, let us recall the purpose of an accounting price (for example, electricity) in project selection. If the accounting price for electricity is high, then the project which uses a lot of electricity is less likely to pass the test, and vice versa—and hence the demand for electricity is less than it otherwise would be. But projects generally last a long time. If the shortage of electricity is merely temporary, it would be wrong to put a scarcity value on electricity when the project will probably be using very little until it is in operation several years hence. Similarly, it would be wrong to put a low accounting price on electricity just because there is, temporarily, excess capacity.

The case of electricity (here assumed to be in the public sector) is therefore one where very temporary considerations of excess demand or supply should not influence an accounting price which had been worked out by the method of 12.3, above. What has gone wrong is not the estimated accounting price, but rather the supply programme.

On the other hand, it does not at all follow that one should always ignore supply and demand. The case might be quite different for construction (assumed to be a private sector activity). If the prices charged by contractors have risen since the estimates of accounting prices were made, this could indicate that the costs, on which the estimates were based, were too low to ensure a sufficient long-run supply. Accounting prices for inputs from the private sector must always be based on actual prices, and consequently a change in actual prices, in response to changes in conditions of supply or demand, will normally indicate a need to change the accounting prices—unless, of course, there is evidence to suggest that temporary conditions are affecting the price. One is always forecasting accounting prices in project selection: and new events often make it sensible to change the forecasts.

It hardly need be added that, in inflationary conditions, frequent reassessments of accounting prices will be necessary. This would not be the case if inflation affected all prices to the same extent, but this is not the case. Also, of course, revisions must all be made contemporaneously. One does not want to use a new price for labour in conjunction with an out-of-date one for electricity.

To conclude, no automatic method of adjusting the accounting prices of non-traded goods can be recommended. Fluctuations of all kinds affect an economy from year to year, and necessarily affect the balance between supply and demand, and relative prices and scarcities. It would not be wise, therefore, to put too much weight upon the events of one year. No year's evidence should be neglected, nor should it be given full weight. One should use caution in changing the forecasts of accounting prices. Otherwise, the fluctuations in the predictions may themselves become so bad that no one would place any confidence in them. Fortunately, there appears to be a certain regularity in the operations of economic systems, sufficient at any rate to allow more success in the prediction of demands and prices than random guessing would allow. It may be hoped that economists and statisticians will be able to provide increasingly satisfactory methods of making these forecasts. Every country should acquire a staff of experts, trained and experienced in these matters. Of course, anything like complete accuracy is impossible, being precluded by the intrinsic uncertainty of economic relationships and reactions. But common sense, and a determination to rely on observations, can take one a long way.

CHAPTER THIRTEEN

The Uses of Income

This chapter is a digression, in which we shall discuss some issues of general principle, which must be considered in order to estimate the marginal social benefits of commodities and shadow wage rates. The problem is how to assign weights to the different uses of social income—consumption of various groups, and government expenditure on investment and public consumption. These weights give expression to the objectives of the government: we have already discussed how they arise in Chapter IV. In a book primarily concerned with practical applications, it would not be right to develop a theory of welfare weights in great detail. We consider only what can reasonably be done, in practice, in the present state of economic knowledge. We think that rather crude and simple weights have to be used in practice, but it is a help to know what one is trying to do: that is what the present chapter is about. Some parts of the chapter are rather technical. The whole of it can be omitted by readers who are willing to take arguments about objectives on trust.

13.1 CONSUMPTION WEIGHTS

In Chapter IX we suggested measuring the social value of any extra goods and services a man (or his family) gets, by multiplying what he spends on them by a number, to be called his *consumption weighting factor*, or *'weight'*, for short. In 13.11 we claim that the consumption weight should normally be independent of the particular kinds of extra goods and services that a man gets. In doing so, we shall draw attention to the most important exceptions to this rule. We then discuss, in 13.12, what the consumption weight ought to depend on —mainly the man's total consumption. Finally, we make some suggestions, with diffidence, about the numerical magnitude of the weights.

To make the discussion less confusing, we shall pretend that the people we are talking about spend all their income on consumption. In practice, one often wants to assess the value of extra *income*, some of which the man will save for the sake of future consumption. Also, it may often be easier to find out a man's income than his consumption. We say something about saving in 13.14.

13.11 *Valuing Extra Consumption*

The procedure we suggest can be summarized as follows. Let u be a man's consumption weighting factor. In other words, u is the social value of an extra rupee spent on this man's consumption. Suppose he gets x units of a commodity, additional to what he would have consumed in any case. He normally buys that commodity at a price p (p is the market price, not the accounting price). Then

The social value of the additional consumption $= upx$.

So long as x is small, and the man's consumption choices are to be respected as serving his own best interest, it can be reasonably assumed that u is independent of the particular commodity considered: this means no more than that a man's welfare would not be significantly changed if one took away one rupee's worth of one commodity and gave him instead one rupee's worth of another commodity which he habitually consumed.

Our formula for the social value of consumption also implies that twice as much is twice as good. So long as the amount remains small, this is reasonable: a little extra makes very little difference to the man, so that the same again must be just about as valuable as it was the first time. The proviso that the consumption change is small is important. If a man's consumption of rice were doubled, it would probably not be a good approximation to estimate the social gain at upx. We shall consider the social value of large changes in consumption in 13.13, below.

The proviso that the man's choices should be presumed to be in his own interest is also important. In many cases, governments do not make this presumption. People are induced by taxation, and in other ways, to increase their consumption of some things such as education and to curb their consumption of others, e.g. tobacco. In such cases, one must reconsider the use of p in the formula: for instance, as we saw in 12.51, it seems right to take the net-of-tax price if the tax is imposed to discourage consumption of something that is regarded as anti-social.

13.12 *What the Weight Depends On*

It is widely accepted that u should be smaller, the more consumption a man has in total: that an extra rupee is better given to a poor man than to a rich man. It may be claimed, in support of this view, that happiness is increased less (or misery reduced by less) with each successive rupee given to a man. Not everyone would accept the truth—or even the meaningfulness—of this claim. Perhaps one should simply say that it seems fair to give the poorer man some priority, since the rich man has already been able to enjoy a rupee equivalent to the poor man's extra one. We take it that most governments, administrators, and advisers would wish to make u depend on the man's total consumption (including what he gives to his dependants), and would wish to have it smaller for men with greater consumption, who are in other respects similar.

But people differ in much more than income: presumably u ought to depend upon age, sex, and family situation at least, and a subtle moralist could quickly list other relevant variables. However, there is no point in considering how u ought to depend upon variables which in practice are not going to be observed by the planners anyway. We therefore restrict ourselves to three sets of considerations:

(i) One group of workers may have more dependants than others —e.g. young female workers in a textile or radio factory as compared with male workers in heavy industry (and the latter will need more calories themselves). As against this, the former may well contribute to the consumption of other family members, though in practice this is not easy to allow for.

(ii) Generally, one considers broad groups, such as the workers in a particular region. Such groups consist of men, women, and children, of all ages and in diverse family groupings. If the two groups contain all these types in closely similar proportions, one may as well take income per head as the basis of comparison. Adjustment is needed only if there are significant differences in the age structure. Then it may be necessary to change the actual numbers to a number of adult equivalents. This involves comparing the consumption of, say, a ten-year-old with a thirty-year-old. It may help to imagine at what relative consumption level a man would think that an extra rupee would have meant as much to him at 10 as it does now at 30 (it is, perhaps, best to put oneself in the shoes of the 30-year-old!). If the answer is one-third, then a ten-year-old should count as one-third of an adult.

We can properly talk about u as depending on the value of the consumption of different groups only if all groups face the same prices when purchasing their consumption goods: otherwise the values of their different 'baskets' of goods are not strictly comparable. Small differences in prices, such as you would find when comparing different households in a town, hardly matter. But, at least in the comparison between townsmen and country-dwellers, price differences may be large. If it were simply that all prices are higher in towns, in the same proportion, we could readily change the figures for consumption so as to make them comparable; but the trouble is that *relative* prices are often quite different.

Presented with this difficulty, one can either say 'Go and look at the different groups and decide what the ratio of their weighting-factors should be'—and that may be quite sound advice, although it demands a judicious cast of mind—or suggest a crude approximation. The short-cut we suggest, which we have no reason to think misleading, is to measure the consumption (per adult-equivalent) of the different groups *at market prices* if they all pay prices that are rather similar (except for overall differences in price level): and otherwise to use *accounting prices*[1] (with an adjustment explained below). In other words, multiply each man's consumption by the appropriate consumption conversion factor, and regard the weight as a function of consumption measured in this way. It must be admitted that this could be misleading: it is possible that two people consuming goods and services worth the same amount at accounting prices nevertheless deserve different weighting factors. Thus two people might in theory have quite different levels of welfare, and yet there be a set of prices (in this case the APs, which are arbitrary from their point of view) which makes the notional value of their consumption the same: nevertheless, common sense suggests that one would not go far wrong in treating them as equal. We shall denote the weighting factor at accounting prices by v, to be distinguished from the weighting factor at market prices which is denoted by u.

The one adjustment we think worth making is to allow for higher prices in towns that reflect the cost of transporting food, etc., from rural areas: if prices in town are higher for that reason, the transport cost (at accounting prices) should be subtracted from consumption. Of course, it will not always be necessary to make such an adjustment.

(iii) It may be thought right to have the weight depend on the circumstances—particularly the consumption—of others. The case for increasing the consumption of a man with Rs. 10,000 a year seems stronger when very many people have that level of consumption than when he is an unusually rich man. Planners and others concerned with consumption weights should not ignore such considerations, which may justify weights that fall off steeply with increasing individual consumption in those societies where income is very unequally distributed. We shall not explore the point in any detail since the current degree of inequality forms part of the back-

---

[1] It would probably be better to use an average of the market prices paid by different groups, but we are reluctant, where a short-cut is our aim, to introduce yet another set of prices into the procedure.

ground against which numerical consumption weights must be discussed.

13.13 *Numerical Weights*

We have discussed what determines *relative* weights, but have made no mention of uncommitted social income, although the weights are supposed to render consumption equivalent to it. We shall be discussing the value of government income relative to consumption in subsequent sections of this chapter. It is best to keep these issues separate from the problems of weighting consumption, and so we introduce the notion of a *base consumption level*. This is the level of consumption, measured at accounting prices, at which a proportional increase in the man's consumption of all goods and services would be socially just as valuable as having these goods and services available for uncommitted use by the public sector. We denote this level of consumption by the letter b.

In the case of any particular group we would proceed in two steps:

(i) Calculate the conversion factor for the group's consumption: that is, find the ratio of the value of its consumption at accounting prices to its value at market prices. It will be convenient to denote the conversion factor—which in principle varies from one group to another, of course—by the letter γ. At the same time, one has calculated the value of the group's per-capita consumption, measured at accounting prices, which will be denoted by c.

(ii) Compare c with b. If c were equal to b, then, by definition of b, the weighting factor v is unity. It follows that u, the weighting factor at market prices, is equal to γ. More generally, we write

$$u = v\gamma,$$

where v (the weighting factor at accounting prices) will be taken to depend only on c, and is equal to 1 when $c = b$.

It may seem that this two-step procedure is cumbersome. But one will usually have to measure consumption in accounting prices for other purposes anyway. The main point, however, is that γ is quite likely to vary from year to year, as taxes, world prices, and the economy's productivity change, while v may be taken to be constant so long as the level of c relative to b does not change much. v and γ are thus determined by quite different considerations.

One way of thinking about how v should depend upon c is to ask oneself how much it would seem right to take away from a man who has consumption b in order to increase by one unit (at accounting prices) the consumption of a man who already has c: the answer to that question gives the value of v corresponding to c.

Another way is to pose the question 'How many men, each with c (say Rs. 300 a month), would have to get an extra rupee for you to regard this as being as good as one man with b (say Rs. 150 a month) getting an extra rupee?' If the answer were say, four, then the consumption weight quarters as the income is doubled, and the v corresponding to Rs. 300 a month is $\frac{1}{4}$.

There are, unfortunately, great difficulties involved in trying to establish consumption weights in the sort of manner suggested above.[1] Ordinary people are very reluctant to commit themselves to any quantification of their feelings on such matters. Politicians may be even less willing, since they cannot easily envisage what the consequences of such judgments might be if translated into terms of economic policy. Yet, as we saw in 4.2, if systematic, consistent, and thorough-going attention is to be paid to income distribution, a system of consumption weights is required. The upshot may well be that systematic, consistent, and thorough-going attention to income distribution is not generally desired by politicians, and is therefore beyond the bounds of of political possibility. However, we can without great difficulty envisage a situation where a rough system of weighting is covertly used to determine such operational variables as the SWR; with the politicians agreeing, provided that they need not commit themselves to any explicit recognition of the weights. Also, we would not wish *ourselves* to rule out explicit use and recognition of a weighting system. On this basis, let us pursue the matter a little further.

Let us first define the 'elasticity', η, of the consumption weight as being the proportionate fall in the weight for a given small proportionate rise in consumption. If this elasticity does not itself vary with the level of consumption, we can write

$$v = (b/c)^{\eta}.$$

By differentiating it follows that

$$\frac{dv}{dc} = -\eta b^{\eta} c^{-(\eta+1)}$$

---

[1] A few economists have sought to measure 'utility'. Even if these measurements could be accepted as roughly measuring something objective, which is very doubtful, there is still the problem that utility thus measured cannot necessarily be equated with the social value to be put on different levels of consumption. The reader may refer to Fellner, 1967, for a discussion of measuring utility. We regretfully do not think that the social planner can get much comfort from this source.

whence
$$\eta = -\frac{c}{v}\frac{dv}{dc}$$

Since $-\dfrac{c}{v}\dfrac{dv}{dc}$ is an expression for the proportionate fall in v for a given proportionate rise in c, it follows that η is the elasticity already defined.

Thus if $\eta = 1$, v falls in the same proportion as c rises: and the answer to our question would be that two men with Rs. 300 each getting an extra rupee would be as valuable as one man with Rs. 150 getting an extra rupee. If η was 2, v falls with the square of the proportionate rise, and the answer would be 'four men'. Similarly, it would be 'eight men' if η were 3.

On admittedly extremely inadequate evidence, we guess that most people would put η in the range 1–3 (if they could be induced to commit themselves at all). The following table shows the consequential weights, for values $\eta = 1$, $\eta = 2$, and $\eta = 3$.

	$\eta =$		
c/b	1	2	3
0·25	4	16	64
0.50	2	4	8
0·75	1.33	1.78	2.38
1·0	1	1	1
1·5	0·66	0·44	0·30
2.0	0·5	0·25	0·125
3·0	0·33	0·11	0·04
5·0	0·20	0·04	0·01
10·0	0·10	0·01	0·001

The above figures depend on the constancy of η. But there is no particular reason why v should fall at the same proportional rate at all consumption levels. Why should twice as much consumption deserve a quarter of the weight, whether consumption is low or high? Of course, there is something to be said for simplicity where views are diverse and ill-formed. There also seem to be arguments going both ways. As soon as some low level of consumption is exceeded, since basic needs are satisfied, it can be argued that the weight need not fall off so fast; as against this, it becomes rather doubtful whether more goods make people happier (though there is no dispute that they want them). Similarly, at very low levels of consumption, the exceptionally poor may be thought to deserve an especially high weight; but it is sadly true that their sufferings may not be much eased by small increases in their consumption.

We present these weights as points of reference, for the reader to consider. For our own part, we would find it hard to select a set of weights which did not support the suggestion, made in 11.2, that the consumption of rich capitalists should normally be given a zero weight in cost–benefit calculations. There would be no point in including a weight of 1% (except perhaps to make the project report sound nicer). These weights would also, in many countries, support the assignment of a large weight to the consumption of agricultural labourers, and peasants with very small landholdings, compared even with unskilled labourers working for the larger urban employers.

Indeed, as a practical matter, we would suggest that it will often be useful to assign weights to only three or four broad groups of consumers. This will make the task of weighting the consumption generated by a project rather easier, since it will only be necessary to split the total into a few parts. For instance, if $b =$ Rs. 150 a month, the above table of weights might be simplified to:

c	v
below Rs. 150	2
Rs. 150–Rs. 600	0·5
above Rs. 600	0

A simple table like this can perhaps be discussed more easily by the many interested parties, but the more detailed table would often be needed to provide a justification.

As we remarked in 13.11, these weights are not perfectly appropriate when a group's consumption changes by a large amount (relative to the consumption they started with). Large changes are important, particularly in developing countries, where the creation of new jobs in organized industry may bring about, in effect, the substitution of a highly paid occupation for a low-paid occupation. For example, it must not be assumed that, because new employment augments the wage bill, the appropriate weight for this commitment to consumption is the weight for an average wage-earner. The weight may well be much closer to that for an agricultural labourer. It is likely to be convenient, for the economic analysis of such cases, to express consumption objectives in terms of 'utility functions'. We define *a utility function V*, by laying down that the social value of changing a man's consumption from c_1 to c_2 is $V(c_2) - V(c_1)$. The consumption weight for a man with consumption c is then the derivative of V with respect to c.[1]

In more concrete terms, we can derive the utility function from the consumption weights by regarding $V(c_1) - V(c_2)$ as the sum of a large number of small contributions to social value, arising from small changes in consumption which gradually change c_1 to c_2, each of these small changes being multiplied by the appropriate weighting factor.[2] This might actually be a better description of the real changes. A new job in the city can, as we have pointed out earlier, cause a large number of people to change occupations, each one slightly improving his consumption. The total effect is the sum of improvements for each person, which are estimated by multiplication of the consumption change by his weighting factor; and that total effect is the same as if one man came straight from the lowest 'rung of the ladder' into the new job.

13.14 *Saving*
The discussion so far has been entirely in terms of consumption. However, as we saw in our discussion of consumption by private capitalists (11.12), it will often be necessary to assess the social value of additional *income* to some group when it is virtually certain that part of that additional income will not be consumed immediately. It is also true that one tends to group people into income rather than consumption groups, but we think it is more natural to make the weighting factor depend upon consumption, when that is possible, rather than income.[3] We do not discuss this minor issue further, but we must say something about the evaluation of extra saving generated by a project. That extra saving may have a different value from consumption by the same person for three reasons:

(i) If the savings finance extra investment, that will possibly

---

[1] So $V(c_2) - V(c_1) = \int_{c_1}^{c_2} v(c)dc$, where $v(c) = \dfrac{dV}{dc}$ is the consumption weight corresponding to consumption level c.

[2] For instance, the utility function corresponding to the weights in the table, with $\eta = 2$, is $V = A - \dfrac{b^2}{c}$, when $\dfrac{dV}{dc} = v = \left(\dfrac{b}{c}\right)^2$.

[3] Income may fluctuate more from year to year than consumption, which may better reflect the lifetime experience and expectations of individuals and groups.

generate extra tax revenue for the government (or involve the government in paying additional subsidies), so that a change in uncommitted social income is involved.

(ii) The extra investment may also generate extra employment, or an increase in real wages.

(iii) It may be to the advantage of the economy to have the man postpone his consumption, for his rate of return on savings may be less than the social rate of return to investment.

These three considerations can all be brought together by means of the techniques discussed in 11.2. The social value of saving by any consumer is worked out in the same way as for a rich private investor, with the difference that the consumption which the poor consumer will get in the future as a result of his investment is more valuable than in the case of a rich investor.

But such calculations naturally require a good deal of work. When, as is usual, the amount of saving is small, a very crude short-cut will be sufficient. We suggest that it be assumed that the value of the saving is half-way between (i), the value of uncommitted social income, and the consumption weighting factor of the saver.

13.2 Public Expenditure on Consumption

Our discussion of consumption weights will not be complete until we have explained how to estimate b, the per capita consumption level (in APs) at which it is thought a man will make as good use of an extra rupee of consumption as would the government with an extra rupee to spend. It is hard to make an intelligent estimate of b, and we shall emphasize the uncertainty of it. But in general terms, we know what has to be done. We have to ask what the government will do with uncommitted social income, and we have to estimate how valuable these uses are by looking at the consumption generated. Of course, the value of the consumption generated depends on b. *We have got b right when the average value of the uses to which the government puts social income is one.*

13.21 *Subsidies to, and Direct Taxes on, Private Consumption*

The estimation of b would be easy if the government used its income solely to subsidize people with a particular income (letting no one fall below that level). Then b would be just this minimum level of income.[1] At least that would be a reasonable presumption if the

[1] If there were administrative costs to these subsidies, equal to a proportion x of the subsidy, the weight for those getting the subsidy should be (at least) $1 + x$: this also allows us to estimate b.

government had no reason to be concerned about the effect of these subsidies on incentives. In developed countries, particularly, it is a matter of some concern that welfare payments made to poor people may discourage them from seeking employment. Similar considerations apply in a developing country, if there is any degree of labour shortage.

Although the whole of public income is obviously not spent on consumption subsidies, an answer can still be reached if we suppose that the government has well considered its various expenditures, so that additional expenditure in any particular field is as valuable as additional expenditure in any other. Then the project planners can deduce the value of b from any single category of expenditure, and one whose social significance is as obvious as consumption subsidies is a particularly suitable means for estimating it.[1] The procedure suggested by this argument is to see whether consumption subsidies are paid to some group, or groups, and to estimate the value of their *per capita* consumption, at accounting prices (with a deduction for transport costs, as indicated in 13.12). Groups for whom the incentive to work is not an issue, because of disability, are the best ones to use for this purpose. Even when, as in the cases to be considered next, b cannot easily be estimated in this way, we would want to know the consumption per head in groups receiving consumption subsidies. It will be useful to denote this figure by b_0.

There are two cases where we may want to look further for our estimate of b. The first is when no group receives consumption subsidies. Even in this case, it can be argued that the income level at which a man just escapes the direct tax net can be used as a basis for estimating b.[2] It is quite plausible that subsidies are only not paid below this 'minimum tax' level, because of the incentive effect —and that the government would consider an increase in such incomes (if it could be achieved in a manner which did not make people rather unwilling to work if they could) as being as valuable as its own expenditures. As against this, it is also true that political expediency as well as the incentive argument may push up the minimum tax level well above b. If the more complicated procedures to be outlined appear to be unworkable, the mid-point between the lowest income at which people succeed in living and the minimum

---

[1] This method for estimating b, the weights based on it, and the shadow wage rate (cf. Chapter XIV), has been used by Maurice Scott for Kenya and Mauritius (see Scott, MacArthur and Newbery, 1974, and Scott, 1972).

[2] This method is also used in Scott, MacArthur and Newbery, 1974.

tax level might be taken. We regard this as another estimate of b_0, and denote it by that same symbol.

The second case is when the hypothesis that consumption subsidies are pushed to a point where such expenditures have a social value equal to the average value of additional government expenditures in other fields is untenable. Although, as already pointed out in Chapter VI, advisers to the government, including project planners and civil servants, will often have to assume that many of the government's actions are and will be well considered, they may reasonably take a different view, either when the government feels itself forced into various expenditures which it would not make in the absence of political pressure or prior commitments, or when the government is in effect seeking advice on whether its various expenditures are of equal social value. Aid agencies may on occasion also wish to look further: for, if the government wastes money, and it is politically possible to embody this consideration in one's estimate, then the value of b is higher than it otherwise would be.

13.22 *Current Government Expenditure*
In theory, with a rational benevolent government, public consumption should be of equal social value to subsidies, as well as to public investment. But it is seldom easy to estimate its value directly. Indeed, the chief items of 'public consumption'—expenditures on defence, justice, police, education, medical care, and facilities for recreation, are the main examples—are notoriously hard to evaluate: and we are making no attempt to provide any guidelines for doing so in this book.

Some public consumption shares with subsidies to private consumption the character of a gift: its value is the total value to the individuals who benefit. Thus it may be possible to apply the principles enunciated in 9.43. A hospital bed, for example, has a social value which is at least the sum of the amounts that the individuals who will use it would have been willing to pay, weighted by the appropriate consumption weights.[1] But in many cases—police services, employment exchanges, and so on—we have only the vaguest ideas of social values, and in all countries conventions

---

[1] Notice that larger weights should be used where individuals would be willing to make payments that are a large part of their incomes—for the gain in 'utility' is then greater than the weighted willingness-to-pay (cf. 9.43). It can further be argued that the value may still be understated, at least in some cases: there are, for instance, external benefits in the case of infectious diseases.

are followed. Until, at least, much more research work has been done, there is little advantage to be had from attempts to measure their social value; except in cases of glaring over- or under-provision, the planners may as well assume that they have the same value, at the margin, as uncommitted social income.

Investment in enterprises producing marketed goods is the part of public expenditure whose value may be most amenable to economic analysis. The remainder of the present chapter is therefore devoted to methods of estimation in the industrial case. A thorough analysis rapidly becomes somewhat technical. We have avoided any deep economics, but many readers may prefer to read only 13.31, which discusses two numerical examples. It would be possible to estimate the value of public investment in a crude way by comparing actual countries with these imaginary examples.

13.3 The Value of Public Investment

The public sector may invest in many fields—agriculture, transport, and large-scale industrial production, for example. Different kinds of investment projects raise different problems when they are evaluated—labour costs require special treatment in the case of agricultural projects; accurate estimation of the value of output will be difficult in the case of transport; and so on. Investment in these different fields may possibly be expected to have different values (say, because of the relative effectiveness of the different ministers involved) but the normal assumption is that they are equally valuable. The discussion that follows is simpler if we assume that all uses are equally valuable in prospect, for we can then concentrate on one kind of investment project. If this seems to be a bad assumption, other kinds of project must be evaluated: the single case we discuss should show how it would have to be done. We concentrate on industrial projects, and consider how one can estimate the social value of funds devoted to such projects.

Industrial projects provide additional consumption directly through employment. In 13.31 and 13.32 we compare the social value of public investment with the social value of current consumption provided through extra employment; and discuss the latter in 13.4. If the social value of public investment can be equated with that of uncommitted social income, then this section will provide us with a method of comparing the latter with the value of the current consumption generated by employment, a method of estimating b which is alternative to that discussed in 13.2.

13.31 *Investment and Employment*

It will be a help in appreciating what is important in this connection if we describe two imaginary countries which represent rather extreme cases.

Country A. In this country the marginal productivity of labour in agriculture is close to zero, for there is year-round unemployment even in rural areas. Population is growing so rapidly that, despite expansion of the industrial sector, and advances in agricultural capital and techniques, the standard of living in the agricultural sector is not expected to grow in the near future. Nor is the industrial wage rate expected to rise (or fall), but it is already so high that an industrial employee and his family enjoy a standard of living twice as high as the average in agriculture. Industrial investment projects are currently yielding 15% in terms of social income, and seem likely to continue doing so. A third of these returns is committed to wage payments, the whole of this representing an increase in consumption, since the marginal product is zero; but virtually all the rest is available for further investment.

It will be recognized that we sketch an extreme case here. Returns to investment are good (though not unattainable, considering the low cost of labour in such a country), yet, because of constraints on saving and government income and expenditure, growth in agricultural output only just keeps pace with population growth. This does not mean there is no growth in output per head in the economy, of course; only that the growth is industrial, and its benefits are distributed by increased industrial employment, rather than through increases in consumption levels in either the rural or urban sector taken separately.

In this country, $1,000,000 of public investment provides, in the first year, $100,000 of further investment and $50,000 of additional consumption for wage earners and farmers:[1] and as the investment grows each year by 10%, so also does the consumption provided. Thus, by giving up a million dollars to investment now, it is possible to get $50,000 of consumption next year, $55,000 the year after that, and so on, growing at 10% each year. After ten years, a total of about $800,000 of extra consumption will have been enjoyed, and the initial million dollars invested has grown to over 2·5 million dollars.

---

[1] We here suppose that the new wage earners were previously members of a rural family and shared in its consumption: so that part of the rise in consumption will be enjoyed by the latter.

On our assumptions, the individuals who benefit in ten years' time are no better off than those of today. It might therefore be argued that consumption in ten years' time is worth as much as consumption today. But the present generation may not think so, and politicians and planners might therefore take a slightly different view. Even so, future consumption could hardly be discounted very strongly. If it is not discounted at all, and if the 2·5 million dollars of investment could in time be converted into at least as much consumption (a very pessimistic assumption implying that the return on investment falls to zero), then the above calculation shows us that a million dollars of investment today is worth at least 3·3 million dollars of consumption. Indeed, if we pursue the calculation another ten years, so as to take in twenty years altogether, and retain the assumption of a 15% rate of return, we shall get a much larger figure. By that time the accumulated total of all consumption, *plus* the accumulated capital stock, amounts to over 9 million dollars. No doubt, it is implausible to assume that by that time neither industrial wages, nor the rural standard of living, will have improved. On the other hand, there is still a lot of the future to come.

For the sake of argument, let us use that figure of 9 million dollars' worth of consumption arising from 1 million dollars of investment today. It is high, but not absurdly high, given the decision not to discount the future for twenty years. Then in Country A uncommitted social income turns out to be 9 times as valuable as consumption committed through industrial employment. In other words, the weight given to present consumption committed through employment should be $\frac{1}{9}$.

Country B. For the second picture, we take the opposite extreme. Rapid growth is expected in both the agricultural and industrial sectors, and there is a shortage of labour in rural areas. Those who might go from rural areas to employment in the towns are consuming goods and services which are, in terms of accounting prices, equal in value to the marginal productivity of labour, m. The consumption of an average industrial worker, c, is only 50% higher than m. Both c and m are expected to grow at 4% per year. Investment is high, since private saving and taxation are quite large, even in the agricultural sector: indeed, it is thought that in ten years' time consumption provided through employment will be as valuable as uncommitted social income. A million dollars in this economy can be sure of providing an annual output, less material inputs, of 25%, i.e. of $250,000; but $150,000 of this has to be paid in wages.[1]

What are the consumption gains from undertaking a million dollars of public investment in this economy? Each year the investment yields 10% that is ploughed back into further investment, so that investment grows at 10% per year for ten years. At the end of that time, it does not matter what is done with the annual output, since investment and consumption are regarded as being equally valuable. The $150,000 paid in wages during the first year provides an increase in consumption of $50,000, the rest being lost through the reduction of agricultural output caused by the removal of labour. (For simplicity, we assume that wage earners pay no taxes and save nothing.) This $50,000 grows by 10% each year, and we can summarize the results, year by year:

1st year:	50,000 dollars
2nd year:	55,000 dollars
3rd year:	60,500 dollars

. . . .

10th year:	117,900 dollars

These figures show consumption during the ten years. After 10 years, investments have accumulated to a value of:

2,593,700 dollars.

This amount can be thought of as being available for consumption in the 11th year.

In the circumstances of this country, consumption ten years ahead is certainly not as valuable as consumption now, since in ten years' time the population will have been enjoying annual increases in average consumption of 4%. This amounts to an increase of 48% by the end of the ten-year period. For this reason alone, quite apart from being later in time, these future consumers should be given a lower weight. Let us suppose that, all things considered, the weight for consumption is made to fall at 10% per year (that is, to use a terminology mentioned earlier, the consumption rate of interest, CRI, is taken to be 10%). In the circumstances, this is a possible figure.[2] Let us consider its implications.

Discounting at 10%, the stream of consumption listed above is worth 1·5 million dollars of consumption in the first year. In other

---

[1] In our notation, $cn = 150,000$, $mn = 100,000$. We suppose that, while c and m are growing over time, labour requirements, n, are falling at the same rate, so that, conveniently, cn and mn remain constant.

[2] The CRI is further considered in 13.43. The discussion there suggests that 10% may be on the high side for this example. We use it here for simplicity.

words it is 50% better to invest, than to commit income to consumption by increasing industrial employment now. The weight for consumption given this way is $\frac{2}{3}$: that is, uncommitted social income has a social value only 50% higher than consumption generated by industrial employment.

There is no point in multiplying examples. These two cases show that the relative weight of consumption and public investment can vary a great deal with circumstances. But they show no more than that, and are not meant to imply that investible funds are always more valuable than consumption. In some countries expertise in devising profitable investments falls short of the funds becoming available, and this situation may continue for some time. For this sort of reason, the authors of some case studies have thought it best to assume that investible funds were worth no more than consumption, for the time being.[1] In Chapter XIV, we shall see that their relative value is quite important for estimating the shadow wage rate, but that the shadow wage rate does not vary nearly as much as this weight, when everything is taken into account.

13.32 *Some Formulae*

The point of the above examples can be made more explicitly, and with additional important details, if we use some symbols for the different effects in year t of making a public investment of one unit in year 1.

r_t = the uncommitted social income generated; it is assumed to be ploughed back into further public investment, and it is less than extra government income by the amount g_t.

n_t = extra employment of unskilled labour.

Other quantities required are symbolized as follows:

c_t = consumption per wage-earner, arising out of wage-payments.[2]

m_t = the marginal productivity of labour in agriculture.

Estimation of these numbers is admittedly difficult. r_t is the social value added in production (with no deduction made on account of labour) *less* the value at accounting prices of additional payments made to labour as a result of the investment. Those payments *include* (though c_t does not) any transport costs of bringing consumer goods from country to town, and any additional payments to labour

---

[1] E.g. Little and Tipping, 1972.

[2] c_t will be measured net of transport costs for goods brought from country to town (cf. 13.12).

already employed as a result of increases in wage rates brought about by new employment. Some part of public income, g_t, may be committed as a result of the project; and the residue is then r_t. n_t is the amount of extra employment in the industrial (or technically advanced) part of the economy—that is, the employment generated by an average project *less* employment reductions elsewhere as a result of upward pressure on wage rates and labour shortage. In the long run, when unemployment problems are of a short-run nature, or in countries where the supply of labour to the urban economy is inelastic, n_t will be zero. When n_t is small or zero, the benefits of investment are distributed mainly through increasing wages, and current government expenditure. But in the following calculation these effects are ignored, and g_t is assumed to be zero—until 13.33.

Thus we now show how to estimate the value of investment, as compared to the value of consumption distributed through new employment, on the assumption that all the new social income made available to the government by the investment is reinvested in further projects of the same kind. Of course this is an unrealistic assumption. Nevertheless the method would give a satisfactory estimate of the value of government income if all its uses—including investment—were equally valuable. We shall explain in 13.33 how it can be modified to take account of non-investment government expenditures, when it is desirable to do so.

In order to do the calculation, we must have a way of comparing the value of consumption in different years. We introduce:

$i_t =$ the *consumption rate of interest* (CRI), which we define specifically as the rate at which the social value of *employment-generated consumption* declines.

This definition coincides with that implicit in other discussions of these matters.[1] The idea is that future consumption (committed through employment) has some weight relative to consumption today. We define

$D_t =$ the weight for consumption committed through employment in year t

and

$$i_t = \frac{D_{t+1} - D_t}{D_t}.$$

For these definitions to be natural, we must suppose that consump-

---

[1] E.g. UNIDO *Guidelines*, Section 13.5.

tion in future is measured in such a way that a unit in future represents the same real goods to consumers as a unit now. Then the way in which D_t varies over time depends on changes in real incomes. To ensure this comparability, we stipulate that consumption measured in money terms be deflated by the appropriate consumer price index, that is by an index of the APs of consumer goods (c and m being measured in APs). Since accounting prices are equal to market prices times conversion factors, the appropriate deflator for historical data is a consumer price index (which is based on market prices) plus the change in the consumption conversion factor. This justifies our definition of the numéraire in 9.12.

Because of reinvestment, an initial unit in year 1 results in additional capital, after t years, of

$$(1+r_1)(1+r_2) \ldots (1+r_{t-1}) \text{ units.}$$

Each unit of this capital yields in current net benefits, extra consumption $(c_t - m_t)n_t$ distributed through additional employment. Thus the net benefit in year t of the initial unit of investment, in terms of consumption, is

$$(1+r_1)(1+r_2) \ldots (1+r_{t-1})(c_t - m_t)n_t.$$

This net benefit is to be discounted back to the present at discount rate i, so that the present value of a unit of investment relative to the current consumption generated by industrial employment, a ratio which we shall call s_0, is given by the following tedious, but essentially simple, expression:

$$s_0 = \frac{1}{1+i_1}(c_1 - m_1)n_1$$

$$+ \frac{1+r_1}{(1+i_1)(1+i_2)}(c_2 - m_2)n_2$$

$$+ \frac{(1+r_1)(1+r_2)}{(1+i_1)(1+i_2)(1+i_3)}(c_3 - m_3)n_3$$

$$+ \ldots \ldots$$

This formula is simplest when $(c-m)n$ is constant over time. Constancy may be a good approximation for a long time, but eventually it is to be expected that $n=0$; and, as n falls, m will become closer to c. However, let us suppose it constant for the moment. Then one is struck by the possibility that if r is always bigger than i, the terms in the series apparently become bigger and bigger so that s_0 is infinite! Which is, as mathematicians have always been fond of saying, absurd.

No sensible country would keep reinvesting at a rate greater than i for ever. It can be shown that, if it did, capital would be accumulated at a uselessly rapid rate. But it would be wrong to jump to the conclusion that r is *always* less than i, convenient though it would be if that were true.[1] r is a number that should be based on facts which have only a remote connection with the growth rates of consumption that most influence i. The planners thus have to estimate r separately, and cannot adjust their estimate after they have compared it with i, just because it would be mathematically convenient to do so. It may be thought that we should be less definite about i, since it involves value judgments, about which disagreement may be particularly wide. As against this, we shall see that it may not depend very sensitively on value judgments. But even if it did, a decision must still be made, which in its turn should be independent of the magnitude of r. Thus planners could perfectly well find themselves estimating current levels of r and i such that r is bigger than i.

Looking again at the expression for s_0, we see that if r exceeds i then the first few terms of the series certainly get larger and larger. At some stage they may get smaller, as $(c-m)n$ gets smaller: but that stage might be rather remote, and it is almost always hard to estimate. The expression does suggest that, in such a case, s_0 is likely to be rather large. s_0 may also be quite large in cases where r is less than i initially, but not much less; or if there is good reason to expect that r will soon be greater than i and will remain so for some time. This latter case would arise if a country were currently reinvesting only a small proportion of profits, but was expected to do much more in the near future.

Before we go on to consider these difficult cases, we can draw two conclusions:

(i) If r is less than i; and the difference between i and r is not expected to change much in the future; and $(c-m)n$ is also expected to be fairly constant for a time, then the value of investment relative to consumption can be obtained from the formula

$$s_0 = \frac{(c-m)n}{i-r}.$$

---

[1] We emphasize this point because the UNIDO *Guidelines*, in Chapters XIII and XIV, though basing themselves on the same analytical ideas, make the mistake of assuming—merely for convenience—that r and i are constant, and that r is less than i.

This formula is obtained from the series derived above by summing the geometric progression:

$$\frac{1}{1+i}+\frac{1+r}{(1+i)^2}+\frac{(1+r)^2}{(1+i)^3}+ \cdots = \frac{1}{1+i}\left(1-\frac{1+r}{1+i}\right)^{-1} = \frac{1}{i-r}.$$

We omit the t-labels from s and the other symbols because in this case everything is constant.

It must be said firmly that that this case arises only when the economy is expected to follow for a long time a fairly steady growth path, with a constant proportion of income being saved, and the balance of the economy between different sectors remaining constant. These assumptions are more likely to be satisfied in the more developed countries.

(ii) If r is expected to be larger than i for a substantial period, there is considerable uncertainty about the value of s_0. A large part of the expected benefit of investment then comes in the fairly distant future, since the reinvestment of profits creates new employment which grows faster than the discount rate the planners apply to the consumption provided by that employment. Even quite small changes in the assumptions made about r and n, would make a considerable difference to the estimate of s_0. We conclude from this that the planners should avoid extreme assumptions—whether of pessimism or optimism—when estimating s_0. The value of s_0 that is wanted is an average over all the possibilities (cf. Chapter XV), some of which would give a very large value of s_0, while others would give quite a low value. Because of the averaging, one can usually say that s_0 ought not to be at one of these extreme values.

13.33 *The Value of Government Income Again*

If one does arrive at an estimate of s_0 that is high, and it could easily exceed 10 using the formula in 13.32, then the estimate of base consumption, b, derived from s_0, will probably be much lower than that derived from the uses of current government expenditure. If, as is implied by the above, investment looks substantially more valuable than current consumption, the calculation of s_0 should probably be drastically modified, on the grounds that, at each stage of reinvestment, part of the government income generated probably 'leaks' into current expenditure.

Suppose then that, at the margin, a fraction g_t of government income is devoted to current expenditure. We say 'at the margin', since we are interested in the effect of *changes* in total government income. A change in its income may induce, or force, the government to

(i) change the levels of subsidization and taxation;
(ii) change the levels of expenditure in areas where there is a contractual or moral commitment, or there are political pressures from within or without the country.

Since we are interested in changes, item (ii) may be sufficiently small to neglect. Then the value of a unit change in (i) may be estimated as $v(b_0)$, where b_0 is the average of the lowest taxed consumption level and the highest subsidized consumption level. If $v(b_1)$ is the weight for consumption distributed through extra employment (cf. 13.4), the value of current government expenditure relative to employment-distributed consumption is $v(b_0)/v(b_1)$, which we shall denote by $\bar{v}$. It may not be a bad approximation to put $\bar{v} = 1$. But in general it might vary over time.

We now want to interpret s_0 not just as the social value of investment (relative to consumption), but as the social value of government income. Then the weight for employment-generated consumption will be $1/s_0$. An initial unit of expenditure will go partly $(1-g)$ into investment and partly (g) into current expenditure, with relative weight $\bar{v}$, so at each stage reinvestment is at a rate $r' = (1-g)r$, and an item $\bar{v}gr$ has to be added to the other current benefits, measured by $(c-m)n$.

The long formula in 13.32 therefore becomes:

$$s_0 = \bar{v}_0 g_0 + (1-g_0)\left\{ \frac{1}{1+i_1}[(c_1 - m_1)n_1 + \bar{v}_1 g_1 r_1] \right.$$
$$\left. + \frac{1+r'_1}{(1+i_1)(1+i_2)}[(c_2 - m_2)n_2 + \bar{v}_2 g_2 r_2] + \ldots \text{etc.} \right\}$$

with $r'_t = (1-g_t)r_t$. Since r'_t is smaller than r_t, there is a better chance now that r'_t will be smaller than i_t, but we would not put too much faith in that possibility. The short formula (valid when r and i, and everything else, are constant over time) becomes

$$s_0 = \bar{v}g + (1-g)\frac{(c-m)n + \bar{v}gr}{i-r}$$
$$= \frac{(1-g)(c-m)n + \bar{v}g(i-gr)}{i-r}.$$

There are, broadly speaking, two ways of estimating s_0. One is to formulate an economic model of the economy, and solve it for an appropriate objective function. The accuracy depends upon the quality of the model used, and satisfactorily realistic economic models are very difficult to construct, either for developing or developed economies. But the method has been used, and is at least a check on the more rough and ready arguments we have been using.[1] Since these methods are highly technical, we cannot go into them further here.

The other way of estimating s_0 is simply to make plausible assumptions about the relevant variables, without fitting them together to form a fully articulated economic model. We suggest the following procedure, which is clearly very crude:

(i) Estimate how long it will take the economy to reach a situation in which the proportion of the labour force employed in urban industry is fairly constant. When such a situation has been reached, it may be assumed that the additional capital would not be used to employ more labour in the modern sector, but rather to provide the same labour force with different kinds of capital equipment. Thus n will be zero at that time. One way of estimating how long it will be before no weight is being given to the creation of additional urban employment is to project current changes in the labour force, and those that are expected in the near future, and find when the proportion of the labour force employed in manufacturing industry will be the same as is observed in more developed countries now. Alternatively, we might expect the planners to formulate a target for urban employment. Since a precise estimate is quite impossible, the planner will be wise to rely on visual extrapolation of current trends using crude graphs. We denote the estimated time until n is zero by T.

(ii) Beyond date T, the value of investment cannot be estimated by its effects on future employment in the modern sector. It seems best to rely on an estimate of the value of social income when used for consumption subsidies by the government, as discussed in 13.21. Therefore the planner should estimate the level of consumption of those who, at T, can be expected to be just deserving of government subsidies. Again, the experience of countries already industrialized can be used to suggest what this consumption level would be, relative to

[1] Cf. Stern, 1972, Newbery, 1972.

average consumption per head in the economy as a whole. Average *per capita* consumption will have to be estimated by extrapolating the current trend rate of growth in consumption per head of the economy. In this way we can estimate the value of public funds at T, relative to the value of consumption through increased employment *now*. (For further explanation of this point see 13.4).

(iii) Estimate the average of r during the next T years. This must be based on evidence of reinvestment by public sector projects. Details of this estimation will be discussed briefly in 14.41. Similarly, g must be estimated. Using the estimate of r, we can work out the total capital that will exist at T as a result of one unit of investment done now. Applying the value of public funds at T (already estimated under (ii)), we get the contribution to s_0 of the capital carried forward at T.

(iv) It remains to estimate the value of the employment generated in the intervening period from now until T. The amount of that employment, n, will have to be estimated on the basis of current observations and well-informed guesses about future trends. Again, we need the *average* value of n over the period (not just the current one). Estimates of c and m will likewise have to be based on current evidence. All this will be discussed further in 14.41. Finally, we need an estimate of i, or rather, its average over the period from now until T. We shall discuss that in 13.4, where we look at the social value of employment in more detail.

13.4 THE VALUE OF EMPLOYMENT

We have explained how to relate the value of uncommitted social income to the value of social income that is committed to consumption through the creation of additional urban employment. Since those who benefit from the new employment have diverse consumption levels, this does not enable us to estimate the base level of consumption, b, until we know how to relate the weight for any particular consumption level to the social value of employment. We discuss this relationship in 13.41, and then use it to determine the consumption rate of interest, i, in 13.43.

13.41 *Employment and Consumption*

Dependants are a complication in trying to assess the social value of employment in terms of the consumption levels of those affected. If the shift of labour is within either the rural sector or the urban sector, it is reasonable to suppose that the earnings of dependants will be unaffected and that their consumption levels will move with that of the head of the family. When a man comes to the town, however, he may bring a family: in that case, since female participation rates are lower in towns than in the country, and since there is widespread unemployment among juveniles, it is likely that the amount of work on the part of dependants would be reduced. But this effect is often rather unimportant, because normally most migrants are young and unmarried: moreover, even if married, many will leave their wife and family behind initially (especially if there are few opportunities for them in town); and most children are likely to be below working age.[1] Finally, although it may be expected that, on average, the dependants get less work in the towns, the marginal product of such work as is obtained will probably be higher than in the country. These factors lead us to the tentative view that changes in dependants' earnings, consequent on new jobs being created for adult males, can probably be neglected: so we shall not go into the adjustments that could be made for dependants if an investigator had sufficient evidence to go on.

In the following discussion we shall therefore neglect dependants, although of course what we call the average worker's consumption will be spread among his dependants. We have not allowed for the fact that the higher the wage, the greater may be the spreading of consumption among dependants. We have no numerical evidence to go on, and the reader can if he wishes himself allow for this effect by choosing a somewhat less egalitarian utility function than he otherwise would (see 13.1), on the grounds that higher incomes are less inegalitarian than they appear.

We now introduce some notation.

c = the consumption that the average wage-earner on the project enjoys, evaluated at accounting prices (net of any transport adjustment).

Notice that a wage-earner's consumption might differ from the wage he receives, because of saving. But it can hardly be very different from the wage (adjusted to accounting prices); either because he

---

[1] Of a sample of over 1,000 male immigrants, aged 15 and over, into eight urban centres in Kenya, 63% were aged 15–24, and $81\frac{1}{2}$% were either unmarried or had a wife in the country. See Rempel and Todaro, 1972.

That migrants are largely young, male, and leave their wives behind, seems to be confirmed in two recent articles published by United Nations organizations (United Nations, 1968, and Economic Commission for Latin America, 1971).

relies on his children to support him in old age, or because he will then consume any savings made earlier, so that the latter are merely postponed consumption.

a = the previous consumption of those who move out of other sectors as a result of the creation of the new job.

This requires some explanation. As a result of the new job there may be a general shift of occupations. Some other sectors (we include unemployment together with those who finance it as a 'sector') will lose bits of a man as a result (the 'average wage-earner' is, himself, of course, a statistical artefact). Thus it is possible that urban unemployment is reduced, say, by one-fifth of a man, and 'unorganized' industry employment by one-fifth, and agricultural employment by three-fifths. If the average consumption per head in these sectors is a_1, a_2 and a_3 respectively then $a = \frac{1}{5}a_1 + \frac{1}{5}a_2 + \frac{3}{5}a_3$. More generally, $a = \Sigma n_i a_i$, and $\Sigma n_i = 1$.

In the simplest case when the final upshot of creating the new job is a shift of one man out of agriculture, a may be regarded as the average standard of living of those rural workers most likely to migrate. As already noted, some authors have suggested that the creation of a modern sector job may pull in more than one man from the country. This does not prevent the n's adding up to 1: if it happens, we assume that the 'unemployment sector' *gains* labour.

Neglecting for the moment any effect on wage levels, we now divide the consumption effect of creating the new job into three parts:

(i) *The effect on people (or firms or government) in the sectors which lose some labour (or some unemployed)*. It may be the case that the departing worker (or bit of a worker) consumed $n_i a_i$, more than the amount $n_i m_i$ (the marginal product) he produced, in which case there is a gain of $n_i(a_i - m_i)$ to people in that sector.[1] Urban unemployed will generally be supported by relatives. The latter gain the whole consumption, $n_i a_i$, of the erstwhile unemployed (with i denoting unemployment in this case). In a few developing countries the government may have paid a dole, in which case it gains that amount (with a weight of unity). If unemployment actually rises, which is a possibility, then there is a *loss* of $n_i a_i$.

Among other urban sectors there is more or less traditional industry and handicrafts, trade, traditional transport, etc. Unless

---

[1] It has been assumed by many authors that family members share equally in the product of the family holding, and that this average product is higher than the marginal product: as against this, it has been suggested that those who leave may well have consumed less than the average product.

the project under consideration is one which may reduce traditional sector output by substituting factory-made for hand-made goods, the possibility that such sectors will lose labour can probably be neglected: for it seems likely that even if new recruits to the modern sector came from this source, then their places will be largely taken by those previously unemployed, or from the country. In any case there is probably no alternative to neglecting this possibility, for information on unemployment and earnings in the 'unorganized' or 'informal' sectors is usually non-existent, and $n_i(a_i - m_i)$ would be impossible to estimate reliably.

In a few countries, government services are heavily overstaffed and m_i can be taken as zero for that sector; sometimes this may even be true of private industry in countries where labour regulations make it hard to get rid of redundant labour. Where government is concerned we have the same case as a dole. Where private industry is in question, the gain of $n_i a_i$ goes to private profits and should be weighted accordingly (see 11.5).[1]

Turning to the rural sectors, the most likely migrants are probably the younger sons of cultivators and landless labourers.[2] Where a family member migrates without the family, it is quite likely that a is higher than m, and that the family will gain $a_i - m_i$. In the case of landless labourers, there is little reason to suppose that a_i and m_i will differ very much, and that there will be a significant gain to the rest of the rural community. Where a whole cultivating family moves, and the land is sold or let (if they were owners), or re-let (if they were tenants), there is again little reason to suppose that the effect on the rest of the rural community could be sufficient to be worth taking into account. However, we recognize that detailed studies might show the above judgments to be unsound. Since so much depends on conditions in the country concerned, and on available information, we find it difficult to offer any general guidance. It seems likely that a, the consumption level of the migrants, will normally be less than the average level of consumption in the countryside, and that m will be still less.

The total gain under this heading can be expressed as $\Sigma n_i(a_i - m_i) = a - m$. As before, we can offer little general advice about the question for which sectors an estimate of $n_i(a_i - m_i)$ is both possible and desirable.

---

[1] It was found that the sources of labour referred to in this paragraph had to be taken into account in Chile. See Seton, 1972.

[2] In the Kenya sample referred to above, 66% owned no land: and 47% either had no father, or had a father who owned no land.

Finally, $a-m$ must be weighted by the appropriate consumption weight $v(a)$: more strictly each (a_i-m_i) should be weighted by that consumption weight $v(a_i)$ which is appropriate to the group which makes the gain. Thus $v(a)(a-m) = \Sigma n_i\, v(a_i)(a_i-m_i)$.

(ii) *The effect on those who move.* Assuming that it is reasonable to suppose that movements consequent on the creation of a new job have no more than a negligible effect on wages, the total consumption gain from movements is $c-\Sigma a_i n_i$. This will not normally accrue to one man: and will only do so if one man goes straight into the new job from the countryside, or from unemployment, and there are no other consequences. But if A takes B's place, B takes C's, and C gets the new job, the gain in consumption is still the difference between that of the new job and that of A—although it is now probably shared between A, B and C. If more than one person comes from the country, then more people move than are absorbed into the new job. We assume that this additional movement goes into unemployment, but it makes no difference to the formula.

Thus the gain in consumption under this heading is $c-\Sigma a_i n_i$ or, for short $c-a$: while that under the previous heading is $\Sigma a_i n_i - \Sigma m_i n_i$. If we put these together we get the result $c-\Sigma m_i n_i$, or $c-m$ for short: and this would reduce in the simplest case, when a single man moves from agriculture, to $c-m_{agr}$. But while $c-m$ does represent the (unweighted) change in consumption, its two components should not in principle be added together, because one may want to attach a different consumption weight to the different parts. If the change were small, one could attach the consumption weight appropriate to a to both parts, and effect the simplification. But if not, the change $c-a$ should be valued as $V(c)-V(a)$ (see 13.13), and the change $a-m$ as $v(a)(a-m)$.

The above formulae take no account of the fact that workers in the modern sector, and perhaps also in some parts of the 'unorganized' urban sector, work for more hours in the year than agricultural workers. If increased consumption were 'bought' entirely by increased effort, it could be argued that there was little or no real increase in welfare. The evaluator might therefore want to reduce c in proportion to extra effort expended. If so, it should be noted that working hours are often not a good indicator of effort: many urban jobs are very light compared to hoeing, for instance. We leave it to the reader, or individual evaluator, to decide whether the extra effort can be measured, and should be allowed for.

(iii) *The effect of an increase in wages.* An increased demand for labour in the urban sector may bring about an increase in real wages, and therefore an increase in c. Among the causes of such a change, we can mention increased union pressure and political pressure by and on behalf of labour, and a tendency for urban wages to be related to a because of a need to attract labour to the cities. In some countries, this effect may be non-existent or at least negligible; but in others it seems to have been important, although governments might perhaps have resisted the tendency more effectively if they had appreciated its consequences. One such consequence could be a reduction in employment by other parts of organized industry— particularly the private sector. If this happens, the creation of one new job in fact increases modern sector employment (L) by less than 1, and all the other gains and losses resulting from the new employment must be reduced accordingly. This is not allowed for in the discussion that follows. Of course, one effect of an increase in c is good—there is an increase in consumption for the employees of organized industry, whose social value is

$$Lv(c)\frac{\partial c}{\partial L}.$$

That is, an improvement for each of the L workers concerned of an amount equal to the change in c resulting from unit changes in L, weighted by the weighting factor appropriate to the group.

Summarizing, the value of the extra consumption created as a result of the new job is

$$v(a)(a-m) + V(c) - V(a) + v(c)L\frac{\partial c}{\partial L}$$

Only if $c-a$ is small can this be reduced to

$$v(a)\left(c-m+L\frac{\partial c}{\partial L}\right)$$

The other effect of increased wages is to increase the commitment of social income to consumption: if the whole of the modern sector were public, uncommitted social income would be reduced by $L(\partial c/\partial L)$, in addition to the reduction occasioned by the increased consumption $(c-m)$ of the new worker. But some of the modern sector will be private, and then the increase in consumption of the workers is at the expense of private profits (provided company taxation is not, as a result, reduced): the resultant effect on social profit can be allowed for by applying the weight, discussed in 11.5, which relates the value of private profit to public profit. This is done in the example that follows.

13.42 *An example*

We shall illustrate how the above might work out in the simple case when it can be reasonably assumed that the final result, after any shuffling of occupations, of the creation of an extra job is that one man comes from the agricultural sector and that there is no change in unemployment.

(i) We suppose the wage rate per annum is Rs. 2500. A reduction of 20% is made to allow for transport costs (see 13.12). From budget studies it is estimated that the conversion factor to border rupees is 0·8, and that no allowance should be made for savings. So

$$c \text{ (in APs)} = 1{,}600$$

(ii) The average consumption level of those adult rural workers in the region most likely to emigrate to the town is thought to be Rs. 750 (after any adjustment by a conversion factor appropriate to rural consumption). Therefore

$$a \text{ (in APs)} = 750$$

(iii) Landless labourers are thought to earn Rs. 600 over the year. Small cultivators are better off, and some of them employ hired labour. Some studies comparing output and labour input on farms for which other important inputs are roughly constant suggest that the marginal product of labour in the region is certainly positive: though such estimates are always very uncertain, the studies would be consistent with taking the marginal product of family labour as Rs. 500 (a little less than the earnings of casual labour, since there is some reason for thinking that the marginal product of family workers is less than that of hired labour). However, having regard to the fact that the lower marginal product of family labour at least partly reflects the advantages of working on the family plot, the real sacrifice may be higher than Rs. 500. We take the compromise figure of Rs. 550. There is no protection or subsidization of agricultural products, so no conversion factor is required. Thus

$$m \text{ (in APs)} = 550$$

(iv) Observing that, in recent years, real wages have tended to rise, the planners assume that some of this increase was the unavoidable result of increased urban employment. While urban employment has doubled, real wages have increased by 50%, during the last ten years. It is assumed that increases of as much as that will not be allowed during the next ten years, and that some part of the increase to be expected will result from the existing power of labour, rather than from increased numbers. It seems reasonable to suppose that a 10% increase in urban employment will cause an increase in c of at least 1%, and that is the figure assumed for the calculations. Thus

$$\frac{L\partial c}{c\partial L}=0 \cdot 1$$

$$\text{and } L\frac{\partial c}{\partial L}=160$$

(v) A 1% increase in real wages will hardly, it is thought, reduce other urban employment by as much as 1%. For illustrative purposes, we shall suppose that the reduction in employment brought about is one quarter of the percentage of real-wage increase. Since a 1% increase in employment causes a $0 \cdot 1\%$ increase in real wages, one new job reduces employment elsewhere by (near enough) $0 \cdot 25 \times 0 \cdot 1 = 0 \cdot 025$. Therefore, we would have to reduce our other figures by only $2\frac{1}{2}\%$: consequently we shall neglect this possible influence.

Let us now recall the formula

$$v(a)(a-m)+V(c)-V(a)+v(c)L\frac{\partial c}{\partial L}$$

and use the weighting function $v(x)=(b/x)^{\eta}$ suggested in 13.13. Then

$$V(c)-V(a)=\frac{1}{\eta-1}\left\{\left(\frac{b}{a}\right)^{\eta-1}-\left(\frac{b}{c}\right)^{\eta-1}\right\}.$$

Suppose it is agreed that $\eta=2$, so that

$$V(c)-V(a)=b\left(\frac{1}{a}-\frac{1}{c}\right).$$

Using the values for a, m, c, and $L(\partial c/\partial L)$ given in the above illustration, we have, as the *social value* of the increase in consumption,

$$\left(\frac{b}{750}\right)^2(750-550)+b^2\left(\frac{1}{750}-\frac{1}{1600}\right)+\left(\frac{b}{1600}\right)^2 160.$$
$$=0 \cdot 00113b^2.$$

We next need to calculate the sacrifice of uncommitted social income, or its equivalent. For the public sector it is:

$$c-m+aL\frac{\partial c}{\partial L},$$

where a is the public share of modern sector urban employment. Supposing $a=\frac{1}{2}$, this amounts to,

$$1600-550+\tfrac{1}{2}\times160$$
$$=1130.$$

In addition, private sector employers pay increased wages of $\frac{1}{2}L(\partial c/\partial L)$. This is converted to our numéraire by applying the weight for the value of private sector profits derived by the methods of 11.5. Taking this weight as 0·5, we arrive at the figure of 40. Therefore,

The increase in consumption in terms of the numéraire $= 1170$

The social value of one rupee of this increase $= \dfrac{0 \cdot 00113 b^2}{1170}$

$$= \left(\frac{b}{1000}\right)^2 \text{ approx.}$$

If one gave a man with an income of Rs. 1000 p.a. in terms of accounting prices (Rs. 1560 in actual prices) a gift of one rupee, this too would have a social value of $\left(\dfrac{b}{1000}\right)^2$. Thus the commitment to consumption arising from providing an urban job at Rs. 2500 has about the same value per rupee in this example as a gift to a man with Rs. 1560. If consumption weights fell less steeply with increasing consumption than we have allowed, the latter figure would be higher; and vice versa.

Recollect that the value of public funds relative to consumption committed through modern sector urban employment has been defined as s. Therefore $1/s$ is equal to the social value of a rupee of such consumption commitment, that is, in the case of our example, $\left(\dfrac{b}{1000}\right)^2$. Thus, once we know s, we can calculate b. Similarly if b is independently assessed by the method of 13.21, then s is determined. For instance, if b were independently assessed as being the level of income of agricultural workers, i.e. Rs. 600 in our example, then $\dfrac{1}{s} = (\frac{6}{10})^2$, and $s = 2 \cdot 8$ approximately.

If s is to be independently calculated, then one needs to know the consumption rate of interest, which is the subject of the next subsection.

13.43 *The Consumption Rate of Interest.*

As we look ahead to consumption provided through industrial employment in the future, we shall want to give it a weight different from the weight we give such consumption now—most probably, we shall want to give it a lower weight. There are three main reasons for this:

(i) *Impatience.* The government may want to give future consumption a smaller weight merely because it is in the future, quite apart from any difference in the standard of living of those who receive the extra consumption. It has often been claimed that this practice is hard to defend, and we have some sympathy with that view. In any case, it would probably not mean an addition to the CRI of more 2% or 3% per year.

(ii) *Growth of wage earners' consumption.* If c rises, while m is constant, then each \$1000 of additional consumption can employ only fewer people. If the difference in consumption is spread over, say 10% fewer people, then the benefit is not reduced by as much as 10%, because each beneficiary gets about 10% more: but it is reduced to some extent, because it is better to use a given sum to benefit more people a little than fewer people more. For instance, the consumption weights given in 13.13, plus an initial difference between rural and modern sector real earnings of 50%, would suggest that this element in the estimate of the CRI might be about one-third to two-thirds of the growth rate of c.

(iii) *Growth of rural consumption levels.* As the lot of those living in rural areas improves, the weight to be given to increases in their consumption falls. If we ignore impatience, then the relative weights should be consistent with the treatment of contemporaries discussed in 13.1. It was there suggested that the welfare weight could be expressed by the formula

$$v = \left(\frac{b}{c}\right)^{n},$$

whence, by differentiation,

$$-\frac{c}{v}\frac{dv}{dc} = \eta.$$

Since the weight is often taken to be synonymous with the 'marginal utility of income', the expression $-\dfrac{c}{v}\dfrac{dv}{dc}$ is called the (income) elasticity of (the) marginal utility (of income).

The CRI is defined as the rate of fall of the weight, i.e. $-\dfrac{1}{v}\dfrac{dv}{dt}$.

Now,
$$-\frac{1}{v}\frac{dv}{dt} = -\frac{c}{v}\frac{dv}{dc} \times \frac{1}{c}\frac{dc}{dt}.$$

Hence, still ignoring impatience,
$$\text{CRI} = \eta g$$
where η is the income elasticity of the weight v, and g is the rate of growth of consumption.

Things get complicated when the consumption levels of different classes are growing at different rates, as envisaged above. It is easiest to decide what to do if all consumption levels are growing at the same rate—or, to be more precise, when c, a, and m are all growing at the same rate. We can then proceed for everyone as in (iii) above, and express the CRI as ηg, perhaps adding something for impatience.

In fact it may be expected that c and a will be growing at different rates. What we suggest planners do is decide what the CRI should be if everything were growing at the same rate as a (which is after all the most important element in the argument), and adjust that figure if c is expected to grow at a different rate from a by subtracting half the excess of the growth rate of a over the growth rate of c. This adjustment is a rough and ready one, based on the notions mentioned in (ii): it is unlikely to make much difference to the result.

We should emphasize that the rate of growth of a will generally be less, and perhaps substantially less, than the rate of growth of average consumption in the economy, taken as a whole. It would be a mistake to base the estimate of the CRI on the growth rate of aggregate consumption per head. Suppose, to take an imaginary example again, that aggregate consumption is expected to be growing at 5% per year, while population grows at 3%: then aggregate consumption per head grows at 2%. Suppose further that 10% of the economy's labour force is employed in the 'modern' sector—industry, government, etc.—at wages three times the level ruling in the rest of the economy; and that employment in this sector is expected to grow at 10%, and the wage rate at 2% per year. On these assumptions, the following figures can be computed:

	YEAR 1			YEAR 2			PERCENTAGE INCREASE		
	Modern sector	Tradi-tional sector	Total	Modern sector	Tradi-tional sector	Total	Modern sector	Tradi-tional sector	Total
Consumption	25	75	100	28	77	105	12·00	2·67	5·00
Employment	10	90	100	11	92	103	10·00	2·22	3·00
Consumption/ Employment	2·500	0·833	1·000	2·545	0·837	1·020	1·80	0·48	2·00

Thus, although overall consumption per head has grown by 2%, that in the traditional sector has risen by less than $\frac{1}{2}\%$, and that in the modern sector by $1\cdot8\%$. Alternative figures would show that a 2% overall growth rate is consistent with a rise of less than 1% in each sector.

If we estimate the CRI at twice $\frac{1}{2}\%$, plus an adjustment (cf. (ii) above) of $0\cdot65\%$, plus 2% for impatience, we get a low figure of only $3\cdot65\%$. If we had, wrongly, used the growth rate of aggregate consumption per head, we should have obtained a CRI of 6%. More egalitarian consumption weights, implying that larger multiples of growth rates should be used, would have given yet larger differences. The moral is that some degree of disaggregation is desirable when estimating the CRI, particularly in countries where a major part of the benefits of development comes through the movement of people from one sector to another.

It will be noticed that these considerations tend to force us to take quite low values of the CRI, except in countries that can anticipate rapid growth in consumption. This is why it is quite possible that i will be less than r for a time, with the result that the value of public investment will be found to be, potentially, large.

13.5 BASE CONSUMPTION AND PUBLIC INCOME

In this section we shall bring the strands of the argument together. We have been discussing an economy in which the government uses its funds both for investment, and for consumption, both public and to some extent private. Of these uses, public investment stands out as the one that creates further public income in the future (this is most likely to be true of urban and industrial projects—hence our concentration on them). Some part of public funds may, perforce, be devoted to purposes of doubtful value, or value less than one can expect from public expenditure. These uses we regard as being less valuable than the numéraire—uncommitted social income. We might then hope to estimate the value of uncommitted social income relative to other uses of social income either by looking at its use for consumption (through e.g. consumption subsidies) or at its use for investment.

Both of these uses pose difficult problems. The first is difficult because the government typically does not know whether it has got the balance between consumption and investment right (within the constraints and pressures acting on it). The second is difficult because it is very complicated. We think that planners should look at the valuation of uncommitted social income both ways. If they have no time or inclination for complications, they will have to use consumption subsidies (and other well-considered uses of uncommitted social income for current expenditure) as the touchstone. Otherwise they should carry out a study of the kind we have sketched in 13.3 and 13.4. This study will estimate s, and then estimate b on the basis of s. If the estimated value of b is not very different from the consumption level commonly thought just deserving of subsidies, we are home: we have a sufficiently consistent estimate of base consumption. If there is a big difference, either this may be taken as useful evidence of the need for more or fewer consumption subsidies (and that would be the right conclusion if the calculations of investment and employment value were thought to be rather well founded) or the calculations of s and the value of employment will need to be checked, since they must have omitted some considerations of importance. If these latter calculations are, as they will often be, rather uncertain, it will be tempting to rely on the consumption-subsidy method of estimating base consumption.

Once we have estimated base consumption, we have the basis for setting up consumption weights. We have been at pains to avoid suggesting that either base consumption, or the weights based on it, can be objectively deduced from facts alone. It is not merely that the facts are uncertain: reasonable men who agree on the facts will disagree about the weights. Fortunately, in many cases, the weights make no great difference to a project decision. In others, where income distribution is a consideration important enough to tip the balance, it is usually best to use rather crude weights, as suggested in 13.13. And in such cases, it will be important to bring out the way in which the project decision will depend upon income-distributional considerations in the project report. (Of course, it is also important to make a definite recommendation.) The other context for which the discussion of this chapter is important is the estimation of shadow wage rates, the subject of Chapter XIV.

CHAPTER FOURTEEN

Shadow Wage Rates and the Accounting Rate of Interest

If planners follow the cost–benefit procedures put forward in this book, they will do much the same as sophisticated businessmen— subtract outgoings from income, discount, and undertake those projects and only those projects that have positive present value. The difference from private calculations is that planners should, where practicable, replace the ordinary prices ruling in the market place by prices—accounting prices—that better reflect social values. An important 'price' to get right is the wage rate. The shadow wage rate may, for reasons indicated in 9.5, be very different from the actual wage rate. At the very least, because the numéraire is foreign exchange, the actual wage should be multiplied by a consumption conversion factor to make wage costs comparable to other costs and benefits. In this chapter we first explain, in 14.1, 14.2, and 14.3, how further desirable adjustments can be made; and then in 14.4, how the accounting rate of interest (ARI) can be estimated. In 14.5 we provide, for professional economists, the analysis of a specific model to show how the various accounting prices are interrelated.

14.1 SHADOW WAGE RATES IN THE ORGANIZED SECTOR

In 13.3 and 13.4, we showed how to compare the value of consumption, committed through increases in urban employment in organized industry, with the value of uncommitted government income. The employment of labour causes changes in both. To work out the real cost of employing labour we must put the cost of the commitment and the value of the consumption together explicitly.

14.11 *The shadow wage formula*
We use the notation s for the value of uncommitted government income, measured in terms of consumption committed through employment. Consequently, $1/s$ is the social value of a unit of consumption so committed (in terms of the numéraire), and we can write

$$\text{SWR} = c' - \frac{1}{s}(c - m) \tag{1}$$

where $\quad\quad\quad c'=$ additional resources devoted to consumption

$\quad\quad\quad\quad\quad c=$ consumption of the wage-earner

$\quad\quad\quad\quad\quad m=$ marginal productivity of the wage-earner.

c' measures the commitment to consumption, and $c-m$ is the increase in the worker's own consumption, plus any surplus consumption accruing to others as a result of his movement into the new occupation (estimated as in 13.41). The second term in the formula can be thought of as a whole, representing the consumption value of employment (we saw in 13.4 that the effects of employment on consumption can be quite complicated). But it is also enlightening to look at it in the way written, as we shall see below.[1]

The following points should be noted:

(i) c', c and m are to be measured in APs. Insofar as the relevant consumption goods and goods produced in the unorganized sectors of the economy are traded, there is no problem in principle; but of course there will almost always be various non-traded goods and services in c', c and m. In the case of these latter, the estimates of the APs depend on prior estimates of the SWR. This apparant circularity can be dealt with either (*a*) by making a plausible initial guess at the SWR in order to estimate the relevant APs, then deriving a better estimate of the SWR from equation (1), and redoing all the calculations with this new estimate so as to get a still better estimate (usually no further improvements in the estimate by repeating the procedure would be worth while); or (*b*) by estimating the APs of non-traded goods in terms of an unknown SWR, w, so that the right-hand side of (1) depends on w, and the equation can be solved to obtain w.

The fact—when it is a fact—that workers consume commodities which are themselves produced partly or entirely by labour which ought to be valued at a shadow wage substantially below the market wage is known as the multiplier effect of employment, because the extra employment generated indirectly is valuable in itself, and

---

[1] Another way of writing this formula shows more clearly how the SWR is made up of different costs:

$$\text{SWR} = m + (c'-c) + \left(1 - \frac{1}{s}\right)(c-m). \quad\quad (1')$$

The first term is the marginal product of labour; the second is the cost which is associated with providing the consumption level c but does not form part of that consumption level (transport costs from country to town, and urban overheads); and the last term is the cost of having an extra amount $c-m$ committed to consumption (since 1 is the value of a unit of resources uncommitted, and $\frac{1}{s}$ the value when committed).

therefore makes the SWR less than it would otherwise have been. The methods we have just mentioned take care of the multiplier effect. They may be an important part of the estimation of SWRs, especially for rural labour.

(ii) The above method (*b*) assumes that all labour should be valued at the same SWR. In fact, there may be quite large differences even among enterprises in the organized sector of the economy. Differences in actual wage rates imply differences in c' and in c (and may often be associated with differences in m: e.g., because workers are drawn from different regions or ethnic groups). In general, when dealing with the organized sector, we would recommend estimating a single *wage conversion factor*,

$$k = \frac{\text{SWR}}{\textit{market wage rate}},$$

to be applied to all wage rates of unskilled labour in order to convert them to shadow wages. This is not to say that the circumstances of particular countries might not justify more subtle procedures.

(iii) We make a distinction between c' and c because, in theory, the difference might be quite large. c' should exceed c by an allowance for the transport cost of goods from country to town (cf. 13.12), and any public costs of urbanization, plus the amount by which total wage costs (in AP terms) are increased as a result of additional employment (cf. 13.41).[1] In practice, it might be hard to estimate the difference, but since there are many reasons for thinking that it costs more in real resources for workers in towns to be as well off as workers in the country, the difference should not be neglected.

(iv) For those who can stomach it, it may be convenient to mention here a more detailed formula for the SWR, which, though based on some special (but not implausible) assumptions, shows how the various relevant considerations operate.[2] We use the notation (cf. 13.41)

$a =$ the previous average consumption of those who move into employment in the organized sector;

$d =$ transport-cost allowance in consumption cost, and other urbanization costs;

$L \dfrac{\partial c}{\partial L} =$ effect of increased employment on wage-earners' consumption;

---

[1] It may also be reduced by the amount of any public costs saved by reducing unemployment.

[2] The formula is based on the analysis of the value of employment given in 13.41.

e = employment premium (to be explained and discussed in 14.13).

Then the formula can be written

$$\text{SWR} = \left[c + d - e + L\frac{\partial c}{\partial L} \right] - \left[V(c) - V(a) + v(a)\,(a-m) + v(c)L\frac{\partial c}{\partial L} \right], (2)$$

where, as before, $v(c)$, $v(a)$ are the consumption weights for people at consumption levels c and a, relative to uncommitted government income.

The first part of the formula, $c + d - e + L\dfrac{\partial c}{\partial L}$, shows in detail how c' is made up, c being the worker's real consumption, d the additional costs of providing it, e the cost-savings (and other public benefits) associated with employment, and $L\dfrac{\partial c}{\partial L}$ the increased commitment to consumption caused by the 'bidding up' of other wages. The second part of the formula shows the *benefits*, to the worker, his family, and other consumers, created by the new job: these are of course set off against cost. $V(c) - V(a)$ is the increased 'utility' of consumption c compared to a (which the worker had received previously); $v(a)(a-m)$ is the extra consumption of the group from which the new worker is drawn, weighted appropriately; and $v(c)L\dfrac{\partial c}{\partial L}$ is the increased consumption of other urban workers, weighted by the weight appropriate to their standard of living. Normally one would take $v(a)$ to be less than one, and $v(c)$ less than $v(a)$. $V(c) - V(a)$ will be less than $v(a)(c-a)$, since the increments in consumption as one moves from a to c accrue to consumption levels higher than a, with weight therefore less than $v(a)$.

14.12 *The Probable Magnitude of Urban SWRs*
In Chapter XIII we argued that the value of uncommitted government income compared to consumption could be given very different values, depending upon the country being considered, and the views of those for whom the evaluations are being done. The other considerations governing the SWRs can vary greatly too, and it must be emphasized that planners could get the costing of labour quite wrong if they made a guess—half the going wage, or something like that—without a careful study of the economy. But very careful and detailed study is not always possible, so that it may be helpful to suggest what values of k might arise in different circumstances.

(i) $c=a,\ \dfrac{\partial c}{\partial L}=0,\ e=0.$

It will often be reasonable to suppose that increases in urban employment will have a negligible effect on wages—e.g. because they are determined by minimum-wage legislation. And sometimes urban workers may be little better off than they were before they moved into the organized sector. Then the consumption-value of extra employment is that it provides extra consumption $c-m=a-m$ to people all on the same standard of living, a, and we have

$$\mathrm{SWR}=c+d-v(a)(a-m). \tag{3}$$

Thus in the extreme case, where the planners are working on the assumption that extra consumption for urban workers is just as good as extra government revenue (so that $v(a)=v(c)=1$)

$$\mathrm{SWR}=m+d, \tag{4}$$

while at the other extreme, where resources for investment and other public expenditures are given maximum priority, $v(c)$ is negligible and

$$\mathrm{SWR}=c+d. \tag{5}$$

Where the government, or other users of public funds, are active and reasonably efficient, but the scarcity of public funds and low total investment means that c cannot be expected to grow rapidly in the near future, we would expect planners to regard $v(c)$ as being a small fraction of unity, so that the SWR would be nearer $c+d$ than $m+d$. In this connection, the reader should recollect that $c+d$ is the wage rate actually paid, multiplied by the appropriate conversion factor.

Some economists have suggested that, even when c is apparently much greater than a, the true difference may actually be much smaller if increased employment draws people from rural productive employment into urban unemployment (because of improved job prospects). In that case m would be a little larger than the marginal productivity of a single rural 'family', since more than one worker and dependants leave the unorganized sectors. It is still the case that additional consumption $c-m$ is distributed to consumers as a result of the new job. If it is thought that the average newcomer attracted to town (who may either get a job or join the unemployed) is as well off as those working in the unorganized sectors, then $v(a)$ may be roughly the right weight to attach to $c-m$. Thus (3) may be a sufficiently accurate formula for the SWR, with $a-m$ replaced by $c - m$. We should add that this theory that new modern sector jobs cause an increase in urban unemployment has not been substantiated, and we do not consider it very plausible for most countries.

(ii) $c > a$, $\dfrac{\partial c}{\partial L} = 0$, $e = 0$.

Where c is definitely greater than a, as seems to be true in most developing economies, we can see intuitively, or from formula (2), that the estimate of the SWR is affected in two ways. In the first place, there is a gain to the person who obtains employment, because he consumes c instead of a (shown by the term $V(c) - V(a)$ in equation (2)). This might be taken to show that the SWR should be lower in the present case than in the previous one. But now $a - m$ is smaller, perhaps much smaller, than $c - m$, so that we might actually have a larger k. Consider the implications of the extreme assumption that $v(a) = 1$. Equation (4) applies if $c = a$; but if $c > a$,

$$\text{SWR} = m + d + (c - a) - (V(c) - V(a)), \qquad (6)$$

and this last term—which is the value in terms of the numéraire of increasing a man's consumption from a to c—will surely be less, and possibly much less, than $c - a$. If, to take the special case we used for illustrations in Chapter XIII, $v(x) = \left(\dfrac{a}{x}\right)^2$, one can easily calculate that $V(c) - V(a) = \dfrac{a}{c}(c - a)$, and we have

$$\text{SWR} = m + d + (c - a)^2 / c. \qquad (7)$$

This last formula might be a convenient first approximation to the SWR, to be adjusted upwards towards $c + d$ when the weight for government income is greater than the weight for consumers at consumption level a, or when income weights fall more rapidly with increasing consumption than our special weighting function assumes.

(iii) $\dfrac{\partial c}{\partial L} > 0$.

No one needs to be told that wages may rise. But industrial wage rates, and the consumption they allow, may rise over time for reasons that have little or nothing to do with the demand for labour by industry. Changes in government legislation, in the strength or success of trade unions, acting either directly or through political action, may push up wage rates quite substantially: the mere fact that wages are known to be rising is not clear evidence that they are rising *because* the demand for labour is increasing.[1] But in time, the increasing demand for labour will bring about increases in wage rates, either as a result of employers competing against one another for labour that is becoming increasingly reluctant to leave the other sectors of the economy, or because a larger labour force strengthens the bargaining power of labour.

If wages have to rise when labour demand increases (if, say, a 1% increase in the requirements of labour by industry increases the wage rate that has to be paid by $\frac{1}{2}\%$) the effect is that an increase in employment, as a result of establishing a particular project, not only leads to increased consumption by those who get the new jobs, but also commits the economy to allowing all wage earners increased consumption. On the particular numerical assumption just mentioned, consumption will increase by 50% more than c. This happens at the expense of investment and other desirable uses of government income. Thus the SWR should be increased, if not by the whole amount of the extra consumption, $L\frac{\partial c}{\partial L}$, then usually by a substantial fraction of it.

Only in a country where there is considerable experience, well recorded, of the relationship between employment and real wage rates can one hope adequately to estimate this effect. Probably it need never be a very important consideration. For, once a country has reached a stage in its development at which wage rates and industrial employment are mutually related, it is likely to be able, if it chooses, to moderate the effect of increased industrial employment on consumption by using the tax system appropriately. Yet, it is another consideration that tells against the presumption that shadow wage rates should be very low.

It will be seen that the size of the SWR depends upon the view one takes about the weight given to c and a, relative to uncommitted government income; but that it may not depend very sensitively on these weights—an estimate using (7) might, for instance, be quite close to an estimate at the other extreme using (5), and one might narrow the range further by arguing, say, that those consuming a should be given a weight not greater than one-half. So one does not need to be very accurate about s. It does need to be thought about,

---

[1] In fact, real wages have remained fairly constant for long periods in some developing countries.

though, and for the main arguments that might be used, we refer the reader to Chapter XIII. In the rest of this section we discuss how to estimate numerical values of c, c', a and m.

14.13 *Estimating Marginal Productivity*

To estimate m properly, a detailed study is needed of each of the main sectors of the economy. This has proved to be difficult even in the most industrialized economies, and would be all the more difficult where most production takes place in rural areas and in small shops, workshops, etc. Wherever good econometric and quantitative studies of marginal productivities are available they should be used, but used with care. If some research institute has estimated the marginal productivity of labour in rice-growing in one region of a country, it is not very likely that this one study will happen to have come up with the average that is needed. One must also make guesses about other regions, crops, and sectors, even though they will be less well informed.

Take the case of agriculture, which is usually the main sector for which m has to be estimated. Suppose no detailed econometric investigation has been done. Some kind of quick method is required. Fortunately, there is almost always some relevant information. For a start, most countries have estimates of total agricultural production, and of the size of the agricultural labour force. These may not be very accurate, but they would usually be better than nothing. From them, one can deduce the average productivity of labour (after converting the figure for agricultural production to accounting prices, as nearly as possible). If inputs to agriculture, such as fertilizers, are important, one should subtract them before calculating the average productivity per man. The loss in production caused by the departure of a man would normally be less than the average production per man: those who remain can work more intensively, and share the work out differently, and some men have more land to work on. Our estimate of m should include any unpleasant extra effort that remaining farmers and workers can be expected to put in (valued in terms of the equivalent consumption), but even allowing for that, the average productivity will be greater than the marginal productivity. Since it could be a lot larger, this does not at first sight seem very helpful; but in many countries the average productivity of labour in agriculture is rather low (compared to urban wages), so that this figure is nevertheless quite a help. If nothing else is possible, one can take half the average productivity as a measure of the marginal productivity, and this may not be far wrong.

But one ought to try to do better than that. Statistics of agricultural wages may be available. During harvest time, and whenever there is an unusually large demand, different farmers may be competing for labour, bidding the wage up against one another, so that it gets close to the maximum amount a farmer would be willing to pay—which is the value of the extra output the man can produce, at market prices. In the absence of other information, it is reasonable to use the wage rate at these times as a measure of the marginal productivity of a man-day of labour. (It should be noted that any payments in kind, including meals provided, for example, should be included in the wage—these being valued at local market prices; and the wage should be adjusted proportionately for any difference there may be between the prices received by the farmer and the appropriate APs.)

At other times of the year there may be many men who would like jobs, but cannot get them. One should be a little careful about accepting the appearance of unwilling idleness for the reality, since a man may be idle because he chooses to be idle, given the current wage rate. On the other hand, he may be idle because he is too ill-fed to be able to work, and in such circumstances the departure of other members of the family could actually increase the family's production. Normally there is some wage-employment in these off-peak periods, and wage rates are established. These could well be taken as estimates of the marginal productivity. At the other extreme, if one is convinced that off-peak wage rates are fixed by convention, the determination of labourers not to let the wage come down, or of employers to have fairly well-fed workers, one might take the off-peak marginal productivity to be zero. As usual the decision lies with the man who knows the situation.

Armed with these estimates, the next step one takes is to estimate the number of days in the year on which labour in the agricultural sector is more or less fully employed.[1] Multiplying the number of days by the per-day marginal productivity, one obtains an estimate of m, the marginal productivity per man-year.

This account neglects many possible complications. Agricultural wage rates often seem to vary considerably from place to place; different kinds of agricultural labour get quite different rates; large plantations pay more than peasant farmers (perhaps to obtain better labour); convention and bargaining power often affect the actual

---

[1] Days when people are working on non-agricultural activities should be included. Even when there is no information on this point, a sensible allowance should be made.

rates paid. Given time and application, one could study data from the agricultural ministry carefully, or even conduct extensive surveys, and carry out quite sophisticated calculations based on the simple ideas we have outlined. Alternatively, one can do a quick sum in one's head, on the basis of hearsay and general impression. It is a question of common sense how sophisticated one should try to be, always bearing in mind that the argument behind the estimate is, anyway, rather crude.

We have devoted most of the space to agriculture because it is usually the most important sector from which labour comes, because there are often useful statistics about it, and because the principles of the method might be applied to other sectors. Generally speaking, it will probably be sufficient to think a bit about whether the first estimate of m, based on agriculture alone, is likely to be biased one way or the other: one should accept that first estimate unless there is real evidence which can be used to correct it.

The chief exception to this rule may be when there is substantial non-agricultural unemployment. The main question to ask then, and it is not likely to be easy to answer, is whether increased employment in the organized sector of the economy will tend to reduce or increase the 'pool' of unemployment, and if so by how much. We have referred several times to the theory that better urban job prospects tend to increase unemployment rather than reduce it, although we doubt whether it is often empirically valid. It is more plausible that hidden or incipient agricultural unemployment spills over into the cities—perhaps because peasants are losing their land. In that case, the main effect of new jobs may be to reduce the pool of unemployment: but we doubt whether most of the effect is usually on unemployment itself.

The marginal productivity of unemployed labour is surely not greater than zero—except that people are seldom entirely unemployed. Although arguments can be advanced for saying it is negative, we recommend assuming it to be zero, unless, of course, there is hard evidence in support of a better estimate.

This does not cover all the consequences of reducing unemployment. If there are unemployment benefits, or similar relief payments, and if disease, crime and violence are related to the volume of unemployment, a reduction in the number of unemployed saves the government expenditures. This saving can be attributed to the project—a deduction e per man should be made from the consumption-commitment cost of the project. This is the *employment premium*, already referred to when we wrote down Formula (2). The employment premium can also be used to encourage increased employment now, if that is an objective of the government over and above the other considerations that have been introduced into the system of project appraisal. It has, for example, sometimes been suggested that a value be given to the reduced risk of political upheaval if unemployment is reduced, though there could obviously be two views about that.

Before a government instructs planners to use an employment premium for these more nebulous reasons, it should consider the extent to which particular kinds of new employment really reduce unemployment, and whether its desire for reduced unemployment is a short-run or a long-run aim. The effect of an employment premium is to encourage reductions in unemployment now, at the expense of resources that could be used for investment and the creation of employment opportunities in the future. It should be used only if there is a more urgent need for employment now rather than later, as might be the case in particularly underdeveloped regions of the economy.

14.14 *Estimating Consumption Levels*

It is easier to estimate c and c' than m, although in some countries most of the relevant data may be lacking. For c' one proceeds in three steps:

(i) Firstly, wage rates paid in the relevant industry are estimated. We want to estimate the probable level of real wages in about five years' time. To do that, the recent history of wage rates, and the prices of goods purchased by wage earners, may be examined. These should make possible an intelligent guess at future real wage rates.

(ii) Secondly, the proportion of the wage that is spent on consumer goods should be estimated. Any income tax, compulsory saving, and social insurance, should be subtracted (but at the same time one ought to add back the average payment made to workers on account of accidents, etc., covered by insurance schemes). Then it may be possible to estimate the average proportion of his income that a wage earner is likely to save—that is, what he does not immediately spend on consumption. It must be remembered in this connection that workers may save in order to spend more only a little later; so that while some are saving at any one time others are dissaving. Since the amount of a wage earner's saving will seldom be at all large, there is no point in spending much effort on making accurate estimates here; and if one knows nothing about saving behaviour, one may perhaps forget about it and assume that the workers' whole disposable income is spent on consumption.

(iii) Thirdly, having obtained an estimate of the wage earner's consumption, it must be revalued in terms of accounting prices instead of actual prices. This can be done by doing a detailed analysis of the average wage earner's consumption budget. (Sample surveys have been carried out in a number of developing countries which show how much of his expenditure a wage earner and his family devote to various categories of consumer goods.) One would then use known accounting prices to evaluate his expenditure on each of the main categories of consumer goods. Alternatively, the standard conversion factor (see 12.34) can be applied to the estimate of his total consumption expenditure, perhaps adjusting it a little to allow for obvious differences between the wage earner's budget and the usual pattern of industrial inputs. At this stage one should subtract any employment premium to obtain c'.

To obtain c, we still have to subtract the transport allowance. The main item here is likely to be the excess of urban food prices over rural food prices, but some deduction on account of the higher housing prices in towns may also be correct. Insofar as these latter result from higher land rents, they often represent additional income for landowners who are much richer than urban wage-earners. Such rents are consequently a cost, which enters c' but should be omitted from c because they reflect no addition to the wage-earners' real consumption.

c and c' may vary greatly from one centre of organized employment to another, and between different jobs. In the former case, one might use the same estimates of m and a in different places, but have different figures for c and c'; but it is likely to be most convenient to work out k for one or two representative cases and then apply the same conversion factor to all unskilled wages. In the case of higher wages, paid to skilled labour or supervisory grades, or in compensation for particular danger, or as an incentive to particular honesty, c and c' may be much higher than for unskilled labour. The simplest thing to do is to increase the SWR for such labour by the amount of the additional consumption. In particular cases, even this might not put the SWR high enough, if there were a shortage of the kind of labour in question. Then a scarcity premium would be justified, as a means of discouraging projects from planning to employ categories of labour that are likely to be in short supply. However, project planners should beware of using scarcity premiums because of temporary shortages: they are justified only if there is some fundamental reason for the shortage—such as a small secondary education system—which is likely to continue for a long time.

Accurate estimation of *a* is unlikely to be easy, since one needs to know where new urban employees tend to come from, and how they used to fare in these diverse occupations. As we have repeatedly emphasized, the question is not where the new employees in organized industry come from immediately, but what occupations are actually reduced by the new employment opportunities, after allowing for all repercussions. The obvious first estimate of *a* must be the average income per head in the economy, after separating out, as far as possible, the incomes of organized industry (including labour incomes), government administration, and richer farmers, bankers, traders, etc. A number of countries have surveys of consumption and income distribution that might be helpful in such an estimation; and elsewhere, what is known about a similar developing country could be assumed true of the one in question.

Ideally, this first estimate ought to be adjusted to allow for the ways in which the occupations vacated are not representative of occupations in the economy generally. This might happen for different reasons. Urban jobs might tend to go to members of one particular group, defined by region, religion, or race, and that group might be relatively prosperous. (In that case, the government would presumably want to encourage projects that employ less privileged groups, and would therefore want to distinguish different *a*'s for different projects.)

On the other hand, one might expect that migration will usually draw on those in less remunerative occupations—landless labourers, members of large families, and so on. In the latter case, the first estimate of *a* should be reduced. It is hard to give any general advice about how this can be done: planners will have to rely upon what they know or can guess of their own country.

14.2 Development of the Economy over Time

Everything we have said so far has been directed at the estimation of the SWR for one particular year. The project analyst needs SWRs for every year of his project. The same methods could be applied for all future years, but it would be intolerable to have to perform the same kind of calculation, along with associated estimations of the marginal productivity of labour in agriculture, the effect on urban unemployment, and s. It would save a lot of trouble if one could justifiably assume that k is unlikely to vary much over the lives of most projects, for then project wage rates could be projected into the future, on the basis of past experience and good economic advice, and the same k applied in all years in order to convert to SWRs.

There is some reason to expect that, in many developing economies, k will remain fairly constant, or change only slowly. Before explaining why this might be, we must consider how the various elements in the formula

$$k = \frac{1}{w} \left\{ c' - \frac{1}{s}(c-m) \right\} \tag{8}$$

are likely to vary over time. Of these parameters, the one that we are least able to forecast directly is s. To see how it is likely to change, we require a lengthy digression.

14.21 *How s Changes*

Recollect that s is the weight given to uncommitted income divided by the weight given to consumption distributed through employment in organized industry.

This definition allows us to deduce the useful relationship

$$-\frac{\dot{s}}{s} = -\frac{1}{s}\frac{ds}{dt} = \text{ARI} - \text{CRI} \tag{9}$$

which tells us that s falls over time at a rate equal to the difference between the accounting rate of interest and the consumption rate of interest. The reason is that the CRI was defined as the rate at which the weight we would now give to future consumption falls over time (cf. 13.32); and the ARI, being the discount rate appropriate to uncommitted income is likewise the rate at which the weight for such income in future falls relative to uncommitted income now. (9) is helpful because it shows us that s will be falling faster if investment is currently highly productive; and less rapidly if incomes are in any case expected to rise fast, for then the CRI will be larger. Notice that the CRI could be large either because rapid growth is expected, or because the government is in any case

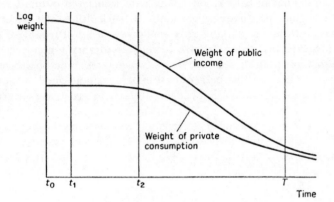

Figure 4

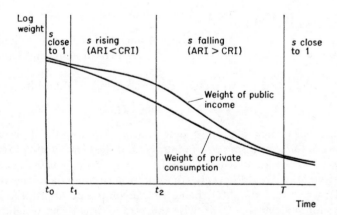

Figure 5

impatient for present consumption benefits; and the ARI could be large either because resources are being used with high efficiency, or because resources are so scarce that only a few high-yield projects can be undertaken.

In general, we expect economies that are very poor or undeveloped to have low ARIs, because they have not yet learned how to use savings channelled through the state and large-scale industry. At that stage the ARI could well be less than the CRI. But as economic administration is built up, the ARI should begin to rise, and may remain above the CRI for many years or decades, because of constraints on the government's ability to tax. In a more 'mature' stage, the ARI can be expected to fall, as labour shortage sets in and wages rise; and the CRI may rise. Eventually the ARI and CRI should be equal, except insofar as it is desirable to tax returns to capital.[1]

We can portray the development of an economy over time in a diagram with the weights of private consumption and public income measured on the vertical axis. If we measure them by their logarithms, the rate of fall of the private consumption line is the CRI, and that of the public income line is the ARI. The distance between the two lines is log s: when it is zero, s is 1. (The weights are to be measured from the present, when the weight of public income is unity, and its logarithm zero; but really the level of the two curves does not matter.)

In Figure 4 we show an economy in which growth is initially (at time t_0) zero, and the government takes the view that, as a consequence, future consumption needs are as urgent as present ones. Thus the CRI is zero. At the same time aid is becoming available, and the tax system is making some public investment possible; yet few projects are available. There might be so few reasonable domestic projects that the country must, at this time, invest abroad. The quite small rate of return so obtained is the ARI initially. But domestic investment opportunities open up, from t_1, and the ARI rises, and remains high despite the growing volume of saving. Indeed, the government would willingly, and rightly, invest more if it could force the rich, the middle classes, and the workers to consume less. But this it feels unable to do, and as a consequence growth in consumption will not be so rapid as to make the CRI equal to the ARI. But, from t_2, consumption growth accelerates, and investment continues to increase, until eventually

---

[1] We do not discuss the situation in developed economies since it is barely relevant to the problems we are concerned with here.

(several or many decades after t_2, no doubt) the government no longer feels itself constrained by a lack of saving, s is close to 1, and the ARI close to the CRI. This point is shown as T. The small gap between the two curves at that stage represents the intrinsic imperfections of the tax system which prevent private and public income from being perfect substitutes.

It is clear in this case that s could be quite large initially, since it is always falling until T. Yet it is not impossible that s could be 1 or close to it at t_0, if it is going to be 1 in the future. This would be reasonable if the government could make the economy invest all that it thought right, for then it could arrange the allocation of resources between private consumption and public expenditure so as to make their weights equal. Some of the oil-rich countries are presumably in this position. When investment prospects improve, consumption will grow faster, so as to keep the CRI and ARI equal.

The absence of a constraint on savings and public income (relative to known ways of using them) is not, however, sufficient grounds for thinking that s is equal to 1. If a constraint is expected to operate in the future (e.g. because of less aid, or better investment possibilities), s may be substantially greater then. Unless the ARI is expected to be less than the CRI in the intervening period, s should be as great now. But if in fact, because currently investment projects are hard to find, current government consumption expenditures will be encouraged, which are, on a long-sighted view, much less valuable than lending abroad in order to be able to invest when good investment becomes possible, then one ought to use a value of s close to 1. Project planners must always make a realistic judgment about the probable uses of the social income they intend to generate!

Another possible situation is portrayed in Figure 5. Here the CRI is initially positive, for growth is already occurring. There are many such cases in the developing world. The ARI is low initially, about equal to the CRI, because projects (and good export markets) are lacking. The first burst of investment lowers it further, and s rises, leading into a phase, from t_1 to t_2, where s is high and the ARI is lower than the CRI. But from t_2 on, the ARI rises (the savings constraint is biting now!) and the CRI does not (for the same reason, allied to agricultural and population drag). Finally the high ARI has generated the possibilities of public income that render the savings constraint irrelevant, and T is reached.

14.22 *Changes in Shadow Wage Rates*
Planners can be guided by the ideas embodied in Figures 4 and 5,

and elaborated in the previous section, when framing their ideas about changes in k over time. It can be seen from Equation (8) that lower s means lower k—provided that everything else remains the same. But we know that in many countries c', c and w have tended to rise over time, and we can expect that they will rise at about the same rate. In the earlier stages (possibly until some time after t_2) m may be very small, and, because of population pressure and low savings, rising very slowly, if at all. But just for these reasons, s should be large, and the term $(c-m)/s$ unimportant in (8). Thus k may be falling as s falls, but only very slowly. By the time s is small enough for $(c-m)/s$ to be significant, m may be rising faster than c: we certainly expect that m would get closer to c in a rapidly developing economy. Thus, in this later stage, it is not at all certain that k will fall, and indeed, as m gets close to c, we would expect k to rise. Broadly speaking, it seems that k ought to be quite close to 1 in the years around t_2, and to c'/w (which in the end may not, because of $\dfrac{\partial c}{\partial L}$, be close to 1) at T. It would be rather less than 1 in the middle years between t_2 and T, but would in any case not change quickly.

The above argument is partly based on guesswork, as must be any view of the economic future. Such simple models as have been constructed to assess the probable movement of SWRs have so far confirmed our view that k would change only slowly.[1] No doubt future research will make better guesses possible.

The practical upshot is that planners should try to estimate k on the basis of estimates projected some years ahead—that is, they should adjust for any factors that seem to be temporary, such as a recent devaluation that has not yet brought about expected money wage increases. They should then assume that k will be constant over time, until, as they undertake new estimates of SWRs in future, they find evidence to support the assumption that k is changing.[2]

14.3 SHADOW WAGE RATES IN OTHER SECTORS

Generally speaking, the difficulty about labour costs in the un-organized sectors of the economy is not that the principles governing the estimation of shadow wage rates are different, but rather that it is often hard to estimate additional employment, and indeed the notion of 'employment' can become quite vague. Also, while it is

[1] Newbery, 1972, Stern, 1972.
[2] The analytical basis for a rigorous treatment of the topics in this section is given in 14.5.

still true that the extra consumption of an employee represents a reduction in uncommitted income, the wages of additional employees usually come out of the profits of a small businessman or farmer, so that the resources in question never had a chance of being uncommitted government income anyway. In fact, it is often most convenient to take a small business or farm as a whole, and not treat labour costs separately. One can estimate additional production, net of inputs purchased, subtract consumption by everyone involved—workers and employing family—and the marginal productivity of those drawn into the activity. Then one can add the consumption benefits, looking at the additional consumption (of employers and employees) as a whole. In other words, it may be simplest not to use a shadow wage rate at all, but estimate the consumption benefits separately.

14.31 *Small-Scale Urban Production*
Production in small firms or by self-employed workers may be of importance for project appraisal either because such production would result from some special industrial assistance programme, or because many non-traded goods are produced in this way. Workers are often paid much less (and may work in worse conditions) than in organized industry, and profits may largely accrue to low-income families, while investment may also be financed out of low incomes, or at very high interest rates. Information about small-scale production is not very easily come by. But it is probably safe to assume that workers do not earn significantly more in real terms than a, the consumption level of the groups from which migrants are drawn, and that it is unlikely that this latter level would be much affected by increased employment in the small-firm sector. Thus we have case (i) of 14.12 above, except that e might not be zero (and could be relatively more significant than in the organized industry case). We take it, therefore, that k for small-scale producers is likely to be lower than for large, and the SWR could be quite low if m and $d-e$ are small.

Yet it must be remembered that the profits of small enterprises, though probably counting for much more than equal profits in large enterprises, would normally receive a weight considerably less than 1. Therefore, in calculating the AP of a non-traded good (such as retail trade), it is essential to include as a cost not only the labour cost (which could easily be as low as half the wage adjusted to APs), but also the profits of the trader, or rather the consumption they make possible, less an allowance for the social value of that consumption. When there is no information about employment in the producing sector, the whole of value added can be treated as profits: this procedure neglects the cost associated with the marginal productivity of labour (which might in any case be very low), but as an offset makes no allowance for employees being poorer than their employers.

14.32 *Rural Labour*

In some cases one will want to cost rural labour in the same direct way as in large public sector projects. For example, in local public works projects, or construction work for irrigation and other agricultural improvements, labourers will be identifiably employed, and paid out of public funds. Then the methods of 14.1 apply, though the numerical values may be different from the urban case, particularly because of lower wage levels, and d being zero. There may still be an employment premium, and sometimes that could be rather important, if there were special reasons for encouraging employment in one particular area of the country.

More puzzling cases arise when it is hard to estimate the employment generated by a project. Consider, for example, a scheme that provides people with land to farm, technical advice, loans, and other agricultural assistance, at the same time insisting that the farmers grow from seed provided by the agency in charge of the project: how does one decide whether such a project is worthwhile?

Take the case of an irrigation scheme. The cost of building it, and administering the scheme, can be calculated just as for an industrial project. To calculate the benefits and costs of the scheme once it is in operation, we need at least estimates of

    (i) changes in the outputs of crops as a result of the scheme;
    (ii) changes in material inputs, such as fertilizers and seeds;
    (iii) changes in the incomes of farmers.

Using (i) and (ii) we can work out the social value added of the project, Y. (iii) has to be estimated separately, since incomes are determined by market prices, not accounting prices, and there may be other changes in income associated with the scheme, such as water charges, or cheap loans. From (iii) one must deduce an estimate of increased consumption (including as usual an allowance for future consumption made possible by current saving) in accounting prices, C. At this stage, the changes in *aggregate* consumption have been estimated, not allowing for the way that changes in wage-employment may affect the local distribution of incomes.

If one is truly able to estimate the changes in all outputs in the area—that is, prepare 'before and after' estimates, which include any likely changes in non-agricultural activities (such as cottage industry)—the changes in labour inputs need be considered only to the extent that there is a change in leisure, or a change in the number of people who can be expected to leave the area of the scheme to work elsewhere if the plan is not adopted. We think that only the latter item can usually be allowed for. The 'cost' of preventing people from leaving the area or attracting others in, can be taken to be m, the marginal productivity of labour generally in the unorganized sector of the economy, including unemployed labour. It can be assumed that this marginal product would have been consumed. Denote the increased number in the area as a result of the scheme by N.

Then the scheme can be evaluated as follows:

$$\text{Social Profit} = Y - C + v(C - mN)$$

where v is the consumption weight appropriate to an average family in the area. This calculation pretends that the consumption benefits of the project are spread evenly among all types of families, rich and poor. There may be no reliable data to allow a more precise calculation, and project planners would be wise to avoid making assumptions about the distribution of benefits on scanty evidence or pure guesswork.

However, it may be possible to use

(iv) changes in labour input, measured in man-days, distinguished according to the season,

to make some estimate of the way in which benefits will be distributed. One could start by classifying the local population crudely into two groups—poor and not-so-poor. These groups will have different consumption weights. The line of division should be drawn so that wage-labour will come from the 'poor' group, while the better-off farmers are included in the other group. Then any changes in labour inputs will represent changes in the income of the lower-income group: the magnitude of the changes will depend upon the season of the year in which the changes in labour demand are expected to occur.[1] Of course, not all the changes in labour

---

[1] Another reason for wanting estimates of labour-input change by season is to check that the labour will probably be available when wanted; and to discover whether (more expensive) labour from outside the area of the project will be required. The latter could be treated like labour employed in a public works project.

input will be observed as changes in wage-employment: in small farms, there may be more work for the family. But, unless there is clear evidence to the contrary, it can be assumed that larger farms will find additional labour from outside. In this way, one can separate C into gains accruing to low-income and higher-income families, and apply different consumption weights to the two components, thus modifying Formula (6).

It will be appreciated that this simple example by no means captures all the special circumstances that can arise in agricultural projects. Resettlement schemes, for example, may bring people in from other areas, and make little difference to the local labour market. But the same method can still be applied.

14.4 THE ACCOUNTING RATE OF INTEREST

We discussed the framework within which project evaluation should be done at length in Chapter V, particularly 5.5, and the role of the ARI in 9.13. While, theoretically, using too low a rate of interest to discount social profits would lead the economy to attempt to invest too much, with inflationary effect, and too high a rate could leave savings unutilized and cause excessive unemployment, a good planning system should maintain some kind of balance between investment and investible resources, even when the ARI · in current use is wrong. But that does mean, to some extent, taking the wrong projects. The right ARI is the one that passes just the right volume of projects: to estimate it, one needs some idea of investible resources available, and how well they can be used.

It is obviously convenient to use a single ARI, rather than discount future social profits at different rates according to their distance in time. We shall therefore concentrate on the estimation of a single discount rate. But it is not altogether impracticable to estimate an ARI that changes with time. The general ideas explained in 14.2 may suggest the long-term movements of the ARI that can be expected. It may also be possible to use available data. For example, it might turn out that project returns had been rising in the past, and could be expected so to continue. Sometimes it may even be possible to devise econometric models that take into account changing export markets, industrial efficiencies, and savings, and deduce from them how the ARI is likely to change in the future. If it were forecast that the ARI should rise, the right way to discount social profits is to use a higher discount rate for more distant profits. If it will be falling, the opposite applies. Perhaps the main case where an economy might be well advised to follow these more complicated procedures is when there has been a catastrophe, whose consequences are likely to continue for some time—such as a drought, or a large movement in the terms of trade. Then the economy might have to reconcile itself to a lower than normal rate of investment for a year or two. But the long-term developments suggested in 14.2 should not be forgotten, though they may be less easy to quantify.

Simply to use a higher ARI would not be the best policy in such circumstances. What the economy ought to do is postpone those projects that can be most readily postponed. Increasing the ARI would concentrate resources on high and quick yielding projects, and discriminate against long-lived ones. An increase in the immediate discount rate, while continuing to use the previous ARI for discounting beyond the next couple of years, will not discriminate against long-period projects, but against those which are easily postponed, or those whose major investment costs come rather soon.

Similarly an economy that is currently enjoying a particularly high capital inflow or favourable export markets should not bring down the ARI so as to encourage very long-lived projects, but undertake more projects now, whether long-horizon or short. This is achieved by having a lower discount rate for the next few years, and a higher one thereafter.

14.41 *The Initial Estimate of the ARI*

If indirect taxes are fairly uniform, with little discrimination between imported and exported commodities, and if the SWR is close to the actual wage rate (in APs), the rate of return currently being earned in the economy should be quite a good guide to the ARI. The rate of return might be estimated from company accounts, or from industrial surveys, or by asking businessmen. But in most developing countries, this would hardly be a sufficiently good estimate.

Otherwise, information about industrial and other investment experience and possibilities is needed. This might be obtained from the following sources:

(i) Projects previously considered or accepted by the government. The reports, both those on the original proposal and on performance (if any), should give at least summary information about inputs, outputs, and their time profile. In fact some of these projects will be obviously unsatisfactory when looked at in the light of accounting prices. Common sense should allow the planners to ignore the more unsatisfactory of their previous decisions.

(ii) Prospective projects. There should always be some proposals that could be examined to gain an impression of current possibilities. Indeed, one of the first tasks of the Central Office of Project Evaluation might be to request information about projects (already carefully checked from the technical point of view) in systematic quantitative form, without evaluation (except for including the relevant border prices where possible). At this stage, it is more important to have a large number of project proposals roughly sketched than a few worked out and evaluated in detail.

(iii) Industrial and agricultural censuses and surveys. These, together with similar information available within government departments, can also provide information on major categories of inputs and outputs. In this case, the planners will not get detailed information about the time-scheduling of particular inputs and outputs, but broadly classified figures for an industry as a whole, including capital stock and depreciation: supplementary information will usually need to be obtained from people familiar with that industry. Just as some past projects were bad, and some not so bad, so industrial data will reflect bad and good performance, bad and good past decisions. The planners must expect that some of the figures would imply a low rate of return and others a high one, and should probably be guided by those that show a relatively good return.

Whatever the source of data, the inputs and outputs must be measured at accounting prices before they can be used. Where non-traded goods with a large labour input are involved, it may be as well to separate the social cost (or benefit) of the commodity into the part that does not depend upon the SWR, and a labour part. In this way, it will be possible to describe a variety of 'test projects' (some of which are simply representations of aggregate data for an industry) in terms of labour inputs and the net value of other inputs and outputs.

If we already have a good estimate of the SWR (derived from a valuation of public relative to private income based on the methods of 13.21, for example) we can find out which of the test projects would be worth doing at various interest rates; i.e. which ones have positive PSV. The first estimate of the ARI should, in principle, be one that would have let through only a few of the best projects in the past (ignoring any projects for which the figures appear, on examination, to be unrealistic). This ARI need not be so high as to frighten ministers. Probably planners would be wise in any case not to start systematic social cost–benefit analysis with an interest rate much higher than has been usual in the past: otherwise the system may not be accepted at all. The ARI can be adjusted upwards as soon as experience clearly justifies it. We also suggest that the initial ARI should not be too low, even when past experience has been bad, because it should be presumed that future projects, at least those subjected to thorough cost–benefit analysis, will do better than past projects.

These test projects can also be used as the basis of a more thorough estimation of the SWR, by working out s from the value of invested public income. The manner in which this could be done was explained in 13.32, where we developed some formulae for s, which required information about likely future investment projects. To keep the formulae simple—and nothing complicated would be appropriate since a very precise estimate of s is not required—we described a typical investment project by r, the uncommitted social income generated per unit of investment, and n, the employment of labour per unit of investment. The data on the test projects can be used to estimate r and n.

Suppose that in one sector, a fairly typical project has an investment cost of Rs. 1,000,000, spread over two years[1] (this being already measured in APs), and yields outputs of value Rs. 200,000 per year for twenty years, while requiring non-labour inputs of Rs. 100,000 per year. 100 men are employed in the plant, at a wage of Rs. 1,000 per year. Taking the unit of investment as Rs. 1 million, we have immediately

$$n = 100.$$

The annual social value added is Rs. 200,000, but this goes on only for twenty years, and includes what is committed to consumption. We have to subtract something for depreciation. The easy procedure is straight-line depreciation: one would subtract, in this case, one-twentieth of the capital cost. But this always overestimates deprecia-

---

[1] If investment costs were spread over a longer period, an interest charge should be included, but it unlikely to make much difference. For simplicity, we are supposing the APs for capital goods are readily available.

tion from the economic point of view, and we would suggest taking half that figure.[1] Thus

Annual depreciation = Rs. 25,000.

Avoiding complications we have already discussed, let us suppose that the entire wage is spent on consumption, and that the conversion factor is 0·8. Then in the present instance the

Annual commitment to consumption = Rs. 80,000.

Subtracting the last two figures from social value added, we obtain

$$r = 95,000 \text{ (per million)},$$

or 9·5%.

Different test projects will of course give different values of r and n, and it would probably be wise to calculate s for several alternatives. We shall not further elaborate the example by introducing measurements of c', c, and m. With these, s can be calculated. This estimate of the value of income in the hands of the government should be considered in conjunction with the other uses of public income, before one decides the value of s, and deduces from it the SWR.

There is a quick way of estimating the ARI from the data on the test project. Denote the SWR by w. Clearly, the discount rate at which the test project breaks even is the annual social value added, minus the wage cost (and depreciation), i.e.,

$$\text{ARI} = r + c'n - wn. \tag{8}$$

This formula shows one thing that is very important, and useful in estimating the ARI: the ARI is at least as large as r. Thus in our particular numerical example, it is at least 9·5%. If the SWR were three-quarters of c' (it would probably not be much smaller when r is as large as this), we should have ARI = 11·5%. While this is very simple and convenient, it is advisable to go through the more thorough procedure outlined above, in which fuller descriptions of a number of projects are evaluated at alternative interest rates, using the estimated value of the SWR. In this way, the final estimate of

---

[1] If the parent project, and other similar ones created out of reinvested funds were to put aside uncommitted funds amounting to

$$R/(e^{RT} - 1)$$

each year, where R is the ARI, and T is project life, a unit of investible funds would be made available after T years, thus allowing continuation in perpetuity. Straight-line depreciation puts aside $1/T$ per year. The correct formula multiplies $1/T$ by the factor $RT/(e^{RT} - 1)$, which is less than one. The factor is equal to one half when $RT = 1·25$, and a sixth when $RT = 3$. In the present example, it turns out that the ARI is over 10%, implying that $RT > 2$. But, in the depreciation formula, R should be *achieved* R rather than the one used to evaluate prospective projects.

the ARI is less sensitive to the particular depreciation procedure that has been used.

14.42 *Adjustments and Other Methods*

The best guide to the proper choice of the ARI is experience. If more projects look acceptable, than there are investible funds available, the ARI should be adjusted upwards; and if too little looks promising, the adjustment should go the other way. In the case of this accounting price, as with most others, such adjustments should be done gradually: the ARI is supposed to reflect long-run possibilities, not to achieve a perfect investment/savings balance week by week. Short-run fluctuations in the availability of resources ought to be met by temporary postponements or advancement of projects, changes in consumption (which may be easier for short periods than for long), and the use of foreign exchange reserves.

It is also possible to estimate the ARI by more sophisticated methods based on input–output tables and other data about the economy's performance and possibilities. If economic models of this kind are to give results that project planners could rely on, or even use as initial estimates, they must include trade possibilities as well as domestic production possibilities. Models of linear programming type have often expressed trade possibilities in a very crude and arbitrary way, by imposing constraints, many of them pure guesses, which have a large effect on the accounting prices estimated. If these difficulties can be circumvented, it should be possible to indicate the sectors that deserve most emphasis in the economy's development, and deduce the ARI that is implied.[1] But any economic model must neglect information that could be available to planners: in order to put the available data together in a consistent and systematic way, excessive detail must be avoided. For this reason, the results of models should not be used without further checking and examination of the most important presumptions about economic possibilities.

The developing economies are so various that we must expect very different ARIs to be right for different countries. If a country is large enough, and economically sufficiently advanced, to be able to contemplate setting up a large-scale industrial plant, and if it can expect to operate a modern industrial plant quite efficiently, it would be surprising if the ARI were less than 10%. After all, the level of wages in the developing countries is usually considerably

---

[1] This has been attempted by Khan and Mirrlees, 1973.

lower than it is in the industrial countries, so much lower that the inevitably lavish use of labour in the developing countries should seldom offset the advantage of low wage rates. If the developing countries could do the same things as the developed countries, and do them as well, they would earn higher rates of return than are enjoyed by industry in the developed countries (quite apart from the results of special protection). Unfortunately, it takes time to learn to operate new techniques efficiently, to produce goods of standard quality, and of the right quality, and to cultivate satisfactory export markets. But even taking all that into account, it would be surprising if the more developed of the developing countries could not achieve a real social rate of return of at least 10%; some may find even 15% more appropriate. But others, less fortunate in their opportunities for large-scale production, less efficient in their industrial operations, may well find that they have to set interest rates as low as 6 to 7%. It would never be worth going below 4 to 5% since returns of that order (after allowing for inflation) can be earned, with reasonable security, in the international capital markets to which any country has access.

14.5 OPTIMUM DEVELOPMENT AND ACCOUNTING PRICES[1]

It is interesting to see how the accounting rate of interest, shadow wage rates, and consumption rate of interest are related in an explicit model. The model will provide a check on our verbal arguments; and it can bring out clearly the necessity of long-term prediction and optimization as a basis for current accounting prices. We shall concentrate, in the model, on what might be termed political constraints on consumption levels, and ignore other considerations that would prevent simple optimizing solutions, such as the intrinsic distortions of tax systems. We shall also omit the private production sector, which would complicate the analysis without enriching the particular lessons we want to elicit here.

14.51 *A Model*
On the production side, we concentrate on consumer goods. The

---

[1] This section is directed at economists. It presents in mathematical terms some of the arguments underlying this chapter and Chapter XIII. Readers not interested in theoretical fundamentals can omit it without disadvantage.

The theory of optimal development in dual economies, of which the analysis sketched here is a generalization, has been developed by a number of authors, stimulated particularly by the fixed-wage models of Dobb, 1960, and Sen, 1962 and 1968. The papers by Marglin, 1967, Dixit, 1968, Stern, 1972, and Newbery, 1972, may be mentioned.

technological possibilities of the economy, and the opportunities provided by international trade, make possible many alternative consumption paths for the economy. The investment plans implied by any such path are to be thought of as undertaken by the government. Just what is possible depends on the numbers of people in various kinds of occupations. We shall use the notation:

C = total consumption goods available
N = total population
n_i = number of people in occupation i
c_i = consumption per head in occupation i.

Each of these depends on the date, t. We have:

$$C = \Sigma n_i c_i, \tag{1}$$

$$N = \Sigma n_i. \tag{2}$$

(1) assumes there are no 'wasted' costs associated with providing consumption to people in particular occupations, such as urban workers—we may as well ignore that complication here. We also appear to have assumed that goods are freely transferable from one person to another, but we shall see how to modify that assumption below. We shall look upon consumption as a single commodity, but the reader can easily interpret C and other consumption variables and prices as vectors so as to cover many consumer goods.

We take the objective to be the maximization of total utility

$$\int \Sigma n_i u(c_i) e^{-\delta t} dt \tag{3}$$

for some increasing, concave function u, and $\delta \geqslant o$ a utility-discount rate. Economists will recognize the limitations of such an objective as (3). It is very convenient for our purposes. We do not at this stage make any time horizon explicit: this point will be discussed below.

The constraints on the maximization of (3) are (1); (2);

$$(C(t), n_1(t), n_2(t), \ldots .) \text{ form a feasible production} \tag{4}$$
plan for the economy, given initial capital stocks;

and

$$u(c_i) \geqslant \bar{u}_i(n_i). \tag{5}$$

The constraints (5) express the 'political' necessity of meeting the needs or demands of different groups—such as workers in organized industry, civil servants, doctors, and so on. $\bar{u}_i$ is the minimum level of utility that must be provided to people in occupation i. These constraints may arise not only from the bargaining power of the occupational group but also from the wish to keep people in the country (in which case $\bar{u}_i$ will probably depend on n_i), or from the desirability of providing workers with sufficient consumption to ensure adequate efficiency,[1] or from the impossibility of taking away (at reasonable cost) what people already have. In the last case, it might be better to regard the constraint as an *equality*, since it is sometimes virtually impossible to give subsidies efficiently. This would be particularly relevant to backward agricultural areas, and we shall take the point up again below.

14.52 *Prices*
It is clear that in the optimal development of this economic model, production will be efficient. We can therefore introduce accounting prices for the variables mentioned in (4). We shall here measure these prices in terms of utility. The notation is

$p(t) =$ price of consumption at t
$w_i(t) =$ price (shadow wage) of occupation i at t.

Then the optimum development path is such that any small change in it (which is feasible from the production point of view, though possibly violating (1), (2), or (5)) leaves

$$\int \{p(t)C(t) - \Sigma w_i(t)n_i(t)\}dt \qquad (6)$$

unchanged (neglecting terms of second order), the prices being kept fixed. It will be recognized that these prices are the accounting prices which if followed would support the optimal development of the economy. Thus in the terminology of the present book

$$-\frac{\dot{p}}{p} = \text{ARI} \qquad (7)$$

$$\frac{w_i}{p} = \text{SWR for occupation } i. \qquad (8)$$

To connect this model with previous work, it may be as well to verify these relations for the one-output neoclassical model, in which capital stocks K_i co-operating with the various categories of labour are related to aggregate consumption through the equation

$$C + \Sigma \dot{K}_i = \Sigma F_i(K_i, n_i). \qquad (9)$$

If the F_i are concave (i.e. no economies of scale), the optimum growth path maximizes

---

[1] Again $\bar{u}_i$ would depend upon the particular development of the economy that is considered optimal, but we may as well suppose that predetermined for the purpose of our analysis.

$$\int_0^T \{pC - \Sigma w_i n_i\}dt$$

$$= \int_0^T \Sigma\{pF_i - p\dot{K}_i - w_i n_i\}dt$$

$$= \int_0^T \Sigma\{pF_i + \dot{p}K_i - w_i n_i\}dt - p\Sigma K_i(0) + p\Sigma K_i(T).$$

Therefore the derivatives of $\{\ldots\}$ with respect to the K_i and n_i are zero:

$$\left. \begin{array}{l} p\,\dfrac{\partial F_i}{\partial K_i} + \dot{p} = 0 \\[2mm] p\,\dfrac{\partial F_i}{\partial n_i} = w_i. \end{array} \right\}$$

The first of these equations says that $-\dot{p}/p$ is the marginal product of capital in all sectors; the second that w_i/p is the marginal product of labour in sector i. Thus equations (7) and (8) are verified in this special case. They are however of much more general validity.

14.53 *The relation of Prices to Utility*
Since we have measured prices in terms of utility, the prices associated with the optimum path can be used to combine outputs and inputs with utility. We can assert that any changes in the development path which, though possibly violating (4), satisfy (1) and (5), will reduce (or at any rate not significantly increase)

$$\int \Sigma n_i u(c_i)e^{-\delta t}dt - \int\{pC - \Sigma w_i n_i\}dt$$

$$= \int \Sigma\{n_i u(c_i)e^{-\delta t} - pn_i c_i + w_i n_i\}dt. \tag{10}$$

Thus the optimum c_i and n_i are such that small changes subject to $n_i = N$ and $u(c_i) \geqslant \bar{u}_i(n_i)$ leave

$$\Sigma\{n_i u(c_i)e^{-\delta t} - pn_i c_i + w_i n_i\}$$

stationary. To take care of the constraints, we introduce multipliers (shadow prices corresponding to the constraints) g and h_i. The derivatives of

$$\Sigma\{n_i u(c_i)e^{-\delta t} - pn_i c_i + w_i n_i - gn_i + h_i[u(c_i) - \bar{u}_i(n_i)]\}$$

with respect to the n_i and c_i are zero at the optimum:

$$u(c_i)e^{-\delta t} - pc_i + w_i - g - h_i\bar{u}_i'(n_i) = 0 \tag{11}$$

$$\left(e^{-\delta t} + \frac{h_i}{n_i}\right)u'(c_i) = p. \tag{12}$$

In equating these derivatives to zero, we are assuming that neither c_i nor n_i is zero. This might be questionable in the latter case, but we need not concern ourselves explicitly with occupations that might or might not exist.

From (11) we have the following expression for the shadow wage rate in occupation i:

$$\frac{w_i}{p} = c_i \frac{u(c_i)e^{-\delta t} - h_i \bar{u}_i'(n_i)}{p} + \frac{g}{p} \tag{13}$$

$$= c_i - \frac{u(c_i) + \bar{u}_i'(n_i)n_i}{pe^{\delta t}} + \frac{\bar{u}_i'(n_i)n_i}{u'(c_i)} + \frac{g}{p} \tag{14}$$

using (12) to substitute for h_i. In some occupations, e.g. industrial ones, $\bar{u}_i'$ may be negligibly small, in which case (14) simplifies.

In order to interpret these first-order conditions (12) and (14), we should recall the meaning of the multipliers g and h_i. g is the value, in utility terms, of an additional person in the economy: it might be positive or negative. Its significance is that it is the same for all occupations. So long as the constraint (5) can be kept as an inequality, we can be sure h_i is non-negative, and zero if $u(c_i) > \bar{u}_i(n_i)$.[1] If $u(c_i)$ has to be equal to $\bar{u}_i(n_i)$ (minimum utility also being a maximum) h_i could be negative. This would be the case for a sector where transfers to and from consumers are impossible, and c_i is a function of $n_i : c_i = f_i(n_i)$.

Such a subsistence sector can form a convenient basis for estimating the SWR. Suppose $i=0$ is the label for such a sector, and that we can estimate the marginal product of labour, $m = w_0/p_0$, in that sector pretty accurately. Then

$$m = c_0 - \frac{u(c_0) + \bar{u}_0'(n_0)n_0}{pe^{\delta t}} + \frac{\bar{u}_0'(n_0)n_0}{u'(c_0)} + \frac{g}{p},$$

with

$$\bar{u}_0'(n_0) = \frac{d}{dn_0} u(f_0(n_0)) = u'(c_0)f_0'(n_0) = \frac{u'(c_0)(m - c_0)}{n_0}$$

in this case, since

$$m = \frac{d}{dn_0}(n_0 f_0(n_0)) = f_0(n_0) + n_0 f_0'(n_0) = c_0 + n_0 f_0'(n_0).$$

---

[1] If there is only one consumer good and $u(c_i) = \bar{u}_i$, with $\bar{u}_i$ independent of n_i and t, then c_i will be constant. This means that $u'(c_i)$ is constant, and the way h_i changes can be deduced from (12). But that cannot be done when there are a number of consumer goods.

Therefore

$$\frac{g}{p} = \frac{u(c_0) - (c_0 - m)u'(c_0)}{pe^{\delta t}}.$$ (15)

We can use this formula in (14) for other sectors now. Take one for which $\bar{u}_i'(n_i) = 0$;

$$\frac{w_i}{p} = c_i - \frac{u(c_i)}{pe^{\delta t}} + \frac{u(c_0) + mu'(c_0)}{pe^{\delta t}} - c_0$$

$$= c_i - \frac{u(c_i) - u(c_0) + (c_0 - m)u'(c_0)}{pe^{\delta t}}.$$ (16)

c_0 here corresponds to the number a that has been used in the main body of these chapters, and c_i to c. Formula (16) corresponds to (2) in 14.11 where $pe^{\delta t}$, being the weight currently assigned to government income, is put equal to 1, V is u, and v, u', and the term $g - e$ allows for considerations absent in the model.

The consumption rate of interest does not have an unambiguous meaning in the model we are discussing, since c_i may vary in different ways for different consumers. In the case of the sector i we have just been discussing, where a new worker is taken from occupation o (in the optimum it does not matter where he comes from), it is natural to define the CRI as the rate of fall of the utility gain from using a unit of consumption to make possible the transfer of people from occupations o to occupations i, i.e.

$$\text{CRI} = -\frac{\dot{q}}{q}$$ (17)

where

$$q = \frac{u(c_i) - u(c_0) + (c_0 - m)u'(c_0)}{c_i - m} e^{-\delta t}.$$ (18)

Naturally,

$$\text{SWR} = \frac{w_i}{p} = c_i - \frac{q}{p}(c_i - m).$$ (20)

q/p is the same as $1/s$ in the main text, and tautologically

$$-\dot{s}/s = \dot{q}/q = \text{ARI} - \text{CRI}.$$ (21)

The real point of introducing the CRI is that q can be calculated directly from (18) without intervening multipliers whose values could not be estimated without fully solving the model.

We can use this notation to show that the procedure using SWR and ARI, which we advocate, is equivalent to the alternative procedure[1] of discounting at the CRI, and valuing increases in and calls upon public income at a premium price. Consider a project that involves changes $\delta C(t)$ and $\delta n_i(t)$ in production and employment. ($\delta C(t)$ will be negative initially, and would then be called investment.) It is optimal to undertake the project if (cf. (6))

$$\text{PSV} = \int \{p\delta C - w_i \delta n_i\} dt = \int p \left\{ \delta C - \frac{w_i}{p} \delta n_i \right\} dt \qquad (22)$$

is positive. Using (20), this can be written

$$\text{PSV} = \int q \left\{ \frac{p}{q} \delta C - \left(\frac{p}{q} c_i - c_i + m \right) n_i \right\} dt$$

$$= \int q \{s(\delta C - c_i \delta n_i) + c_i \delta n_i - m\delta n_i\} dt, \qquad (23)$$

using the notation $s = p/q$, as above.

In this expression we are discounting by a factor q, i.e. with the CRI as discount rate. The quantities being discounted are calculated by separating net output into the part going to (or coming from) government funds, $\delta C - \Sigma c_i \delta n_i$, and the part going to consumers, the first part being valued at a premium price s. The cost of labour is measured by taking the marginal product as the shadow wage in this case. The inconveniences of the method are, first, the need to revalue government income, and, second, the necessity of discounting at different rates, etc., if different occupations are involved. In fact, over the economy as a whole it would not be right to use the same q and the same CRI for different sectors.

14.54 *Calculation of the Optimum Path*

Conditions (7), (8), (12) and (14), in conjunction with the constraints (2), (4) and (5), provide what looks at first sight like a complete characterization of the optimum path. But it is not. The problem can be brought out most clearly by considering the one-output model described in (9), with the additional assumption of constant returns to scale in every sector. This latter assumption implies a fixed relationship (the factor–price frontier) between the ARI and the SWR:

$$\frac{\dot{p}}{p} = Q_i \left(\frac{w_i}{p} \right) \quad (i = 1, \ldots, I). \qquad (24)$$

w_i/p is known, from (14), as a function of the c_i, n_i, g and p. Further-

---

[1] This is the procedure used in Marglin, 1967, and the UNIDO *Guidelines*.

more, in each sector the capital–labour ratio, k_i, is a definite function of w_i/p, so that we have, with $K(o)$ the initial capital stock,

$$\Sigma n_i k_i \left(\frac{w_i}{p_i}\right) = K(o). \tag{25}$$

Recollect also that

$$\Sigma n_i = \mathcal{N}, \tag{2}$$

and that, since either $u(c_i) = \bar{u}_i$ or $u'(c_i) = p$, the c_i are determined by the n_i and p. All this means that we have $I+2$ equations in $I+3$ unknowns—the n_i, g, p, and $\dot{p}/p$. In other words, we seem to be able to find a path satisfying all our equations given *any* initial value of p.[1] (Investment in K is determined residually from (9).)

This problem is well known in the theory of optimum growth. It expresses the entirely plausible proposition that we must know where the economy ought to be going (i.e. what K should be at some future date) before we can decide how it ought to start off. The optimization problem must therefore be solved as a whole, perhaps for an infinite time-horizon, if we are to know what the ARI and SWRs ought to be in the immediate future. This does *not* mean that the answer will be sensitive, within sensible limits, to what is assumed about the distant future; only that one must assume something, and work the whole problem out, before one has any idea about initial policies. The moral is, that optimum growth calculations in solvable models are the only satisfactory way of telling at what level current accounting prices should be put.[2] There is no reason to think that complicated models are better for this purpose than simple ones,[3] but much research on that question remains to be done. In particular, realistically specified versions of the general model of this section (including a private production sector) have not yet been used. We shall not go into the computational problems of solving optimum growth models here.

In the absence of adequate guidance from computed models, presumably one should be able to make fairly sensible guesses about the general long-term development of the economy, and work backwards from these guesses to estimates of the SWR and the ARI in the present. In effect, that is the procedure we have proposed in this book.

---

[1] If p were too small initially, the path would not be possible, because it would run capital down to zero.

[2] Stern, 1972, Newbery, 1972.

[3] Mirrlees and Stern, 1972.

14.6 SUMMARY AND CONCLUSION

The accounting prices discussed in this chapter are central to a system of project appraisal. The shadow wage rates and the accounting rate of interest tie different investment decisions together in a consistent way, and they express, especially through the shadow wage rates, the objectives of the country in the ways that are most likely to affect project decisions. It is not therefore very easy to evaluate a single project in a situation where the government has never seriously worked out these controlling shadow prices. It is always possible for a scholar, an adviser, an aid agency, or a government department to apply its own opinions and values; and no doubt there are many hints in this chapter about the levels of shadow wage rates we would normally want to see applied. But if the result of the evaluation is sensitive to the assumptions made, then there is not much to be said about the project on its own, before a study of the whole economy has been done, and an attempt made to express the objectives of the government and country in the ways required for economic analysis. This is certainly not to say that project evaluation is useless before a well-researched system of accounting prices exists. Many very bad choices can often be eliminated. Moreover, applying the methods of cost–benefit analysis is a way of asking the most pertinent questions, and bringing out choices that might have been neglected. At the very least it is a step towards knowing what to expect, and finding out what is going on.

We hope that this chapter has brought out what kinds of considerations are involved in choosing the SWR and ARI. Even crude methods need a lot of information and hard work. It is no light matter to decide how much urban employment should be expanded, to what extent rural projects should be used to redistribute income, whether to concentrate on long-term or short-term projects, on agriculture or industry, and so on. Accounting prices are there to help in making better decisions, both on such broad fronts and more narrowly. The fact that they are hard to estimate with sufficient accuracy is no reason for casually adopting the first numbers that one thinks of. Since in practice the numbers do not need to be *very* accurate, some research and thought is likely to be well worth while.

Uncertainty

It is not unnatural to discuss investment projects, as we have done in earlier chapters, on the assumption that their costs and benefits are known in advance. Most people dealing with industrial projects are prepared to put some kind of figure to the quantities of outputs and inputs that a project is likely to provide and require. But one can never be certain of the outcome. Sometimes the estimates even of quite important costs and benefits are no better than informed guesses. Project planners ought to pay some attention to this uncertainty. In this chapter, we consider what they should do about it.

The uncertainties of particular projects are often rather insignificant when measured against the total performance of the economy, important though they may seem to those responsible for the decisions. Usually it will do little harm if no specific allowance is made for uncertainty, although there are some important exceptions to this rule. Furthermore, it still has to be decided what particular figure to put to costs or benefits when uncertainty is present, a problem we have ignored in earlier chapters. There is no guarantee that the estimates which the engineers provide are, even approximately, the correct average of the various possibilities. We must decide what kind of average is appropriate, and how to get it: and also what to do when the uncertainties are, for one reason or another, so important that they cannot reasonably be ignored.

The theory of choice under uncertainty is a difficult subject, and there is some disagreement among economists and statisticians on quite fundamental issues. We shall avoid the more controversial and difficult parts of the subject, and try to take the most sensible view of what is relevant to practical decision-taking, even when our suggestions would not be universally accepted. The reader will have to decide whether he finds our arguments convincing.

15.1 THE VARIETIES OF UNCERTAINTY

The uncertainties of a particular project arise from many unpredictable influences. One cannot perfectly predict future technology or tastes, or the actions of the government: any of these can quite easily falsify the assumptions upon which the project design and appraisal

is based. And of course the project itself may not perform in the way expected.

It is important to bear in mind this distinction between uncertainties about the project itself and uncertainties about the environment in which it operates—that is, about the rest of the economy and the rest of the world. These two sources of uncertainty will often act independently of one another. The price of the output, for instance, may depend on what is happening to the demand for that commodity in the industrialized countries, whereas the quantity of output that *can* be produced depends upon the success with which the project is being operated.

But the quantity of output that *will* be produced certainly depends upon what happens to prices. The project managers may decide to operate it in a way different from what was originally intended, because economic conditions turn out differently—indeed they might even decide to close it down. Similarly, the prices paid for some of the inputs might depend upon the project's demand for them, which in turn depends upon how well it operates. So there is a process of mutual adjustment between the economic environment and the performance of the project, which implies that prices and quantities depend upon one another. It is, nevertheless, useful to think of the uncertainties about prices and quantities separately.

Many of the troubles of industrial firms producing consumer goods arise from the competition of too many firms trying to supply a limited potential market, or from trying to sell a new design or invention of uncertain appeal. The more basic consumer demands can be predicted with tolerable accuracy, apart from temporary fluctuations. Indeed, the unpredictability of consumers' tastes is often exaggerated as a source of uncertainty. Moreover, a consumer product is as likely to prove more popular than planners expected, as it is to be less popular—provided the planners have made a reasonably objective assessment of possibilities. We shall see that, normally, this would justify the planners in making no further allowance for uncertainty.

Uncertainties in export markets may be rather large, in part because of unexpected changes in the tastes of foreigners. Yet the cases that spring to mind arise mainly from changes in technology or from government actions. Changes in tin-plating techniques affect the demand for tin; developments in plastics threaten disaster for jute producers; new import restrictions can destroy a market overnight.

It is understandable that the governments of developing countries should get the impression that such changes are usually adverse to them. Even although the prices of primary products have not shown, in the long run, any clear tendency to fall relative to the prices of manufacturers, technological developments have usually seemed to be unfavourable. It is difficult to tell whether this is true, or an illusion. Certainly, at some time, new inventions and industrial processes created the demand for petroleum, rubber, bauxite, and so on; but that era may have passed. On the other hand, new technological developments may be as likely to increase as decrease the value of the new industrial products that the developing countries are beginning to produce.

The important lesson to be drawn from past experience is not so much that the developing countries live in a very risky world: as a group, their risks in international trade may be no greater than the risks of the industrial countries. The lesson is that there are risks and uncertainties which can be taken account of. One should not assume that things will turn out for the best. The various plausible possibilities can be weighed up, and the prospect of high or low prices (or high or low sales) assessed. It is usually possible to make some guess at the kinds of changes in world technology that can affect the value of a project. In fact, it is quite normal to consider the most important of them when discussing a new project. The temptation to be avoided is that of putting detailed figures only to the most favourable of the likely possibilities: mere worry about the other possibilities is an inadequate way of allowing for them. When risks are considerable, a systematic description of all the likely possibilities is a sensible preliminary to a detailed evaluation of the project.

Before turning to the details of such a description, it is worth emphasizing that, while some uncertainties are outside the control of planners, others can easily be influenced by their policies. The extent of the risks associated with a project may be reduced either by making advance arrangements to deal with adversity—as with life-boats on ships, or by insurance (e.g. with foreign countries), or by substituting a less risky alternative for the one first considered, or in many other ways. If the insurance arrangements are worth-while, the value of the investment project plus insurance arrangements will be greater than the value of the project taken alone. Special expenditures to meet adverse contingencies will be worth-while investments in themselves, and will enhance the value of the main project. We shall assume for the sake of argument that proper decisions concerning such risk-avoiding possibilities have been taken, so that we can concentrate on the evaluation of a single specification of the project, and refer directly to the possible control of uncertainty only occasionally. But it is always to be remembered that careful planning against particular undesirable contingencies may be better than replacing a risky-looking project with a more timid alternative.

15.2 THE DESCRIPTION OF UNCERTAINTY

For each possible future of the project, and the economy, one can in principle calculate the present social value. With some trouble, all reasonable possibilities could be allowed for in this way, and one would have estimates of the range of possible PSVs. We shall later consider whether this is a sensible practical procedure. Practical or not, it is certainly not sufficient. It takes one some way towards describing the prospects for the project, but not far enough for a decision (unless it cannot possibly have a positive PSV, or cannot possibly have a negative PSV). This has to be emphasized, because it is sometimes suggested that a sensitivity analysis—consisting of a number of calculations, in particular PSV calculations, on the basis of alternative assumptions—helps to get more sensible decisions made in the face of uncertainty.

But it remains unclear how the sensitivity analysis is supposed to affect the decision. Possibly, projects that have a very wide range of present values are to be rejected. If that were the effect of sensitivity analysis, countries might be better off without it. We shall be arguing below that the rejection of exceptionally risky projects, simply because of their riskiness, could be a most unfortunate policy. At least it should certainly not be adopted unthinkingly. A sensitivity analysis *can* be a great help in deciding whether a more careful examination of the various possibilities is desirable, so as to reduce uncertainty before a decision is made, but it does not do more than that.[1]

A list of possibilities is thus only the beginning of an adequate description of an uncertain prospect. The description must be completed by means of the quantitative language of probabilities. In the right context, no one concerned with investment decisions has any difficulty in understanding probabilities: they provide the natural language for describing games of chance, and for describing those risks that businesses are accustomed to insure against. But some people doubt whether probabilities can be used to describe the main uncertainties involved in investment decisions. How, it

---

[1] Sensitivity analysis has been more fully discussed in 8.4 and 8.5.

may be asked, can one hope to estimate the probability that the price of jute bags will have risen next year, far less estimate the probability that it will have risen by between 10% and 11%?

Yet one really cannot fully compare different investment projects without estimating the probabilities of the different outcomes or possibilities. In some cases there is no great difficulty—as, for instance, in the case of a dam, where the main uncertainties about rainfall in the catchment area can quite easily be described by probabilities. But the dam has to be compared with other projects, in the export trade, for instance, where one is unaccustomed to using probabilities. There may be no more uncertainty about the second project; merely unwillingness, because of the *kind* of evidence available, to use probabilities in describing it. How then can one decide between two such projects, far less compare either with the whole population of potential projects?

One could, like a board of directors, listen to an account of some of the relevant evidence about future possibilities; or merely hear a rather vague account of someone's views on the possibilities, perhaps on the most probable course of events. Then a decision might be made without any formal analysis. But this is an unsatisfactory procedure. All the reasonable possibilities may not have been fairly considered: evidence about the probable course of events may have been mixed up with particular value judgments about the alternatives. Since the procedure is undisciplined, its logic is incapable of further check.

Managers, in both public and private industry, frequently make judgments about uncertain projects which are intuitive. There is plenty of evidence that most people's intuitive responses to uncertainty are irrational and inconsistent, even when there is no doubt about the probabilities involved. Techniques of investment appraisal are designed to reduce irrational behaviour. The use of numerical probabilities is a step in the right direction. Once one becomes accustomed to describing uncertainties in this way, it seems quite natural. A gambler understands betting odds, and, with practice, might even offer sensible odds on the occurrence of an earthquake or a war. The trick is to think of possibilities that seem equally likely, and are mutually exclusive; these can then be used to get a probability. One might, for example, imagine very broadly three different kinds of future for a country, the third of which leads to civil war; and then decide the first can be split in two, all four possibilities being more or less equally likely. Then the probability of civil war is a quarter. Obviously that is a very rough procedure, but it makes sense.

People often make the mistake of thinking that they ought to be sure of probabilities. They will say that probabilities suggest 'spurious precision'. As an argument, that deserves to rank with the one about being able to prove anything with statistics. Numbers can be used without pretending to be absolutely sure they are right: if one said Delhi was five thousand miles from Oxford, one should not be accused of 'spurious precision', because it is not precisely true. Similarly, if one says there is a 25% chance of civil war, one is not insisting that the probability is not 24%—merely that it is fairly likely, though far from certain.

As in the rest of cost–benefit analysis, one tries to use sensible numbers, without striving for correctness beyond what is possible in the time and with the techniques available. The use of probabilities, as a way of expressing the bearing of the known evidence on the quantities in question, is justified by the fact that one probability description is often *clearly* better than another. For instance, the statement that the terms of trade of developing countries in Asia are as likely to rise as to fall during the next decade, is certainly a better description of the possibilities than the statement that they will deteriorate by 5% per year during that time. Many probability descriptions of any particular prospect can be rejected out of hand, and one can usually find a description that is at least as good as any other. There is no other usable way of expressing empirically based knowledge about uncertain possibilities in a way that is independent of opinions about the goodness or badness of the possible results.

15.3 Using Probabilities

Some knowledge of the theory of statistics is desirable when the particular probabilities to be used play a very important part in the final decision. If they do not, it is still helpful to have in mind the main ways in which probabilities can be estimated, even when very rough approximations are adequate (as is frequently the case). The following methods are worth distinguishing, although from some points of view they are similar to one another:

(i) Probabilities may be available from actuarial evidence, or can be simply allowed for since the risks in question are normally insured against. This is the model that one copies in order to have a general language for uncertainty. If large numbers of similar instances have happened in the past, insurance companies can predict with high probability the number of claims they will have to meet in the year, and are therefore willing to make a fixed charge for the promise to pay in the event of loss. Fire insurance is a well-known example. The probability of a fire destroying a factory building is known, within relatively small limits. The firm may not want to take out all the insurance it could—it may carry some of the risk itself; or it may have taken special precautions, or have special knowledge that suggests the probability is actually less than the insurance company uses for factories chosen at random. Indeed we should not usually recommend a public enterprise to take out insurance: the state may as well bear the risks itself. But it is clear that there are risks of this kind, where estimating probabilities is not difficult.

(ii) Even if the risks would not be easily insurable, so many instances may be known from past experience that the appropriate probability can be estimated without significant disagreement. For instance, if planners kept good records, the results of projects could be compared with those predicted. Once a reasonably large body of experience had formed, and provided that the period considered was not exceptional in some obviously relevant way, the frequency with which the original figures overestimated and underestimated actual social profit could be established. Specifically, one might find that in two cases out of ten social profit exceeded predicted social profit; in four out of ten, it was not more than 5% less than predicted social profit; in another three out of ten it was between 5% and 50% less than the predicted level. This kind of information would clearly be helpful in allowing probabilities to be estimated. In a particular project, special information may modify or override the general evidence. But for frequently occurring items, like construction costs, delays in completion, repair time of equipment, and so on, such information could be used directly. We shall see shortly that in many cases one can simply make an adjustment in the initial estimate of cost or benefit, rather than use a whole probability description; but the principle is worth bearing in mind.

(iii) Statistical techniques can be used to establish *probability distributions*. The probability distribution of some quantity— say export sales of tea—is the whole probability description of its possible values: for example, a statement of the probabilities that the variable will be greater than any stated number. Statistical methods usually assume that the probability distribution has some general kind of shape— e.g. a 'normal distribution'—and then use the available evidence to decide which particular form of this distribution is the correct one. Since these methods are technical, we shall not pursue them further here.

(iv) Those responsible for estimating the probable course of the project may simply agree upon probability distributions for future social profits—and thus on a probability distribution for the PSV—as a fair, but approximate, expression of their opinions or hunches. When there is evidence that cannot be dealt with in any of the ways mentioned above, this method can be very useful. Non-statistical evidence can also be given quantitative expression. For instance, the managers of the project might well be willing to agree that there is a five to one chance against a particular piece of equipment arriving on time. Many important kinds of relevant evidence— impressions about the trustworthiness of contractors, rumours about future developments in the markets, knowledge of the difficulties of breaking into new markets—can be brought to bear in this way. Fortunately, a very precise knowledge of the probabilities is not required in the assessment of most projects. What is important is the estimation of 'average values', to which we now turn.

If a man has equal chances of winning or losing \$1 in some gamble, the *expected value* of the gamble is zero; if he had had a 2/3 probability of winning, the expected value would have been \$1/3. The minimum premium a fire insurance company can charge is the expected value of the claims it must meet: it is obtained by multiplying each possible size of claim by its probability, and adding the result. In other words, the expected value is the natural average value: the value that is to be expected on average, taking one possibility with another. Whenever probabilities can be assigned to the various possible values of a variable, then the expected value can be calculated in the same way. In symbols: if the variable X can take the values $x_1, x_2, x_3 \ldots$, its expected value is defined to be $p_1 x_1 + p_2 x_2 + p_3 x_3 \ldots$, where p_i is the probability of taking the value x_i.

So, once we have estimates of the probability distributions for social profits in all the years of the project's potential life, we can, in principle, calculate the expected value of social profit—the *expected social profit*, for short—in each year. Similarly, we can estimate the *expected present social value* (EPSV). This is, in many ways, the most natural summary measure of the prospects of the project, either year by year, or as a whole. Yet it is not the whole story. A project about whose prospects there is very great uncertainty might have the same EPSV as a project whose results were known with near certainty in advance. On the face of it, one would not expect to regard the two projects as having an equal claim on investment funds: the relative uncertainty of different projects seems to be relevant to the investment decision. Indeed, it may be tempting to say that very uncertain projects are very undesirable, unless their EPSV is very high.

The above point of view is, no doubt, sensible for an individual, who may dislike excessive uncertainty as such, and will almost certainly attach less weight to an increase in his wealth than to an equal decrease, so that equal probabilities of an increase and an equal decrease may provide a prospect less satisfactory than the certainty of unaltered wealth. But it does not follow that the same considerations are appropriate, or have the same force, in the case of production decisions by a public enterprise. The question therefore arises whether a producer, taking his decisions for the good of society, should pay any attention to the extent of uncertainty involved; or should simply attend to the EPSV.

15.4 Investment Criteria: the Simplest Cases

Suppose that in a particular year a project has equal probabilities of making a million rupees of social profit, and of making zero social profit. Perhaps it is a bicycle factory, and it is hoped to sell its output in a new export market; if that falls through, the bicycles will have to be sold at home where the market is already well supplied, so that the social profit would be, say, zero. The factory may be producing a substantial proportion of the country's bicycle output, but the social profit will, at best, be only a small proportion of the total value of production in the economy.

As we saw in Chapter IX, social profit measures the value of the project in the following sense. If the government had available to it an equal amount of purchasing power, which it could use to purchase goods and services in world markets for the purposes it thinks best, that would be just as good as having the project operating. Thus the social profit is measured in terms of convertible foreign exchange, i.e. general purchasing power not committed to the provision of consumption. The bicycle factory itself makes only a small contribution to the total production available to the economy, measured in these terms. Suppose the government's annual budget, similarly measured, is Rs. 1,000 million. Then the project is equivalent to either an increase in the budget of 0·1 % or no change. With small changes of this magnitude, two successive increases of Rs. 500,000 would have the same value, near enough. Thus a project that would, with equal probability, produce a gain of Rs. 500,000 or a loss of the same magnitude, is of zero value to the country; and the bicycle project is therefore worth Rs. 500,000 a year. In saying this, we are abstracting entirely from the fun of gambling, or the nastiness of risk-taking, as such—neither of which should be relevant to decisions taken for society.

Another way of looking at this argument is to compare one man considering a risky investment, with a partnership of many men, each as wealthy as the first, undertaking a similar investment. The first man may reject the investment, because failure would have grave consequences, whereas the partnership would go ahead since no one of them stands to lose much even if the project fails. The more who share in the project, the less does the risk element matter. Insofar as the consequences of investment projects are spread widely and fairly evenly among the population, the risks are not important.

The reader may still feel uneasy. If public authorities ignore the risk aspect of their investments, will they not plunge the economy into terrible uncertainties and fluctuations? Surely a government ought not to ignore uncertainty if that implies a serious risk of negative economic growth; nor could an aid agency encourage such behaviour. Such arguments make the mistake of seeing individual projects as though they were the whole economy. But risks do not add up the way that profits do. If a hundred projects each ran a 25 % risk of making a loss, it does not at all follow that the projects taken all together have an equal risk of making a loss. Indeed, if the uncertainties about these projects are fairly independent of one another, the probability that the sum of their profits is negative would be very small: although it is very likely that some projects will make a loss, it is very unlikely that almost all of them will make a loss; and when some make losses, others will be making positive profits, and some will be making quite large profits.

This appeal to the 'law of large numbers' is easily justified by looking at the fluctuations in the national income of some particular country from year to year. Usually, the level of the national income is at most 2% or 3% different from what would have been expected two or three years before. Considering that many projects turn out very much worse than expected—a large anticipated profit turning into a large loss when the figures are counted up—there is a very striking difference between overall uncertainty in the economy, and the uncertainty associated with particular production projects.

This, then, is our first rule: *in the absence of special reasons to the contrary, one should measure the value of a project to the economy by its expected present social value.* One might conveniently measure the EPSV by estimating the expected level of all the various inputs and outputs, then evaluating them by means of the expected accounting prices, and discounting in the usual way. This assumes that any uncertainty about the accounting prices is essentially independent of uncertainty about the level of outputs or inputs: an assumption that is not strictly correct, since project performance can be adjusted to adverse circumstances. But that is usually a small consideration.

15.5 MORE DIFFICULT CASES

In certain cases, for one reason or another, some of the assumptions on which the above argument is based will be false.

(i) The accounting price of one of the outputs (or inputs) may depend quite sensitively on the amount being produced (or used). For example, the price at which a bicycle factory can expect to sell its products abroad may depend on the number it is trying to sell. In that case, we want to value the output by the expected earnings of foreign exchange (making allowance for any change in consumption commitments when necessary), and that need not be the same as the expected output multiplied by the expected accounting price. For example, the price of bicycles might fall off quite sharply if more than a certain number are sold, but not increase very much if fewer are sold. If the output to be achieved is rather uncertain, one must make due allowance for the relatively small contribution that an excess of production over the expected level would make to foreign exchange earnings.

Once the problem is stated, the solution is of course clear: one should, in such a case, not think in terms of valuing expected output, but estimate directly the expected level of foreign exchange earnings. Since this kind of situation arises mainly with exportable commodities, its treatment is fairly easy. But one can imagine more difficult cases. Then one must estimate the social value directly under various alternative assumptions about the outcome of the project.

(ii) The output of the project may be closely related to the overall performance of the economy. For instance, it may be more useful if there is a substantial increase in consumer incomes; or, perhaps, it will be more useful if, say, poor rains spoil the harvest, with a substantial fall in the national income. What one should do here is to estimate the expected value of the product of the quantity produced multiplied by the accounting price. If the project is likely to produce a lot under just those conditions when the output is worth most, its value is naturally greater than that estimated by taking the expected output and multiplying it by the expected accounting price. For, when prices and output are not independent, this latter procedure does not properly estimate the expected social profit; whereas calculating the social profit directly, and estimating its expected value does.[1] Probably this case seldom arises when dealing with industrial projects, but can be quite important in some agricultural and transport projects.

(iii) Uncertainty about the results of a particular project may actually be undesirable in itself. We are on the edge of irrational feelings here, but it must be admitted that sometimes uncertainty as such is unpleasant or may have deleterious consequences. For example, the project may be tied to foreign aid from some particular government, whose future attitude to the country may be strongly influenced—however irrationally—by the performance of its own pet projects. In this case, some weight must be given to projects that are more likely to perform 'satisfactorily'. (Of course, it is also possible that the country would react so well to an extremely successful project that it is worth taking special risks for the sake of such a reaction.)

Again, the failure of a project might have unpleasant consequences for the particular area in which it is sited, whereas its success would lead to increased incomes in a rather more diffused and evenly distributed way. It would not be unreasonable in such a case to attempt to insure against such failure: although it might well be cheaper to adopt a risky project, with the promise of special aid, or priority in the siting of new projects, if the first project should be a failure.

On the whole, the above kind of argument should be used with caution, since it is seldom likely to be of great importance. If it does seem to be important, some kind of *ad hoc* adjustment or allowance

---

[1] See 15.8 for a technical justification.

must be made, since the task of carrying out a precise analysis would be exceedingly complicated.

(iv) The extent of uncertainty may not be small in relation to the national income. This might be true of a very small country. There are countries where the value of annual production in a single enterprise accounts for more than a quarter of the national income: fluctuations in the export price of the commodity produced—copper, aluminium, or asbestos—may be a large part of the uncertainty of national income.

In general, people give more weight to a substantial reduction in their income than to an equal increase. This is proved by their willingness to take out insurance, and the fact that they frequently prefer securities with a low yield and low risk to risky stocks and shares that have a high expected return. Consequently a government must, acting on behalf of the citizens of the country, tend to prefer a more certain *national* income, even at some cost in terms of a lower expected value. It is therefore right that projects which add significantly to *aggregate* uncertainty in the economy should be somewhat penalized in the system of project evaluation. No government would want to insist that all farmers in the country should adopt a new crop variety as yet largely untested, even though it offered the prospect of much higher yields: the risks of crop failure would be too great, and the possible consequences too awful.

Our earlier argument turned to a great extent on the assertion that most projects, uncertain though they may be in themselves, bring about an insignificant increase in the aggregate uncertainty of the economy's prospects. In that case, one can avoid the awkward question of putting a figure to the social cost of the uncertainty. Fortunately the case of a project which is very large in relation to the economy will arise only rarely; nevertheless something must be said about this controversial question.

The difficulty is that, on the one hand, there is no way of dealing with the problem precisely, without bringing in the mathematical theory of probability; while, on the other hand, the answer must depend upon the extent to which a country ought to avoid uncertainty—a disputable matter. This latter question turns upon the extent to which it seems desirable to take a chance of getting higher incomes at the risk of actually getting lower incomes: a consideration like that of giving up some present lower income to get a larger increase in future higher income. But it can be said with some confidence that, on almost any plausible weighting, it is unlikely that a large allowance for uncertainty ought to be made. A reduction in the value of the project by a few per cent is the most that one would expect.[1]

(v) Considerations similar to (iv) arise when the project, though not large relative to the country's national income, has a substantial effect on the incomes of particular groups. For example, if irrigation is brought to an area previously dependent on local rainfall, farmers and farm-labourers in that area will probably gain substantial increases in their incomes. Of course it might be better if the benefits (or costs) could be widely distributed within the economy, but that often happens only to a very limited extent (through additional tax revenue, water charges, etc.) in most actual irrigation projects; and, because of administrative costs and the need to provide adequate incentives to the farmers, it is unlikely that one would want to design the project so that it had only a small effect locally. If that is so, the risks of the project will be borne locally, and

---

[1] The following example, in which we use the notion of 'utility', shows the orders of magnitude involved. Suppose a country's national income is \$400 million. A large project is being considered. In the year in question, the planners have estimated that it will provide the economy with:

> \$125 million, with probability one quarter;
> \$100 million, with probability one half;
> \$ 75 million, with probability one quarter.

The utility of national income x is taken to be $A - \dfrac{1,000}{x}$ million. (The constant A is actually irrelevant.)

In terms of this assessment of the relative utility of the different prospects, we see that the country can expect:

> utility level $A - 1 \cdot 905$ with probability one quarter;
> utility level $A - 2$ with probability one half;
> utility level $A - 2 \cdot 105$ with probability one quarter.

Averaging, we compute its expected utility level to be:

$$A - 2 \cdot 0025.$$

This is the utility that would have been provided by a sure prospect of a national income of \$499·375 million, corresponding to a project yielding \$99·375 million for certain. Thus the correction that must be made to the average social profit of the project on account of uncertainty is only \$625,000—less than 1% of the project's expected value.

Even if the project had been much more uncertain, yielding \$50 million, \$100 million, and \$150 million with equal probabilities, the deduction to be made from the expected social profit of \$100 million on account of uncertainty is only \$3.25 million. It is hard to believe that projects of this relative size and uncertainty ever present themselves for consideration by the governments of developing countries.

This topic is treated mathematically in 15·8, which is a technical appendix to the chapter. It is there shown that the deduction to be made from profits on account of uncertainty should be

$$\frac{\text{Variance of profits}}{\text{Expected national income}}$$

multiplied by a constant, which may reasonably be taken to be unity.

the project evaluator must use the ideas mentioned in (iv) above.

(vi) When a project brings about irreversible effects, the EPSV may seriously overstate its value; for the project will then exclude other (generally later) projects which might have a higher EPSV. This argument holds, even if at the moment no alternative use of the resources that are in danger of being committed appears as good as the one proposed; for, with time, new information will become available, which may reveal better uses—and the value of that information is lost when the project is undertaken. The best examples are projects involving the destruction of works of art (such as beautiful buildings) or the natural environment (such as landscapes); and projects, such as the development of ports, that may impose a system that will later prove to be regrettable. In such cases, the question is whether it may be better to postpone the irreversible aspect of the project for, say, five years (in the first instance) because of the value of the information, about people's tastes or technical developments, which may become available in the meantime.

We think that this problem is of great importance only in a few cases. It is hard to allow for the costs of irreversibility; but a rough estimate can be made by considering what sorts of developments might make the irreversible action regrettable, and putting a value to the alternative plan of postponing the action for five years and then following the new development if that has become feasible. By putting a probability to the new development, one can in this way estimate the EPSV of postponement. This should be counted as a cost against the project. It might well make an alternative design of the project superior.

15.6 PRACTICAL METHODS

Although the project planner should have the exceptions of 15.5 in mind, it remains true that the EPSV of the project must be the starting-point of his evaluation. But the EPSV is not simple to estimate, and its definition depends on being able to describe uncertainty by means of numerical probabilities. Indeed, it looks as though its estimation would require a great deal of difficult guess-work and extensive calculation. Therefore we must now consider how it might be estimated in practice. We succeed in concluding that the difficulties are not so bad as they may seem!

There are three things to consider when contemplating the potential of a project. Firstly, there is uncertainty about both prices and quantities of inputs and outputs: and these uncertainties arise from different causes. Secondly, it will be possible to adjust the day-by-day and year-to-year running of the project so as to take fullest advantage of, or suffer least disadvantage from, the actual development of accounting prices. Thirdly, the project will have been designed to perform best—in terms of social profit—when prices are at their expected levels: it will not be possible later to take as full advantage of relatively unexpected price movements as would have been possible if the project had been designed with them in view. In other words, the flexibility in operation that any project provides is limited.

How do these various considerations influence expectations about the performance of our imaginary bicycle factory? We estimate the expected value of future prices: balancing one possibility against another, we think that the accounting price of a bicycle will not fall very much, and we have made predictions of the shadow wage rate, the border price of steel, and so on. It is possible that the accounting price for bicycles will rise: in that case, the output would not only be worth more, but would also be stepped up beyond the planned rate of production (at the expense of more cramped and less efficient working conditions, more frequent machinery breakdowns and replacements, the use of less satisfactory labour, and so on). Thus the social profit in a year when the price of bicycles was above its expected value would be greater both because of the increased price, and also because advantage would be taken of it. If, on the other hand, the price of bicycles was lower than its expected value, it might not be worth while to replace worn-out machinery, or to continue operating capital equipment for quite so long. Machinery becomes obsolete earlier when its output is less valuable, since rising labour and repair costs more quickly reach the level where the value of output ceases to cover them.

The same kinds of consideration apply if the price of the steel used is unexpectedly high or unexpectedly low, or if the shadow wage rate moves more or less than was expected. If steel turns out to be unusually expensive, it may be possible to change the design of the bicycles so as to use less of it; if labour is unexpectedly cheap (in terms of the shadow wage), it may be possible to make more use of it, and less use of machinery.

If the world price of bicycles fell very low, the factory might be better used for some different purpose; or it might even be abandoned. On the other hand, capital equipment is often used long after one would have expected its useful life to be over, either because it has proved more durable or efficient than had been thought at first, or because the demand for its products has been unusually high. If the factory is used for some other purpose, it will naturally not be as suitable as if it had been designed specially for this different kind of operation when it was first built. Similarly, although a machine or a factory may be used for longer than its anticipated life, a different kind of machine or factory would have been chosen in the first place if the conditions resulting in this longevity had been correctly foreseen.

The extent to which the project has flexibility that will allow advantage to be taken of relatively unexpected developments in the structure of accounting prices will vary from project to project. A bicycle factory consists of such a varied assortment of buildings and bits of equipment, that there will usually be plenty of scope for making quite good use of it whatever happens—provided there is good management. On the other hand, a power station imposes on its management a rather rigid relationship between the output of electricity and the inputs. Production may not turn out as expected, but there is relatively little that can be done to adjust production performance to the developing price structure, except that the length of time for which it is operated each day, each year, and over its working lifetime, can be varied. Projects that provide no flexibility are extremely rare: nevertheless, the economy must to some extent put up with the existence of unsuitable capital equipment, and can do nothing about its regrets that it had not known what would happen to prices before the investment decisions were made.

We can now consider how to prepare the necessary evaluation of the project. It can be done at various levels of sophistication, depending on the reliability of the data, the importance of the project, and so on. We suggest three methods, of varying thoroughness:

(i) When estimating inputs, outputs, and accounting prices, the project evaluator has to think in terms of estimating *expected* inputs, outputs, and accounting prices. To repeat our earlier discussion, this implies that he must average the various possibilities, using as weights the probabilities that these possibilities will occur. But, in order to do this fairly accurately, it is not usually necessary actually to set down all the possibilities, and assign probabilities to each. It will be enough if he has a clear idea what magnitudes he is trying to estimate: these are *the expected outcomes*, and *not* the most probable ones. He should not be optimistic—giving too much weight to the more favourable possibilities; nor should he be pessimistic, giving too much weight to the less favourable. It does not require much practice to avoid unreasonable estimates, which no one would accept as estimates of the expected outcomes. Very often, there is little significant disagreement about an estimate, once it is understood what one is after, and that great accuracy would be out of place.

In a few cases it may be desirable to ask oneself, say, what level of output has only a one in ten chance of being exceeded, and of not being exceeded; and what level of output is as likely to be exceeded as not. When one has a clear notion of the probable spread of possible results, in this kind of way, one can roughly estimate the expected value—say, by giving a 20% weight to each of the two extreme estimates, and the remaining 60% weight to the medium estimate.[1] In other words, the various inputs, outputs, and accounting prices, are estimated in more or less the same kind of way as was described in detail in Chapter XII, except that one takes some care to make the estimates 'medium' ones, in the precise sense of 'expected values' as defined by probability theory. Having done so, one can work out the PSV.

The figure, worked out in the above manner, will normally be an underestimate of the EPSV, since the various estimates of social profit will be underestimates of expected social profit, especially for later years when prices are likely to be considerably different from expected prices, and the scope for adjustment to take advantage of the prices therefore greater. In cases where flexibility is low, and extremely careful evaluation of the project is inappropriate, the first straightforward calculation of social profit may be accepted as a good enough evaluation of the project. If flexibility is likely to be of some importance, one might adjust the estimate upwards by some reasonable percentage. But if the adjustment one is tempted to make is at all large, a more careful evaluation must be done. A rough adjustment of this kind is best made by using an interest rate a little smaller than the accounting rate of interest, since it is in more distant years that the gains from flexibility are likely to make the most important contribution to the project. A reduction in the interest rate of no more than 1% would certainly be large enough for this purpose.

(ii) If more care is needed, the evaluator should examine various possible developments of the project in detail. At least three alternatives should be considered: one in which prices move more

---

[1] Suppose output is as likely to be above 100 as below, has a probability 1/10 of being above 200, and a probability 1/10 of being below 50. The idea is to assume that the lowest 1/5 of possibilities averages roughly around 50, the next 3/5 around 100, and the top 1/5 around 200: giving expected output = 110.

favourably than the expected possibility, one in which prices move less favourably, and the expected movement itself. Of course, as we have seen, there are many different prices relevant to the decision about a particular project, and each of them can change in many different ways; it is no easy task to choose three sensible possibilities, especially when one remembers that not all prices will move more favourably than the expected movements, nor will they all be less favourable than expected.

It is best to deal with social profit in each period separately, first calculating it on the assumption that prices are at their expected levels, and outputs and inputs at the levels intended: in addition, calculate estimates of social profit on adverse assumptions, and on favourable assumptions. In making the favourable assumption one might assume that all the relevant prices are a little more favourable than their expected values—say, at such levels that there is a probability of about a third for each one that the price might have been even more favourable. Using these prices, and estimating the expected inputs and outputs that will be used and produced under these circumstances, one will get a *very* optimistic estimate of social profit. Similarly, one can prepare a very pessimistic estimate of social profit by assuming that all prices are somewhat less favourable than their expected levels. One cannot without considerably more trouble say precisely what is the probability that social profit would be even higher than the optimistic estimate, or even lower than the pessimistic estimate. But these two probabilities will be roughly equal, and one will therefore have a good idea of the range of probable social profits. One might give the two extreme estimates weights of 25%, and the mean estimate a weight of 50% in averaging to estimate the expected social profit. Once expected social profit has been estimated, one has only to calculate the PSV in the usual way, and the evaluation is complete.

Clearly this same method can be carried out with closer attention and greater accuracy, but some expert knowledge of probability theory and statistics would seem to be required for very thorough calculations. In any case, the extra accuracy obtained by the attention to extreme cases which we have suggested will almost certainly be sufficient for all but the most important cases.[1]

(iii) Finally, it may occasionally be necessary to deal with the exceptional cases in which the spread of risks is relevant to the

---

[1] Some of the considerations are discussed in a simple manner in Reutlinger, 1970. See also Pouliquen, 1970, for an explanation and judicious assessment of the use of 'Monte Carlo' methods for estimating the distribution of the PSV.

investment decision. It is, unfortunately, much more exacting to estimate the probabilities of alternative levels of social profit or social present value than to estimate the expected levels. For these probabilities arise from the coincidence of many different events, each with its own probability. Yet it is desirable to have some kind of estimate of the degree of uncertainty of the PSV of a project—that is, of the extent to which the PSV is likely to differ from the EPSV. The only simple procedure available is to use the pessimistic and optimistic estimates of social profit prepared in the way described above, and discount them so as to get pessimistic and optimistic estimates of the PSV. It must be emphasized that these estimates would be *extremely* pessimistic and optimistic, since they are calculated on the assumption that—in the optimistic case, for example—everything goes a little better than expected in every period. Since there are sure to be many adverse circumstances, the calculation is very optimistic even if the individual price and quantity levels used are independently quite probable.

For this reason, the above sort of estimate of the probable spread of the PSV around its expected level is not altogether satisfactory. However, it can still be a useful indication of the *relative* riskiness of different projects, provided it is borne in mind that it may give to the casual observer an exaggerated impression of the risks involved. Let us call the difference between the pessimistic and optimistic estimates of social present value the *range* of the project. On the assumption that the range is likely to be about six standard deviations, the calculation of 15.8 (referred to in a footnote above) suggests subtracting $\frac{1}{36} \times \frac{(\text{range})^2}{\text{GNP}}$ from the EPSV to allow for risk. We think this gives the right order of magnitude. As we have remarked, the correction need not often be applied, and would seldom make a significant difference.

15.7 COMMON RULES OF THUMB: SOME COMMENTS

One rule of thumb that will be familiar to many who have to do with investment projects is the use of the 'pay-off period'. If this method for choosing investment projects is used, projects are accepted only if their profits will pay for the initial investment cost within a specified period of time—two to five or more years, depending upon the industry. The rule may be used in conjunction with other methods. For example, projects whose present value is greatest may be preferred, but the profits will still have to pay for the initial investment cost within the specified time. A similar, but not identical, method is often used in the centrally planned econo-mies. The method is sometimes justified on the grounds that one must have some rule for choosing among investment projects, and this is really the simplest possible. One may agree that it is the simplest possible, without thinking that much of an argument when other methods, particularly that of discounting profits, are quite simple and capable of being given a much more satisfactory justification. It is also recommended as a way of avoiding paying too much attention to the later profits of the project, which are often thought to be much more uncertain than profits in the first few years of the project's life.

The method has little to recommend it. It allows no satisfactory way of comparing projects in different industries, where different pay-off periods must often be used. It gives altogether too little weight to what is likely to happen after the pay-off period has elapsed. To take only one example: many project choices are affected by the life of the investment—a brick factory, say, is a better investment if there is likely to be a continuing and growing construction programme in the immediate neighbourhood than it would be if the relatively certain immediate demand was unlikely to be continued into the more distant future. It is hard to see what advantage there is in ignoring such considerations, or in allowing for them in a merely *ad hoc* way.

The other quite common rule of thumb for allowing for uncertainty is the use of a risk premium. The rate of return of the project is calculated; then a few percentage points are subtracted from it, more if the uncertainty seems to be large, less if the prospects seem fairly dependable. This procedure amounts to calculating the present value of the investment project using a rate of interest that is larger than the basic rate of interest used for relatively riskless projects. The addition to the rate of interest reflects the project planner's impression of the degree of uncertainty involved: it is not derived by any formal argument or use of the evidence. But the mere fact that it is a rough and ready method, relying on impression rather than analysis, is not necessarily a conclusive argument against it, since the relevant evidence is in any case rather hard to interpret.

Our objection to this method is that it may well lead to unjustifi-able results, in particular an undue reluctance to undertake risky projects. To see exactly what sort of influence on project choice the use of risk premiums may have, let us consider how it might be justified. Clearly, the estimates of profits used in applying the method cannot be the expected value of profits: for, as we have argued above, one would scarcely ever want to discount future expected profits by more than the accounting interest rate, and might sometimes want to discount them by less. Admittedly, the profit estimates that are to be discounted at this inflated interest rate are those based on engineers' estimates of the project; and it may be assumed that these are, compared with expected profits, optimistic estimates. If the risk-premium method is to be justified, it must be argued that the engineers' estimates of profits are more optimistic the further ahead they look—because discounting reduces estimated profits more the farther in the future they lie.

At first sight this is quite a plausible suggestion. To a large extent, engineers are accustomed to assume that existing prices and circumstances will continue into the future. It may be thought that changes are likely to be unfavourable to the project, since it is designed with today's circumstances in mind. Then it will not be surprising if engineers' methods, being somewhat short-sighted, are over-optimistic about the more distant future. This argument might be supported by the general impression that preliminary estimates of project cost and benefits often turn out to have been over-optimistic when one looks back over the history of a project.

There may well be something in this argument (although a lot depends not only on the particular engineers who are preparing the estimates, but also on the particular circumstances of the industry in question, rather than its degree of uncertainty as such). But there is one particular consideration suggesting that this is the wrong conclusion to draw from any apparent tendency for projects to turn out worse than the fond hopes of their designers had suggested. It seems to be much more generally true that the initial costs of projects are serious underestimates than that the eventual running costs are underestimated (in real terms, after allowing for inflation). Construction and development costs are notoriously subject to error, especially in the developing countries, but not only there; there are everywhere complaints about unexpected delays—delays of a kind that are less likely to occur when the project depends on regular deliveries of raw materials, instead of once-for-all deliveries of pieces of special equipment. Designers, it is often suggested, are inclined to underestimate the number of special problems that will have to be overcome before the project will be working properly, and the time that will be required to trace the faults and find satisfactory remedies for them. Of course, the regular running of established projects also throws up difficult problems; hesitations and delays are not unknown in mature plants.

But it is hard to see why one should expect later costs and benefits to be more optimistically estimated than earlier ones, even if there is perhaps more excuse in the former case.

It seems much better, therefore, to try to consider the various elements in the situation systematically, and to prepare, quite deliberately, estimates of the expected level of costs and benefits throughout the possible life of the project. In the first place, these must be based on the designers' estimates. But it will often be possible to get further information, and to consider circumstances peculiar to the industry, when revising these initial estimates into estimates of expected social profit. It is in any case an extremely important part of the project planner's job to consider critically the various elements of the designers' estimates: he should expect to make a complete revision of the original estimates as he goes along.

The use of rules of thumb such as we have been discussing is based on a general impression of the relationship between initial estimates and final performance. The rules make some attempt to adjust the initial estimates for biases inherent in them. Although we advocate a more searching analysis of the estimates, we should also like to emphasize the great importance of using information about the relation between initial estimates and actual performance. We have drawn attention to this matter already, when we suggested that it might be possible to adjust initial estimates of construction costs to take account of any observed general tendency to underestimate them. It is possible to keep careful and systematic records of previous experience, so that this kind of adjustment could be made in a systematic and verifiable way: there is no need to rely on hunch and impression entirely, although they will always play some part in investment appraisal.

15.8 A Theoretical Analysis of Investment Decisions under Uncertainty

This section is an appendix to the chapter, intended primarily for professional economists. Its purpose is to state formally the arguments for using the mathematical expectation of social profit as a measure of social value under uncertainty, and to indicate more precisely the conditions under which that rule is valid.[1]

---

[1] An analysis of this kind was presented in the OECD *Manual*, on pp. 266 and 267. An essentially similar case, more rigorously argued, is put forward by Arrow and Lind, 1970. Related results can be found in Malinvaud, 1969. The argument we now present interprets the mathematics somewhat differently, and is, we think, somewhat more compelling, since it does not depend on propositions that hold only in the limit, as the projects considered become negligibly small.

To bring principles out clearly, we keep the model simple. In particular, we assume that the effects of the project are confined to a single time-period: this clearly does not affect the validity of the argument, so long as irreversible effects are excluded. We also assume that there is a single commodity. It is not so clear that this assumption is innocuous, but arguments of the same kind can be given for the many-commodity case. We use the notation

Y = national output in the absence of the project,
X = net contribution of the project to national output.

These are random variables, with means $\bar{Y}$ and $\bar{X}$. For the present X and Y are assumed to be stochastically independent.

The contribution of the project should be thought of as accruing to the government, both costs and benefits being, in effect, widely distributed within the population. Assuming that no weight, positive or negative, is attached to uncertainties about national income *as such*,[1] we can represent the social value by the expectation of social utility:

$$EU(Y), \qquad (1)$$

with U an increasing, concave function ($U' > 0$, $U'' < 0$). If the project is adopted, this is changed to

$$EU(Y+X). \qquad (2)$$

The project should be undertaken if (2) is greater than (1). The question is when we can be pretty sure that (2) is greater than (1). To answer it, we introduce a notion of certainty-equivalent: x is a number (not a random variable) such that

$$EU(Y+X-x) = EU(Y). \qquad (3)$$

Clearly the project should be undertaken if x is positive, and not undertaken if x is negative.

The utility function may reasonably be assumed differentiable as often as we like, and indeed one expects to be able to derive a Taylor series:

$$U(Y+X-x) = U(Y) + U'(Y)(X-x) + \tfrac{1}{2}U''(Y)(X-x)^2 + \ldots$$

Taking expectations, and using (3), we obtain

$$E\{U'(Y)(X-x)\} + \tfrac{1}{2}E\{U''(Y)(X-x)^2\} + \ldots = 0. \qquad (4)$$

---

[1] Such weight would have to mean, e.g., that gambling with the national income is intrinsically wrong, or that the risk of war or famine is intrinsically exciting. Neither view is appealing. For the theory of risk preferences, see Arrow, 1971.

By our independence assumption, this may be written

$$EU'(\bar{X}-x)+\tfrac{1}{2}EU''E(X-x)^2+ \ldots =0, \tag{5}$$

where EU' is $EU'(\Upsilon)$, etc. Since

$$\begin{aligned}
E(X-x)^2 &= E(X-\bar{X}+\bar{X}-x)^2 \\
&= E(X-\bar{X})^2+(\bar{X}-x)^2 \quad (\text{since } E(X-\bar{X})=0) \\
&= \text{Var } X+(\bar{X}-x)^2,
\end{aligned}$$

(5) implies that

$$\bar{X}-x= -\tfrac{1}{2}\frac{EU''}{EU'}\text{ Var }X-\tfrac{1}{2}\frac{EU''}{EU'}(\bar{X}-x)^2 + \ldots \tag{6}$$

Now $-\Upsilon U''/U'$ is a rather natural index of 'risk-aversion' (known as the relative risk-aversion index). It is the elasticity of marginal utility with respect to income, and in other contexts one expects that it will be a number not so very far from 2 (say between 0 and 4). In the case of risk preferences, 2 is generally thought to be on the high side, but it has been suggested that relative risk-aversion increases with income,[1] and evidence tends to be based on the behaviour of the rich. However that may be, it seems that EU''/EU' should be taken to be of the same order of magnitude as $1/\bar{\Upsilon}$:

$$\frac{EU''}{EU'} = -\frac{A}{\bar{\Upsilon}}, \tag{7}$$

where A is a positive number, perhaps in the region of 2, although it could be rather larger.

Inserting (7) in (6), and rewriting slightly, we have

$$\frac{\bar{X}-x}{\bar{X}} =\tfrac{1}{2}A\frac{\text{Var }X}{\bar{X}^2}\frac{\bar{X}}{\bar{\Upsilon}} +\tfrac{1}{2}A\left(\frac{\bar{X}-x}{\bar{X}}\right)^2\frac{\bar{X}}{\bar{\Upsilon}} + \ldots \tag{8}$$

For most projects, $\text{Var }X/\bar{X}^2$ is less than 1, and $\bar{X}/\bar{\Upsilon}$ is small—1% or less. Thus the first term in (8) will normally be very small. Treating that as a first approximation to $(\bar{X}-x)/\bar{X}$, we see that the second term will be completely negligible, and the same can be expected for the remaining terms of the series. A good approximation to x is given by:

$$x=\bar{X}\left\{1-\tfrac{1}{2}A\frac{\text{Var }X}{\bar{X}^2}\frac{\bar{X}}{\bar{\Upsilon}}\right\}. \tag{9}$$

This argument is not, it must be admitted, a rigorous one. The chief doubt it leaves concerns the magnitude of A. To dispel that

---

[1] Arrow, 1971.

doubt, consider a rather large project, with $\bar{X}/\bar{Y}=0\cdot1$ and Var $X/\bar{X}^2=1$. Such a project would certainly be quite risky,[1] and planners may be expected to require a significant risk premium. That is, $x/\bar{X}$ should be less than 1. Suppose we think that $x = \frac{4}{5}\bar{X}$. Then (8) would hold (neglecting the unlisted terms of the series) if $A=3\cdot8$. In our view the suggested risk premium here is rather large: certainly we would not apply so large a premium to comparable cases in the conduct of our own affairs. But even with $A=4$, it is clear from (9) that $x=\bar{X}$ is a good approximation for most projects.[2] In other cases, planners can use (9) with $A=2$, or, if they are cautious, 4.

The major modification to this analysis is when X and Y are not independent random variables. The simplest case is when all activity in the economy is affected by common influences. In that case, X/Y is independent of Y, and we should seek a certainty equivalent ξY for X. It can be proved, on the same lines as the above analysis, that ξ is accurately estimated by the mean of X/Y. The project should therefore be undertaken if this mean is positive.

More generally, when X and Y are mutually dependent, we can obtain directly from (4) the first approximation

$$x= \frac{EU'(Y)X}{EU'(Y)}, \tag{10}$$

the project to be undertaken when this is positive. (10) is a weighted average of the project's outcome. If $U'(Y) = Y^{-\eta}$, a good approximation to (10) is

$$x=\bar{X}-\eta \frac{\text{Cov}(X,Y)}{\bar{Y}}, \tag{11}$$

where Cov (X, Y) is the covariance $E\{(X-\bar{X})(Y-\bar{Y})\}$. η and A will be approximately equal.

---

[1] An example of such a project with $\bar{Y}=100$ is one for which $X=3$ with probability $\frac{1}{2}$, and 17 with probability one half. A risk premium of 20% implies that the planners are indifferent between taking this risk and being assured of 8.

[2] The argument of this paragraph can be made rigorous by supposing that, within the probable ranges of Y and $Y+X$, U'' is bounded above and below by numbers that are not very different, and applying the second mean-value theorem instead of relying on the rapid convergence of the Taylor series.

Part Four

SOME RELATED ISSUES

CHAPTER SIXTEEN

External Effects

16.1 INTRODUCTION

The concept 'external economies' has been widely used in cases where the social profitability of a project is thought to be higher than the profitability from the point of view of the enterprise: sometimes rather regardless of the exact reason for such a supposed difference. Similarly, 'external diseconomies' may be used to refer to the opposite case. But it is the external economies which have been emphasized for developing countries: especially in the case of industry, in defence against criticism that industrialization is over-emphasized in developing countries. In this chapter we shall not concern ourselves with all such differences, for the good reason that our system of cost–benefit analysis is precisely supposed to allow for many of them. The question that arises is therefore 'what costs and benefits, if any, have escaped the analysis which has been propounded?'

We have proposed a system of valuing the inputs and outputs of a project according to a set of accounting prices supposed to measure social costs and benefits. The question of the previous paragraph can thus be divided into two questions:

(i) Are there inputs and outputs which we have failed to include —what we may call extraordinary inputs and outputs to distinguish them from the ordinary ones which we have certainly included?

(ii) Have we misvalued the obvious inputs and outputs, because they themselves have extraordinary benefits or costs for society?

We shall discuss these questions primarily in relation to industry, because it is the alleged external economies of industrialization which have been most stressed in the literature on developing countries: but we shall also draw attention, in 16.2, to external economies in agriculture; in 16.5 we address ourselves briefly to infrastructural projects.

Certain external economies are sometimes attributed to industrialization in general; for example, the inculcation of disciplined working habits: these are closely related to those external economies which are required to validate what is known as the 'infant industry' argument, an argument which has long been used to justify the protection of, and special fiscal treatment for, any newly established industries or firms. In brief, the argument relies, mainly if not wholly, on the premise that the entrepreneur in a new line of activity is inadequately rewarded for the high cost of acquiring technical knowledge and skills (including the training of managers and workers), because such learning and training has benefits which he cannot keep to himself, and charge for.[1] This kind of externality is discussed in the next section, which deals with outputs.

16.2 EXTERNAL ECONOMIES RELATED TO OUTPUTS

16.21 *Extraordinary Outputs*

As already suggested, the first possibility is that there are outputs not ordinarily counted as such, which may consequently be overlooked. The most obvious case in industry of a beneficial extraordinary output seems to be labour-training (including skilled labour). In general, people improve their skills by being employed, in a manner which increases their value to other employers, or sometimes to themselves if they leave and set up their own business. When a man leaves a firm, the latter will thus have added some value to him. Is it in any way recompensed for this 'product'? The answer is, only to the extent that it may have got the man cheap in the first place in anticipation of the training (e.g. apprenticeship). For even if the man stays with the firm that trains him, the latter is likely to have to pay him more as a result of the training it itself has provided, in order to keep him. It should be possible to make a rough quantitative estimate of this external economy when appraising a project. The main question is whether it is worth doing. Our impression is that the present value of such training is usually likely to be small compared with other project items.[2]

The second possibility is the cornerstone of the infant industry argument. If a firm starts a new product or new process, it may make it easier for other firms to do likewise, and the initiator's benefit may then fall short of the social benefit. Patent laws are intended to ensure that the inventor or patent-purchaser is sufficiently protected, by ensuring that external economies are *not* realized, for a while. But the industrial innovator relies very often

---

[1] The infant industry argument is discussed more fully in Little, Scitovsky and Scott, 1970, pp. 118–121.

[2] This point is distinct from the question whether training itself has a positive PSV. An attempt at answering the latter question is made in Chakravarti, 1972.

more on secrecy than on patents, and on retaining a monopoly of the 'know-how', sometimes with the aid of (probably unenforceable) service agreements. Even when there is no mystery, and little problem in acquiring know-how (and therefore no question of a leakage), the successful innovator may, especially in a developing country, stimulate others to try their hands at the same game.

In the industrialized countries, much more attention is now paid to extraordinary bad industrial outputs than to possible external benefits. Pollution has found its way from academic text-books to the popular imagination. Developing countries are nervous of this change of emphasis, and some regard it as a phenomenon only of a high level of industrialization (although it is, perhaps, now more obvious in some towns in the developing world than in most of those of the industrialized countries).

Turning to agriculture, it seems to us that external economies at the farm level are more obvious than in industry. The classic example of an external economy—the fruit-farmers who produce blossom and so aid bee-keepers—comes from agriculture, just as the classic example of an external diseconomy—smoke—comes from industry. More important, it appears that the spread of know-how in agriculture comes from direct imitation to a greater extent than in the case of industry. This is sometimes implicitly recognized when new agricultural inputs are subsidized: while the most important output of a demonstration farm is supposed to be its external effect. Equally one can say that the externality of training in industry is recognized by the institution of training centres, institutes of technology, and management schools.

What has all this to do with project analysis? If a government believes that industry has more net external benefits than other sectors, and that these come about mainly as a result of employment, then it can, through COPE, give a general 'bias' towards projects in this sector: and the most appropriate way would seem to be the choice of a lower SWR than otherwise. But such a blanket measure seems hard to justify, and it may well be thought by some that it gives inadequate recognition to the special externalities of new industries (and most governments in developing countries give some tax incentives for new enterprises in 'non-traditional' lines of activity). Should some industries be more favoured than others? We are not aware of any research which would permit the project evaluator to incorporate any allowance for the comparative knowledge-spreading effects of new industries, products, and processes. *A priori* it would seem that the process must be skill-intensive, and that the skill cannot be easily learned except on the job; and, if the skill or knowledge is very specific to the product, it must be expected that the number of firms using the process will be increasing, and will somehow acquire access to the experience of the innovator. If the skill or knowledge is not very specific then there is a potentially wider spread of benefit, but learning on the job is likely to be less essential.

For ourselves, we confess to a certain cynicism about those supposedly important commercial 'spin-offs' which are always claimed, but seldom if ever substantiated, when a government supports a new technology such as atomic energy or supersonic transport.

16.22 *Undervaluation of Ordinary Outputs*

It is quite common for certain outputs to be sold for less than their social value, for administrative or political reasons. This is most usual in the case of infrastructural projects. Thus roads are usually supplied free. Irrigation water is either free, or sold for less than its worth. Public electricity undertakings as often as not lose money. No one conducting a cost–benefit analysis would think of ignoring such divergencies between the price charged and the social value of the output, which must then be estimated by some other means. In manufacturing and agriculture, deliberate undercharging is less common. It is also unusual for it to be administratively difficult to charge people as much as they would be willing to pay.

More subtle reasons why one might underestimate the value of some industrial outputs have been suggested. These suggestions concern the domestic output of intermediate and capital goods. In this connection, the concept of 'forward linkages' has received wide attention, a 'forward linkage' being a relationship between two firms considered from the seller's point of view, while a 'backward' linkage is a relationship seen from the buyer's point of view.

Consider a new project which uses a cost-reducing innovation. Now it is possible that in practice some of the benefit of the cost-reduction will be passed on (or forward) to other industries. But there is no reason, so far, why a project analysis should go wrong: the output would be normally valued at the old price, which would properly account for the benefit.[1] It has been suggested, not so much

---

[1] This assumes that the new investment is small. If the investment is one which realizes economies of scale, and is large, then the anticipated price of the output after the investment may be significantly less than before—as a result of increased supply. In this case the new price is taken into consideration by the private producer: but the mean of the two prices is a better measure of benefit in an appraisal from the social point of view (see 10.1).

that the benefit of a given project may be underestimated, as that the size of the investment is likely to be too small, because increased demand arising as a result of the cost reductions passed on to other firms or industries (called, sometimes, pecuniary external economies) will not be allowed for by private industry.[1] This argument raises the whole question of investment planning, and of whether, when information is inevitably limited, planning or the price mechanism produce better results for investment. But it does not seem to be a very strong argument in the context of external economies; for investments generally anticipate increasing demand, and that part of the increased demand which is caused indirectly by the investment is likely to be inconsiderable in relation to the total increase. In investment planning, much depends on the market conditions facing the investor, and his attitude. At all events, excessive investment in capacity often arises in industries where one might expect the opposite, according to the above argument. There seems to be nothing in this argument which should make us want to modify what has been said: that demand should be estimated as well as it can be, with or without the help of planning.

Still on the subject of 'forward linkages', it has been maintained that the production of intermediates encourages others to make investments which use these inputs, and that this is an advantage. What is undeniable is that lack of an input can inhibit otherwise profitable and socially beneficial investment. This is the essential argument for providing a suitable infrastructure, which can be commonly used by manufacturing firms, in the case of non-traded inputs which can best be produced on a scale which requires their use by many customers. But there is nothing here which implies that the rules suggested for the production of non-traded inputs require any modification. Such things as transport and power should be available at prices which equal the marginal social cost or benefit of providing them (see 12.3 and 12.4). But it should not be thought that the mere provision of such things will result in any use being made of them. There is a number of monuments to this mistake in developing countries.

The same argument has been extended to traded goods, particularly steel. Domestic production of steel is supposed to be more conducive to the use of steel and hence more of an encouragement to investment in socially profitable steel-using industries, than imports of steel. Why should this be the case? If it were true, then

---

[1] See Scitovsky, 1957.

domestic steel should be valued at a somewhat higher accounting price than would be arrived at by the methods explained in 10.1 or 12.2. Several reasons may be suggested: first, that imports are unreliable because quotas may be imposed; second, that domestic suppliers will be keener to sell, and so may offer special terms; third, that smaller stocks can be held if a closer-to-hand supply is available.

Take the first reason. Our position is that if steel passes the project selection criterion, *which takes full account of any scarcity of foreign exchange,* then domestic steel will be available; but if it does not, then foreign exchange will be available to import it. In that case, there is no reason for government restrictions on imports. Admittedly, one must allow for some fluctuations in foreign exchange earnings, and for miscalculations of its availability: and temporary import quotas may therefore become desirable: but the last things which should be allowed to suffer from such quotas are basic materials and intermediates. The government is certainly handling the economic affairs of the country badly if restrictions have to be imposed which do damage to domestic production. Despite this, we are well aware that the governments of many developing countries have given higher priority to imports for creating new capacity than to imports of parts and components, with resultant under-utilization of existing capacity. Nevertheless, as already remarked, it is extremely difficult to produce rational criteria for project selection on the assumption that governments will behave irrationally (in very varying ways about which it is difficult to generalize). Finally, of course, if a government both creates a shortage of steel and it is known that this policy is immutable, then steel has to be treated as non-traded and be valued accordingly.

Turning to the second reason advanced above, it must be said that the main commercial factor in promoting sales of intermediate goods is undoubtedly the price. A domestic producer is not likely to be able to promote the use of his product much more than an importer of the same product, unless he can offer a comparable price. But if, to be competitive with imports, a price has to be charged for the product, e.g. steel, which is less than the properly calculated social cost of making it, then the encouragement given to the use of steel is a cost, not a benefit, to society, unless steel-using industries show a social profit large enough to offset the social loss involved in supplying the steel; that is, unless these industries would pass the project selection criterion when valuing steel at its marginal import cost. But, if this proviso is the case, then these industries would (or should) be started anyway, either because they would be directly chosen in the public sector, or because the government was giving sufficient encouragement to industrialization in the private sector in the ways discussed in 5.5. In short, the desirability of starting industry A, which uses the output of B, is no good reason for starting B, if B does not pass the test. Industry A can always be started using imported inputs.

Finally, one must remark that, in practice, the above 'forward linkage' argument almost always works the opposite way to that supposed. Wrong intermediate industries are established and excessive protection is put on to let them survive: the result is that the output is sold at a price which is higher than the socially optimum price, so that industries which use the product are put at a disadvantage. Only occasionally is this disadvantage recognized, and the intermediate good supplied at border prices.

The final argument suggested was that steel-using industries can hold smaller stocks if there is a domestic source of supply. It is often true that larger stocks of imported goods than domestic goods need to be held somewhere. In general, imported goods may require additional services, such as port-handling, as well as more stock-holding (internal transport can go either way), compared to domestic goods. In principle, of course, these domestic services should be allowed for in the accounting price.

This argument about stock-holding is a special case of a more general one. It is often more advantageous to have a close source of supply, rather than a distant one—quite apart from the transport cost, which is allowed for in our methods of evaluation. This is particularly the case with non-standard items, which cannot be ordered from a catalogue or by written specification; where the purchaser needs to discuss his requirements with the manufacturer; or where services are required only occasionally, but then urgently— e.g. repair services. These advantages of proximity will normally be reflected in the price which the supplier can charge: a local repair-shop, or a manufacturer who will make a one-off piece of equipment to experiment with, can charge more than a distant or mass-producing firm could, while remaining competitive. In general, this can be allowed for if there is evidence that firms will pay more for local supplies than imported supplies. If, for instance, there is market evidence that there is a 'natural' 5% preference for local supplies of some good, then its accounting value can be set 5% above its c.i.f. value.

It should be noted that the above is likely to apply *least* to goods of standard specification like oil products or steel; and more to non-standard engineering products, textile materials, and any goods where technical changes in the manner of their use, or changing consumers' tastes, play an important role. It is also worth noting that imported supplies are often preferred in developing countries, rather than the reverse. This may be because the imported article, though nominally the same, is of better quality. It may be because the local supplier more than offsets his natural advantage by being unreliable in delivery, quality, and generally by failing to keep his promises. On the other hand, the preference for imports may sometimes be due to prejudice. In this latter event, the producer under free trade would not be able to obtain as much as the c.i.f. price: the prejudice is thus allowed for by valuing his output at the c.i.f. price.

The advantages of proximity may apply rather less to a country, than to a region or town. Sometimes it is easier to get something from abroad promptly, than it is to get it from another part of the country. We consider this again briefly in 16.4.

16.3   EXTERNAL ECONOMIES RELATED TO INPUTS

16.31   *Extraordinary Inputs*

In theory, if a project receives some beneficial inputs for which it does not pay, this should be counted as a cost, and the producer of the benefit should receive an equal recompense: and similarly if it is harmed, e.g. by another's smoke, its costs should be reduced by an appropriate amount. We are not aware of cases where such adjustments would have a very important effect on costs.

16.32   *Wrong Valuation of Inputs*

It is possible that the general development of the economy will reduce the real cost of some of the inputs of a project. But this is a matter of proper estimation of future accounting prices and is not an 'external effect', unless the initiation of the project itself causes changes in the real cost of its inputs. This can happen if the demand of the project for an input is either (*a*) sufficient to result in the establishment of a socially profitable project to produce the input, or (*b*) sufficient to realize economies in the production of the input, when the latter is already produced domestically. These kinds of effect, via new demand for inputs, are often referred to as economies resulting from backward linkages.

The first case could arise if there was previously no domestic demand for the input, while it could not have been produced for export with adequate social profitability because of transport costs or foreign protection. But, given a domestic demand, the input can be produced at a lower social accounting cost than the import price. Now the project under consideration might show inadequate social profitability if the input were reckoned at the c.i.f. price (there being no domestic production); but it would pass the test if, anticipating its production, one treated the input as a non-traded good (*ex hypothesi* its accounting cost is then lower than the c.i.f. price).

To illustrate the above paragraph, it might be socially profitable to produce refrigerators together with electric motors; but if one evaluated a refrigerator project based on imported motors, and an electric motor project without the refrigerator demand, neither separately would pass the test.

Now, supposing that the refrigerator project is under examination, the methods of evaluation proposed need no modification, provided that it is realized that domestic electric motor production will spring up as a result: given this, the proper accounting price will be put on the motors. If, say, the main project (refrigerators) is in the public sector, and the input-supplying project or projects will be in the private sector, it may be as well to ensure that it or they in fact get started by offering long-term contracts, credit, etc. If there is no question of either project being in the public sector, it can happen that neither gets started since each waits upon the other. In this case no question of project appraisal will arise, but an opportunity is missed. But that such opportunities can be missed is no proof that they often are; after all, either the refrigerator man can decide to make motors himself, or the motor man can make refrigerators. True, such 'vertical integration' requires more capital, and this might be a stumbling block: on the other hand, if each of the men can raise capital for his own part of the business, it is not inconceivable that they should amalgamate their projects, or at least make a contract.

A very similar situation arises when some of the inputs of the project are already made at home. In this case, the increased demand for them may result in economies of scale, and these economies may be external to the project. They will be external if the resulting benefit is not passed back in the form of lower prices. Does our method of project appraisal, as described in earlier chapters, automatically take account of this kind of benefit? Probably 'yes', but let us consider the matter further. Suppose some

343

of the input is imported and will continue to be so for some time. In this case, it is valued at its c.i.f. price, which makes no allowance for induced economies of scale; but this is correct, for if the good is still imported, then the economies of scale could in any case have been realized by further import substitution, and are not attributable to the project. On the other hand, if the import price tends to fall as less is imported, complete import substitution may not have been a correct policy despite domestic economies of scale (in this case we would have used the marginal cost of importing as the basis for the accounting price of the input, and not the c.i.f. price). Similarly, when the input is an export commodity, economies of scale can arise as a result of the project, if the export market is not perfectly elastic. Economies of scale can also arise if the good is not traded at all. Thus the question whether our methods already take account of such economies boils down to the question of whether they will be correctly anticipated, if they arise, and so be allowed for in the *future* accounting prices of inputs. There is really no matter of principle involved. The more important question is whether they are likely to be very significant, and whether it is sensible to spend much time on enquiries and research which would enable one to make some sort of rough estimate.

Much has been made of the benefits to be expected to result from backward linkages. It has often been claimed that a project which was manifestly socially unprofitable at the time would become socially profitable when the heavy dependence on imported components was reduced—without any evidence being offered, as if the matter was self-evident. Again, it is sometimes argued that motor-car assembly must be a good thing for developing countries to promote, because it leads to the manufacture of the component parts. Governments may require that increasing percentages of the value of the final product result from domestic manufacture as time goes on.

Some warnings are in order. If the establishment of backward linkages is sought for its own sake, without economic appraisal, then the social profitability of a project, whose costs consist to a considerable extent of the purchases of parts, is likely to be reduced, not raised. For instance, some parts may need to be made on a much larger scale than is required for their assembly into a particular final product. This seems to be notably the case in the motor-car industry.[1] It is for this reason that it is often referred to as essentially

---

[1] See Baranson, 1969.

an assembly industry. It is also worth remarking that it seems to be increasingly the case, even in industrialized countries, that imported components are incorporated in a final 'national' product. Even so considerable a component as the engine is sometimes of foreign manufacture, where the scale of output is small. This is still more notably true of aircraft. Since slogans such as backward and forward linkages seem to be influential, it might be as well to add the slogan 'trade in intermediates'. Finally, it should not be imagined, even when it seems likely that small-scale manufacturers could supply components for a new venture, that there is anything automatic about the development of backward linkages. Sometimes it happens: but often it does not.

We shall end this section by asking whether there is any way of deciding *a priori* how important the external effects arising from backward linkages might be. Let us make up a very simple hypothetical project. All figures are in accounting prices. Rs. 50 million of capital is spent in year 1: thereafter, in every year for ever, sales are Rs. 15 million and current costs are Rs. 10 million. Discounted at 10% this flow of social profit gives Rs. 50 million of present value, equal to the capital expenditure. Hence the PSV is zero.

Now suppose that 10% of current costs is in respect of purchases of a component, not subject to economies of scale, which was previously wholly imported, but which is now going to be made domestically as a result of our project. The project thus spends Rs. 1 million per annum on this item, at c.i.f. prices. Now the new domestic production is unlikely to reduce social costs by more than, say, 15%. If the component could have been made much more cheaply than this, it is reasonable to assume that it would have been worth making for export. Let us suppose that production of this component starts at the same time as the project. This is a very favourable assumption, because if this really were to happen its production would have to be planned in conjunction with the project—in which case any sensible project appraisal would reckon in these external benefits, which we are now assuming to be forgotten or at least ignored. On these assumptions, annual current costs are overestimated by Rs. 150,000 per annum.

Assume now that a further 10% of costs is in respect of purchases of inputs which are not specific to the project (i.e. have other uses), where economies of scale are consequently realized. The increased demand is thus Rs. 1 million. How large a percentage increase in output of the item or items this represents, depends on the previous size of the market. It would seem to be extreme to assume that average costs might fall 20%, as a result of such increased demand. Nevertheless, this might happen if the increased demand was, say, in respect of one item whose output was thereby doubled: so this is the assumption we shall make. But Rs. 200,000 of consequent saving cannot be reckoned for every year of the life of our project. Since the item is non-specific, the general development of the economy would have caused the realization of the economies of scale anyway. The project under examination only advances the realization. Its contribution to these economies of scale thus falls away from the maximum figure of, say, 20%, after a year or two (when the new capacity is created to meet the increased demand caused by the project) to a negligible amount after, say, 20 years. As a rough allowance for both the delay in the realization of such economies, and their decreasing importance, one might reckon that the 20% mentioned is the equivalent of 10% for every year of the life of the project. Consequently another external economy of Rs. 100,000 is realized.

This adds up to a total of Rs. 250,000 external economies per annum for ever: which compares with projected sales of Rs. 15 million, a projection which is most likely to have a range of at least *plus* or *minus* 10%, i.e. Rs. 1½ million. This example, designed to show how one might make a quantitative estimate of this particular externality, does, despite its hypothetical nature, make one wonder whether it is worth spending a lot of time on trying to estimate external economies. It may be far more important to spend the time improving the ordinary estimates of sales and costs.

16.4 INDUSTRIAL AND SPATIAL COMPLEXES

Both of these have been mentioned *en passant*. The manufacture of refrigerators and electric motors could be considered as a rudimentary 'complex'. Any set of plants such that one buys most of the output of all the others, or all but one or two plants sell most of their output to another member or members of the set, seems to be what is meant by this rather vague term. People, for instance, speak of a petro-chemical complex. Where such a set of linked projects can be set up, it may be advisable to do a cost–benefit appraisal of the whole complex. This is because the situation already discussed in the refrigerator and electric motor example may arise. In other words, a set of plants may be sufficiently socially profitable; but taken one by one, and without the local market provided by other plants, no constituent plant would be socially profitable. In extreme cases, this is obvious enough, as when a product is very expensive to transport, and can be used only as an input into another process— e.g. some of the gases in a petro-chemical complex. But, with such a complex, it is also advisable to look at each plant separately whenever the result is not obvious—whenever, that is, an input can be purchased outside the complex, or an intermediate output sold outside it. The complex should not be regarded as technically determined. Sometimes, an input might be better imported. Sometimes, it might be profitable to produce more of some intermediate than needed by the complex, and sell it as well as the final product.

We have also briefly mentioned the economies that can result from physical proximity, independently of vertical technological linkages. This is what we mean by spatial complexes. If one is designing a spatial industrial complex from scratch, like decorating a completely bare room, then it becomes useful to know what benefits derive from proximity. What industries or plants gain by being close to each other? There appears to be very little empirical work indeed which helps to answer this question. Ordinary transport economies are obvious enough; so also are the diseconomies, e.g. locating oneself near any input may mean increasing one's distance from the market for the final product. Other slightly less obvious economies arising from proximity are all analogous to transport economies. They arise from the need, for technological or commercial reasons, of rapid communication, often face-to-face with other firms; or from the need to acquire a special service very quickly, as when a machine breaks down.

But the above sort of economies are not, usually, external economies: that is, a firm in an industrial cluster can charge appropriately for the services it renders locally; and it would take account of the benefits it would receive, and pay for, as a result of joining such a cluster, when deciding on its own location (as already seen, the benefit of being able to draw on a trained labour force may be an exception, and constitute the receipt of a genuine external economy). Thus locational problems arise more if one has to *design* a spatial complex *ab initio*, for then one has to anticipate and allow for a whole pattern of relationships which need not be 'external'. Similar difficulties arise, of course, in the planning of towns, agricultural settlements, and even buildings. These are problems which lie beyond the scope of this book.

16.5 EXTERNAL CONSIDERATIONS AFFECTING INFRASTRUCTURAL PROJECTS

As already mentioned, the ordinary outputs of many infrastructural enterprises are supplied either free or at prices which are clearly not intended to reflect either cost or benefit. If one calls everything an externality where a difference arises between benefits and receipts, then, for instance, it follows that one classifies all the benefits of a free road system as external effects. The terminology does not matter very much: what matters is simply that every important effect is envisaged and, if possible, valued. The ordinary purpose of a transport project is transport: and the evaluator is not going to forget, in evaluating a road, such things as reduction in traffic costs, time savings, and accident prevention (however difficult it may be to put a value on them, in the absence of a market); in estimating demand he also has to consider the generation of new traffic, and consider the effects on the existing network. It is more likely that things which have nothing to do with transport will be neglected— e.g. noise, harming or improving the landscape, etc. Admittedly, such neglect may seem implausible now that there is so much emphasis on the environment, but it has certainly happened in the past.

Great projects, involving large areas of land and changes in water use, may have major ecological effects which are unforeseen by the planners. This, for instance, is said to be true of the most recent Aswan dam. Similarly, some people fear that the great extension of irrigation may in the longer run have severe diseconomies through increasing soil salinity. Envisaging such effects, which may be better called unintended than external, is outside the realm of economics; although, once their probability is established, the economist may be called upon to appraise them.

16.6 CONCLUSIONS

Bearing in mind that we are essentially comparing projects with each other, we feel that differences in those external effects, which are not in any case allowed for in our type of cost–benefit analysis, will seldom make a significant difference. We believe that this conclusion may be more readily acceptable in the light of our recommendation that where linkages between projects are very close, then they should be examined together (as well as apart), the whole being regarded as a 'complex'.

If, however, the project analysers have a suspicion that there may be rather powerful external effects to an individual project, one way or the other, then they should try to quantify them, however roughly. Even a back-of-an-envelope calculation may serve to show either that the initial suspicion was unjustified, or that further work might need to be done. If it is thought that the presence of external effects will be strongly claimed by opponents or proponents of a project, every effort to achieve a sensible, albeit rough, quantification should be made. Otherwise, wild exaggeration is all too easy.

There will no doubt sometimes remain possibilities of strong external effects, which nevertheless defy any attempt at plausible quantification. There is, finally, no alternative to mentioning such possibilities in a qualitative or literary manner.

CHAPTER SEVENTEEN

The Balance of Payments

In our experience, readers of the OECD *Manual* have found some difficulty in understanding whether any special assumptions were required concerning a country's management of its balance of payments if the advocated methods of project appraisal were to be valid; and also difficulty in understanding exactly how proper allowance was made for a shortage of foreign exchange when no apparent use was made of a shadow exchange rate. This chapter explains how our system of accounting prices is related to the balance of payments and foreign currency shortage, and it is hoped that all doubts will be set at rest.

Consider first a well-managed socialist economy, whose objective is consumption, and which is selecting its investments according to the principles suggested in this volume. The government succeeds in keeping full utilization of domestic capital, and it is also allowing just as much consumption from year to year as it thinks right, this being achieved by a combination of taxation and its system of accounting prices in project selection. If there is, in these circumstances, a balance of payments deficit, the only remedy is to reduce real domestic expenditure, since output cannot be increased. The government might decide that consumption can be cut back below the planned level to rectify the deficit: it is much more likely that the planned level of investment will also be reduced, even if it is decided that consumption can be cut to some extent.

In order to reduce investment, the appropriate action is to raise the ARI, for this reduces the number of projects which will gain acceptance. However, it may be possible to be more subtle than this, for 'the ARI' is a sort of short-hand for rates of discount which may be different for different time-periods. Thus it might be appropriate to raise the rate of discount for certain periods and not others—this was discussed in 14.4. It may also be necessary to tighten up investment-budgeting where this is used.[1]

But how does trade policy, and the rate of exchange, fit into the above picture, which was drawn only along the lines of real resource utilization? The answer is that the right combination of trade policy

---

[1] See 6.3.

and the exchange rate is required to make good the assumption of a reasonably full use of domestic capacity.

A certain level of total savings (domestic, plus foreign in the form of aid or a reliable long-run private capital inflow) would be forthcoming if the economy were producing as much as it could. If investment is no higher than this, then balance of payments trouble can arise only because there is too much use of foreign resources and not enough use of domestic capacity. Thus the basic way of ensuring full use of domestic capacity is to see that the effective competition of foreign goods is not so great that the level of domestic output is less than it might be. If domestic prices and wages are inflexible and do not fall when there is excess domestic supply, then the main weapons available to the government are the familiar ones of the exchange rate, tariffs and quotas, and export subsidies. Thus, if there is excess domestic capacity due to insufficient demand, the appropriate means of curing a balance of payments deficit is to change foreign trade policy so as to engineer a rise in domestic output. But if there is more than adequate demand for domestic products, then consumption or investment is too high, and one or both must be reduced.

Just as the ARI in our system is used to control the aggregate level of investment, so must the accounting prices for commodities and labour be determined in such a way that new investment will tend to promote just the right balance of use of domestic resources and foreign exchange. How has this been achieved?

First, all traded goods have been given APs which measure (or, at least, are intended to measure) the foreign exchange costs or earnings to which they give rise. Thus far it is clear that the system will minimize the foreign exchange cost or maximize the foreign exchange earnings of a project: for the cheaper foreign input and the more rewarding export will always be preferred. Second, payments for or receipts from non-traded goods can always be split into payments for or receipts from traded goods (and here what was said above still applies), plus APs for domestic factors of production (including profits). These payments to domestic factors might cause no change in domestic incomes: this would be the case if markets were perfect, prices reflecting opportunity costs. In fact, of course, some incomes will increase. These additional incomes give rise to consumption, and possibly also to savings and hence investment— all these expenditures having some effect on the balance of payments.

Let us deal with labour incomes first. From a purely production point of view, the opportunity cost of labour in terms of foreign exchange is m, which measures labour's contribution to foreign exchange in its alternative employment. Thus, *if production resulted in no commitment to consumption*, m would be the correct shadow price for labour from the point of view of the maximum savings of foreign exchange; and this value for the SWR would in turn tend to lead to the correct accounting price for the non-traded commodities into which it enters as a cost. It should be no surprise that, in these circumstances, an SWR of m would lead to maximum social profit as well as to maximum savings of foreign exchange: for we are, after all, measuring social profit in terms of uncommitted foreign exchange.

But normally one has to assume that the employment of labour commits the economy to providing some increased consumption—which when measured in APs is designated c. In terms of total foreign exchange cost the extra consumption is $(c-m)$. Adding this to the production cost of m, we see that the total foreign exchange cost of employing a man is c. Thus, allowing for the commitment to consumption, the correct shadow price for labour if the aim were to maximize savings of foreign exchange would be c. This is also the SWR which would be appropriate if the aim were to maximize the growth of the economy (when the saved foreign exchange from each project is immediately ploughed back into further investment). We argued in 4.1 that such extreme aims are seldom if ever appropriate. Therefore the SWR is chosen so that new investments are encouraged to use labour instead of imported inputs, direct and indirect, to the maximum *desirable* extent.

To a lesser degree, increased demand for or supply of non-traded goods may affect other incomes. Capitalist income may be raised, or reduced—which changes capitalist consumption and savings. On our principles, any rise in capitalist consumption is counted fully as a cost, and, being measured in APs, this cost is also a measure of the actual cost to the balance of payments—and *vice versa*, for a fall. Salary earners are similarly treated.

Capitalist savings are treated partly as a cost. So long as these savings (measured in APs) do not result in further investment, they save foreign exchange: to this extent we underestimate our project's contribution to the balance of payments; as against this, it is proper to assume that they will be invested, in which case our valuation of the savings is designed, just as in the case of the original project, to reflect the actual effect on the balance of payments (except insofar as the SWR is less than labour's consumption—but by now any difference in this respect will have certainly become negligible).

The upshot is that, if the SWR is put equal to c, then the resulting estimate of social benefit is also as exact a measure as one could hope for of the *actual* effects on the balance of payments. But this is not a good argument for putting it equal to c, even in the case of a donor agency, or the IBRD, which may be worried about the liquidity of the economy. The reason is that the commitment to consumption arising from use of a lower SWR has been so valued that it is *equivalent to*—i.e. *as good as*—the country's gold and foreign exchange reserves. The need for liquidity has, in principle, already been fully allowed for.

The above account remains the same whatever the manner in which the balance of payments is handled, provided full capacity is maintained. If it is by the price mechanism (the exchange rate, or multiple exchange rates, with or without tariff and export taxes or subsidies) the accounting prices of goods and services, that is their foreign exchange cost or savings, are relatively easy to estimate. If quotas are extensively used, so that it becomes doubtful as to whether a good should be categorized as traded or non-traded, with the added difficulty of not knowing who gets the extra monopoly profit which usually arises when demand for a quota input is increased, then it becomes harder to assign the correct accounting price which measures the (indirect) foreign exchange cost: but the function of the accounting price is not altered. Deflationary methods of dealing with the balance of payments are considered later in this chapter.

How do our methods compare with the use of a shadow exchange rate which is sometimes used by project analysts when the balance of payments is managed by controls (and less often when the balance of payments is not so managed, but a devaluation is regarded as imminent)? With this system, direct earnings and uses of foreign exchange (plus some of the most obvious indirect uses or earnings— e.g. when the output is regarded as an import substitute) are counted in dollars, and all other transactions in rupees. The dollars are then converted to rupees by applying the shadow exchange rate. Suppose that the shadow rate used is 10 rupees to the dollar: this is implicitly saying that 10 rupees earned or used by the project are the equivalent of earning or using $1—in other words, that these 10 rupees earned or used, save or cost the economy $1.

How is this shadow rate arrived at? Various methods have been suggested, including using black market rates determined by smugglers and illicit currency dealers. More careful analysts would usually suggest some kind of an average of APs and domestic prices. The question arises as to whether it is reasonable to estimate that the foreign exchange cost of spending 10 rupees on domestic inputs for our project should be estimated to cost the economy one dollar, just because some overall average expenditure of 10 rupees would cost the economy one dollar. The answer is that such an estimate may be a very bad one: our project's expenditure of 10 rupees may be for a particular item whose use can be directly estimated to cost the economy as much as, say, $3 (or as little as, say, 50 cents).

The difference between the shadow exchange rate method (anyway as sometimes used) and the methods we advocate is like that between a blunderbuss and a sniper's rifle. This is not to say that grape-shot does not have its uses. In previous chapters we have suggested the use of a number of conversion factors. These are indeed averages. Thus the worker's consumption conversion factor is an estimate of the foreign exchange cost of an average unskilled worker's consumption. Let us suppose that we estimate that 10 rupees of such consumption costs the economy one dollar, and that the official exchange rate is 5. Since we convert domestically used rupees to a rupee's worth of foreign exchange at the official rate, our conversion factor would be $\frac{1}{2}$. This could be called a shadow exchange rate of twice the official rate (10 rupees to the dollar instead of 5).

The upshot is that our method advocates using direct estimates of foreign exchange use or earnings for all important inputs, whether of domestic or foreign provenance: and that we resort to conversion factors, which are inverted shadow exchange rates, only where the use of averages seems appropriate. It is the inappropriate use of a single shadow exchange rate, or general blunderbuss, which we deprecate.

Despite what has been said above some economists and others may still not feel satisfied that our methods make proper allowance for a weak balance of payments in all circumstances. They probably have in mind one or both of two by no means unknown situations.

In the first situation, the country is living with a balance of payments deficit by reducing reserves and borrowing abroad. But this cannot go on for ever, and a devaluation must be anticipated within a year or two. Now clearly, if a devaluation will take place, and will have some differential effect on the social profitability of different projects, then this should be reflected in the choice of projects now. This is, indeed, very much the situation in which project evaluators in developed countries may resort to the use of a shadow exchange rate: they act or choose as if foreign exchange is worth more than its present price suggests. The government may

directly encourage foreign sales by the public sector, and discourage the purchase of foreign goods (e.g. public airlines may be forced to buy indigenous aircraft, and the defence authorities may be refused permission to buy foreign weapons, and so on). In this way more use is made of domestic labour, and less use is made of foreign inputs, provided that the additional consumption of new wage earners is not too great.

With us, traded goods are valued directly at their foreign exchange equivalent. Devaluation makes no difference. What, then, is the equivalent in our system of anticipating a devaluation by using a shadow rate of exchange? A *successful* devaluation operates by reducing the value of consumption at world prices, thus reducing the foreign exchange cost of employment. In our system, a successful devaluation would, therefore, reduce the shadow wage: and, if a devaluation is anticipated, a lower shadow wage than otherwise must be employed; in principle also lower values should be used for other domestic incomes where these enter the calculations. This, in turn, will reduce the accounting price of all non-traded resources. In fact, all non-traded resources will be 'devalued', which is as it should be.

The second situation is that in which the balance of payments is kept under control by deflation which reduces the demand for traded goods and non-traded goods alike, so that a situation of general over-capacity develops. This is rather different, in that the objection is probably not so much that our methods result in projects which do too little for the balance of payments, but rather that they will generally restrict investment too much, given the low real cost of domestic resources when overcapacity exists. A difficulty with this is that the government may have deliberately engineered a fall in investment (perhaps by raising the ARI or by investment budgeting) in order to create the deflation. As against this, it may be argued that the government would be pleased to have more investment provided the programme could be so slanted as to have little negative impact in the construction phase on the balance of payments, and be such that earnings (reckoned as always in terms of foreign exchange) would be quickly realized. In a developing country, the sort of investment required would be that which employed very few people directly, used inputs from excess capacity capital-intensive industries, and reached the production stage quickly. This slant to the investment programme would imply three things for accounting prices: first, a high ARI (already carried out); second, a low accounting price for the output of the excess capacity capital-intensive industries; this too would be carried out, for when it can be anticipated that some demand would be met by a domestic industry with no export potential and some excess capacity then the AP would consist only of the foreign exchange equivalent of the labour, fuel, and materials entering into the product (see 9.4); third, a high SWR—because the relative value of uncommitted social income, which can be retained so as to improve the balance of payments, is high.

It may be argued that multiplier effects should be taken into account in the above situation, because of excess capacity. We have seen (in 14.11) that some multiplier effect is already allowed for in the SWR in an economy where wages exceed the value of the marginal product of labour, even when there is full capacity working. Excess capacity would increase this allowance insofar as it raised the relative labour component and reduced the foreign exchange component of consumption: which would reduce the SWR, offsetting the increase implied by the argument of the previous paragraph—so that in principle the SWR could be either higher or lower than in a situation where there was no cause to use deflation to maintain a viable balance of payments. Some allowance for an increase in non-wage incomes, and the consequential balance of payments cost, would also need to be made.

Finally, it is important to remark that it would be unwise, especially having regard to the lag between appraisal and an operating project, to change project appraisal rules unless the deflationary situation was expected to continue for many years, which is unlikely. This is because the slant given to investment to tailor it to a deflationary situation would produce the wrong projects if the situation were to be remedied either by devaluation, or by instituting controls, higher tariffs, export subsidies, etc. If the latter methods are used with sufficient force to permit a full use of domestic capacity then one is back in the situation envisaged in the body of this book. It has already been sufficiently explained how our rules take proper account of the balance of payments in such a situation. Here it is worth adding only that controls, etc., operate to make it possible to have full capacity working by reducing the foreign exchange cost of employing labour; in this respect they are similar to a devaluation.

The deflationary situation discussed above occurs in developing countries from time to time, especially those which are semi-industrialized, but it is not very common. It must not be confused with that under-utilization of capacity which is highly prevalent but is not the result of any general deficiency of demand. Such under-utilization has many causes. Partly it is because capital in many developing countries is excessively cheap, while labour laws and practices inhibit multi-shift working. Partly it results from exchange controls which make it difficult to get spares or materials. Sometimes it is due to technical failure, or incompetent management. Sometimes it is due to labour troubles. In short, it is frequently true that an increase in demand would be satisfied by imports, although excess domestic capacity in that industry appears to exist, in that machinery is idle a lot of the time.

To sum up, one may say that the essential point is that we revalue *all* resources in terms of the foreign exchange cost which their use results in (or which their production saves). Once such revaluations have been adopted, the right way to control the balance of payments is to concentrate on high-yielding projects, and not try to do more investment than private saving, tax policies, and the inflow of foreign capital, allow. In conditions of emergency, it may be possible to cut consumption by more than would normally have been feasible. This may perhaps make some investment projects previously entered into, making refrigerators or motor-cars, for instance, temporarily redundant. But usually what is felt to be a chronic balance of payments crisis is just a situation in which one wishes one was better off, and is conscious of the projects one would like to see undertaken, for which no resources are being made available. The best solution is more foreign assistance or improved opportunities for exporting. Failing that, a high ARI or increased taxation must, be used.

CHAPTER EIGHTEEN

A Comparison with Other Methods of Project Analysis Involving Accounting Prices

18.1 The UNIDO *Guidelines*[1]

We are not here concerned with detailed differences of emphasis, or relatively small points of economic analysis. The intention is to help the reader of both works to understand what appear to us to be the substantial similarities, and differences if any. One broad distinction, which makes it sometimes difficult to know if any difference of economic treatment exists or not, is that the present book is often more specific in its recommendations and guidelines than the *Guidelines*, which seems to be to us more theoretical and to offer rather less practical advice.

The most striking difference lies in the choice of numéraire. Ours is 'uncommitted social income measured at border prices', and that of the *Guidelines* is 'aggregate consumption measured at domestic market prices'. These numéraires have already been dealt with in 9.12, and their merits will not be further discussed. Here we want to point out only that the difference of numéraire often makes what is an identical formal analysis look different.

To give just one example, suppose for the sake of argument that border prices and internal market prices are the same, so that one can concentrate on the effect of using uncommitted social income and aggregate consumption as numéraires.

Using the symbols of this work where possible, the UNIDO formula for the shadow wage is

$$swr = m + (\textit{Capitalists' Saving Rate}) \ (s-1)w$$

(UNIDO equation 15.8)

---

[1] *Guidelines for Project Evaluation* (UNIDO, 1972), was published three years after the OECD *Manual*, which was the forerunner of the present book. P. Dasgupta has written a paper comparing the analysis of the UNIDO *Guidelines* and the OECD *Manual*, Dasgupta, 1972. In this chapter we have drawn on Dasgupta's analysis, but his comparisons cannot be taken always to apply to the present book, which in certain respects is substantially altered.

Let us now suppose that it is a public sector project, and that the government's saving rate is 1. The formula thus becomes

$$swr = m + (s - 1)w$$

The formula of this book can, on the UNIDO assumption that workers save nothing, be written as

$$swr = \frac{m}{s} + \left(1 - \frac{1}{s}\right)w.$$

Clearly the UNIDO formula is s times the formula of this book, for the reason that the UNIDO numéraire is $\frac{1}{s}$ times as valuable as our numéraire.

It should be noted that we have substituted s (the price of un-committed social income in terms of consumption) for the UNIDO P^{inv} which is the price of investment in terms of consumption.[1] This, however, is justified on our present assumption that the whole of the surplus thrown up by a public project is uncommitted social income for us: while, for UNIDO, to call it investment requires the assumption, also made, that the government uses new uncommitted social income entirely for investment. In this connection it is worth noting that in principle UNIDO distinguishes the social value of government investment, government consumption, private invest-ment and private consumption. But, when simplifying to make the system more practicable, as in the case-studies contained in the *Guidelines*, the line of division drawn is simply between investment and consumption. In this book, the main line of division is between public and private funds. We believe that the latter is better (*a*) because a rational government will so far as possible equalize the social value of public consumption and investment, and (*b*) because private investments may be worth much less (or more) than public investments.

We turn now to the use of border prices in our numéraire, and domestic market prices in the UNIDO numéraire. It must be first emphasized that both works use both border prices and internal prices for commodities. Corresponding sums of money can be kept separate and be called 'border rupees' and 'domestic rupees'. UNIDO then revalues border rupees in terms of domestic rupees (by a shadow exchange rate): this volume adopts the reverse

---

[1] We are, incidentally, not fully in agreement with the UNIDO discussion of P^{inv}. See 13.32.

procedure (by conversion factors). As thus stated, the difference is clearly trivial.

Substantial differences could arise for two reasons,

(i) because different recommendations are given as to when border or internal prices should be used; and

(ii) because different procedures are recommended for converting border rupees into domestic rupees, or vice versa.

The first difference is closely related to the distinction of traded and non-traded (or partially traded) goods, which is explicit in the present work and implicit in the *Guidelines*—and here it seems to us that there is little difference between the text of the *Guidelines* and the present work, although the latter stresses the advantages of using border prices more than UNIDO: but from the case-studies it would appear that the UNIDO authors are more prone, when in doubt or when further research is not indicated, to value 'domestic materials' at their domestic market price. This assumes that the market prices of all goods so classified correctly reflect their contribution to consumption. Since the admitted distortions in wages and foreign exchange spread to most commodities in the economy (and there are other distortions as well), we regard this assumption as unjustified and therefore one which should be made as little as possible. Valuations based on the present work would tend to make much less use of domestic market prices (i.e. less use of the classification 'domestic rupees'), either because the goods were classified as traded; or because, if non-traded, it would be assumed that supply would respond, so that the domestic cost of the input would be broken down into its own cost components, which would mainly consist of border rupees and labour costs.

It is easiest to understand the effect of the above difference of emphasis by an example, which uses border rupees as numéraire (but with domestic accounting rupees in parenthesis). Suppose the official exchange rate is 1 rupee to a dollar, and the shadow exchange rate (SER) is 2 rupees to a dollar, and that 100 domestic rupees are spent on a 'domestic material'. If a 'domestic rupee' classification is adopted then the accounting price is 50 border rupees (100 domestic rupees). If this is a mistaken classification in that trade is mainly affected, then the proper accounting price is 100 border rupees. Next suppose that it is not the traded/non-traded classification that is wrong, but the implicit assumption that supply does not respond. If supply responds, it may be that the 100 domestic rupees could be broken down into 40 border rupees, 45 labour costs, and 15 domestic rupees. Assuming that the SWR is $\frac{1}{3}$ (this figure of $\frac{1}{3}$ includes the adjustment of the wage to border prices: in terms of domestic prices the shadow wage is $\frac{2}{3}$), the accounting price would be calculated as follows:

	Conversion to border rupees	AP in border rupees	Conversion to domestic rupees	AP in domestic rupees
40 border rupees	none	40	multiply by SER	80
45 labour cost	multiply by SWR ($=\frac{1}{3}$)	15	multiply by SWR ($=\frac{2}{3}$)	30
15 domestic rupees	multiply by SCF (or divide by SER)	$7\frac{1}{2}$	none	15
100		$62\frac{1}{2}$		125

In this example the use of the classification 'domestic rupees', and its necessary companion, an SER or SWR, has been much reduced, which is what we recommend. (See also Chapter XVII.) The change has raised the AP in domestic rupees from 100 to 125—exactly double the AP in border rupees, which is as it should be.

The classification 'domestic rupees' would be used only (*a*) for items where both the supply of a good was clearly inelastic and the marginal product of that supply could not be directly expressed in terms of border rupees, and (*b*) for small items where the extra work involved did not seem justifiable.

This brings one to the second possible cause of differences—different procedures for calculating the SER. In principle the SER appropriate for UNIDO is the inverse of our 'consumption conversion factor', i.e. the change in the border value of imports and exports caused by a marginal change in aggregate consumption measured in domestic market prices.[1] This is, of course, a difficult thing to measure: and there is a danger that much less appropriate procedures will be used (and, indeed, in the *Guidelines*' case-studies the SER is apparently estimated in a casual manner). The same conclusion as before emerges—the less it has to be used the better.

A second, possibly important, difference between the UNIDO *Guidelines* and the present work lies in the treatment of taxes on

---

[1] For some reason which we do not understand, and believe to be mistaken, the *Guidelines* suggests that capital goods should be left out of the calculation.

final non-traded consumer goods. As explained in 12.5 we believe it is almost always correct to value such outputs net of tax. The *Guidelines* does not appear to deal explicitly with this rather important matter. But with its emphasis on domestic market prices one has to assume that the output would normally be valued gross of tax, the tax being added back to the amount received by the project. Exceptions might be made to this on the ground of 'demerit wants', but there is no guidance given as to when the tax might or might not be added back.

Another considerable difference is the emphasis given in the *Guidelines* to 'bottom-up' rather than 'top-down' procedures. This has been discussed in 8.53. In short, we doubt whether the process of trying to arrive at important accounting prices by letting them emerge from decisions on project analyses which leave the values of these prices undetermined is likely to get very far: another important reason for the opposite emphasis is that the design of projects can hardly be affected by accounting prices unless these percolate from the top down.

Despite the above, and some differences which may not be important in practice, there is no doubt that the two works adopt basically the same approach to project evaluation. Both treatments single out the values of foreign exchange, savings, and unskilled labour, as crucial sources of a distorted price mechanism. Both go on to calculate accounting prices which will correct these distortions, and both carry out these corrections in an essentially similar manner. Both advocate DCF analysis, and the use of PSVs. The treatment of externalities and risk seem to be very much the same. Finally, both works advocate making explicit allowance for inequality. This latter agreement marks out the present work and UNIDO as differing from some practitioners of social cost–benefit analysis, who believe that economists do better not to introduce this consideration. It is also worth noting that a French school of thought believes that economists should also abjure accounting prices.[1]

Subject to the reservation made earlier in this section, the present authors will be pleased to learn that a country has set up an OCPE using the *Guidelines*, just as we hope that the *Guidelines* authors will be pleased to learn that a country has set up a COPE using L/M methods.

18.2 OTHERS

The two other methods which have been advocated are essentially

---

[1] E.g., Prou *et al.*, 1963, 1964 and 1970.

short cuts. They may be called the Domestic Resource Cost or Bruno method,[1] and the Effective Protection method.

18.21 *The Domestic Resource Cost or Bruno Method*

The essence of the Bruno method is to divide annual costs (including capital costs) into foreign exchange and labour, whether by input/output or cruder methods. As the name of the paper referred to implies, the output is always valued in terms of foreign exchange. Since capital is involved as an input into the project, and also into other sectors insofar as capacity is expanded to meet the demands of the new project, a rate of interest has to be assumed in order to give annual direct and indirect capital costs. The labour cost per unit of foreign exchange saving (conceivably dissaving) is then calculated. This yields an own exchange rate for the project—the local currency cost per dollar saved. This may be compared with an estimated shadow rate (just as the IRR may be compared with an ARI), and the project selected or rejected accordingly.

The numéraire of the Bruno method is thus 'domestic (labour) rupees'. This is, of course, readily transferable to our numéraire of foreign currency by calculating 'dollar savings per unit of local currency cost' instead of vice versa, in which case comparison would be made with a conversion factor. This would be the conversion factor for labour—i.e. an SWR. As used in Israel, which is not a 'surplus-labour' country, there is no SWR because no disequilibrium is assumed to exist in the labour market (this is not an essential feature of the Bruno method, which could easily be adapted for use in a 'surplus labour' country), and because the numéraire is the value of labour itself.

Switching to our numéraire, we can say that the Bruno method ranks projects by the SWR required to achieve a certain given rate of profit, which can be identified with our ARI. It is, of course, more usual to estimate an SWR (or a shadow exchange rate) and rank projects by their profitability. It makes no difference to project selection which method of ranking is used. This can be illustrated by a simple example, which assumes that capital goods are all imported. Let X be the foreign currency earned or saved, directly and indirectly, as a result of the project's use of current inputs and outputs. Let K be the direct and indirect use of capital, expressed in foreign exchange. Let W be the direct and indirect wage bill.

---

[1] See Bruno, 1967. Bruno states that the essentials of the method had been in use in Israel for ten years.

Then the Bruno ranking measure, expressed in our numéraire, is

$$\frac{X - K(\text{ARI})}{W}$$

If a target SWR is set, then a marginal investment would satisfy the relation $\dfrac{X - K\,(\text{ARI})}{W} = \text{SWR}$, and the annual benefit from the project can be written

$$X - K\,(\text{ARI}) - W\,(\text{SWR}).$$

It plainly makes no formal difference whether we say that an acceptable project must satisfy the relation

$$\frac{X - K\,(\text{ARI})}{W} \geqslant \text{SWR}$$

or the more usual form

$$\frac{X - W\,(\text{SWR})}{K} \geqslant \text{ARI}.$$

In a small economy like Israel, which borrows very extensively abroad, the ARI may reasonably be thought of as determined by the borrowing rate. It was probably this which made the first form of the relationship seem the natural one to use.

In practice (and this echoes our comparison with UNIDO), much depends on how the essential division between foreign currency and labour (assumed to be the only primary domestic factor) is carried out. In the paper cited much reliance is placed on input/output methods. This amounts to an assumption that domestic inputs are non-traded, and that the supplying industries will always be expanded, with the same current and capital coefficients, to meet project demand. This assumption is clearly at variance with the present volume (and also with UNIDO which tends to assume, as we saw, that non-traded goods are in fixed supply). Any practical use of the Bruno method in most developing countries could hardly employ such methods, and the division between foreign exchange and labour might in practice be made in much the same way as we advocate.

The Bruno method is a short-cut method, because it considers a single year's full capacity operation only. The time profile of the project can then be allowed for to a very limited extent only by the inadequate device of depreciation allowances (which make a rough allowance only for the life of the project). This short cut also precludes use of the present value criterion, so that its validity is limited to compatible projects.

Apart from being a short-cut method it is also limited in its application, since it concerns itself only with projects which produce fully traded, or nearly fully traded, outputs. Moreover, it makes no allowance for disequilibrium in the labour market, or for a shortage of savings. It is concerned only with trading distortions, arising from tariffs and wrong exchange rates.

In our opinion it is valuable for quick looks in the field of manufacturing and agriculture, more as a way of deciding which are promising fields for fuller analysis than as a good substitute for such analysis.

18.22 *The Effective Rate of Protection*
This has been suggested as a selection criterion, those industries or projects with the lower rate of effective protection being preferred. It resembles the Bruno method in two respects: that it aims to deal only with trade distortions, and that it is a short-cut. But, without modification, it could be very misleading. The following simple example suffices to make the point.

A government is considering two public projects, A or B. Each requires the same investment, and employs the same amount of domestic labour. Capital does not depreciate. All inputs and outputs, except labour, are traded. A and B have value added at domestic prices (VAD) of 40 and 20 respectively. Value added at border prices (VAW) is 20 and 16 respectively. By definition the percentage rate of effective protection is $100 \left[\dfrac{VAD}{VAW} - 1 \right]$. Thus A has effective protection of 100%, and B 25%. Now consider social profit. A saves or earns the country (and the government) $20 in respect of current commodity inputs and outputs: the corresponding figure for B is $16. Since each has the same domestic capital and labour inputs, it is obvious that A, the more highly protected, is better. The fact that A is more highly protected than B does not prove that a given investment in A will not yield more value added at world prices than it would in B. The basic failing of effective protection as a criterion stems from the fact that value added is a measure only of the output of domestic primary factors. No good investment criterion can dispense with comparing outputs with inputs.

Professors Bela Belassa and D. M. Schydlowsky, who have advocated effective protection, in some sense, as a criterion recognize that the (unmodified) measure takes no account of distortions in the domestic factor markets.[1] It seems to us that if the proper modifica-

---

[1] See Balassa and Schydlowsky, 1968 and 1972.

tions are made, then it is no longer an effective protection measure but a modified version of the Bruno method. The authors' criticism of the Bruno method concerns the separation of domestic from foreign resource costs by input/output methods. As already indicated in 18.21, we fully agree with this criticism.[1]

---

[1] Professor Bruno himself compares the 'domestic resource cost' method, and effective protection, in Bruno, 1972.

CHAPTER NINETEEN

The Economics of the Second Best

It is a theorem of economics that, under certain assumptions which amount to saying that perfect competition is possible and externalities are absent, an optimum can be a competitive equilibrium, provided that wealth has been suitably redistributed. Perfect competition, it will be recollected, is a state of affairs in which prices are established for all commodities, and no one, consumer or producer, exerts monopoly power or bargaining strength. It should also be emphasized that the competitive equilibrium contemplated is one in which there are no taxes or subsidies (beyond the initial 'lump-sum' redistribution of wealth). The theorem appears to commend the use of the price system, and in particular to imply that any public production decisions should be taken so as to maximize profits (more generally, expected present values) measured at ruling and expected prices.

The interpretation of this theorem has often suffered from one or other of two serious errors. The first error is the belief that it justifies any change in the direction of perfect competition, such as equating marginal cost and price for some commodity. This may not be desirable when the other conditions of perfect competition are not satisfied. Awareness of this difficulty has led economists to attempt to develop economic analysis of the *second-best*,[1] that is to say, of situations where some or many of the marginal conditions implied by the general theorem (of the 'first-best') fail to hold. Certainly in the foreseeable future no country could hope for more than a second-best optimum. Therefore any proposals for methods of public decision-taking must be judged as proposals for achieving the second-best. Some readers, noticing that a number of arguments advanced and principles urged in this book seem quite similar to those associated with first-best welfare economics, may think that problems of the second-best have been ignored. This brings us to the second error.

It is tempting, but clearly fallacious, to suppose that when a theorem has been deduced from certain assumptions, these assumptions are *necessary* for all the conclusions of the theorem. In the case

---

[1] Haberler, 1950; Little, 1950; Meade, 1955; Lipsey and Lancaster, 1956; Green, 1960.

of the fundamental theorem of welfare economics, the usual assumptions are very far from being necessary for all the conclusions of the theorem. For example, the usual assumption of convex preferences is quite unnecessary if the number of consumers is large; if there are economies of scale in some sectors of the economy, it is still desirable that other sectors should behave in a competitive manner; and some kinds of consumption externality can be allowed. The particular conclusion that we should concentrate on, since it is equivalent to the desirability of using (accounting) prices, is that of productive efficiency—marginal rates of transformation should be equal in all production sectors, or, in the case where there are no economies of scale or indivisibilities, all producers should maximize present values measured in terms of the same prices and interest rates. This conclusion still holds under many kinds of constraints that impose a second-best optimization.

The chief constraints that render the attainable optimum a second best are:

    (i) The presence of taxes and subsidies that are not lump-sum in their operation—i.e. which consumers and producers can to some extent avoid by changing their economic behaviour.

    (ii) The existence of external economies and diseconomies, including public goods.

    (iii) The presence of monopolists, and the existence of markets in which prices are determined by bargaining.

    (iv) Irrational behaviour (particularly likely in response to uncertainty).

It seems likely that the first of these is, in practice, considerably more important than the others. (ii) and (iii) can of course be affected, and their impact ought to be reduced, by government policy through taxes, subsidies, and quantitative controls. But let us allow that all four kinds of 'imperfection' are present, and consider how *public sector* production ought to be controlled.

Suppose the public sector, as a whole, produces and uses goods and services, which we may write as a vector $z = (z_1, z_2, \ldots z_n)$, with inputs written as negative numbers. The question is, how valuable z is to the economy. That depends upon how public sector inputs are obtained, and how public sector outputs are disposed of. Outputs might be given away, and inputs taken by law or force; or, as is more common, they may be bought and sold (in which case they may be subject to various taxes and subsidies). Generally speaking, however it is disposed of, one presumes that additional output (if obtained without increasing any inputs or reducing other outputs) will cause an improvement in the economy. One can think of exceptions: more roads may be (or seem to be) good for motorists, but bad for those who live near them, so that there could be disputes about whether there is an improvement or not, all things considered. But surely if it is possible to have more of some goods without less of any others, the government *could*, if it wished, dispose of them in a way that is unambiguously an improvement (e.g. by reducing suitably chosen taxes). Furthermore, if public production is inefficient, it is very likely that *some* change in production plans is possible, which would improve matters for everyone. Thus, on the assumption that the government is prepared to use commodity taxes and subsidies optimally, we are led to the conclusion that if public sector production is optimal, it is efficient.

Formally, we are arguing that, if objectives can be expressed as the maximization of a function $W(z)$, and z^* is optimum public production, then there is some i such that

$$W(z_1^*, \ldots z_i, \ldots z_n^*) > W(z_1^*, \ldots, z_i^*, \ldots, z_n^*)$$

if z_i is a little greater than z_i^*. If that is so, no such $(z_1^*, \ldots, z_i, \ldots, z_n^*)$ can be feasible. Therefore z^* is on the production frontier.

It should be emphasized that this proposition, though very plausible, is rather far-reaching in its implications. It implies that accounting prices can be associated with the optimum, these same accounting prices to apply to all undertakings in the public sector. In particular, taxes on transactions between public sector undertakings are undesirable. And if foreign trade can be regarded as part of the public sector—there is every reason why it should—the marginal costs of importing and marginal revenues of exporting should be equal to these accounting prices (except insofar as the interests of other countries are to be counted).

The basic proof of the efficiency proposition[1] assumed that the public sector traded goods and services with the rest of the economy at uniform prices, the rest of the economy not necessarily being subject to any other taxes, and that these prices and wage rates were chosen optimally. The proof also assumed that consumers' preferences were to be respected, that there were no externalities, and no monopoly. But it can easily be seen that even these assumptions are far from necessary for the conclusion. For example, if some

---

[1] Diamond and Mirrlees, 1971.

consumer prices are fixed, by convention, political pressure, or irrational policies, the efficiency result still holds (because this constraint does not prevent additional production from being disposed of in an improving way). This weakening is quite an important result for cost–benefit analysis, since a tariff applied to a constant import price yields a constant market price. Thus the presence of non-optimal tariffs which are uninfluenced by domestic production levels or the volume of international trade in these commodities does not disturb the conclusion that border prices should be equal to accounting prices. What it comes to is that, in the main, only weak assumptions need be made to justify efficiency: if a departure from efficiency is urged, the onus of proving its desirability lies on those who urge it.

Having said that, we should like to point out two kinds of argument that might imply that departures from efficiency are desirable. The first is based on the costs of running a tax system, and administering public enterprises. Very little useful work has been done on these problems. In a general way, it is easily seen that a departure from public sector efficiency, even in a fully socialized production system, could produce a more desirable set of final consumer good prices, provided that it is either impossible or administratively costly to distinguish between sales to producers and sales to consumers. Petroleum has already been instanced as a possible case in point. But at the same time, there is a lot to be said on grounds of administrative simplicity for keeping any departures from efficiency to a minimum—for the pursuit of efficiency in a definable sense is itself conducive to efficiency, and will tend to avoid possibly rather arbitrary decisions on the part of public enterprises.

The second way in which some might be led to recommend aggregate inefficiency is when considering production as a whole, in a mixed economy. (We are not, for the purposes of the present book, discussing those parts of the production sector where production decisions would not in any case be subject to public control, but rather the organized sectors, where production is on a relatively large scale.) It has been shown that aggregate production efficiency is still desirable if private producers act like perfect competitors, and any profits they make, over and above the normal return on capital, are negligible or paid to the government (e.g. through a very large tax on excess profits).[1] One can also argue,

---

[1] Diamond and Mirrlees, 1971.

if a private sector project is subject to government approval, and the decision will not affect other production plans in the private sector (except in ways that are socially marginal), that it can be regarded as a public sector project, except that it will increase the wealth of private capitalists. This latter effect can be dealt with separately and assessed independently of the production plan. If the private sector, or a part of it, can be made to behave approximately like perfect competitors, earning only a normal profit for its owners, then it is desirable that it be made to do so. That is what the efficiency theorem implies. Departures from aggregate efficiency are justified only as a way of affecting the prices that govern, or are governed by, producers who are not subject to such control.[1] Even when one wants to influence a price in this way, it may often be quite easy to do so without affecting public sector efficiency. For instance, if it is hard to tax private enterprise adequately in other ways, it might make sense for a public airport authority to charge a large fee, well in excess of marginal cost, for executive jet movements; but there would be no need to charge the Air Force similarly.

It seems to be impossible to make general rules about desirable lines of departure from public sector efficiency: this being the case, there is a certain danger of undesirable exceptions being carried out in an *ad hoc* and even chaotic or corrupt manner. Governmental administration of the foreign trade sector—here regarded as part of the public sector—is a case in point, and is one of the major arguments in favour of a straightforward system of taxes on final sales.

We have suggested above that foreign trade ought to be regarded as part of the public sector. The reason is that the government can determine the terms on which producers (and consumers) have access to foreign trade. Foreign trade is like an industry that uses exports as inputs and produces imports as outputs: the 'production decision' is a decision about the levels of imports and exports, which will be made by importers and exporters, on the basis of the prices they face and the other controls on foreign trade that the government may be operating. If, as the efficiency result implies, it is desirable that these foreign trade decisions be made so as to maximize the 'profit' of foreign trade, measured at accounting prices—i.e., the value of imports less the value of exports at these prices—this will be done by trading in each line to the point where the marginal cost of an import is equal to its accounting price and the

---

[1] See Dasgupta and Stiglitz, 1972, and Mirrlees, 1972, for further discussion of the private sector.

marginal revenue from an export is equal to its accounting price. If an import is bought at a fixed border price, then the accounting price must be adjusted so as to be equal to it.

This argument does not at all depend upon assuming that world trade is optimal, or that monopoly is absent in world markets. In fact, the argument completely ignores the interests of foreign countries and companies, and assumes that they should be exploited to the maximum benefit of the home country. For developing countries, this may often be a right position to take. But the argument might be modified to allow, say, for cooperative action between developing countries. For example, two countries exporting the same primary commodity might agree on a common trade policy, which would imply a smaller marginal revenue from exports for each than would have applied if each had been pursuing its own interest without regard to the other.

We claim that some of the basic principles of welfare economics hold in circumstances that are altogether more realistic than those that used to be found convenient for textbook exposition. We have gone into a little detail, so as to show that welfare economics can be applied in real-world circumstances, and to indicate how one could hope to go further to deal with more difficult cases. But however far one goes in weakening assumptions, it is certainly true—and should also be emphasized—that assumptions are required if the procedures suggested by welfare economics are to be valid. The circumstances in which efficiency principles can be applied are not *intrinsically* unrealistic, except in the sense that no specific assumptions are likely to be satisfied exactly in the real world. In the discourse of some economists, that is what the second-best argument comes down to: 'You have reached conclusions, therefore you have made assumptions; it is extremely unlikely, whatever the apparent evidence, that specific assumptions hold exactly; therefore your conclusions are almost certainly wrong.' Perhaps that can be a useful argument in a debate, but it does not get one very far for practical purposes.

The real issue is whether one should approach policy questions with a set of principles and theoretical procedures in mind, or take each question as it comes and judge it without reference to models and theories. We suspect the latter method is not possible, and we do not observe people doing it. When they would claim to be doing it, they are relying on simple models and theories so crude they would be too embarrassed to state them explicitly. Perhaps the alternative, of starting from a clear and definite framework, would also be very unsatisfactory if one had to pretend that the world was like the perfectly competitive economies with ideal wealth distribution on which economists cut their teeth. Fortunately, the cost–benefit analyst and the planner can approach their problems with models that are not wildly unrealistic, and basic rules that are very serviceable. When the evidence is available, these rules may be modified. But we have noticed that, when one tries to pursue the further repercussions of production plans, as any departure from the basic rules requires, one is seldom sure which way the evidence urges modification on balance.

The world as it is, then, does not allow an ideal distribution of goods to people. At best, and in the long run, it can allow some kind of second-best outcome. Economists now know a great deal about these second-bests. But, in the short run, there is much confused action, and third-best may be as much as can be attained. In our opinion, the pursuit of second-best policies will in the short run do little worse, and perhaps much better, than attempts to capture that Will-o'-the-Wisp third-best. In the long run, these second-best policies will be taking economies in the right direction.

List of References

Arrow, K. J., *Essays in the Theory of Risk-Bearing*, North-Holland Publishing Company, Amsterdam, 1971.

Arrow, K. J. and Lind, R. C., 'Uncertainty and the Evaluation of Public Investment Decisions', *American Economic Review*, June 1970. (Reprinted as Chapter II in *Essays in the Theory of Risk-Bearing*; see above.)

Balassa, B. and Schydlowsky, D. M., 'Effective Tariffs, Domestic Cost of Foreign Exchange and the Equilibrium Exchange Rate', *Journal of Political Economy*, May-June 1968.

Balassa, B. and associates, *The Structure of Protection in Developing Countries*, Johns Hopkins Press, 1971.

Balassa, B. and Schydlowsky, D. M., 'Domestic Resource Costs and Effective Protection Once Again', *Journal of Political Economy*, January–February 1972.

Baranson, J., *Automotive Industries in Developing Countries*, World Bank Staff Occasional Papers No. 8, Johns Hopkins Press, Baltimore, 1969.

Bos, H. C., Sanders, M., and Secchi, C., *Private Foreign Investment in Less Developed Countries; Evaluation of Some Macro-Economic Effects*, D. Reidel Publishing Co., Dordrecht, 1973.

Bruno, M., 'The Optimal Selection of Export-Promoting and Import-Substituting Projects', in *Planning the External Sector: Techniques, Problems and Policies. Report on the First Interregional Seminar on Development Planning.* New York, United Nations, 1967.

Bruno, M., 'Domestic Resource Costs and Effective Protection: Clarification and Synthesis', *Journal of Political Economy*, January–February 1972.

Chakravarti, A., 'The Social Profitability of Training Unskilled Workers in the Public Sector in India', *Oxford Economic Papers*, March 1972.

Commission on the Third London Airport. *Report*, London, H.M.S.O., 1971.

Dasgupta, P., 'A Comparative Analysis of the UNIDO Guidelines and the OECD Manual', *Bulletin of the Oxford University Institute of Economics and Statistics*, February 1972.

Dasgupta, P. and Stiglitz, J. E., 'On Optimal Taxation and Public Production', *Review of Economic Studies*, January 1972.

Diamond, P. A. and Mirrlees, J. A., 'Optimal Taxation and Public Production', *American Economic Review*, March and June 1971.

Dixit, A. K., 'Optimal Development in the Labour-Surplus Economy', *Review of Economic Studies*, January 1968.

Dobb, M. H., *An Essay on Economic Growth and Planning*, Routledge & Kegan Paul, London, 1960.

Dupuit, J., 'De la Mesure de l'Utilité des Travaux Publiques', *Annales des Ponts et Chaussées*, 2nd Series, Vol. 8, 1844. English Translation in *International Economic Papers*, No. 2.

Economic Commission for Latin America, 'Population Trends and Policy

Alternatives in Latin America', *Economic Bulletin for Latin America*, 1971.

Fellner, W., 'Operational Utility: the Theoretical Background and a Measurement', in *Ten Economic Studies in the Tradition of Irving Fisher*, Wiley, New York, 1967.

Green, H. A. J., 'The Social Optimum in the Presence of Monopoly and Taxation', *Review of Economic Studies*, October 1961.

Haberler, G., 'Some Problems in the Pure Theory of International Trade', *Economic Journal*, 1950.

Harris, J. R. and Todaro, M. P., 'Migration, Unemployment and Development: A Two-Sector Analysis', *American Economic Review*, March 1970.

Khan, A. R. and Mirrlees, J. A., *Optimal Prices for a Developing Economy*, mimeo, Nuffield College, Oxford, 1973.

Lal, D., *Wells and Welfare*, OECD Development Centre, Paris, 1972.

Lal, D., *Appraising Foreign Investment in Developing Countries*, Heinemann, London, 1974.

Lipsey, R. G. and Lancaster, R. K., 'The General Theory of Second Best', *Review of Economic Studies*, Vol. XXIV (1), 1956–7.

Little, I. M. D., *A Critique of Welfare Economics*, Oxford University Press, 1950, (2nd ed., 1957).

Little, I. M. D., 'On Measuring the Value of Private Direct Overseas Investment', in Ranis G. (ed.), *The Gap Between Rich and Poor Nations*, Macmillan, London, 1972.

Little, I. M. D. and Mirrlees, J. A., *Manual of Industrial Project Analysis, Vol. II*, OECD Development Centre, Paris, 1968.

Little, I. M. D., Scitovsky, T. and Scott, M. FG., *Industry and Trade in Some Developing Countries*, Oxford University Press, London, 1970.

Little, I. M. D. and Tipping, D. G., *A Social Cost–Benefit Analysis of the Kulai Oil Palm Estate*, OECD Development Centre, Paris, 1972.

Malinvaud, E., 'First Order Certainty Equivalence', *Econometrica*, Oct. 1969.

Manne, A. S. (ed.), *Investments for Capacity Expansion, Size, Location, and Time-Phasing*, George Allen & Unwin, London, 1967.

Marglin, S. A., 'The Rate of Interest and the Value of Capital with Unlimited Supplies of Labor', Ch. VIII in Shell, K. (ed.), *Essays on the Theory of Optimal Economic Growth*, Massachusetts Institute of Technology, Cambridge, 1967.

Marglin, S. A., *Public Investment Criteria*, George Allen & Unwin, London, 1967.

Meade, J. E., *Trade and Welfare*, Oxford University Press, 1955.

Mirrlees, J. A., 'On Producer Taxation', *Review of Economic Studies*, January 1972.

Mirrlees, J. A. and Stern, N. H., 'Fairly Good Plans', *Journal of Economic Theory*, April 1972.

Newbery, D. M. G., 'Public Policy in the Dual Economy', *Economic Journal*, June 1972.

OECD, *Fiscal Incentives for Private Investment in Developing Countries*, OECD, Paris, 1965.

OECD, *Manual of Industrial Project Analysis, Vol. II*, by Little, I. M. D. and Mirrlees, J. A., OECD Development Centre, Paris, 1968.

OECD, *Investing in Developing Countries*, OECD, Paris, 1972.

Pouliquen, L. Y., *Risk Analysis in Project Appraisal*, World Bank Staff Occasional Papers No. 11, Johns Hopkins Press, Baltimore, 1970.

Prest, A. R., 'The Role of Labour Taxes and Subsidies in Promoting Employment in Developing Countries', in *Fiscal Measures for Employment Promotion in Developing Countries*, International Labour Office, Geneva, 1972.

Prou, Ch., Chervel, M., et Gardelle, J., *Établissement des Programmes en Économie Sous-Developpée*, editions Dunod, Paris, Tomes 1, 2 et 3, 1963, 1964, 1970.

Rempel, H. and Todaro, M. P., 'Rural to Urban Labour Migration in Kenya', in *Population Growth and Urban Development in Africa*, Ominde, S. H. and Ejiogu, L. N. (eds.), Heinemann, London, 1972.

Reuber, G. L., with Crooknell, H., Emerson, M. R., and Gallais-Hamonno, G., *Private Foreign Investment in Development*, Oxford University Press for OECD Development Centre, 1973.

Reutlinger, S., *Techniques for Project Appraisal under Uncertainty*, World Bank Staff Occasional Papers No. 10. Johns Hopkins Press, Baltimore, 1970.

Scitovsky, T., 'Two Concepts of External Economies', *Journal of Political Economy*, April 1954.

Scott, M. FG., *Estimates of Accounting Prices for Mauritius*, Nuffield College, Oxford, mimeo, April 1972.

Scott, M. FG., MacArthur, J. and Newbery, D. M. G., *Project Appraisal in Practice: The Little/Mirrlees Method Applied in Kenya*, Heinemann, 1974.

Sen, A. K., *Choice of Techniques*, Basil Blackwell, Oxford, 1962 (3rd Edition 1968).

Seton, F., *Shadow Wages in the Chilean Economy*, OECD Development Centre, Paris, 1972.

Stern, N. H., 'Optimum Development in a Dual Economy', *Review of Economic Studies*, April 1972.

Stern, N. H., *An Appraisal of Tea Production on Small-Holdings in Kenya*, OECD Development Centre, Paris, 1972.

United Nations, 'Urbanization: Development Policies and Planning', *International Social Development Review*, No. 1, United Nations, New York, 1968.

UNIDO, *Guidelines for Project Evaluation*, written by Dasgupta, P. S., Marglin, S. A., and Sen, A. K. United Nations, New York, 1972.

Vernon, R., *Sovereignty at Bay*, Basic Books, New York, 1971.

Annotated Bibliography

The following suggestions for further reading and reference are restricted to works bearing directly upon the main topics we have discussed.

1. Economic Principles

The literature on welfare economics and its applications to public investment decisions is enormous and wide-ranging. The collection, *Readings in Welfare Economics*, ed. Arrow, K. J. and Scitovsky, T., Allen and Unwin, for the A.E.A., 1969, is a useful compendium for the professional economist. Others may pick up a great deal from general works on investment criteria, such as the Joint Economic Committee of Congress volume mentioned below.

1.1 Investment Criteria in General

Joint Economic Committee of the U.S. Congress, *The Analysis and Evaluation of Public Expenditures: the PPB System*, Volume 1, U.S. Government Printing Office, Washington, 1969, contains papers by economists, which avoid technical analysis, and cover many of the issues. A quick survey is provided by Musgrave, R. A., 'Cost-Benefit Analysis and the Theory of Public Finance', *Journal of Economic Literature*, September 1969.

Among books that deal specifically with the problems of developing countries, we mention:

Hansen, B., *Long- and Short-Term Planning in Underdeveloped Countries*, North-Holland, Amsterdam, 1967.

Marglin, S. A., *Public Investment Criteria*, Allen and Unwin, 1967.

Two books reflecting a standpoint that is, on many issues, very different from ours, are

Harberger, A., *Project Evaluation*, Macmillan, London, 1972.

Mishan, E. J., *Cost-Benefit Analysis*, Allen and Unwin, London, 1972.

In 1.2–1.8 we list a number of papers and books dealing with particular aspects of investment decisions. Most of them assume acquaintance with economic theory.

1.2 Discount Rates

Arrow, K. J., 'Discounting and Public Investment Criteria', in *Water Research*, ed. Kneese, A. V. and Smith, S. C., Johns Hopkins, Baltimore, 1966.

Diamond, P. A., 'The Opportunity Costs of Public Investment: Comment', *Quarterly Journal of Economics*, November 1968.

Baumol, W. J., 'On the Discount Rate for Public Projects', in *The Analysis and Evaluation of Public Expenditures*, see 1.1 above.

Sandmo, A. and Drèze, J. H., 'Discount Rates for Public Investment in Closed and Open Economies', *Economica*, November 1971.

Kay, J. A., 'Social Discount Rates', *Journal of Public Economics*, November 1972.

1.3 *Externalities*

Chase, S. B. (ed.), *Problems in Public Expenditure Analysis*, The Brookings Institution, Washington, 1968.

Papers by Davis, O. A. and Kamien, M. I., Kneese, A. V. and d'Arge, R. C., and Margolis, J., in *The Analysis and Evaluation of Public Expenditures*, 1.1 above.

Mishan, E. J., 'The Postwar Literature on Externalities: An Interpretative Essay', *Journal of Economic Literature*, March 1971.

1.4 *Large Projects*

Manne, A. S., *Investments for Capacity Expansion: Size, Location, and Time-Phasing*, Allen and Unwin, London, 1967.

For an explanation and discussion of consumer surplus, the reader can consult Mishan's *Cost–Benefit Analysis*, 1.1 above.

1.5 *Uncertainty*

In addition to the works referred to in Chapter XV, we mention:

Hirshleifer, J. and Shapiro, D. L., 'The Treatment of Risk and Uncertainty' in *The Analysis and Evaluation of Public Expenditures*, 1.1 above.

Raiffa, H., *Decision Analysis*, Addison-Wesley, 1970. The latter provides a wide-ranging and entertaining discussion of decision-taking under uncertainty.

1.6 *Wages in Developing Countries*

For different views and their implications, see the papers by Fei, J. C. H., Ranis, G., Jorgenson, D. H., and the comment by Marglin, S. A., in Adelman, I. and Thorbecke, E. (eds.), *The Theory and Design of Economic Development*, Johns Hopkins, Baltimore, 1966.

Systematic development of different theories is contained in

Stiglitz, J. E., 'Alternative Theories of Wage Determination and Unemployment in Less Developed Countries, I, II and III', *Quarterly Journal of Economics*, 1973 and 1974.

1.7 *Programming Models*

A valuable survey is provided by

Manne, A. S., *Multisector Models for Development Planning: A Survey*, Technical Report 91, Institute for Mathematical Studies in the Social Sciences, Stanford University, California, March 1973.

For examples of programming methods and applications, see:

Adelman, I. and Thorbecke, E., *The Theory and Design of Economic Development*, Part 2 (1.6 above).

Goreux, L. M. and Manne, A. S., (eds.), *Multi-Level Planning: Case-Studies in Mexico*, North-Holland, Amsterdam, 1973.

2. *The Practice of Cost–Benefit Analysis*

2.1 *Financial Analysis*

Two standard works on the analysis and appraisal of investments, without shadow pricing and special reference to developing countries, are:
Merrett, J. A. and Sykes, A., *The Finance and Analysis of Capital Projects*, Longmans, 1963.
Bierman, H. and Smidt, S., *Capital Budgeting Decision*, Collier-Macmillan, 2nd ed. 1970.

2.2 *Discussions of Cost–Benefit Analysis*

Prest, A. R. and Turvey, R., 'Cost–Benefit Analysis: A Survey', *Economic Journal*, December 1965, reprinted in *Surveys of Economic Theory, Vol. III: Resource Allocation*, Macmillan, London, 1966.
Hirschman, A. O., *Development Projects Observed*, Brookings Institution, Washington, 1967; a stimulating essay on the theme that any assessment leaves things out.
Schultze, C. L., *The Politics and Economics of Public Spending*, Brookings Institution, Washington, 1968.
Williams, A., 'Cost–Benefit Analysis: Bastard Science and/or Insidious Poison in the Body Politick?', *Journal of Public Economics*, August 1972, and in *Cost–Benefit and Cost Effectiveness*, ed. Wolfe, J. N., Allen and Unwin, London, 1973.
The February 1972 number of the *Bulletin of the Oxford Institute of Economics and Statistics* was a symposium on the OECD Manual containing articles by Dasgupta, P., Gutowski, A. and Hammel, H., Healey, J. H., Joshi, H., Joshi, V., Stern, N. H., Stewart, F., and Streeten, P., together with an introduction by the editors and reply by the authors.
Sen, A. K., 'Control Areas and Accounting Prices: An Approach to Economic Evaluation', in the *Economic Journal*, March 1972 (Supplement), is concerned with the political assumptions of economic evaluation with special reference to the OECD Manual.

2.3 *General Manuals for the Appraisal and Evaluation of Investments in Developing Countries*

The forerunner of this book was Little, I. M. D. and Mirrlees, J. A., *Manual of Industrial Project Analysis in Developing Countries, Vol. II, Social Cost–Benefit Analysis*, OECD Development Centre, Paris, 1968. Two other much briefer manuals have been based on it: these are the British Overseas Development Administration's *A Guide to Project Appraisal in Developing Countries*, H.M.S.O., 1972, and *Grundlagen der Cost–Benefit Analyse bei Projekten in Entwicklungsländern*, Kreditanstalt für Wiederaufbau, Frankfurt, 1971 (it is believed that an English translation is now obtainable). But the book most nearly comparable in scope to the present one is *Guidelines for Project Evaluation*, UNIDO, 1972, which has been discussed in the present text, especially in Chapter XVIII.

2.4 *Case Studies and Other Works Using Little/Mirrlees Methods*

Two industrial case-studies were published in the OECD *Manual* (*op. cit. sup.*). Four others were separately published by the OECD in 1972, these being:

Lal, D., *Wells and Welfare, An Exploratory Cost-Benefit Study of the Economics of Small-Scale Irrigation in Maharashtra*.

Little, I. M. D. and Tipping, D. G., *A Social Cost–Benefit Analysis of the Kulai Oil Palm Estate, West Malaysia*.

Seton, F., *Shadow Wages in the Chilean Economy*.

Stern, N. H., *An Appraisal of Tea Production on Small-Holdings in Kenya*.

Apart from these OECD publications, there are:

Karunaratne, N. D., *Techno-Economic Survey of Industrial Potential in Sri Lanka*, Industrial Development Board of Ceylon, 1973.

Khan, A., and Mirrlees, J. A. *Optimal Prices for a Developing Economy*, Heinemann, forthcoming. This is an application of the method to industrial sectors rather than projects.

Lal, D., *Appraising Foreign Investment*, Heinemann, 1974. This deals with a number of foreign industrial investments in India and Kenya.

Scott, M. FG., MacArthur, J. D. and Newbery, D. M. G., *Project Appraisal in Practice: The Little/Mirrlees Method Applied in Kenya*, Heinemann, forthcoming, the most thorough application of shadow pricing to any economy which has yet been carried out, is particularly concerned with an evaluation of the White Highland agricultural settlements, and with cattle fattening.

Lal, D. and Duane, P., *A Reappraisal of the Purna Irrigation Project in Maharashtra, India*, World Bank Staff Occasional Paper (forthcoming).

3. Sectoral Studies

Few of the works mentioned below are specifically concerned with developing countries, and none of them deals adequately with the problems of shadow pricing in developing countries. But most sectors give rise to specialized problems which need to be, and can be, discussed independently of shadow pricing—although the best solutions generally depend on shadow pricing. The works selected have generally been chosen because they are recent and themselves contain further references so that they can be used as a lead-in to the literature. We do not mention manuals which are primarily checklists of points to be covered in submissions and are obtainable from donor agencies such as the FAO, AID, and others. As in the main work we ignore town planning, health, education, and defence, despite the fact that cost–benefit methods have been used for these sectors, in some cases extensively.

3.1 Transport

Transport, like electricity generation, is a sector where systems effects should generally be taken into account when examining any element in the system: thus a new road will affect traffic on other roads, and also other modes of transport. It is also a sector, like water-resource development, where investment decisions are often mutually dependent or incompatible: a new airport requires land access, and cannot be crossed by a new railway-line. For such reasons, large sections at least of a transport system should often ideally be planned together. There are also special problems in estimating demand, and in valuing the benefits: thus the value to be placed on time savings and accident reduction is uncertain and controversial, and it is even difficult to measure such a mundane item as the reduction in user–costs resulting from road improvements. In some cases, there are also important externalities, such as congestion and the noise from aircraft or an urban motorway.

Heggie, I. G., *Transport Engineering Economics*, McGraw-Hill, U.K., 1972, is a valuable recent work on transport projects and planning, which seeks to bring together the more theoretical and practical considerations and literature. It contains a fairly large select bibliography, and numerous further references to most problems likely to be encountered.

Two World Bank Staff Occasional Papers in the field are: de Weille, J., *Quantification of Road User Savings*, and Adler, H. A., *Sector and Project Planning in Transportation*. The latter is a brief introduction to the subject, containing a short bibliography. There is also Adler, H. A., *Economic Appraisal of Transport Projects*, Indiana University Press, 1971: this is cursory on methodology and shadow-pricing, but contains fifteen useful illustrative case-studies.

The British Transport and Road Research Laboratory (Tropical Section), Crowthorne, and the U.S. Highway Research Board, Washington, have many publications concerning the planning and evaluation of roads.

Turning to more general transport problems, the Brookings Institution, Washington, has published a series of books on developing countries. These include Fromm, G. (ed.), *Transport Investment and Econom c Development*, 1965 (containing an extensive but now rather dated bibliography), and Haefele, T. (ed.), *Transport and National Goals*, 1969. Munby, D. (ed.), *Transport*, Penguin, 1968, is a useful collection containing many references. Georgi, H., *Cost-Benefit Analysis and Public Investment in Transport*, Butterworths, 1973, is a useful survey of the literature but not specifically concerned with developing countries. Beesley, M. E., *Urban Transport: Studies in Economic Policy*, Butterworths, 1973, contains the famous study of a new underground line in London, and discussion of other urban transport problems. The main journal in the field which publishes many case-studies and more general articles is the *Journal of Transport Economics and Policy*.

3.2   *Agriculture* (other than water-resource development)

Price Gittinger, J., *Economic Analysis of Agricultural Projects*, 1972, is a publication of the EDI, the teaching branch of the IBRD. It is a fairly elementary text on cost–benefit analysis, with rather little special agricultural orientation, despite the title. The cursory treatment of shadow-pricing should be taken to be in line with the past rather than the present philosophy of the IBRD. Some cost–benefit studies following Little/Mirrlees methods have already been listed in 2.4 above. There seems to be a dearth of works on planning the agricultural sector. We mention only Weitz, R., *From Peasant to Farmer*, Columbia University Press, 1971, and Mosher, A. T., *To Create a Modern Agriculture*, The Agricultural Development Council, New York, 1971. The former contains many references, and the latter is concerned largely with the organization of agricultural planning.

3.3 *Forestry*

Watt, G. R., *The Planning and Evaluation of Forestry Projects*, Commonwealth Forestry Institute, University of Oxford, 1973, is a compact survey of the literature on forestry planning and projects, and contains an extensive bibliography.

3.4 *Water Resources* (see also 2.4 above)

Lieftinck, P. *et al.*, *Water and Power Resources of West Pakistan—A Study in Sector Planning* (3 volumes), Johns Hopkins Press, 1969, is the most detailed account of actual economic planning and appraisal available in this sector. James, L. D. and Lee, R. R., *Economics of Water Resources Planning*, McGraw Hill, 1971, and Kuiper, E., *Water Resources Project Economics*, Butterworths, 1971, are two recent textbooks with numerous references to the very large literature in this field. Bergman, H., *Guide to the Economic Evaluation of Irrigation Projects*, OECD, 1973, is a compact manual of narrower scope. It contains a bibliography in French, German, and English.

3.5 *Electricity Supply*

Turvey, R., *Optimal Pricing and Investment in Electricity Supply*, Allen and Unwin, 1968, is concerned primarily with the former, but also shows how optimum capacity expansion depends essentially on optimum pricing. He considers a system which is large enough for additions to capacity to be considered to be marginal. Where this is not the case, reference may be made to Manne, A. S., *op. cit.* Hydro-electricity is also not considered: this is briefly dealt with in James and Lee (*op. cit. sup.*) where further references can be found. The choice between hydro and thermal power is considered in van der Tak, H. G., *The Economic Choice Between Hydro-Electric and Thermal Power Developments*, IBRD, 1966. The reader may also find helpful the various articles on public utility pricing policy in Turvey, R., *Public Enterprise*, Penguin, 1968, where further references can be found.

Index

Index

Index